C000131808

CARMARTHEN CASTLE

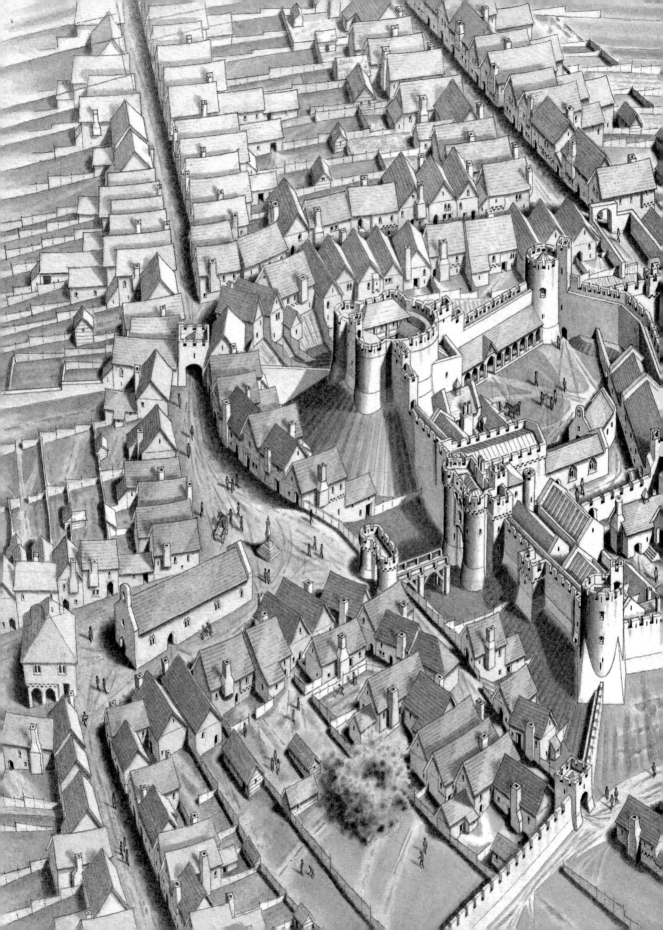

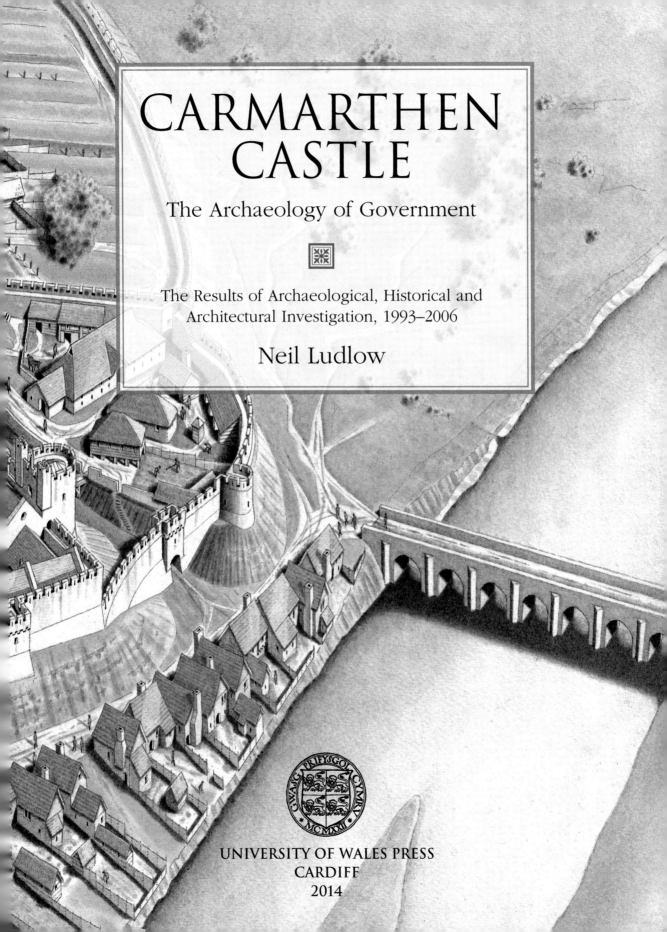

CARMARTHEN CASTLE

The Archaeology of Government

The Results of Archaeological, Historical and
Architectural Investigation, 1993–2006

Neil Ludlow

UNIVERSITY OF WALES PRESS
CARDIFF
2014

British Library Cataloguing-in-Publication Data.
A catalogue record for this book is available from the British Library.

ISBN   978-1-7831-6012-9
eISBN 978-1-7831-6013-6

Funding for this publication is gratefully acknowledged.

Designed and typeset by Chris Bell, cbdesign
Printed by CPI Antony Rowe, Chippenham, Wiltshire

CONTENTS

FOREWORD

BY EIFION BOWEN,
CARMARTHENSHIRE COUNTY COUNCIL

OVER THE last forty years Carmarthen has become familiar with visitors arriving to see the castle, mistakenly thinking they are at Caernarfon (120 miles to the north). Perhaps more surprising was the number of local people who, in response to a County Council public consultation, said, 'I didn't know Carmarthen had a castle,' Only glimpses of the castle were possible through the surrounding buildings and, even then, only ivy-clad remains could be seen. In addition, rarely did Carmarthen appear in books on the castles of Wales. It seemed to have vanished, and been forgotten.

Changes began in the early 1970s when the council demolished the Swan Inn, in Nott Square, to reveal more of the gatehouse. Slowly but surely, over the following thirty years, further schemes revealed more and more of the impressive remains. Hand in hand came a wealth of information from the archaeology. The information from below ground was also matched by that from the depths of the written record.

This book is the fruit of painstaking excavation, survey and research work by Neil Ludlow and others. It includes a detailed history of the castle with a rare depth of analysis. The strategic importance of this site is evidenced not only in battles for its control throughout the Middle Ages, but in its persistence as a seat of power for 900 years. The description of its long history is enriched by references to similarities with other castles in Britain, and the trade connections with continental Europe revealed by the documents and pottery remains.

With the views and access now afforded to the public, Carmarthen Castle is on the map in its own right, and is moreover recognised as one of the most important in the history of Wales and beyond. This has been made possible through the dedication, expertise and professionalism of a multi-disciplinary team of archaeologists, architects, planners, surveyors, engineers, contractors, accountants and archivists; through the funding of the grant- making bodies; and through the vision of the County Council.

Eifion Bowen
Head of Planning, Carmarthenshire County Council
August 2012

FOREWORD

BY KENNETH MURPHY
DYFED ARCHAEOLOGICAL TRUST

FROM ITS foundation in 1975 until 1994, Dyfed Archaeological Trust was based in Carmarthen – Wales's oldest town and the focus of political and economic life in south-west Wales for two thousand years. One of the Trust's early priorities was to obtain a clearer picture of the town's archaeological resource, resulting in the 1980 publication of a pioneering survey by the late Terry James. At the same time, Heather James of the Trust began large-scale excavations within Roman Carmarthen. The Trust's commitment to the town continued with an equally ambitious excavation by Terry James on the site of the medieval Franciscan Friary in the 1980s. Opportunities to investigate the castle were, however, limited – though I had the chance to help excavate part of the site, again under Heather and Terry James, in 1980.

The situation changed in 1993 with the commencement of a thirteen-year scheme of enhancement work at the castle, under the county council, accompanied by a full programme of archaeological investigation by Dyfed Archaeological Trust. The results of excavation and recording by Duncan Schlee, Pete Crane, Neil Ludlow and others, are described in this book, and assessed alongside Neil's extensive research work to provide a full account of the castle's history and development. We see the officials and other occupants of the castle, and look at their activities; the castle buildings are examined, along with the uses to which they were put, and how they changed through time. This study makes a major contribution to the history of one of Wales's great towns.

Kenneth Murphy
Dyfed Archaeological Trust
December 2013

LIST OF FIGURES

LIST OF TABLES

LIST OF ABBREVIATIONS

BBCS	*Bulletin of the Board of Celtic Studies*
Cal. Inq. Misc.	*Calendar of Inquisitions Miscellaneous (Chancery)*
CarmJ	*Carmarthen Journal*
Carms. Antiq.	*The Carmarthenshire Antiquary*
Carms. Hist.	*The Carmarthenshire Historian*
CAS	Carmarthenshire Antiquarian Society
CBA	Council for British Archaeology
CCC	Carmarthenshire County Council
CCcR	*Calendar of Chancery Rolls*
CChR	*Calendar of Charter Rolls*
CCR	*Calendar of Close Rolls*
CFR	*Calendar of Fine Rolls*
CLR	*Calendar of Liberate Rolls*
CPR	*Calendar of Patent Rolls*
CSPD	*Calendar of State Papers (Domestic)*
CRO	Carmarthen Record Office
DAT	Dyfed Archaeological Trust
END	Extended National Database
HER	Historic Environment Record
HMSO	Her Majesty's Stationery Office
JHC	*Journal of the House of Commons*
LB	Listed Building
NLW	National Library of Wales
NMW	National Museum Wales
NMR	National Monuments Record
NPRN	National Primary Record Number (NMR)
OUP	Oxford University Press
OS	Ordnance Survey
PRN	Primary Record Number (DAT)

PRO	Public Record Office
RCAHMW	Royal Commission on the Ancient and Historical Monuments of Wales
SAM	Scheduled Ancient Monument
SMA	Society for Medieval Archaeology
TCASFC	*Transactions of the Carmarthenshire Antiquarian Society and Field Club*
TNA	The National Archives
UWP	University of Wales Press
WWHR	*West Wales Historical Records*

Short-title referencing is applied throughout the main text with the exception of the Appendix, where author-date referencing is applied for ease of use.

ACKNOWLEDGEMENTS

MANY GRATEFUL thanks are offered to the host of people involved in the project. First and foremost to staff at Dyfed Archaeological Trust (DAT), past and present, especially Duncan Schlee, Nigel Page, Pete Crane, Belinda Allen, Hubert Wilson, Richard Ramsey, Gwilym Bere and Jemma Bezant, all of whom undertook fieldwork at the castle; support was willingly given by Louise Austin, Lucy Bourne, Charles Hill and Phil Poucher, while special thanks go to successive Trust directors Don Benson, Gwilym Hughes and Ken Murphy. Many thanks also to the specialists involved in the post-excavation – Dee Williams (formerly of DAT), Astrid Caseldine and Catherine Griffiths (University of Wales, Trinity St David), the late Paul Courtney, Lorrain Higbee (Wessex Archaeology) and Phil Parkes (University of Cardiff). Special thanks to Mark Redknap (National Museum Wales), who so willingly gave his time and who acknowledges his gratitude to Edward Besly for looking at the coins; Rebekah Pressler for comments on the ceramics; James Wild and Robin Maggs for photography; Mark Lewis for identifying species identification of the leather; and Paul Atkin and Robin Wood for wood identifications.

The initiative for the recent works came from Dyfed County Council's Planning Department, who acted as coordinators and advisers throughout. Beginning in 1993, the work continued under Carmarthenshire County Council's Planning Division, following local government reorganisation in 1996. The design and supervision was initially carried out by Dyfed County Council's Architects Department, but was taken over by TACP (Wrexham), who remained consultants for all subsequent phases of work. Carmarthenshire County Council offered continuing support, and enthusiasm, for the archaeology – which could serve as a model for projects of this kind – and contributed to the publication costs of this book; Eifion Bowen, John Llewelyn, Brangwyn Howells and Kevin Davies are particularly thanked. The main contractors on site were John Weaver Construction, Opus International Consultants UK (formerly Veryards Ltd), T. J. Construction, Abbey Masonry & Restoration Ltd and Alun Griffiths Contractors Ltd.

Additional documentary research was undertaken by Stephen Priestley (now of Border Archaeology). Richard Ireland (University of Aberyswyth) very kindly provided pre-publication proofs of his *'A want of good order and discipline': Rules, Discretion and the Victorian Prison* (UWP, 2007) and Charles Griffiths (curator of Dyfed-Powys Police Museum) provided much additional information relating to the Old Police Station.

Special thanks go to Heather James, the late Terry James (both formerly of Dyfed Archaeological Trust), Rick Turner (Cadw), John Kenyon (National Museum Wales), and Edna Dale-Jones (CAS), for reading through and commenting on early drafts, and for much additional information and guidance. Chris Caple (Durham University) provided information on his recent work at Nevern Castle, Roger Turvey kindly explored the issues surrounding Welsh occupation of the castle with me, Bob Higham (University of Exeter) discussed shell-keeps, and Charles Hill (DAT) offered a number of valuable suggestions.

Most of the illustrations and photographs were supplied by Dyfed Archaeological Trust and the author; however, RCAHMW supplied the aerial photograph (Figure 4), Ken Day (MO Design) provided four photographs (Figures 42, 78, 102 and 155) and Mrs Suzanne Hayes kindly permitted Figure 134 to be used. The antique maps, plans and prints were drawn from the collections at the National Library of Wales, Carmarthenshire Archive Service and Carmarthenshire Museums Service, from which Terry Wells, John Davies and Gavin Evans are particularly thanked. I am also very grateful to Bernard Nurse (Society of Antiquaries of London) for providing copies of David Cathcart King's notebooks, and to Tom Lloyd and Julian Orbach who gave much general support. Finally, many thanks to all at UWP.

CHAPTER ONE

INTRODUCTION
'a certain good donjon'

*There is a certain castle in which is a certain good donjon
constructed from five small towers.*
(from a Chancery Inquisition on the Manor
of Carmarthen, 1275)

THE REMAINS OF Carmarthen Castle, though impressive, are of modest extent. They do not immediately announce its former importance. Yet Carmarthen was not only one of the principal castles of medieval Wales, but also among the largest. A springboard for the Anglo-Norman annexation of south-west Wales, Carmarthen Castle became the centre of Crown authority in the region and was one of a very small number of royal castles in an area predominantly given over to Marcher lordships. Its status as Crown holding and centre of government, formalised in the late thirteenth century and paralleled in the north at Caernarfon Castle, was of a very different character from that of contemporary Marcher castles and had a profound influence on its development.

Like many royal castles, Carmarthen continued to be used in civil administration after the Middle Ages, and is still the site of a centre of government. It was used as the County Gaol throughout the post-medieval period, but was acquired by Carmarthenshire County Council in the twentieth century, when the gaol was replaced by the present County Hall. This continuity, and its urban setting, have inevitably had a negative impact on the castle's physical remains, but all three incarnations have been fundamental in defining the cultural identity of the region. The hub around which the historic borough of Carmarthen developed, the castle still dominates the townscape and its surrounds.

Although repair and maintenance work had been undertaken by the council since the late 1960s, the castle had seen little archaeological investigation prior to 1993, when a large-scale programme of enhancement works got under way.[1] The castle remains were consolidated, and their visual setting was improved through selective demolition of derelict

Figure 1 *Aerial photograph of Carmarthen Castle from the south-east, taken in 1993*
(© Dyfed Archaeological Trust, DAT AP 93/48.2)

housing. The scheme was accompanied by a full programme of archaeological recording, undertaken by Dyfed Archaeological Trust (DAT). The archaeological project design was largely dictated by the overall scheme of works, concentrating on the standing remains and below-ground areas that were affected, but opportunities arose for more targeted investigation. In addition, a structured programme of post-excavation, including research and finds analysis, was built into the project. The research design moreover encompassed all periods of the site's history from the foundation of the castle until the twentieth century.

As a result, a detailed account of the castle site can be presented, its layout can be suggested and a developmental sequence can be proposed. The site will doubtless continue to change and develop, and further information will come to light. This book describes the story so far.

A BRIEF OVERVIEW

I have had a fascination with Carmarthen Castle ever since I began working at Dyfed Archaeological Trust in 1981. It was, after all, one of Wales's 'forgotten' castles. Nevertheless I had only a vague idea how much we really knew about it. I knew that archaeological investigation had been very limited, particularly intrusive work, but was unaware that so little analytical study had been published and that structured research had been minimal. Whilst frustrating, this also presented a marvellous opportunity – the castle was, to a large extent, unknown territory and nearly all elements of the recent project yielded new discoveries. These were chiefly revealed through standing building analysis, topographic study and limited excavation, considered alongside primary sources, relating to site development, and antique maps and plans. This book describes those discoveries and the questions asked of them; it is hoped that it may also provide some of the answers, and place them in context.

In style, it is by no means radical. Its layout, in fact, is to a certain extent traditional. The results of the recent work are ordered thematically, broken down consecutively into topics that are broadly historical, descriptive, comparative and curatorial. As this is the first systematic study of the castle, and much of it results from primary research and interpretation, it seemed the most appropriate approach. The thinking that underpins the interpretations is hopefully, however, less tradition-bound. Social identity, administrative demands, manorial economics and the politics of prestige loom large in the following pages.

A degree of determinism may creep in, but as an instrument of deliberate Crown policy, Carmarthen Castle's story was always, to a certain extent, determined; sufficient resources were normally allocated to ensure that this was so. Politics and war were rarely far away; from them emerged the castle's administrative role, and in consequence they remained a constant influence upon its development. Nevertheless, as Charles Coulson reminds us, 'fortresses were only occasionally caught up in war, but constantly were central to the ordinary life of all classes: of the nobility and gentry, of widows and heiresses, of prelates and clergy, of peasantry and townspeople',[2] and I have tried to keep to this spirit. Our primary concern will be the archaeology of Carmarthen Castle, its buildings and its layout – what those buildings were, how they functioned, and how they developed to meet the demands of its various roles and inhabitants. We shall, however, also meet some of those inhabitants, and analyse those roles.

The themes are presented in seven chapters:

• Chapter 1 is an introduction, including a general description of the site, its physical setting and its relationship to earlier settlement. It also contains a summary account of previous archaeological work.

• The political, administrative and economic history of the medieval castle is discussed in Chapter 2. It is broken down into four main themes: the castle's origins, a brief review of its military and political history, its role as the centre of Crown administration and government in south-west Wales, and its interaction with its hinterland and the wider landscape, including sources of supply and materials.

- Chapter 3 is a description of the standing remains of the castle, and a full account of the archaeological investigations between 1993 and 2006. Earlier investigations, where known, are also discussed. The site is broken down into five areas within which the evidence, from all periods, is presented chronologically.

- The results of this archaeological work are discussed in Chapter 4. They are assessed alongside contemporary and later source material, including historic map and print evidence, to establish, for the first time, a comprehensive reconstruction of the layout and development of the medieval castle, and the influences on its development that arose from its various roles. Its social organisation, as a residence, is also examined.

- Chapter 5 is a description and history of the site during the post-medieval period. In it I have attempted to chart the castle's progress through an important period of transition, which had hitherto received little attention. From sixteenth-century decline and disuse, and disposal in the early seventeenth century, it saw reuse during the Civil War but, it is suggested, was eventually slighted, possibly in 1660. The layout of the site during its subsequent use as the County Gaol is examined. The new gaols of the eighteenth and nineteenth centuries are discussed, along with the evidence for the various uses to which the rest of the site was put. The chapter ends with a short description of the present County Hall.

- The stratified finds and artefacts recovered during the recent work are described and discussed in Chapter 6.

- Chapter 7 is a summary and conclusion. Carmarthen Castle's place in British castle development, and in the wider world of castle studies, is reviewed. Its cultural significance, and its remaining archaeological potential, are assessed.

- Transcripts of surviving building accounts, relating to the castle's structural development, form the Appendix.

HISTORIOGRAPHY

The relative dearth of published works is surprising, given the former importance of Carmarthen Castle, and its central location – and seniority – within one of the most 'becastled' regions of Wales. It received little attention from the scholar-travellers of the early nineteenth century like Sir Richard Colt Hoare and Richard Fenton, and none at all from Victorian castellologists such as G. T. Clark. Its workaday aspect – largely hidden by housing and used as a gaol – doubtless lacked appeal for the Romantic sensibilities of the time; it just could not compete with the likes of Carreg Cennen, Kidwelly and Llansteffan. But this is surely not the only reason. Castle-studies pioneer Ella Armitage limited her attention, in the early twentieth century, to two brief notes,[3] while later in the century the likes of Allen Brown, Douglas

Simpson and Cathcart King had little to say about the site; when they did mention it, it could be in somewhat disparaging tones.[4] Its fragmentary nature must be partly responsible, but from the point of view of the castle's historical significance, more interest might be expected.

No comprehensive account of the site had been attempted, and no real study of its medieval development, layout and buildings. What exists is dispersed among a large number of publications, often as short descriptions, brief transcriptions, or summary notes detailing a specific aspect or document. This is all the more surprising, given that the primary source material for the medieval period has been extensively published. As a Crown possession, Carmarthen Castle figures in all the transcripts of royal administration – the Pipe Rolls, Patent Rolls, Close Rolls etc. – while an extensive body of documents was transcribed by Edward Lewis and published by Francis Green in 1913–14 (see Chapters 2 and 4). Little new manuscript material emerged during the study, but a number of documents in The National Archives (TNA: PRO) were previously unpublished, including several valuable surveys and building accounts, while some notebook and journal entries came to light.

Brief descriptions can be found in the Royal Commission Inventory,[5] Cathcart King's *Castellarium Anglicanum*[6] and the *History of the King's Works* in which the source material is briefly summarised.[7] The castle plays a prominent role in Sir J. E. Lloyd's *History of Carmarthenshire*,[8] and provides the stage for Professor Ralph Griffiths's definitive account of the machinery of royal government in late medieval south Wales.[9] A number of published studies of the medieval *town* of Carmarthen also describe the castle in outline. Chief among them are the comprehensive survey undertaken by Terry James of DAT,[10] Professor Griffiths's historical review[11] and a useful summary, incorporating much recent thinking, by Heather James of DAT.[12]

Antiquarian accounts are somewhat sparse, but short entries relating to the castle and gaol were a constant feature of *TCASFC*, the local antiquarian journal. Otherwise the post-medieval history of the site has been similarly neglected, and until the publication of Richard Ireland's social history,[13] little else had been written about the County Gaol. Similarly, much of the source material relating to the development of the site during this period was previously unpublished, and mainly comprises documents, maps and plans held by Carmarthenshire Archive Service at CRO, and at NLW.

Primary sources are listed at the beginning of each chapter, along with a review of the relevant secondary sources and a summary of the new research. In Chapters 4 and 5, they are assessed alongside the archaeological evidence in order to chart the development of the castle. All consequent interpretations, conclusions – and errors – are the author's.

LOCATION, SETTING AND EARLY SETTLEMENT

Carmarthen Castle (NGR SN 413 199) lies 20 m above sea level, on the summit of a bluff with a steep southerly downhill slope towards the River Tywi, which enters the Bristol Channel 17 km to the south-west. The castle lies at the lowest bridging point of the river, and 3.5 km downstream from its tidal limit.

The physical setting (Figure 2)

The River Tywi meanders through a broad floodplain that extends south-westwards for over 50 km, from Llandovery to the wide estuary at Llansteffan. Subject to periodic flooding, its alluvial soil represents one of the most fertile regions of Carmarthenshire, and its meanders appear to have been historically stable between Carmarthen and Llandeilo, where traces of ridge-and-furrow can be seen. Its flanking foothills and steeply incised hinterland however remained thickly wooded until late in the medieval period.

The Tywi Valley has long been one of the great route corridors through south Wales, both by water and by land. It lies between the coast and the higher ground of the central Wales *massif* and all overland routes through south Wales must still pass through Carmarthen. The A40 corridor, running along the interface between the Tywi floodplain and the rising ground to the north, was the line of the main Roman road through the region and may perpetuate a much earlier route. Its line was more or less followed by the later routeway, which was known as 'The High Road' in the eighteenth century.[14] However, a more southerly route, by ferry across the estuaries of the Tywi and the Tâf between Ferryside and Laugharne, was also in use during the medieval period and is described by Gerald of Wales.[15]

Carmarthen lies between the junction of the Tywi with two of its tributaries, the Tawelan Brook, 1 km to the west and the River Gwili, 1.8 km to the east (Figure 2). The solid geology is represented by Ordovician shales of the Arenig system, beneath a drift deposit of stiff glacial boulder clay.[16] Fluvio-glacial activity has left an overlying gravel terrace between the Gwili and the Tywi. Strongly defined, the terrace broadens out to the south-west as a long, low ridge, which lies between 15 and 20 m above sea level, averages 200 m in width and terminates at the bluff on which the castle stands. It forms the spine of the historic town of Carmarthen, and was a natural choice for defence and settlement.

A stream, now culverted – the Wynveth Brook – formerly ran along the north-western flank of the terrace, flowing into the Tywi to form a natural barrier around the north and west sides of the town. North of the town, it flowed through a natural basin which was formerly an extensive area of marsh. Known as 'the Gors(e)' in the medieval period,[17] and later as 'the Wide Ocean' or 'the Wilderness',[18] it remained a wetland, studded with clumps of willows, until it was drained early in the nineteenth century. In addition, a stream, now also culverted, ran into the Tywi from Cwmoernant, 1 km north-east of the town.

Continuous occupation: from Roman to medieval Carmarthen (Figures 2 and 3)

Carmarthen has been occupied, if not continuously, since the first century AD. Its strategic setting was appreciated by the Romans who established a fort in *c*. AD 75.[19] Like the castle, it was situated on the gravel terrace, to command a north–south routeway where it crossed both the River Tywi, and the main east–west Roman road (Figure 2). Both routes continue to be used today. In addition, the Tywi was navigable as far as the bridge, enabling communication by sea. The Roman bridge may have occupied the same site as its medieval and modern successors, but instead of the bluff on which the castle stands, the level ground immediately to the north-east was chosen for the fort.

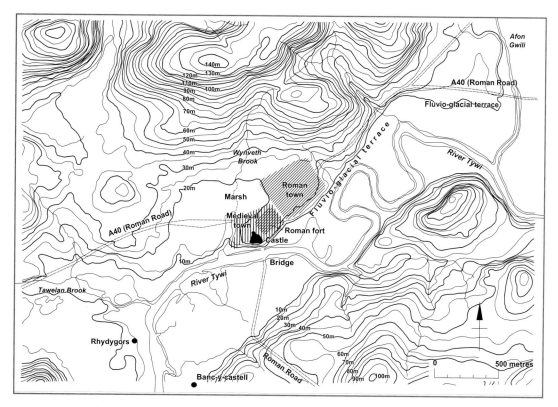

Figure 2 *Site location map showing topography*

The fort had been abandoned by the early first century, but was succeeded by a town. It too occupied the gravel terrace, immediately to the north-east of the fort and either side of the modern Priory Street. Like the fort, it was named *Moridunum*, i.e. 'sea fort', and was later formalised as the *civitas* capital of south-west Wales.[20] It was given timber defences, probably in the late second or early third century, which were remodelled in stone in the third or fourth century.[21] The ramparts remained an upstanding feature as late as the seventeenth century, when they may have been incorporated into the town's Civil War defences (Figure 3; see Chapter 5), and are still defined by modern streets. Much of their masonry facing was robbed during the medieval period, but a document of 1356 makes reference to the 'wall' of *Old* Carmarthen.[22]

The town was abandoned in the fifth century.[23] A monastic house was subsequently established immediately to the east, and was later reorganised as an Anglo-Norman Augustinian priory.[24] Its name, Llandeulyddog, may contain a variant form of the name Teilo, and it has been suggested that the abandoned Roman town was granted to St Teilo in the sixth century as an episcopal centre;[25] the monastery was certainly in existence by the eighth century. No contemporary secular settlement is currently known, but the area was known as 'Old Carmarthen' during the medieval period, when it was a Welshry, subject to the priory and independent of the Anglo-Norman town that developed around the castle (Figure 3).[26]

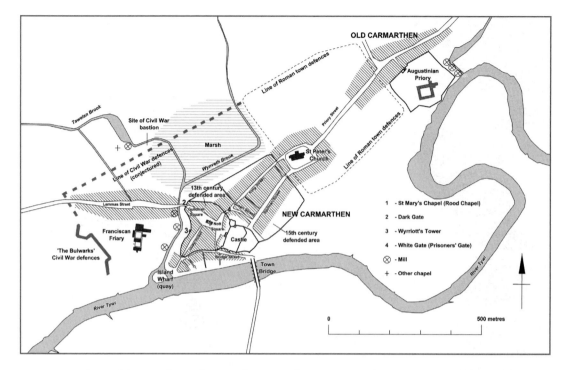

Figure 3 *Plan of the castle and town showing the Roman infrastructure, 'Old' and 'New' Carmarthen, town walls, churches and chapels, and Civil War defences*

So two medieval towns, constitutionally separate, existed at Carmarthen. The Anglo-Norman borough was a deliberate plantation, established at the castle gate between 1106 and 1116, and called New Carmarthen to distinguish it from Old Carmarthen. The two towns were physically, legally and ethnically distinct. The castle, and the marketplace outside its main gate, were the hub for the new settlement which developed towards the quay, also established at an early date. Carmarthen became an important port and experienced rapid growth in the thirteenth century. It was initially walled in the early thirteenth century, but the defended area was more than doubled in size in the early fifteenth century.

AN INTRODUCTORY DESCRIPTION (Figures 4 and 5)

Comprising a motte and two baileys, and formerly occupying a total area of nearly 1.4 hectares,[27] Carmarthen was one of the largest castles in Wales. Initially established as an earth-and-timber castle in *c.*1106, it experienced episodes of Welsh control during the conflicts of the twelfth and early thirteenth centuries. Some rebuilding in stone may have begun during the twelfth century, but it remained largely of timber until the 1220–1230s, and sources from the mid-thirteenth century onwards consistently mention the castle's 'five towers', presumably referring to the inner ward. The interior was crowded with buildings, even by the standards of the day. The accounts mention the 'King's Hall' and 'King's Chamber', lodgings

Figure 4 Aerial photograph of the west side of the castle, from the north, taken in 2005. All the surviving masonry can be seen (© Crown Copyright: Royal Commission on the Ancient and Historical Monuments of Wales, RCAHMW AP 2005/0825)

for knights and esquires, and a chamber for the queen. In addition there were buildings for government, developed during the early fourteenth century to include extensive complexes for the royal officials and their courts – a courthouse, an exchequer and lodgings for the justiciar and chamberlain of south Wales. And there were several kitchens, at least two chapels and three stables – as well as the more mundane buildings that get no mention in the accounts.

However, only fragments still survive above ground (Figures 4 and 5). Over 75 per cent of the site now lies beneath County Hall and its car park; the standing remains, which belong to the masonry defences of the inner ward and motte, are confined to the west, north-west and south-west sides. The underlying earthworks, too, have variously been removed, built over or otherwise obscured. A substantial portion of the site, along its east and south sides, has moreover been lost to road widening. Nevertheless, it is still clearly

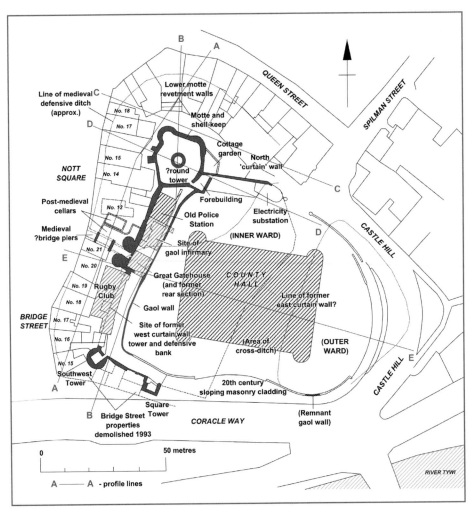

Figure 5 *Overall plan of the castle site showing the surviving remains*

defined, and is respected by modern roads and boundaries. And in addition to the medieval masonry, fabric survives from the late eighteenth-/nineteenth-century gaol.

The medieval castle

The medieval castle[28] comprised an inner ward to the west, and an outer ward to the east, divided by a cross-ditch running beneath County Hall and its car park. The motte still survives, at the north-west corner of the former inner ward, but its south-east quadrant was later removed and further alterations took place during the post-medieval period. It is still partly revetted by the remains of a masonry shell-keep, originally from the late twelfth or early thirteenth century but substantially rebuilt during the eighteenth and nineteenth centuries. Footings for internal buildings, and a possible half-timbered round tower, were revealed through excavation in the interior.

The north and west sides of the inner ward are still partly defined by high masonry walls which may represent the medieval curtain wall-line. The external ditch has been filled in, but its course is still respected by Nott Square and Bridge Street, while Queen Street follows the line of the motte ditch. The steep scarp slope down to the Tywi still defines the southern edge of the site, but the medieval south curtain has gone.

The southern side was fully exposed, for the first time in over 250 years, when derelict housing in Bridge Street was demolished in 1992–3. It was seen that the south curtain had been replaced by a post-medieval revetment wall, connecting two medieval towers, the South-west Tower and the Square Tower. The former is a substantial, spurred drum tower from the thirteenth century, of at least three storeys, at the south-west corner of the former inner ward. The Square Tower now comprises just a single storey, but was probably once taller, and is of late medieval date. Both towers were much affected by domestic encroachment during the post-medieval period.

Selective clearance of domestic properties also took place in front of the Great Gatehouse in 2001–2, enhancing its views from the town. This was the main entry to the castle, connecting the inner ward to the town, but a second gateway at the south-west end of Spilman Street formerly led into the outer ward. The Great Gatehouse is a complex twin-tower structure of two storeys, of which only the front half now survives. It was built in 1409–11, but may incorporate the remains of an earlier gatehouse. Excavation immediately to the west, in 2003, revealed the possible remains of a medieval bridge.

All internal structures, including the inner ward east curtain, have gone. However, the remains of masonry domestic buildings were excavated by DAT in 1980, in the south-west corner of the inner ward, and more may survive beneath County Hall car park. No structures or deposits relating to the outer ward have been revealed, while the outer curtain was almost entirely removed by the road widening mentioned above.

Post-medieval remains

Much of the castle's administrative importance disappeared with the passage of the Act of Union in 1536, and direct Crown ownership was relinquished in the early seventeenth century. Central to Carmarthen's defences during the Civil Wars of 1642–8, it appears to have been deliberately slighted, and indeed the Buck engravings of the 1740s show little more fabric than currently survives (Figures 126 and 127).

The remains however continued to be used as a gaol. This was largely confined to the surviving medieval buildings until 1789–92, when a new county gaol was built on the site by John Nash,[29] whose more notable designs include Brighton Pavilion and work at Buckingham Palace. Like its predecessor, Nash's gaol was confined to the north-west quarter of the castle site, that is, the northern half of the former inner ward; the southern half was a garden. Nash's gaol was largely swept away in 1868–72 when the gaol was extended to cover the entire castle site, removing the last traces of the division between the inner and outer wards. The gaol was demolished in the 1930s to make way for the present County Hall, designed by Sir Percy Thomas and completed in the 1950s.

Various elements of the gaol still survive, including a section of wall from Nash's infirmary building. It is 'fossilised', along with further Nash-period walling, in the perimeter wall of 1868–72, a length of which survives on the west side of the site where it divides the castle remains from the County Hall car park. The old county police station (or 'Castle House'), lying between the two, has undergone little alteration since it was built in the 1880s.

Post-medieval domestic activity around the periphery of the site has had a profound impact on the castle fabric, particularly upon the motte and, as noted, the South-west and Square Towers. In addition, the 2003 excavation revealed three nineteenth-century cellars within the castle ditch.

Previous archaeological work

No systematic review of the standing remains had been undertaken before 1993 and, with one exception, no structured intrusive work.[30] There are some reports, from the late nineteenth century, of features and finds uncovered during groundworks for the gaol,[31] but these are often contradictory and difficult to resolve. Part of the shell-keep wall collapsed in 1913, revealing the motte in section; this was recorded and reported on in the pages of *TCASFC*.[32] Considerably more intrusive groundworks – the construction of Castle Hill in 1936–7, of Coracle Way in 1963–4 and of County Hall itself – took place without any archaeological recording.

The situation changed in 1975 with the establishment of a professional, regional archaeological unit, Dyfed Archaeological Trust. An early priority for the Trust was an accurate audit of the historic resource within Carmarthen town, leading to the publication, in 1980, of Terry James's *Carmarthen Survey*, in which the importance of the castle was stressed.[33] The same year saw the first controlled excavation in the castle, noted above. A photographic record of the Great Gatehouse exterior was made in 1984, again by DAT. The shell-keep was consolidated and repointed in the 1980s, and part of the shell-wall was rebuilt in the early 1990s; both campaigns were accompanied only by *ad hoc* archaeological recording, by Terry James of DAT. The full potential of the site has yet to be fully assessed, having been sampled only in a few small areas, while deposits beneath County Hall car park have yet to be investigated. Chapter 3 includes a review of all previous archaeological work known to me.

NOTES

1   Phase 1 of these works, undertaken between 1993 and 1995, was jointly funded by Dyfed County Council and Cadw: Welsh Historic Monuments. Phase 2, which ran from 1995 to 1996, received a Regional Development Grant from the European Community, grant-aid from Cadw and funding from both Dyfed County Council and CCC. Phase 3 was carried out between 2001 and 2003, and was funded by the Heritage Lottery Fund, Cadw and CCC.

2   C. Coulson, *Castles in Medieval Society: Fortresses in England, France and Ireland in the Central Middle Ages* (OUP, 2003), pp. 1–2

3   E. Armitage, 'Carmarthen Castle', *TCASFC*, 2 (1907), 196–7 and *TCASFC,* 3 (1908), 14–15.

4   See, for example, D. J. C. King, 'Carmarthen Castle', unpublished field note-books held in the Society of Antiquaries of London Library, Burlington House, Piccadilly, 1 (1949), 19–20, and 2 (1950), 53.

5   RCAHMW, *Inventory of Ancient Monuments*, V: *County of Carmarthen* (London: HMSO, 1917), pp. 249–52.

6   D. J. C. King, *Castellarium Anglicanum* (New York: Kraus International, 1983), p. 54.

7   H. M. Colvin (ed.), *A History of the King's Works*, 2: *The Middle Ages* (London: HMSO, 1963), pp. 600–1.

8   J. E. Lloyd (ed.), *A History of Carmarthenshire*, 1 (London: London Carmarthenshire Society, 1935).

9   R. A. Griffiths, *The Principality of Wales in the Later Middle Ages: The Structure and Personnel of Government*, 1: *South Wales 1277–1536* (Cardiff: UWP, 1972).

10   T. James, *Carmarthen: An Archaeological and Topographical Survey*, CAS Monograph 2 (Carmarthen, 1980). It is among the best archaeological studies of a British small town.

11   R. A. Griffiths, 'Carmarthen', in R. A. Griffiths (ed.), *Boroughs of Mediaeval Wales* (Cardiff: UWP, 1978), pp. 130–63.

12   H. James, 'Carmarthen', in E. P. Dennison (ed.), *Conservation and Change in Historic Towns*, CBA Research Report 122 (1999), pp. 158–68.

13   R. W. Ireland, *'A Want of Order and Good Discipline': Rules, Discretion and the Victorian Prison* (Cardiff: UWP, 2007). An outline description of John Nash's gaol and a plan also appeared in R. Suggett, *John Nash, Architect in Wales* (Aberystwyth: RCAHMW/NLW, 1995), pp. 25–30.

14   A. H. T. Lewis, 'The Early Effects of Carmarthenshire's Turnpike Trusts', *Carms. Hist.*, 4 (1967), 41.

15   L. Thorpe (ed.), *Gerald of Wales: The Journey through Wales/The Description of Wales* (Harmondsworth: Penguin, 1978), p. 138.

16   A. Strahan, T. C. Cantrill, E. Dixon and H. H. Thomas, *The Geology of the South Wales Coalfield*, Part X: *The Country around Carmarthen* (London: Memoirs of the Geological Survey, 1909), p. 229.

17   T. James, *Carmarthen Survey*, p. 42

18   W. Spurrell, *Carmarthen and its Neighbourhood* (Carmarthen: Spurrell and Co., 1879), p.103.

19   H. James, *Roman Carmarthen: Excavations 1978–1993*, Britannia Monograph Series, 20 (London, 2003), p. 29.

20   Ibid., p. 21.

21   Ibid., p. 196.

22   Lloyd, *History of Carmarthenshire*, p. 317, from Crown Pleas, 29 Ed. III.

23   A large, V-shaped ditch, from which a fifth-century radiocarbon date was obtained, was discovered during recent excavations at the south-west end of Spilman Street (H. James, *Roman Carmarthen*, p. 40). It suggests that a late or post-Roman ditched enclosure may have occupied the area later chosen for the Anglo-Norman town and castle.

24   T. James, 'Excavations at the Augustinian Priory of St John and St Teulyddog, Carmarthen, 1979', *Archaeologia Cambrensis*, 134 (1985), 120–61.

25   J. W. Evans, 'Aspects of the early Church in Carmarthenshire', in H. James (ed.), *Sir Gâr: Studies in Carmarthenshire History* (Carmarthen: CAS, 1991), pp. 246–7, 251.

26   Old Carmarthen is first mentioned in 1180–4, when an earlier twelfth-century grant of the 'old city of Carmarthen, with all its appurtenances', to the prior, was confirmed: J. R. Daniel-Tyssen (ed.), *Royal Charters and Historic Documents relating to the Town and County of Carmarthen* (Carmarthen: William Spurrell, 1878), p. 4.

27   The total area of the medieval castle, including ditches and banks, was around 13,380 m². The walled area formerly occupied *c.*8,524 m², of which *c.*7,290 m² now survive.

28   PRN 57 in the regional HER for Carmarthenshire, Ceredigion and Pembrokeshire (curated by DAT); NPRN 95084 in the NMR (curated by RCAHMW).

29   NPRN 100074; no overall DAT PRN.

30   David Cathcart King described those remains that were accessible to him – the shell-keep, curtain walls and gatehouse – in his unpublished notebooks (King, 'Carmarthen Castle', 1949 and 1950).

31   For example J. F. Jones, 'Carmarthen "Mount"', *Carms. Antiq.*, 5 (1963), 188.

32   W. L. Morgan, and W. Spurrell, 'Carmarthen Castle Mount', *TCASFC*, 10 (1915), 61–2.

33   James, *Carmarthen Survey*, pp. 26, 35–6.

CHAPTER TWO

CARMARTHEN CASTLE AND ITS PLACE IN MEDIEVAL WALES

CARMARTHEN CASTLE was a deliberate foundation of King Henry I, as a centre from which an Anglo-Norman territory could be carved and delineated, then defended and governed. It was the centre of royal government in south-west Wales, from which the ambitions of the native Welsh princes and the neighbouring marcher lords could be monitored and checked. It therefore fulfilled a number of different functions. It was primarily a centre of administration. It was the residence of Crown officials and their households. It was the base for Anglo-Norman military interventions in the region. It was the centre of a manor and, like all administrative centres, it was a gaol. Except for episodes of Welsh rule during the twelfth and early thirteenth centuries, and a period in the 1220–30s when it was reconstituted as a marcher lordship for royal favourites, the castle and lordship remained Crown territory throughout the medieval period. Its military, political and economic significance meant that its custody became an important appointment for servants of the Crown, and it was frequently used as a political reward. Royal administration was formalised and strengthened in the late thirteenth century, when a justiciar was appointed to control the judicial and political machinery of south-west Wales, along with a chamberlain, responsible for its fiscal management, and a sheriff to oversee local administration, all of whom were based at the castle. Its use as a gaol persisted into the twentieth century, and it is once again an administrative centre.

This chapter comprises a themed review of the castle's history until the sixteenth century. It is broken down into four separate but interconnected narratives which examine its varied functions and identities, its role in the history of Wales and its influence on urban development and the wider landscape. Primary sources used include contemporary chronicles such as the *Brut y Tywysogyon*,[1] *Brenhinedd y Saesson*[2] and the *Annales Cambriae*,[3] which are still the main source for much of its political and military history during the twelfth and thirteenth centuries. As a Crown possession, Carmarthen Castle figures in all the accounts of royal expenditure and administration, for example the Pipe Rolls, Patent Rolls, Close Rolls, Chancery Rolls, Charter Rolls, Fine Rolls and Liberate Rolls, along with Ministers' Accounts, Exchequer Accounts, Acts of the Privy Council and Miscellaneous Inquisitions etc.; a considerable body of these records was published by the West Wales Historical Society in 1913–14.[4] They have been augmented by other published primary source material[5] and, for example, the documents relating to Carmarthen held at NLW that were transcribed by Alcwyn Evans[6] and J. R. Daniel-Tyssen; the latter includes the invaluable Chancery Inquisition of 1275, the 'Extent of the Manor of Carmarthen'.[7] I examined other relevant entries in the rolls, and contemporary chronicles, while transcripts of additional, unpublished records in TNA were kindly provided by Stephen Priestley. The comprehensive collection of acts issued by the native rulers of Wales, compiled by Huw Pryce and Charles Insley,[8] was also examined, particularly for material relevant to the twelfth- and early thirteenth-century episodes of Welsh rule.

Two main secondary sources have been used as a general outline. Volume 1 of Lloyd's *History of Carmarthenshire* is a detailed account of the region's political history during the Middle Ages which has yet to be fully superseded;[9] it includes an extensive section dealing with the administrative history of the castle. Much of the latter was revised and updated by Ralph Griffiths, in his *Principality of Wales*, which deals with the structure and personnel of government, after the Edwardian conquest of 1284,[10] and is drawn on in the administrative history below. Further secondary works have been consulted, alongside those listed in Chapter 1.[11] This account attempts to summarise, synthesise and rationalise the information from all the above sources, with comparison to other, similar sites. New conclusions, and any disagreements with published accounts, are indicated in the notes. In addition, aspects of the castle's economic history are examined, and compared with the other major excavated medieval building in the town, Carmarthen Friary.

ORIGINS

The conquest of south-west Wales was a piecemeal affair, largely undertaken by the Anglo-Norman aristocracy on its own initiative. It was not until the reign of Henry I that the Crown established a permanent foothold in the region, firstly with the acquisition of the castle and lordship of Pembroke in 1102 (see below), and then, more significantly, with the commencement of Carmarthen Castle in c.1106. A castle, however, had earlier been built in the neighbourhood of Carmarthen, at 'Rhydygors'.

Rhydygors

By the late eleventh century, the basic territorial unit of Welsh administration had been established, represented by the *cantref*, which was normally subdivided into three or more *commotes*. The Carmarthen region lay within Cantref Gwarthaf, which itself was one of the 'seven *cantrefi* of Dyfed'. Dyfed was a subkingdom corresponding to present-day Pembrokeshire, and Carmarthenshire west of the Tywi estuary and the River Gwili. To the east of these rivers lay the subkingdom of Ystrad Tywi, comprising Cantref Mawr, Cantref Bychan and Cantref Cydweli lying either side of the Tywi (Figure 6). The two subkingdoms,

Figure 6 Map of south-west Wales showing pre-Conquest administrative divisions relative to the twelfth-/thirteenth-century lordship of Carmarthen

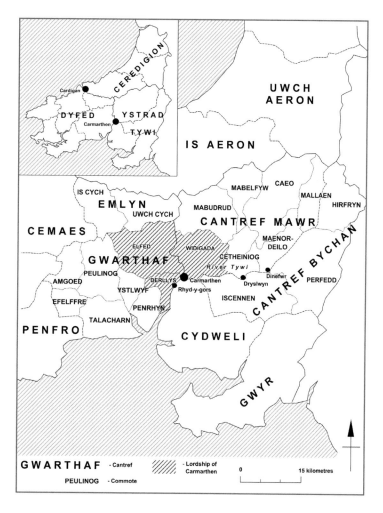

along with areas corresponding to Ceredigion and Breconshire, constituted the eleventh-century kingdom of Deheubarth.

On the eve of the Norman Conquest, Dyfed and Ystrad Tywi were under the control of King Rhys ap Tewdwr, whose overlordship extended throughout Deheubarth. His death in 1093 led to a free-for-all among both the Anglo-Normans and the Welsh princes. The Norman Earl of Shrewsbury established a castle at Pembroke, while the sheriff of Devon, William Fitz-Baldwin, apparently on the order of the Norman king William II, built an earthwork castle at 'Rhydygors'.[12] Fitz-Baldwin's choice of site may have been purely military: the name Rhydygors ('the ford on the marsh'), first recorded in 1094,[13] suggests that it commanded the ford from which it took its name – presumably one of the crossing-points in the main east–west route corridor through south-west Wales. In a volatile environment, within which the hold on Rhydygors was at first tenuous, it seems that control was eventually asserted over a substantial area.

The location of Rhydygors is however unknown, and our two sources for its history appear to contradict each other. The *Bruts* record that in 1102, in return for supporting King Henry I during the unsuccessful rebellion of the Earl of Shrewsbury, the Powys chieftain Iorwerth ap Bleddyn was promised 'Powys, Ceredigion and half of Dyfed – the other portion was in the hands of FitzBaldwin – and Ystrad Tywi, Cydweli and Gower'.[14] As Iorwerth's 'half of Dyfed' was west Dyfed, i.e. the earl's forfeit lands based on Pembroke,[15] the phrasing and punctuation of this account suggest that FitzBaldwin's territory was limited to east Dyfed, wherein, we may infer, Rhydygors lay (i.e. west of the River Tywi). *Brenhinedd y Saesson*, however, is phrased rather differently. Here we are told that Iorwerth was promised 'Powys, Ceredigion and half of Dyfed. And the other half came to FitzBaldwin, together with Ystrad Tywi and Cydweli and Gower.'[16] If Ystrad Tywi/Cydweli was indeed held by or promised to FitzBaldwin, then Rhydygors may instead have stood *east* of the Tywi.

The castle is traditionally regarded as occupying the east bank of the Tywi, 1.4 km south of Carmarthen, where the place-name Banc-y-castell is marked, on a map of 1831, next to a symbol that may represent a motte (SN 409 186; see Figures 2 and 6).[17] The site now lies beneath a railway-line. However, as the *Bruts* and the *Brenhinedd* both allow for a location in Dyfed, a site on the west side may be more likely.[18] A late medieval farmhouse called Rhydygors formerly overlooked the marshes 1.3 km south-west of Carmarthen (SN 403 191). It occupied a low promontory, simple to fortify, and indeed Ella Armitage may have hinted at earthworks in 1908.[19] It is named after the ford, and it lies close to the main Roman road (Figures 2 and 6). Moreover, it formed the nucleus of Carmarthen Castle's demesne holding of 'Redcors' (see Figure 9); the possibility therefore exists that the very location of the castle's demesne – south-west of Carmarthen, concentrated around Rhydygors – was derived from its origins as territory immediately appurtenant to Rhydygors Castle, from which it was also provisioned. It will be seen further on that, for political reasons, a site at Carmarthen itself may at first have been deliberately avoided.[20]

In the settlement that followed the Shrewsbury rebellion, Henry retained Pembroke and west Dyfed, while the rest of the lands promised to Iorwerth were instead granted to a rival Welsh chieftain, Hywel ap Gronw.[21] The grant included 'Ystrad Tywi and Rhydygors and their bounds', presumably as a foil to the FitzBaldwins, and perhaps implying that Rhydygors and Ystrad Tywi were indeed separate entities; Rhydygors's 'bounds' may mean east Dyfed. Hywel was nevertheless ejected from Rhydygors by FitzBaldwin's forces in 1105, and killed by them the following year.[22]

Foundation and consolidation, *c.*1106-1136

The death of Hywel ap Gronw released his territories to Henry I, giving the king considerable scope for intervention in the region, and it was probably shortly afterwards that he took the Carmarthen district into his own hands. He had clearly played the Welsh chiefs and the emerging marcher lords off against one another, particularly after the Shrewsbury rebellion. Rhydygors and the FitzBaldwin presence in west Wales are moreover last mentioned in 1106, suggesting that the castle was vacated on the orders of the king (and possibly slighted) when he assumed control of the region. I suggest therefore that Carmarthen Castle was built on its present site shortly afterwards. Most authorities propose a later date, in 1109,[23] when the king sent Walter FitzRoger, sheriff of Gloucester, to Wales with an army to 'go to defend Carmarthen',[24] but this phrasing suggests that the castle had already been established.[25] Its name, clearly pre-existing, was derived from the Roman town i.e. 'Caer Moridunum'.

The new castle appears to have been built on a virgin site, some distance from both the Roman town and the monastery at Llandeulyddog (see Chapter 1). It has been suggested that the king was, initially, anxious to avoid upsetting local sensibilities;[26] in fact, some kind of accommodation with the native Welsh appears to have been deliberately sought, rather than outright dispossession,[27] while the continued independence of Old Carmarthen appears to have been encouraged.[28] But the compromise came with a strategic advantage: we have seen that the site chosen for the castle was naturally strong, since it both blocks the historic route to the west and overlooks the bridging point. Visibility may also have played a key role. Moreover the site may not have been entirely 'virgin'; it may in part have been occupied by a late or post-Roman ditched enclosure, discovered in 1988, but of unknown extent and nature.[29] Norman authority through economic control was in addition exerted via the planted town – a settlement warranting the description of *villa* had developed at the castle gate by 1116, when it was burnt.[30]

Henry I then set about the reorganisation of its administration along Anglo-Norman lines. Carmarthen Castle had, by 1130, become the *caput* of a compact Crown lordship which comprised the commotes of Elfed and Derllys, both in Cantref Gwarthaf, and Widigada commote in Cantref Mawr (Figure 6). It therefore straddled the old subkingdoms of Dyfed and Ystrad Tywi, whose boundaries were otherwise largely respected by the new Anglo-Norman lordships. For most of the twelfth century, it was the only Crown lordship in west Wales. Pembroke was demised to Gilbert de Clare in 1138, remaining thereafter in marcher hands,[31] and the next royal foothold in the region was not to be established until 1200, when King John acquired Cardigan Castle.

From Carmarthen, the king was able to exercise considerable influence throughout west Wales, granting the commote of Cydweli to the bishop of Salisbury, Henry I's justiciar, and the lordship of Gower to the Earl of Warwick. Anglo-Norman interests were furthered by the establishment of additional Marcher lordships centred on the castles at St Clears, Llandovery, Narberth, Newport and Cardigan. By the second decade of the twelfth century west Wales was almost entirely under Anglo-Norman control, Cantref Mawr alone remaining in Welsh hands. Carmarthen's importance to the king, in this rapidly changing political landscape, was highlighted from the first: from it he could claim ultimate jurisdictional authority over the marcher lords.

Nevertheless, as a frontier castle, Carmarthen was subject to Welsh attacks. Gruffudd, son of Rhys ap Tewdwr, launched a major campaign in 1116, in which the ambiguous relationship between native and invader, and between the Welsh princes themselves, is clearly shown. The defence of Carmarthen Castle had been placed, in rotation, in the hands of three local Welsh chieftains,[32] when Gruffudd ap Rhys led a night attack. Ultimately unsuccessful, the bailey was burnt but the keep held out.[33] The nascent town was also burnt.[34]

POLITICS AND WAR

Carmarthen Castle was established by an invading power, in hostile territory, and its first two centuries were dominated by the struggle between the English Crown and the neighbouring Welsh princes of Cantref Mawr. It was a military base during the thirteenth-century Welsh wars, and during the Glyndŵr rebellion of 1402–6, when it was targeted as an important centre of government. This is a brief, chronological round-up of the most significant events in the castle's military and political history, focusing on its role in Crown strategy.

Welsh resurgence, 1136–1158

The Anglo-Norman hold over west Wales was consolidated following the defeat of Gruffudd ap Rhys in 1116. Much was however lost in the widespread Welsh resurgence following Henry I's death in 1135, including Carmarthen Castle, and it was not until the accession of Henry II in 1154 that the Crown was again in a position to intervene in Wales.

Carmarthen Castle was taken and burnt in 1137,[35] remaining in Welsh hands for twenty years. The effect of Welsh control on its early development is unknown, but the chronicles state that the castle was 'built' following its brief recovery by Gilbert de Clare, Earl of Pembroke, in 1145,[36] suggesting that it had been left in ruins, and vacant, during the interim. However, by the mid-twelfth century the Princes of Deheubarth, like other Welsh leaders, were repairing the castles they took and were shortly to start building their own.[37] Indeed Gruffudd ap Rhys's son, Cadell, 'repaired' Carmarthen Castle in 1150, 'for the strength and splendour of his kingdom'[38] – that is, Deheubarth, which then comprised Ystrad Tywi, Ceredigion and east Dyfed. The town of Carmarthen may, however, have been destroyed. Cadell's hold on Carmarthen was never seriously threatened, and a siege in 1147 was unsuccessful.[39] In 1155 Cadell's lands passed to his brother, Rhys ap Gruffudd,[40] the 'Lord Rhys', the leading figure in Welsh politics in the late twelfth century.

Recovery and loss, 1158–1223

It was not until 1157 that Henry II could turn his attention to Welsh affairs, and the castle and lordship of Carmarthen probably remained in Rhys's hands until his submission to Henry in 1158.[41] The castle was munitioned for the king in 1159,[42] but later that year Rhys rebelled and 'conquered the castles (in) Dyfed and burned them all', except Carmarthen which was relieved.[43] Although Henry was forced to concede Rhys's rule over Deheubarth in 1171,[44] subsequently appointing him 'justiciar' of Wales, Carmarthen Castle and lordship were retained by the Crown; the expenditure of £160 in 1181–3 may relate to an upgrade of its defences (see Appendix).

Carmarthen Castle was again munitioned in 1189,[45] in response to the rebellion of the Lord Rhys on the death of his patron, King Henry. It was soon besieged, but was again relieved by a force led, this time, by the future king, Prince John.[46] By 1193 all west Wales, except Carmarthen and Pembroke, had been brought under Rhys's control. Finally, in 1196 Rhys 'fell upon Carmarthen . . . and burnt it to the ground'.[47] The chronicles are unclear on the extent of the damage. The *Red Book of Hergest* suggests that the town was destroyed, but the castle – or perhaps just the keep – escaped ('eithyr y castell ehun').[48] However, Pen. MS 20, the *Brenhinedd* and *Annales* all state that 'Carmarthen was burnt', suggesting that destruction was total.[49] Either way, it does not appear to have been held by the Welsh,[50] and their campaign petered out following the death of the Lord Rhys in 1197.

A second royal foothold in west Wales was moreover acquired. Discord among Rhys's sons, between whom his territories were divided, resulted in a number of Anglo-Norman gains, of which the most significant was Cardigan Castle. Strategically, a similar site to Carmarthen, it was ceded to King John by Maelgwn ap Rhys, in 1200,[51] and was to be held in common custody with Carmarthen until the 1280s.

Both were granted to William Marshal I, Earl of Pembroke, in 1214, under terms in which he held them essentially as a marcher lord,[52] in reward for his loyalty to King John. In the meantime, however, Llywelyn ap Iorwerth of Gwynedd, 'Llywelyn the Great', had assumed overall leadership of the Welsh princes, launching an offensive against south-west Wales. In a pre-emptive action, the 'bailiffs and burgesses of Carmarthen burnt their town' in 1213.[53] Successful over much of south and west Wales, Llywelyn finally appeared at Carmarthen in 1215. The castle surrendered after five days and was 'razed to the ground'.[54]

Deheubarth was once again entirely under Welsh rule. It was divided between Rhys ap Gruffudd's successors, although Llywelyn initially retained Carmarthen in his own hands and only later conferred it upon Maelgwn ap Rhys.[55] The evidence suggests that the castle was rebuilt and occupied, and when Llywelyn's suzerainty was recognised in 1218, he was formally appointed custodian of Carmarthen and Cardigan during the minority of John's son and heir, Henry III.[56] King Henry III was thus in a difficult legal position on attaining his majority in 1223 and although Carmarthen was recovered, it was not until Llywelyn's death in 1240 that he could permanently annex the castle to the Crown.

Marcher rule, 1223–1240

In 1223, Henry III sent a large army of reconquest to west Wales, under Marshal's son William, also Earl of Pembroke. Carmarthen and Cardigan castles were both recovered,[57] and though Llywelyn sent a force to reclaim them, the ensuing battle, on Carmarthen Bridge, was inconclusive and both sides retired.[58] William Marshal II was granted formal custody of the two castles, and his tenure, which is discussed below, appears to have been that of a semi-independent lord.[59] He was commanded to use them as a base against Llywelyn,[60] and both were garrisoned in 1226.[61] Carmarthen once again became the centre of Anglo-Norman strategy, a role it never subsequently lost.

Marshal relinquished custody of the two castles later in 1226. In 1228, they were granted to the royal favourite Hubert de Burgh, Earl of Kent, justiciar of England and major landowner in south Wales, as a fully independent Marcher lordship (see below). This release of direct royal control must be assessed against not only the king's legal position but also, as with Marshal, against de Burgh's loyalty and military prowess. The castle was again garrisoned in response to the renewal of Llywelyn's campaign in 1230–1,[62] but Cardigan was captured.[63] De Burgh finally fell from favour in 1232, and Carmarthen again reverted to the Crown.

The castle underwent a further siege in 1233 when Marshal's brother and heir, Richard, with support from the Welsh lords under Llywelyn, rose against Henry III. It held out for three months before being relieved by a fleet from Bristol led by the king's lieutenant,

Henry de Turbeville, who was subsequently appointed custodian.[64] The rebellion ended with Marshal's death later in the year. Nevertheless Carmarthen, and nominally Cardigan, were granted – again as a Marcher lordship to the third Marshal brother, Gilbert, in 1234.[65]

The political situation in west Wales changed dramatically in 1240–1, with two events of great significance. Llywelyn ap Iorwerth died in 1240 and, with no overall leader, the Welsh lords were obliged to pay homage to Henry III, including the Lord Rhys's grandson Maredudd ap Rhys Grug for his lands in west Wales.[66] Secondly, Carmarthen and Cardigan were recovered by the Crown on the death of Gilbert Marshal in 1241.[67] Simultaneously, marcher power had been curbed, and the Welsh princes were placed under a feudal obligation to the Crown, via fealty at Carmarthen and Cardigan castles.[68] Carmarthen was never again demised to a Marcher lord, and, apart from a brief period during the Glyndŵr rebellion, never again experienced Welsh rule.

Crown strategy, 1241–1301

Hostilities, however, resumed as Llywelyn's claim to the overlordship of Deheubarth continued under his descendants. Carmarthen town was apparently burnt in 1244.[69] Garrisons were maintained at Carmarthen and Cardigan castles throughout 1245 and 1246,[70] but Carmarthen town was nevertheless 'ravaged' by Maredudd ap Rhys Grug in 1246[71] and, while there is no direct reference to damage to the castle, 'rebuilding' works were apparently undertaken the following year.[72] Henry III's overlordship was nevertheless again formally acknowledged at Woodstock the following year.[73]

In 1254, King Henry granted all Crown lands in Wales – that is, Carmarthen and Cardigan, along with the more recently established lordships of Montgomery and Builth[74] – to his fifteen-year-old son Edward, the future King Edward I.[75] Edward transferred them to his ten-year-old brother Edmund in 1265,[76] who held them until 1279, when they were quit-claimed back to the Crown, under Edward as king.[77]

It was during this period of indirect rule that Llywelyn ap Gruffudd, grandson of Llywelyn the Great, began the campaign of reconquest that was to see Deheubarth once again subject to Gwynedd. In 1257, the experienced commander Stephen Bauzan was sent to Carmarthen to assert Crown authority, but his army suffered a comprehensive defeat at Coed Llathen, near Llandeilo,[78] resulting in a four-year truce. However, skirmishes continued throughout the Tywi Valley. There was fierce fighting around Carmarthen[79] and in 1258, £567 was spent on munitions for Carmarthen and Cardigan castles.[80] Henry's strategy for west Wales was unravelling, a process that accelerated during the political unrest of the 1260s and culminated with the recognition of Llywelyn as Prince of Wales in 1267, supported by the Welsh lords of Deheubarth.[81] Cantref Mawr was held by Maredudd ap Rhys Grug, from Dryslwyn Castle, who remained an ally of the Crown, and his brother, Rhys Fychan, also Lord of Cantref Bychan, who was allied to Llywelyn.[82]

One of Edward I's three military bases in his wars against Llywelyn,[83] Carmarthen Castle ultimately became central to his policy, and administration, in Wales. The submission of Cantref Mawr and Cantref Bychan was obtained after Edward's victory in the war of 1277.

In return for homage to the king, the Welsh lords of Cantref Mawr were permitted to retain their lands,[84] although their centre at Dinefwr Castle, with its commote of Maenordeilo, was seized by the Crown – along with the whole of Cantref Bychan – and entrusted to the constable of Carmarthen and Cardigan castles.[85] Deheubarth nevertheless rallied to Llywelyn during the second war of 1282–3. Edward's forces again mustered at Carmarthen in June 1282, under his deputy Robert Tibetot,[86] but their advance along the Tywi against the castles of Cantref Mawr met a serious reverse near Llandeilo.[87] Welsh resistance, however, collapsed with Llywelyn's death in 1282.

Edward's Welsh strategy was sealed in 1284 by the Statute of Rhuddlan, under which the conquered lands were forfeited to – and in the main, directly annexed by – the Crown. Cantref Mawr was attached to the lordship of Carmarthen to form a new county, Carmarthenshire. Cantref Bychan however was granted to John Giffard of Brimpsfield, Gloucestershire.[88] Ceredigion was added to Cardigan to form a second new county, Cardiganshire. Carmarthen Castle became the formal centre of government for these new territories, and of Crown authority in the Marcher lordships, under a staff of officials headed by a new agent, the 'justiciar of south Wales'. The new administration, which both consolidated and centralised the power of the Crown, was to last, in one form or another, until the Act of Union of 1536. King Edward stayed at Carmarthen Castle for three days in 1284 during his triumphant tour of the newly conquered dominions.[89]

But it was not until the next decade that Cantref Mawr was brought completely under the control of the Crown. Maredudd ap Rhys Grug's son Rhys, Lord of Dryslwyn, had, like his father, remained an ally of the Crown and had kept his lands. However, he effectively ruled as Edward's subject, compelled to appear at the courts at Carmarthen and in 1287, apparently dissatisfied with limited rewards for his support, he rebelled. Dinefwr and Carreg Cennen castles were taken by Rhys, and Carmarthen was 'burnt to the gates', though the castle held out.[90] Rhys's campaign ultimately failed, however, bringing independent Welsh rule in Wales to an end.[91] Cantref Mawr was now at the king's disposal and, in 1290, was formally annexed into Carmarthenshire. The justiciar's position, moreover, was only strengthened, and Carmarthen was largely unaffected by the Welsh revolts of 1294–5 and 1314–16.[92]

The fourteenth century

Thus enlarged, the Crown lands in Wales – the Principality of Wales – were granted to Edward's eldest son, Prince Edward, in 1301 (see Figure 7).[93] With the effective suppression of Welsh resistance, Carmarthen Castle's role became predominantly administrative, although fleets and troops mustered at Carmarthen during the Scottish campaigns of the early fourteenth century.[94]

The castle was instrumental in the Mortimer rising of the 1320s. Edward II's favourite, Hugh Despenser, had been granted Cantref Mawr as a Marcher lordship, one of the grievances that led the justiciar, Roger Mortimer of Chirk, into open rebellion against the king in 1321.[95] Forced to surrender Carmarthen Castle to the king's officers, Mortimer – with

Welsh support – seized Cantref Mawr.[96] The castle was once more put in a state of readiness and its arms and armour were repaired.[97] The rebels were defeated in 1322, and Mortimer imprisoned, dying in 1326.[98] His nephew and ally, Roger Mortimer of Wigmore, Earl of March, recovered the office of justiciar and regained Cantref Mawr for the county, following his deposition of King Edward in 1327,[99] but the Crown, under Edward III, resumed direct control of Carmarthen on Wigmore's downfall in 1330.[100] In 1342 Carmarthen, Emlyn and Cantref Mawr were leased to Henry of Lancaster, Earl of Derby, for ten years,[101] but Edward the Black Prince received the former, as Prince of Wales, the following year,[102] while Cantref Mawr remained in Henry's hands. The Principality reverted to the king on the prince's death in 1376, but was held in dower by his widow, Joan.[103]

Like other coastal castles, royal and baronial, Carmarthen was put in a state of readiness in a more or less coordinated response to the French invasion threats of the fourteenth century. It was repaired, victualled and garrisoned against the French in 1338,[104] and was again garrisoned in readiness for reprisals when Edward III embarked on his French winter campaign of 1359–60.[105] No preparations appear to have been made for the threatened invasion of 1367, but the castle was again garrisoned on the resumption of hostilities in 1369.[106] The invasion scare of 1385, though ultimately called off, was reckoned the most serious threat so far. The Constable of Carmarthen was ordered to muster his tenants,[107] and his garrison ultimately included twenty-four bowmen, with ten crossbows, 12,000 quarrels and forty lances.[108]

The Glyndŵr rebellion and aftermath

As the seat of Crown influence, and English government, Carmarthen Castle inevitably represented the main target – both strategic and symbolic – of the Glyndŵr campaign in south-west Wales, and it was twice taken by the rebels. Glyndŵr first appeared in Carmarthenshire in August 1401, withdrawing in October on the arrival of an army under King Henry IV.[109] Carmarthen, though not threatened, was particularly vulnerable at this time having been, since 1399, under the control of the Prince of Wales (the future Henry V) rather than the Crown.[110] The justiciar's office, moreover, had begun to lose its military credibility; William de Beauchamp, Lord of Abergavenny, justiciar when the rebellion broke out, was in fact removed for negligence later in 1401, and Henry IV took direct control, creating a new post, 'Royal Lieutenant in north and south Wales', as his personal appointment.[111]

In July 1403 a large force led by Glyndŵr moved westwards down the Tywi Valley and, after some resistance, Carmarthen Castle was surrendered by its constable, Roger Wigmore, after the town had been burnt.[112] It was recaptured by the king in September[113] and a garrison left behind, in accordance with his strategy. However, it was insufficient to subdue the hinterland, where rebel sympathisers were still at large, and was therefore vulnerable;[114] the accounts are full of pleas for more soldiers, and relief.[115]

The flaws in King Henry's garrison strategy became apparent when Glyndŵr next appeared in Carmarthenshire in August–September 1405. Landing in Milford Haven in

August 1405, he marched east with an even greater force of 10,000 men, accompanied by 2,800 French troops. Carmarthen Castle once again fell, surrendered either by the constable, John Scudamore, Glyndŵr's son-in-law, or his deputy.[116]

Glyndŵr maintained his hold on the castle and county of Carmarthen until 1406, when the region gradually yielded to the king.[117] Driven from the south by vastly superior forces, Glyndŵr eventually withdrew to Caernarfonshire and the rebellion had largely died down by 1408. However, the threat remained. Prince Henry had been appointed Royal Lieutenant in 1406, but was successively reappointed until 1411[118] when at last the garrison at Carmarthen Castle was stood down. Areas of Carmarthen town had been destroyed during the rebellion. In 1408, all rents in the borough were pardoned by Prince Henry,[119] while it was said that 'the (town) walls have been razed by the Welsh rebels, and the inhabitants are robbed at night for want of enclosure.'[120] Substantial parts of the castle, too, had been severely damaged, including the gatehouse, while the demesne lands were apparently 'devastated'.[121] The Welsh of Carmarthenshire endured the fines and other penalties that were imposed throughout Wales.[122]

We do not appear to see at Carmarthen the same decline in overall status, condition and defensibility that is evident at Caernarfon and the other royal castles of north Wales.[123] Though the justiciar's authority may have declined, the castle remained militarily active throughout the fourteenth and fifteenth centuries, with no apparent reduction in either defence expenditure or military complement; indeed some of its largest garrisons were recorded both before the Glyndŵr rebellion, during the late fourteenth century, and afterwards, during the Wars of the Roses (see below). Nevertheless, the castle had a quiet time during the latter conflict, though it frequently changed hands, and saw no further action until the seventeenth century.

A CENTRE OF GOVERNMENT

This section looks at the tenurial and administrative history of the castle, which profoundly influenced its structural development, from its foundation until the Act of Union in 1536. Carmarthen Castle was the centre of Crown government, and the judicial and fiscal administration of medieval south-west Wales. During the twelfth and early thirteenth centuries the lordship of Carmarthen was intermittently demised to Marcher lords, or vested in its Welsh conquerors, but after 1241 was retained by the Crown as a feudal county. Following the enhancement of government under Edward I, its identity shifted from primarily seignurial, as the head of a feudal holding based on the castle, to civil. However, it remained the head of the manor and lordship of Carmarthen, while the Crown officials, their households and staff were all based at Carmarthen Castle; Griffiths's *Principality of Wales* includes a full list of these offices between 1284 and 1536.

The chief officials had extensive lodgings built at the castle during the early fourteenth century, which were enlarged and extended throughout the medieval period with the addition of new administrative buildings. As many as six courts were operational by second quarter of the fourteenth century, when a purpose-built courthouse was added. Many of the towers, it appears, could be used as prisons. The constable also maintained a residence at the castle. However, we must be careful to distinguish between the office-holder – who was often absentee – and the junior or deputy, who actually undertook his duties, and who would normally have been resident at the castle (discussed in Chapter 4). These buildings were largely abandoned during the sixteenth century, becoming derelict, as the castle was relieved of its administrative status.

The difference in quality of the records after the Edwardian reorganisation in the late thirteenth century is particularly marked with respect to its administrative history. There are few contemporary accounts of the workings of the administrative system in its early years; after 1284, it was as clearly recorded as the administration of England.[124]

The lordship of Carmarthen

The territory acquired from the castle after *c*.1106 (Figure 6) is referred to by a number of terms in twelfth- and early thirteenth-century sources – usually as 'lordship', often as 'honour' and occasionally as 'castlery', all essentially describing the feudal lordship held directly of the Crown.[125] Unlike the lordship of Pembroke, which was also held by the Crown from 1102 to 1138,[126] it does not appear to have been formally administered as an Anglo-Norman county until the mid-thirteenth century, and no sheriff appears to have been appointed until the Edwardian reorganisation. As a foundation of Walter, sheriff of Gloucester, the lordship was instead attached, for fiscal purposes, to the Earldom of Gloucester, as in the Pipe Rolls of 1130 (in which the return was made by Walter's son and successor Milo),[127] 1178[128] and 1189.[129] Nor did it have its own financial administration. Expenditure came via the issues of various exchequers in England; the rebuilding work of 1180–1 was, for example, financed through those of Nottingham and Derby.[130]

For administrative purposes, the lordship of Carmarthen, a compact holding occupying roughly 350 km², comprised an 'Englishry' and a 'Welshry'. The former, or 'English County' as it became known, was represented by the castle, the demesne lands appropriated to it, and the borough. The commotes of Widigada, Elfed and Derllys (Figure 6) constituted the Welshry, or 'Welsh County' (*comitatus Wallensium*), within which native law and custom, or *Walecharia*, was maintained.[131] Their inhabitants were reckoned subject to the Lord of Carmarthen and his court. Their obligations were recorded in an 'Extent' of the lordship undertaken in 1275.[132] They paid their tribute of food and cattle in kind to the king, as their lord, and were bound to follow the king's banner in any war in Wales at their own expense – a persistence of former obligations to their native lord.

The castle and lordship were normally held on behalf of the Crown by keepers or 'custodians' (*custodes*) for fixed terms, and for a fee. Custodians had full feudal powers on behalf of the king, whom they represented as a marcher lord in his own right. They were in fact temporary governors of the whole region, appointing their subordinate officers, superintending works and fortifications and provisioning the garrison, as well as accounting for receipts of rents and profits due to the Crown for the resources placed at their disposal by the various exchequers. They also officiated over the courts of the lordship, held at the castle by the later twelfth century at least, and presumably from the earliest days.[133]

It is clear that these custodians were also regarded as constables in the sense that they were the king's military deputies. Feudal terminology is blurred and interchangeable in twelfth- and early thirteenth-century documents, and the first use of the term 'constable' at Carmarthen was in the 1170s, when it was applied to the custodian Roger Norreys.[134] After the Edwardian conquest, by contrast, the constable became a separate, and subordinate office, appointed by the justiciar.

Few custodians are recorded by name in twelfth-century accounts. It appears however, that they were not normally drawn from the highest ranks of the aristocracy.[135] With few estates or responsibilities elsewhere, they may – unlike their successors, who largely functioned by deputy – have been primarily resident at the castle. They included Roger Norreys in 1174–6, Reginald Norreys in 1177–8[136] – presumably a kinsman – Richard Revel in 1180–3,[137] William de St Leger in 1189[138] and, in 1199–1200, John of Torrington.[139] The situation changed after the Crown's acquisition of Cardigan in 1200. Carmarthen and Cardigan castles were henceforth held jointly, by custodians who could now be of higher status, like William de Londres, a kinsman of the Lord of Kidwelly, custodian 1207–10.[140]

However, they were not always held directly by the Crown. We have seen above that the grant to William Marshal I, in 1214, was essentially as a Marcher lord. His son, William Marshal II, appears to have enjoyed at least quasi-independent status, 1223–6, contributing towards rebuilding work at both castles from his own purse (see Chapter 4). And Crown control was entirely relinquished during 1229–32 when Carmarthen and Cardigan were turned into a new Marcher lordship for the justiciar of England, Hubert de Burgh, 'to be held by de Burgh and his heirs by the service of five knights'.[141] Gilbert Marshal also held them as a lordship, 1234–40, 'by the service of one knight', in lieu of his lost possessions in Normandy; he was to hand them back to the king if his French lands were ever recovered.[142] These periods of Marcher rule need not have had any radical implications for the machinery of government; each lord will have had his own custodian and staff to maintain the feudal courts, as such courts and franchises operated in the independent marcher lordships like Pembroke.[143] Gilbert's brother Walter succeeded to his estates and offices on the former's death in 1241. However, Carmarthen and Cardigan were withheld, becoming permanent annexations to the Crown.[144]

Welsh rule

The effect of Welsh control on the developing identity and administration of the lordship, castle and town in the twelfth century is unclear. During the first half of the century, the Princes of Deheubarth had normally destroyed the conquered Anglo-Norman boroughs and driven out the burgesses.[145] This policy later changed. We have seen that Cadell ap Gruffudd rebuilt Carmarthen Castle in 1150, and the burgesses of Cardigan and

Llandovery, which were captured by the Lord Rhys in the 1160s, enjoyed his patronage and protection, the boroughs continuing to function as normal.[146] This was, however, *after* his tenure at Carmarthen, which had been ceded to Henry II in 1158. Carmarthen's economic significance, in fact, was probably secondary to Cadell and Rhys, who during the 1150s were primarily concerned with consolidating their hold on Deheubarth, to which Carmarthen was peripheral; it has been suggested that they realised they could not hold on to it for the long term and that it would have to be surrendered in return for other concessions.[147] There is moreover little to suggest any continuing relationship between Rhys and the town after it was ceded to the king.[148] So it is also doubtful that the princes used the castle in any administrative context. Indeed, Welsh and Welsh-held castles of the period seem nowhere to have replaced the administrative role of the native *llys*, or courthouse.[149] Welsh law and custom still obtained throughout the greater part of the lordship of Carmarthen, the Welshry, and administration was presumably undertaken through the commotal courts.

We can be more certain of the situation between 1215 and 1223. Unlike Cadell and Rhys, Llywelyn ap Iorwerth held Carmarthen as an officer of the English Crown: in 1218 he was formally appointed custodian of the castles and honours of Carmarthen and Cardigan, 'as royal bailiff, taking the profits and paying the expenses', and he immediately confirmed the burgesses' liberties.[150] The castle maintained its role as regional administrative centre, and under Anglo-Norman systems, the terms of the appointment requiring Llywelyn to 'hold the king's court in the aforesaid castles and lands according to English law for the English, according to Welsh law for the Welsh'.[151]

The early county

After the resumption of direct Crown rule in 1241, the lordship of Carmarthen, along with Cardigan, was administered as a feudal county.[152] John, Lord of Monmouth, was granted custody, and in 1242 was appointed 'chief bailiff of the counties of Carmarthen and Cardigan'.[153] Like their predecessors, the mid-thirteenth-century custodians were the chief executive officers in the county, with more or less sole responsibility for government. They continued to hold the courts, which met monthly at the castle for one day by at least 1280,[154] and are also variously referred to as the 'governor', 'seneschal', 'justice',[155] and sometimes as the 'king's justiciar in south Wales', reflecting wider royal claims.[156] Moreover, with the exception of a stray reference in 1223 – that is, *before* the county was formalised – no sheriff is recorded before the Edwardian reorganisation of the 1280s.[157] The jurisdictional claims of the county court were recorded in the 'Extent' of 1275.[158] Although the authority of royal officials was, until 1284, restricted in practice to the lordships of Carmarthen and Cardigan, claims to overlordship were made over a wider area, including the Marcher lordships of Laugharne, Llansteffan and St Clears (see below). The lordship of Kidwelly, however, was acknowledged to have been lost to the county.

The mid-thirteenth-century custodians were, at first, usually professional officers of the Crown. John of Monmouth was replaced in 1245 by Nicholas de Meules, formerly a governor of Gascony.[159] In 1248, he was replaced by Robert Waleran, hitherto keeper of the Marshal estates in west Wales,[160] a busy official of Henry III and sometime custodian of the castles at Marlborough, Rochester and St Briavels, Gloucestershire.

Like their predecessors, they were also constables – military deputies, with additional responsibility for the castle gaol.[161] They continued to be responsible for financial administration, in conjunction with the relevant exchequers; no separate exchequer, or chamberlain, existed at Carmarthen until the late thirteenth century, and – significantly – the county continued to be assessed alongside Gloucester in the Pipe Rolls.[162] And although Carmarthen and Cardigan, with their adjoining demesnes, constituted manorial 'stewardships',[163] no separate post of steward is mentioned in the sources before the Edwardian reorganisation of the 1280s, when it was an appointment to the commotal courts. Prior to that date, the use of the term 'steward' appears to be as a synonym for the custodian[164] – who, incidentally, also held the manorial courts at Llanllwch (see below). Assistants, however, were of course necessary from an early date; bailiffs are referred to in e.g. 1223[165] and 1233,[166] while Richard de Underleach and Robert de Chandos were named as bailiffs, at Carmarthen and Cardigan respectively, serving John of Monmouth and Nicholas de Meules.[167]

There was little change under Princes Edward and Edmund, 1254–79. They held Carmarthen and Cardigan as the Crown, and the counties were administered by the king's officials.[168] Under the princes, however, custodians were mainly Marcher lords. Waleran was removed, and by 1258 the Lord of Kidwelly, Patrick de Chaworth, held the post.[169] In 1263, a professional, Hugh de Turbeville, was appointed,[170] but the following year was replaced by Guy de Brian, Lord of Laugharne,[171] while Patrick de Chaworth's son and heir, Payn, received custody when Carmarthen and Cardigan were returned to the king in 1279.[172] Moreover, a separate constable appears to have at last been appointed in early 1277, perhaps as a preparation for the Welsh war, in the person of John de Beauchamp.[173] He was to have the additional responsibility of administering Cantref Bychan and Dinefwr after their acquisition later that year.

The justiciar of south Wales

Edward I's acquisition of Carmarthen brought direct Crown control back to the county, and a consolidation of royal power in the region. One of his first moves was to initiate a new office, that of justiciar, in 1280,[174] to replace the custodian. We have seen that some custodians had been referred to informally as justiciars, and in many respects the new officer's powers were no greater. They were however fully formalised. The justiciar was the chief political and judicial officer of south-west Wales. His authority, which was greatest in the generation after 1280, extended throughout the English-held regions of south and west Wales where he was the supreme governor, exercising vice-regal powers.[175] The post-Conquest environment required military men, and accordingly the first justiciar, Bogo de Knovill, was a veteran lieutenant of Edward's and a former sheriff of Shropshire.[176] He was in office for just a year before being succeeded by Robert Tibetot, justiciar 1281–98,[177] another of the king's military companions, and ex-governor of Gascony.

The office was based at Carmarthen Castle where, like the custodians, the justiciar held the county court. He also appointed the constables of Carmarthen and Cardigan castles – which were made separate and subordinate posts – and other royal officials in west Wales including, until 1341, the sheriffs.[178] The early justiciars were, like the custodians, the chief financial officers, but with a new autonomy, free from external control, in which they maintained their own treasury and submitted their own accounts to Westminster.[179] They also collected escheats,[180] undertook other tasks such as arranging military finances[181] and, initially, kept the gaols in Carmarthen, Cardigan and Aberystwyth castles.[182] Their many duties, however, meant that they were often absentee,[183] and from an early period, much of the judicial work was undertaken by deputies; in 1291, the constable Walter de Pederton, himself justiciar 1298–1300 after Tibetot's death, was also holding the courts on his behalf.[184]

The later county: Carmarthenshire

Under the Statute of Rhuddlan the feudal counties of Carmarthen and Cardigan were reorganised, and enlarged, as shires. They were neither components of the English realm nor incorporated into its parliamentary system, but were instead held directly by the Crown, and administered on its behalf by the justiciar.[185] Crown authority in south-west Wales was thereby visibly enhanced. Carmarthen Castle was formalised as their centre of government, housing its principal administrative offices until the sixteenth century,[186] as was Caernarfon Castle in the three new counties of north Wales (see Figure 7).

However, it was not until Cantref Mawr was finally brought under the direct control of Edward's officials, in 1290, that the provisions of the Statute could be fully implemented in Carmarthenshire. Cantref Mawr was annexed to the royal demesne – as 'the other part of the English county' rather than the Welshry – and was initially administered by the constable of Carmarthen Castle.[187] While reorganised on English lines, with the introduction of English criminal law, the commote was retained as its unit of government, and it retained its own beadle (Figure 8).

Crown tenants were obliged to attend the county courts at Carmarthen and Cardigan, and lay tenants-in-chief were obliged to perform military service.[188] However, the extent of the Crown's jurisdiction was often challenged. Nominally, it included the two new shires – including Cantref Mawr – and Giffard's Cantref Bychan,[189] extending over the lordships of Laugharne, Llansteffan, St Clears, Ystlwyf and Emlyn Uwch Cych (Figures 6 and 8),[190] over which claims to overlordship had been made by the feudal county in 1275.[191] The lordship of Kidwelly, lost to the county by 1275, was regained after 1284, but in 1327 it joined the Duchy of Lancaster, independently of Carmarthen, and held its own courts.[192] (We shall see that in the sixteenth century all the above lordships were joined to the thirteenth-century shire to form a new, much larger county of Carmarthenshire.) Jurisdiction was intermittently claimed over Swansea and Gower, too, resulting from their attachment to Carmarthen in the 1214 grant to William Marshal.[193]

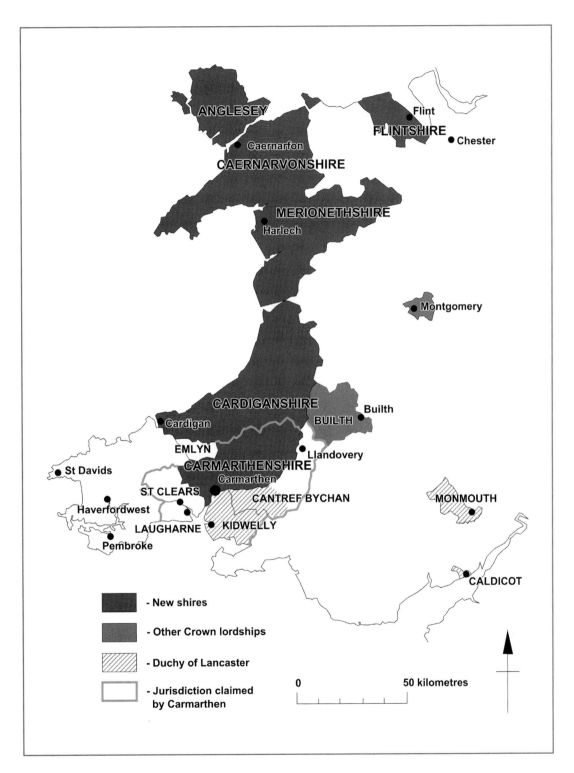

Figure 7 The Principality: Crown lands in Wales, c.1300

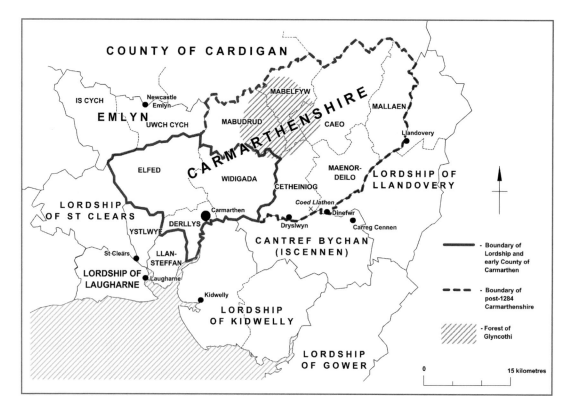

Figure 8 *Map of the post-1284 county of Carmarthen (showing sites mentioned in the text)*

The courts and officials

The administrative system was overhauled during the tenure of Edward II, first as Prince of Wales (1301–7), and then as king (1307–27), with radical implications, both functional and structural, for Carmarthen Castle. There had been hitherto only one court at the castle, the county court, which was extended from one to two days every month in 1280,[194] and which was probably held in the Great Hall (or 'King's Hall'). By the mid-fourteenth century the number of courts had been increased to six, and the 'County Hall' referred to in 1339–40 may describe a second, purpose-built courthouse (see Chapter 4).

Separate county courts for the Welshry and Englishry were established under Prince Edward in 1301, with their own beadles or bailiffs. Initially, both were held by the sheriff.[195] The annual Justiciar's Sessions, held by the justiciar himself or his deputies,[196] were probably introduced at the same time.[197] They were the highest court in south-west Wales, within which Crown pleas were heard, and through which the justiciar emerged as a primarily judicial figure, rather than military.[198] They were at first semi-itinerant, meeting at Carmarthen, Cardigan and Aberystwyth castles, but by 1327 had become fixed at Carmarthen[199] – possibly the context for the construction of the new county courthouse mentioned above.[200]

As a result of abuses under the Mortimers – justiciars during the early fourteenth century (see below) – reforms were introduced in the 1330s. They included an additional monthly court, the Petty Sessions, introduced in 1332–3 and meeting at Carmarthen Castle under the deputy justiciar.[201] Two further courts were established – the Court of Fresh Force, in 1335–6, held by the sheriff to hear land disputes, and the Court of Obligations (1337–8), held by the deputy justiciar, which dealt with debts to the Crown and was primarily used by the chamberlain.[202] Both were short-lived.

The office of sheriff, apparently introduced to south-west Wales after 1284, was a relatively minor post, held by men from obscure backgrounds.[203] Their powers further declined in the fourteenth century; the Welsh county court was taken over by the constable in 1349,[204] the English Court by the deputy justiciar in 1352–3,[205] while the Court of Fresh Force was soon dissolved.[206] The sheriff was henceforth confined to general policing duties.[207] A Crown escheator and coroner was appointed in 1323 to relieve the justiciar, becoming permanent in the 1340s;[208] like all the above officials and/or their deputies, he was based in Carmarthen Castle (cf. Caernarfon; see Chapter 4).

The medieval gaol

Carmarthen Castle had served as a gaol since at least the late twelfth century,[209] and like other castles could presumably have served in this capacity from the first. Proceedings in its own courts could lead directly to imprisonment: in the 1320s, for instance, one John Caperiche, found guilty of conspiracy in the Justiciar's Sessions, was held 'in the prison of the castle of Carmarthen for three years'.[210] But it also served a wider area, sometimes acting as a collection point. For example, eighty 'Welshmen', taken after the revolt of 1294–5, were ordered to be taken to the castle and delivered to the constable, 'who was to keep them there until they were taken to Bristol Castle'.[211] Such political prisoners may also have included the Welsh prince Rhys Grug who was seized at Carmarthen in 1213, and put in the 'king's prison'.[212]

Prisoners were initially the responsibility of the custodian, and after the Edwardian reorganisation, the justiciar, via the castle constable.[213] One of the towers of the inner ward, probably built in the 1220–1230s (see Chapter 4), was referred to as a prison in 1321,[214] and it is possible that it had functioned as a gaol since its construction. However, the number of inmates in the 1290s was far too large for any one tower, and it is apparent that, from an early date, much of the castle accommodation could be used *ad hoc* for confinement. Indeed, an account from 1390–1 suggests that the lower chambers, at least, of all five towers in the inner ward could be used – '(to) locks and keys for divers doors of the five towers, and for gyves, bolts, wedges and other irons, 8s 2d'.[215] In addition, a prison 'below the constable's kitchen' is mentioned in 1360–1,[216] while a further prison may have been added by 1414 (see Chapter 4).

The 1390–1 account also lists 'iron for making fetters etc.' Stocks were mentioned in 1306[217] and 1490–1.[218] The following year saw the purchase of 'iron for making fetter-chains and handcuffs'.[219] However, escapees seem to have been a constant problem and are recorded in 1339,[220] 1376[221] and 1506.[222] Executions could also take place at the castle – the 1491–2 account also mentions the costs of 'making a new gallows'.[223]

The constable of the castle

We have seen that the pre-Edwardian custodian of Carmarthen Castle was occasionally referred to as 'constable', and that in 1277 the post was created as a separate, formalised office as the king's military deputy in south-west Wales.[224] From an early date, however, it was not always held as a separate appointment. The first constable, John de Beauchamp, was succeeded in the post by the justiciars Bogo de Knovill, Robert Tibetot and Walter de Pederton.[225] The holder of the post was subsequently appointed by, and was under the command of, the justiciar (and was occasionally referred to as his 'lieutenant'),[226] and was frequently held by the deputy justiciar during the fourteenth and fifteenth centuries.[227] And while, in theory, a constable was appointed for each of the royal castles of Wales, by the fifteenth century men like John Scudamore (or Skidmore) were acting as constables of castles as far apart as Carmarthen and Grosmont, Monmouthshire,[228] in line with the multiple appointments widespread in England.[229] Constables were normally drawn from the lower gentry, sometimes in the fourteenth century from Welsh stock, but from 1342 onwards, aristocrats began to hold the post in plurality with other offices, and functioned by deputy. In this, Carmarthen was unusual: at only four other castles did the higher aristocracy see service, all important Crown holdings including Wallingford and Dover.[230] Joint constables were appointed in 1399-1402, a practice normally coinciding with national crisis,[231] in this case, Richard II's deposition.

The constable assisted in mustering troops during military campaigns, in garrisoning and provisioning the castle, and was captain of the garrison in time of conflict.[232] He also had civil duties. Like the earlier custodians, he held the manorial court and, after 1349, presided over the Welsh county court. He managed the king's wine store,[233] and we have seen that he was also the castle gaoler on behalf of the justiciar.

As in many any other castles, the constable's residence lay above the great gatehouse, at least from 1356–7 when 'the Constable's Chamber over the large gate' is mentioned. When the gatehouse was rebuilt in the early fifteenth century, one (or both) of its towers may have been named after the constable at the time – 'John Skidmore's Tower' is mentioned in an account of 1409–10.[234]

Normally a short-term appointment of a few years, the constable could be repeatedly reappointed. Scudamore, for example, was constable in 1405–9 (when the castle was surrendered to Glyndŵr), and again from 1409 to 1421,[235] and was reappointed 'for life' 1423–33.[236]

The exchequer and chamberlain

The thirteenth-century justiciars were assisted by financial deputies. Part of the 1288–9 Pipe Roll return was submitted by Robert Tibetot's 'valet', one Alnet,[237] who was clearly more than a servant. A treasurer, Hugh de Cressingham, had been appointed by the 1290s,[238] and in 1299 an entirely separate financial office, that of 'Chamberlain of South Wales', was created;[239] an exchequer had been built at the castle by 1306 (see Chapter 4).

The chamberlain was an appointment of the king or the Prince of Wales, but was under the control of the justiciar and his deputies.[240] He directed the collection of revenue, and its expenditure, in south-west Wales,[241] and was also responsible for the payment of all royal officials.[242] He also kept the records of administrative and judicial proceedings, and the exchequer also came to be known as the chancery.[243] Alongside the deputy justiciar, he controlled the sheriff and commotal officials.[244] Assisted by the constable, he managed Carmarthen's garrison and provisions, and those of the other royal castles of south-west Wales.[245] He also provided logistical support for the king's military campaigns, providing transport and troops as required.[246] In addition, he was responsible for repairs at Carmarthen Castle from the issues of his office, under the direction of the justiciar.[247] As with other posts, it could be held in plurality with other offices; this had occurred by the 1320s,[248] but became particularly prevalent during the later Middle Ages.

The chamberlain thus soon acquired a staff. Much of his work was being undertaken by deputies by the late fourteenth century,[249] and his team of clerks, employed in the exchequer, effectively represented the king's secretariat in south-west Wales.[250] The exchequer also housed the treasury.[251]

Like the constable, the chamberlain's term was normally short, comprising a few years, but he could be reappointed many times, and the post was largely held by the prior of Carmarthen during the first three decades of the fourteenth century. Other appointments were normally of clerks in the household of the king or prince, for example Thomas of Goodrich Castle, chamberlain under Edward III and the Black Prince.[252] So the chamberlain was not himself necessarily fully resident at the castle. Nevertheless his was a prestigious office and he had extensive lodgings built at Carmarthen Castle in the early fourteenth century (see Chapter 4), which served his staff. While the justiciar initially kept the counter-rolls, two auditors were appointed in 1349,[253] travelling from Westminster to conduct an annual audit at the castle to which, as we shall see, a purpose-built Auditor's Hall had been added by 1419.

The fourteenth-century justiciars

Prince Edward's administrative changes continued after he became king in 1307. A single justiciarship, serving all Wales, was created in 1308 for the leading Marcher lord Roger Mortimer of Chirk.[254] He held office until 1315, and again from 1317 to 1322.[255] His extended remit, and his marcher responsibilities, meant that he too was frequently absent, and like the chamberlain he largely functioned through his deputies. Nevertheless, like the chamberlain, he commissioned a suite of lodgings appropriate to his position, the 'Justiciar's Mansion', at Carmarthen Castle (see Chapter 4). After his death in 1326, the Principality was once more divided between two justiciars. However, the office of 'pan-Wales' justiciar was recovered by Roger Mortimer of Wigmore, Earl of March, on his return with Queen Isabella; he held it from 1328 until 1330.[256]

Many complaints against the regime of both Mortimers, in which oppression and abuse of the office were rife, were submitted to Parliament.[257] However, pan-Wales justiciars were once again employed under the Black Prince from 1337 to 1376,[258] contributing, through absenteeism and reduced contact with the population, to a gradual loss of their authority.[259] The importance of the deputy justiciar, often a Welshman, consequently increased. The English Court, the Petty Sessions and the Court of Obligations were all under his control, and he assisted in the array of troops from Carmarthen to Scotland and France during the fourteenth century.[260]

The later Middle Ages

The structure of government in southwest Wales changed quite markedly from the mid-fourteenth century onwards, not always as a result of deliberate intervention. The reforms introduced in the 1330s met with little success. The sessions began to be used primarily as a source of revenue; justice became secondary to income,[261] while the increasing number of courts and deputies reduced the justiciar's authority. By 1343 the chamberlain had begun to assume some of his duties,[262] while Edward the Black Prince began the practice of directly appointing castle constables. They generally served longer terms, throughout his holdings, suggesting a desire for stability.[263]

From the late fourteenth century onwards, the justiciar's office (now often termed 'justice', or 'chief justice' to distinguish it from the deputies) was frequently granted as a sinecure to high-status aristocrats as a reward for loyalty to the Crown. In addition, it was often held in plurality with the offices of chamberlain and constable, and absenteeism became the norm. For example, Richard II appointed his tutor, Simon Burley, as constable of Carmarthen Castle 'for life' in 1377.[264] In 1383 he was created justiciar, again for life. He was succeeded in both posts by Nicholas de Audley, Lord of Cantref Bychan, in 1385;[265] he in turn was replaced in 1390 by Roger Mortimer, Earl of March,[266] who was also appointed chamberlain of south Wales, bringing all three posts together under a leading baron. In addition, the post of steward (or 'Steward of the Commotes'), which was a relatively minor office created in the early 1290s to hold the local, commotal courts in Cantref Mawr,[267] and to act as head forester in Glyncothi Forest (see below), had, by the later Middle Ages, become 'honorary', held in plurality with the offices of justiciar or constable.[268]

By the late fourteenth century the justiciar was a figure of increasingly nominal status, and not normally resident at Carmarthen Castle. We have also seen that he was increasingly unable to undertake effective military command. Moreover, in the political turmoil of the later fifteenth century, such powerful magnates could no longer be relied upon to uphold the king's rule in the region. Henry V's brother Humphrey, Duke of Gloucester, was justiciar during the 1430–1440s, and in his absence it was his deputy, the Lancastrian Gruffudd ap Nicholas, of Dinefwr, who became the leading political figure in west Wales.[269] Thoroughly unscrupulous, he not only maintained the office as his personal fiefdom but dissolved the sessions entirely.[270] In 1455, Richard, Duke of York, as Protector of the Realm under Henry VI, took upon himself the offices of constable of Carmarthen Castle and steward of

Cantref Mawr[271] in order to re-establish Crown – and Yorkist – authority in the area, and ap Nicholas was ejected.[272] In 1457, the constableship was surrendered to the Lancastrian Jasper Tudor,[273] but in 1460, Richard of York assumed the title of Prince of Wales and received Carmarthen Castle.[274]

After Edward IV's victory in 1461, Sir William Herbert, of Raglan, was appointed justiciar and chamberlain, and the prominent Yorkist John Dwnn of Kidwelly was installed as constable.[275] Lancastrian sympathies, however, still ran high in Wales, and a garrison was maintained at the castle.[276] Herbert was executed after the Earl of Warwick's victory at Edgecote in 1469, the latter himself assuming the title of justiciar, chamberlain and constable.[277] In the ensuing confusion, Carmarthen and Cardigan castles were briefly seized by Gruffudd ap Nicholas's grandsons.[278] Edward IV quickly regained control of the realm, ordering his brother Richard of Gloucester (the future Richard III) to 'reduce and subdue' the two castles.[279]

Carmarthen was temporarily restored to Lancaster in 1470–1, but after Henry VI's defeat at Barnet in April 1471 the chief offices were granted to William Herbert's son, another William,[280] who reappointed John Dwnn as his constable;[281] the two officials were retained when Edward IV's son Edward received Carmarthen, as Prince of Wales, in 1473.[282]

Multiple appointments had become a formality by 1495 when the two main offices of justiciar and chamberlain were vested in Henry VII's supporter Sir Rhys ap Thomas, grandson of Gruffudd ap Nicolas and head of the House of Dinefwr;[283] he may also have been acting constable by 1520.[284] He governed uncontested at Carmarthen until his death in 1525, and was often at the castle – the Chamberlain's Mansion was at least partly rebuilt for him (see Chapter 4). In the uncertain judicial climate, however, the inhabitants of west Wales had, by 1435, begun taking their cases directly to Westminster, where, in addition, the courts were both cheaper and perceived as less biased.[285] And then, in 1471, the Council for the Marches of Wales, at Ludlow, assumed control of all judicial business in Wales, with a subsequent loss of revenue for the Carmarthen courts.[286] The Justiciar's Sessions were nevertheless intermittently held at Carmarthen Castle until its governmental role went into terminal decline after the Acts of Union of 1536 and 1543.

THE CASTLE IN THE LANDSCAPE

Carmarthen Castle exerted a powerful influence on the regional landscape, and in a number of different ways. Quite simply, it was first of all a landscape feature by virtue of its dominant location and physical presence. Fundamental in the landscape of consciousness too, it was particularly visible from the Tywi Valley to the east, from which it would have been approached from the Welsh territories of Cantref Mawr. With its high motte and towers it represented the imposition of a hostile, alien culture, sitting astride the way to the west, as well as being a visible symbol of royal prestige and authority.

This section looks at the castle in its physical and economic landscapes, reviewing its effect, as a prestige centre and seignurial residence, on the surrounding region. Demand

and consumption are examined, along with the relationship between the castle and its demesne manor at Llanllwch, and other principal sources of supply. Using contemporary accounts, sources of building materials are suggested. The castle's location in relation to the town, and its influence on urban development, are also reviewed.

The castle in the town (Figure 3)

The castle is central to the town of New Carmarthen and the hub around which it developed. The mercantile heart of the town – the market in Nott and Guildhall Squares – focused on the castle gate and the 'dynamic interface' between the castle and town is particularly apparent in the development of Nott Square. The historic interdependence of town and castle is preserved not only in the street plan, which is coaxial to the castle gates, but also in the system of present property boundaries, medieval in origin, which originate from the castle site along Bridge Street, Nott Square and particularly Queen Street, where they radiate from the motte, emphasising its centrality. The castle of course also represents the origin of the town in a more practical sense, as the source of much of the stone from which its buildings were constructed.

It has been observed that the familiar Anglo-Norman association of castle and town 'conceals a dichotomy that exists between them – a town is a community living off of commerce, [while] a castle is essentially a private institution'.[287] In the Welsh castle-boroughs, however – and particularly in governmental centres like Carmarthen, in which the castle was also a civil institution – this divide could be ill-defined.[288] The borough formed part of the demesne, annexed to the castle, with the king as its lord. It was obliged to provision the castle in time of war and, under the chamberlain's command, provided ships and provisions against the French and Scots during the fourteenth century.[289] The custodian, and later the justiciars, moreover claimed the right of jurisdiction over the borough. This inevitably led to the usual conflicts with the burgesses in their repeated attempts at self-government.[290] Neither was the physical envelope entirely static; the periphery of the castle was dynamic, subject to late medieval domestic development against its walls and within the surrounding ditch, while its later defensive features – two possible barbicans – might intrude into the town.[291] The administrative separation of castle and town however became more apparent after the borough's incorporation in 1386, and was finalised through the Acts of Union of 1536 and 1543 when the castle became 'county' property sitting within the borough (see Chapter 5).

The 'castle-borough'

Settlement, motivated by privileged status and the control of trade and markets, had begun at New Carmarthen by 1116. Its compact, nucleated plan, deliberately based around the market in Guildhall Square/Nott Square, and focused on the castle gate (Figure 3), suggests that it may have been a 'castle-borough' like that at Kidwelly, with a defined (and possibly defended) area laid out at the same time.[292] Unusually, both Old and New Carmarthen were served by the same parish church, St Peter's, which lay between the two towns and was a possession of Carmarthen Priory.[293] However, the most persuasive evidence for planning is the former St Mary's, or the 'Rood Church', which had been established beside the market cross, as a dependency of St Peter's, by 1252.[294]

New Carmarthen's morphology was, like that of the Roman town, dictated by the topography. It developed to the west and south, downhill towards the Tywi and the Wynveth Brook, at the confluence of which lay the quay, which was undoubtedly a primary feature. In its plan, defences and economic role, Carmarthen can be compared with Kidwelly and other Marcher boroughs like Haverfordwest and Pembroke, and like them too it was a port;[295] its layout moreover was almost exactly paralleled at Cardigan, which was also laid out in the years following 1110. Carmarthen profited from its position relative to Bristol which had, by the early twelfth century, established itself as the capital of the west. It was the leading military port in west Wales, receiving munitions, provisions and sometimes armies from Bristol. It was also an important trading centre, particularly in wine, wool and hides, and from 1343 was the sole staple port in Wales.[296]

Although regarded as a borough from an early period, New Carmarthen had to wait until the reign of Henry II before it received its first charter (cited in the confirmations), while its status was not formalised until 1257 and the issue of a new charter.[297] Like many other boroughs, it experienced tremendous growth later in the thirteenth century and expanded by nearly a third, from 181 burgesses in 1275, to 281 in 1300.[298] The burgesses accordingly sought a measure of self-government and petitioned that they should elect their portreeve, by choosing four suitable burgesses and allowing the castle constable to select one.[299] In 1313–18, nevertheless, the justiciar was still refusing to recognise their right to be impleaded before their own portreeve, 'in their Guildhall',[300] but they had evidently succeeded by c.1330.[301] By 1370 the portreeve had been replaced by a mayor,[302] but it was not until 1386 that the borough became incorporated.[303] Borough and county administration thereafter became increasingly separate.

Market rights were also claimed by Old Carmarthen, and although they could not be proved, they were exercised from an early period, and were confirmed in 1318.[304] Conflict was inevitable here, too; complaints were frequently made by the burgesses of New Carmarthen, and tensions arose between the early fourteenth-century priors, as chamberlains, and the justiciar.[305]

Town defences

Carmarthen may have been a 'castle-town' from an early date – the possibility cannot be dismissed that it received earth-and-timber defences before it was walled in stone in the thirteenth century. Work on the masonry wall may have already begun when it was subject to its first murage grant in 1233,[306] as the 'walls of Carmarthen' were mentioned in a document from earlier in the year.[307] Murage grants were renewed, on average, every three years until 1340.[308] The town wall joined the castle, at its south-west and north-west corners, to enclose an area of c.2.2 hectares (Figure 3), which was entered by four gatehouses. It may be that not all built-up areas were enclosed (cf. Bristol), as suburbs had developed, at an early date, either side of Lammas Street, lower Quay and Bridge Streets, and along King

Street. The walls were apparently 'razed' during the Glyndŵr attack in 1405, and were at least heavily damaged, while extra-mural development flanking King Street and Spilman Street also suffered badly.[309] The defences were consequently extended to the north-east to take in this area (an additional *c*.4.4 hectares), the new wall featuring another two (or three) gatehouses.[310] However, the Lammas Street suburb was not to be defended until the mid-seventeenth century (see Chapter 5).

Late sixteenth-century records show that Carmarthen was, by then, divided into wards,[311] but they seem to have disappeared at an early date. While urban wards were not necessarily always medieval creations – their origins and interpretation are still a matter of debate – many were, originating as divisions in which 'a mixture of judicial, financial and military functions were organised', and 'units within which manpower was organised for manning the [town] walls where necessary'.[312]

The town walls are depicted on the Speed plan of *c*.1610 (Figure 112). They were apparently slighted, along with the castle, after the Civil War, but the town gates survived until their demolition between the 1760s and 1790;[313] evidence for the line of the walls now survives only in property boundaries and the street plan. The bridge over the Tywi was first mentioned in 1220,[314] when it was presumably of timber. It was apparently destroyed in the siege of 1233,[315] and the murage grant of that year may partly relate to its masonry successor (see Figures 112, 126 etc.),[316] which was replaced by the present bridge in 1936.

The castle in the countryside

The castle's influence is strongly apparent in the development of the surrounding landscape, but its impact varied. In the Welshries, which constituted the majority of the lordship, pre-existing patterns of tenure and agriculture by and large persisted throughout the Middle Ages.[317] However, much of the 'English County' was physically transformed, i.e. the borough itself, with the demesne manor of Llanllwch, and later the royal forest in Cantref Mawr.

The Manor of Llanllwch (Figure 9)

The core of the English county occupied the parish of St Peter (Figure 9), which encompassed the borough of New Carmarthen and the Manor of Llanllwch, along with Old Carmarthen, the open fields and commons of both towns, and much priory land.[318] Little is known of the uses of the borough land;[319] Carmarthen's environs may have been primarily pastoral in the later twelfth century, as according to Gerald of Wales it was 'surrounded by woods and meadowlands'.[320] Evidence that Anglo-Norman agricultural systems were practised in New Carmarthen's holdings, however, survives in the form of ridge-and-furrow. None has so far been recorded in those of Old Carmarthen, which were presumably held under native tenure.

The Manor of Llanllwch was directly held of the castle, by which it had been acquired by at least 1125.[321] It was an administrative rather than a territorial unit; all arable land,

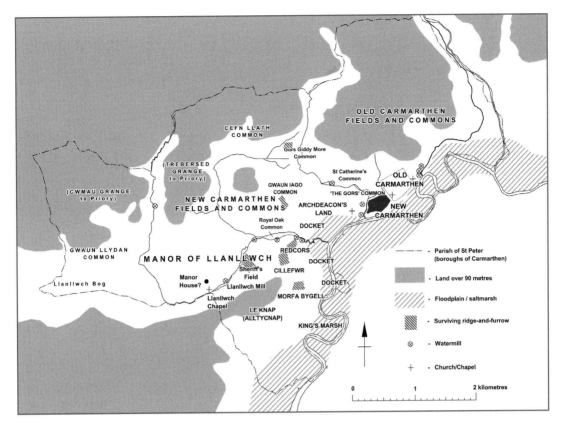

Figure 9 *The parish of St Peter, showing Llanllwch Manor and other demesne lands, and town fields and commons* (adapted from T. James (1980), Figure 4.8)

fisheries and mills in the Englishry were assessed within it. The manorial core was concentrated 2.7 km west of Carmarthen (Figure 9), with a courthouse, mill and chapel-of-ease, around which a settlement had developed by the fifteenth century at least.[322] Little management is recorded before the 'Extent' of 1275,[323] when land held in demesne included 100 acres of arable 'in divers places', including Llanllwch itself, Allt-y-cnap and Cillefwr, along with 29 acres of meadow and separate pasture moor.[324] Their locations, where identified, are shown in Figure 9. Another 'extent', from an Exchequer Record of March 1280, is more detailed and includes, in demesne, 20 acres of land called 'Archdeacon's Land', 12 acres in Cillefwr and another 78 acres of land including meadow in 'Redcors' (Rhydygors) and Dockett.[325] Other chattels included two salmon streams and a fishery, rents of four town mills, and the pleas and perquisites of the county.[326]

Manorial land of Llanllwch was held and worked by Anglo-Norman tenure, and further areas of ridge-and-furrow have been identified at e.g. Cillefwr (Figure 9). It can be seen, however, that much of it was pasture, particularly on the tidal saltmarsh of the Tywi below the castle, over some of which the burgesses of New Carmarthen had been granted grazing rights, for a fee, by the fourteenth century.[327] Llanllwch had its own manorial court – held by the custodian, or later the constable, of Carmarthen Castle[328] – and a reeve.[329] The manor ceased to be worked directly from the castle by the late thirteenth century when, like much Crown land throughout Wales, it was rented out to 'customary' tenants, becoming a source of considerable profit.[330] However, it was badly affected by the Black Death, and its value and tenurial arrangements altered accordingly; it was treated as a single holding in subsequent grants and leases.[331] The manor was, moreover, 'totally destroyed and devastated' during the rebellion of Owain Glyndŵr, and its value dropped considerably.[332] By the mid-fifteenth century, all links with the castle had been finally severed and, as the 'Lordship of Llanllwch', it was leased to a succession of individuals.[333]

The Forest of Glyncothi (Figure 8)
The wooded nature of Cantref Mawr was remarked upon by a number of contemporary writers; Gerald of Wales, for example, described it as 'a safe refuge for the inhabitants of south Wales, because of its impenetrable forests'.[334] The Crown consequently ordered extensive felling on either side of the Tywi Valley corridor, for military purposes, during the 1270s and 1280s.[335] With the final absorption of the entire *cantref* into the demesne in 1290, over 8,500 hectares of its interior, comprising both woodland and moor, was turned into a royal forest, the Forest of Glyncothi (see Figures 8 and 10).[336] It was removed from commotal administration and, with its own forest courts, was administered by a royal forester, an office which was held by the steward of Cantref Mawr (see above)[337] and was ultimately controlled by the justiciar. The forest provided building timber for the Crown, which was used at Carmarthen and other royal castles, but its primary use was as a source of leisure for the king's agents at Carmarthen Castle, and for the king himself should he visit. It was a hunting forest, managed for game, subject to forest law, and its landscape was maintained for that purpose until the close of the medieval period.[338] No further (or earlier) forest, chase or park is recorded in association with the castle.

The remainder of Cantref Mawr, though joined to the English County and held in demesne, continued to be held and worked under native tenurial systems,[339] but the burgesses of New Carmarthen were granted free common and felling in the remainder of its woods, 'on account of robberies and murders', in 1313.[340] As in Llanllwch manor, a considerable amount of land in Cantref Mawr was leased, alienated or otherwise lost by the Crown during the later Middle Ages, a process happening elsewhere, e.g. in the lordship of Kidwelly and other Lancaster holdings.[341] For example, in 1580 we find that 'rents and profits' were being taken from demesne lands in Glyncothi Forest, from pasturage on the 'wastes of the forests' and 'from great woods'.[342] However, Glyncothi retained its status as a protected, legally autonomous forest until the seventeenth century.[343]

Supply and consumption
Basic provisioning was local, from the lordship of Carmarthen. The castle was supplied both from the demesne lands described above and from the Welshries which were, for example, obliged to render an annual tribute of seventeen cows to the 'king's larder' at Carmarthen

Castle, as recorded in 1275.[344] However, these lands were, for the first two centuries, an island in potentially hostile territory, and supply from further afield was vital from the first. The castle was sited with a view to accessibility by sea, and Carmarthen's origins as a port lie in its provisioning. The importance of maritime supply was confirmed during the later medieval period, as the demesne lands were increasingly leased out and food tributes were commuted into cash payments, while demand greatly escalated with the rapid escalation of the castle population after the 1280s (see Chapter 4).[345]

Records, as usual, are scant in the early years. However, during the twelfth century, imported provisions appear to have been mainly supplied from the Honour of Gloucester, within which Carmarthen was assessed; the Pipe Rolls record that Gloucester supplied 20 bacons and 200 cheeses in 1189,[346] possibly for a garrison rather than the permanent household. However, Bristol was increasingly to be the main entrepôt for the provisioning of the castle, as during the siege of 1233, and in 1234 when it supplied wheat, beans, bacon, salt and wine.[347] We shall see that Bristol also supplied building materials, particularly lead.

Carmarthen was the base for royal armies in south Wales during both Welsh Wars of the late thirteenth century and the Glyndŵr rebellion, when it was supplied by a number of West Country ports. In 1277, corn and other victuals were conveyed by the 'sailors of Bridgwater, Totnes and Dartmouth'.[348] A Bristol ship, *La Margaret of Bristol*, was impounded in May 1404 to provision the castle and town of Carmarthen during the Glyndŵr campaign,[349] while in August of that year, customs officials in Bristol were ordered to provide the Carmarthen garrison with food, including wheat and wine, to the value of £130.[350]

Bristol also supplied military *matériel*. In 1288, forty-four crossbows 'and all their tackle' were taken to Bristol Castle, to be delivered to Carmarthen Castle for use against Rhys ap Maredudd's castle at Dryslwyn,[351] and 'a certain ship' was hired in Bristol to carry crossbows, quarrels and 'other armour' to Carmarthen.[352] In *c*.1298, six crossbows and '120 fathoms of hair cords for springalds' were bought at Bristol 'for the stores of Carmarthen Castle',[353] in a rare reference to artillery at the castle, if not necessarily intended for use there. Like other royal castles, Carmarthen was also munitioned from St Briavels Castle, Gloucestershire, the 'arms depot' for the Crown in the great ironworking centre of the Forest of Dean. For instance, it supplied 6,000 quarrels to Carmarthen and Cardigan castles, 'for their protection', in 1230,[354] while during the siege of Dryslwyn, 5,000 quarrels were sent.[355] In 1234, twenty crossbows were supplied from the Tower of London itself.[356]

In time of war, the burgesses of Carmarthen were also called upon to assist in provisioning the castle, as in 1234 when they were ordered to supply the custodian with victuals, should he run out 'before further provision is made to him', for two or three weeks, 'out of their own . . . they can be certain the king will fully repay them'.[357]

Wine was an important component of the castle's stores, and not only for use by the household – it was observed above that Carmarthen Castle was a depot for the king's 'prize' wines.[358] Most of it was shipped from Gascony (Bordeaux) and Portugal, in a trade which also became of great commercial importance to the port of Carmarthen during the thirteenth century, and which reached its peak during the fourteenth century. In 1305–6, nine ships put in at Carmarthen with eighteen casks of wine,[359] while forty-four ships brought wine to the town between 1302 and 1324.[360]

Supplies, including much of the castle's building material, generally arrived by water. Leland recorded that, in the mid-sixteenth century, silting of the Tywi at Carmarthen Quay meant that ships of deep draught had to anchor below Green Castle, some 3 km downstream from the town (Figure 10), and transfer their goods to barges and lighters.[361] Silting had begun to be a problem by the fifteenth century and we find, in 1435–6, wine being unloaded at Green Castle for boatage to the quay.[362]

It is unfortunate that opportunities for retrieving archaeological data on diet and consumption at Carmarthen Castle were limited. Of the animal bone recovered during the recent investigations, the only assemblage that was subject to specialist examination came from the 2003 excavations in the west ditch (see Chapter 3) from which the small assemblage was mainly recovered from eighteenth-century deposits.[363] No full analysis was undertaken on plant remains, which were also largely confined to later deposits in the west ditch.

Chapter 6 includes a discussion of the various sources of the pottery, and other artefacts, recovered during recent archaeological work

Sources of building materials (Figure 10)

A full petrological analysis of the building stone at Carmarthen Castle has never been undertaken. However, the surviving structures appear overwhelmingly to be constructed from local building stone. This is mainly Carboniferous limestone, which outcrops as a long ridge across south-east Carmarthenshire, south of the Tywi Valley (Figure 10). A slightly lesser amount is represented by Devonian Old Red Sandstone, mainly from red beds – particularly in work datable to the late medieval period – but also from green beds. Outcrops of both occur between the limestone ridge and the Tywi itself (Figure 10), while both limestone and sandstone beds are exposed along the shores of the Tywi estuary. These materials may be compared with those used at Carmarthen's Franciscan Friary (see Figure 3), excavated by Terry James during the 1980s, in work dating from the mid-thirteenth century through to the sixteenth century.[364] Here, Old Red Sandstone was the principal material, very little limestone being present; locally quarried Pennant stone was also used, but this has not been certainly identified at the castle.

Only a very small percentage of the site has been investigated, while excavated areas were, in the main, peripheral. Nevertheless, no worked stone, or building stone of any kind, was recovered, and very little roofing material was identified. The main source of information regarding building materials lies, therefore, in the contemporary documentation.

Stone, lime and sand

The Carboniferous limestone belt lay within the Lancaster lordships of Kidwelly and Cantref Bychan (Iscennen), which were held by the Crown after 1399. It has been extensively worked in modern times but there is unfortunately no record of quarrying for building stone during the Middle Ages, or in the earlier post-medieval period; sixteenth- and seventeenth-century

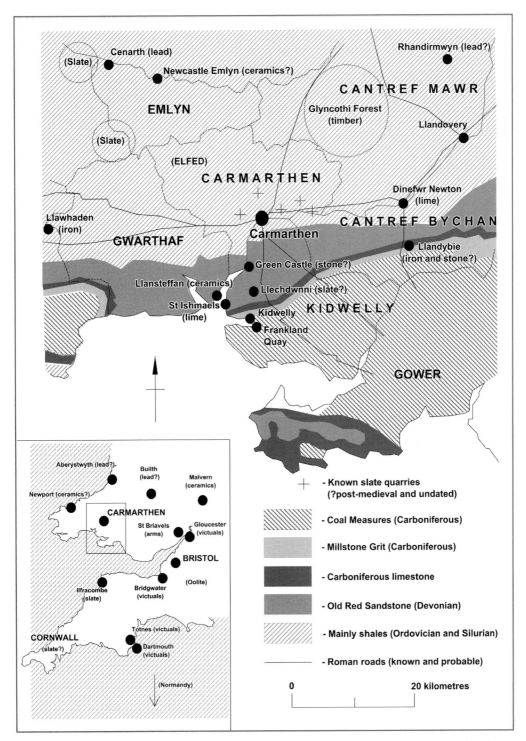

Figure 10 *Map showing sources of building materials for Carmarthen Castle, also showing geology and transport infrastructure*

references, for example, are confined to lime-burning.[365] However, quarrying was clearly ubiquitous in the area, if unrecorded, and virtually every parish has evidence for past stone extraction in the form of small-scale workings.[366] A quarry was purchased by the Duchy of Lancaster, in 1388–9, for new work on the gatehouse at Kidwelly Castle,[367] which is similar to, broadly contemporary with and perhaps by the same architect as that at Carmarthen (see Chapter 4). Further payments for stone at Kidwelly are mentioned in the Duchy accounts, but no quarries are specifically named.[368] However, the stone used at Kidwelly similarly appears to be locally sourced, and is mainly limestone.

Post-medieval quarries of Old Red Sandstone occur at Green Castle (see above), which lay within the lordship of Carmarthen (Derllys commote), and the exposure continues south along the Tywi to Llansteffan. Old Red Sandstone also outcrops south-east of Carmarthen in the lordship of Kidwelly, but being inaccessible by water is an unlikely source.[369]

The records are normally unspecific, as is well illustrated by an account of works at Carmarthen Castle in 1424 in which payment was made for materials including lime, and 'digging three barges of stones at *the quarry* [my italics]'.[370] When quarries are named in the sources, they cannot be identified with certainty. However, 'nine boatloads of broken stone' were conveyed from 'La Blak' to the castle, to repair the outer curtain wall, in 1338–9.[371] 'La Blak' possibly means Black Pool, in the Tywi anchorage immediately below the Old Red Sandstone exposure at Green Castle;[372] as the record makes no mention of transport of the stone to the boats, it can be assumed to have been coastal. If this identification is correct, it may indicate that quarrying was undertaken at Green Castle during the Middle Ages, which otherwise has yet to be demonstrated;[373] however, the reference may be to trans-shipment onto barges rather than primary supply.

Very little non-local stone can be identified within the surviving castle fabric. The exception is the Jurassic oolitic limestone, from the West Country – from a currently unknown source – used in the early fifteenth-century dressings of the Great Gatehouse.[374] The 10 tons of 'freestones, bought at Bristol', for work on the Justiciar's Mansion in 1448–9, may similarly have been West Country oolite.[375] Oolite was also used at the Friary, but the quarries are similarly unidentified.[376]

Lime for mortar was brought, *inter alia*, from St Ismaels in the lordship of Kidwelly, some 12 km south of Carmarthen on the Tywi estuary.[377] It was also taken from 'Newton', on the Tywi,[378] possibly meaning Dinefwr Newton, near Llandeilo, which became part of the castle demesne in 1277. Both references clearly relate to kiln sites, rather than the stone source. Sources of building sand are generally not given, but an account of 1435–6 mentions the 'boatage of a barge of sand from *Hueghpoule*',[379] a place-name that has not been identified, but the 'pool' element may again suggest trans-shipment rather than supply.

Roofing material

Although a large quantity of slate was revealed through excavation, it was, in the main, very fragmentary. Little of it could be positively identified as roofing material, and most was discarded. In general, the slate observed was a greenish phyllite, characteristic of the Preseli and lower Teifi Valley areas (Figure 10), where a large number of quarries were recorded during the post-medieval period,[380] and which has, in recent times, been used to great effect at County Hall. Extraction here has a much longer history, however; while no quarries were documented during the medieval period,[381] Preseli slate was the most common roofing material at Carmarthen Friary, where it formed 43 per cent of the total slate assemblage.[382]

Nevertheless, the few quarries identified in Carmarthen Castle's records were located elsewhere. In 1387–8, for instance, '4,500 stone tiles' for the castle were 'dug in the quarry at Elfed', in the lordship of Carmarthen.[383] The terminology presumably refers to slate, rather than tile-stone. The solid geology of Elfed commote is almost entirely Ordovician, and mainly comprises shale, but while no slate quarries are known,[384] there are a number of 'slate' or 'slab' place-name elements (e.g. llech). However, the known sources of roofing material within the lordship instead lie around Carmarthen itself, in commotes Derllys and Widigada, where more durable Ordovician shales outcrop, if of rather poor quality. Five small workings have been identified in this area, two of which were recorded in the eighteenth century while another two are undated (Figure 10),[385] and it provided 35 per cent of the Friary assemblage.[386] Similar material was unearthed at the castle, but was undiagnostic.

Old Red Sandstone is almost unknown as a roofing material in the Carmarthen area.[387] However, a long exposure on Mynydd Myddfai, south-east of Llandovery, has been extensively worked for tile-stone, although it is uncertain whether extraction has medieval origins, while stone slates from Old Red Sandstone marls in Pembrokeshire were formerly made into roof tiles.[388] Of interest is an order, from 1578, for the purchase of 36,000 'Laughdony' slates and three dozen 'crests' (i.e. ridge-tiles), for use at Carmarthen Castle.[389] It is possible that 'Laughdony' represents Llechdwnni, in the lordship of Kidwelly, which occupies the Old Red Sandstone belt (Figure 10) and contains a 'slate/slab' element in its name, and that stone tiles are meant, although no quarries are recorded here.[390] It is possible, too, that the ridge-tiles were local, of 'Carmarthen Bay' manufacture (see below and Chapter 6).[391] In 1435–6, moreover, 'tile-stones' had been carried from the dock below 'ffre(n)s';[392] this might be identifiable as Frankland Quay, on the River Gwendraeth Fawr, 2 km south-east of Kidwelly, which has probable medieval origins.[393] The latter reference may therefore indicate that the tile-stones were quarried nearby, i.e. in the lordship of Kidwelly. However, it may equally refer to trans-shipment of materials from elsewhere, and perhaps to slate rather than stone – if so, possibly slate from Cornwall or Devon. Devon was a major source of roofing slate for prestige buildings during the medieval period, while also producing ridge-tile (see below), and was easily accessible by sea – 20,000 slates were shipped from Ilfracombe to Kidwelly, in 1478–81, for use at the castle.[394]

There are, however, insufficient data from the castle excavations to establish whether any imported slate was present. No Devon slate appears to have been used at Carmarthen Friary, where the remainder of the slate comprised micaceous sandstone, possibly from the Saundersfoot area (Pembrokeshre) or the east Carmarthenshire coalfield (14 per cent), while the small amount of imported blue slate (8 per cent) may have been post-Dissolution.[395]

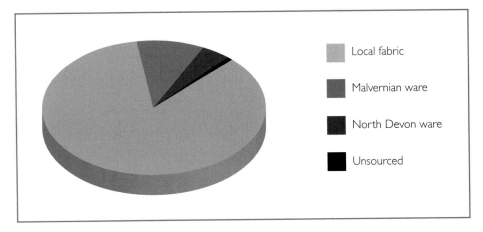

Figure 11 *Percentages of ridge-tile types from all excavations at Carmarthen Castle*

However, 126 fragments of ridge-tile were retrieved during excavation at the castle (fabrics etc. are discussed in Chapter 6). The overwhelming majority of them – 118 sherds (94.5 per cent) – were from the castle west ditch, but largely occupied secondary deposits (see Chapter 3); the remainder came mainly from the shell-keep. Most were in the local Dyfed gravel-tempered fabric (107 sherds; 85.5 per cent – see Figure 11), which was produced during the medieval and early post-medieval periods but has, as yet, no dated type-series; it is currently thought to have been in production from the thirteenth century through to the late sixteenth or early seventeenth century.[396] These tiles generally have a green glaze and simply cut crests. A major centre of manufacture was at Newport, Pembrokeshire, but only one sherd was identified with any certainty from these kilns, which are in fact probably early post-medieval.[397] None were identifiable as Carmarthen Bay/Llansteffan ware, which was extensively employed at Carmarthen Friary.[398] Twelve fragments (9.6 per cent) were imported Malvernian ware, datable to the fifteenth–sixteenth centuries, and five (4.1 per cent) were in North Devon gravel-tempered fabric, from the sixteenth–seventeenth centuries. The latter were confined to the west ditch. The percentages can be compared with those from the Friary, where local wares accounted for nearly 60 per cent of the ridge-tile, Malvernian ware for 20 per cent and North Devon wares for 15 per cent.[399]

Timber (Figure 10)

Timber was of course an important resource throughout the castle's history, particularly during the twelfth and early thirteenth centuries when it was the main building material. The 1280 'Extent' records the obligation imposed on the inhabitants of the Welshries, presumably from the first, to 'carry timber to the castle . . . when the lord orders it', clearly for building work;[400] in 1355, it was alleged that the Priory's weirs in the Tywi 'prevented the carriage by water of timber for the repair of the castle'.[401] The commotes also provided craftsmen to work the timber – in 1288, 'certain carpenters of Elfed and Widigada' were paid 20s. 'for making planks, joists, boards and other timber'.[402] Timber from Elfed also provided fuel for lime-burning etc.[403]

With the absorption of Glyncothi Forest into the demesne in 1290, a whole new resource became available (Figures 8 and 10). 'Timber from Glyncothi' was used for repairs in 1306,[404] while in 1424, payment was made for '1,000 laths from the king's woods there'.[405] In 1424–5, two tables and eight benches were 'made anew . . . from timber of the king's forest of Glyncothi',[406] while Glyncothi timber is also mentioned in building accounts from 1461–2 and 1464–5.[407]

Structural metalwork (Figure 10)

Where iron and lead existed locally, they were mined, but mainly on a small scale. The extraction of both is recorded in Cantref Mawr, near Talley, in an *Inquisition Post Mortem* of 1317 when each mine was worth 40s. annually.[408] Iron was also mined near Llandybïe, in Cantref Bychan (held by the Crown from 1399) and in the Marcher lordship of Llandovery.[409] An important lead mine lay in Crown land near Aberystwyth, from which the king received a ninth of the output and the right to purchase any additional lead.[410] By the thirteenth–fourteenth centuries, there were further lead mines at Rhandirmwyn (Llandovery lordship), and in the Crown lordship of Builth.[411] In addition, a licence was granted to search for lead for Carmarthen Castle at Cenarth (Emlyn), in 1542, while iron nails were bought at Llawhaden.[412]

Of much greater importance than any of these local sources was import, again chiefly from Bristol. Where nails are mentioned in the accounts they were normally supplied from Bristol, along with raw iron. In *c.*1250, for example, '1,000 nails called spikings, 4,000 floor-nails and 2,000 wall-nails' were sent from Bristol to Carmarthen;[413] a very similar order, from *c.*1279, included the same quantities of each.[414] Bristol supplied other building materials, particularly lead (see Appendix). In 1252, the bailiffs of Bristol were ordered to buy four fothers (around four tons) of lead 'and carry them to Carmarthen Castle',[415] while 8 hundredweight of iron, 6 seams of lead (each seam of four cartloads), and 3,000 nails were sent in 1265–79.[416] In 1279, six smiths were ordered to be sent from Bristol, 'together with forty *summae* of iron and four *magnae carratae* of lead',[417] and another fourteen carats of lead from Bristol Castle were used in rerofing 'the houses of [Carmarthen] castle' in 1287–8.[418] However, apart from a handful of nails and lead clippings, which were not diagnostic, no structural metalwork was recovered during the recent excavations.[419]

Other materials

Few other materials are mentioned in the sources, or were recovered through excavation. However, a fragment of 'Normandy-type' floor-tile was unearthed in the shell-keep (five more were retrieved from the west ditch, outside the gatehouse, but from post-medieval, secondary deposits derived from an unknown source, discussed in Chapters 3 and 6). The type is datable to the early sixteenth century and also occurred at the Friary;[420] export from Normandy and Le Havre is well documented.[421] In addition, a fragment of plain floor-tile, in local gravel-tempered fabric of probable medieval date, was also retrieved from the ditch where, like the Normandy tile, it may not have been a primary deposit.

A number of accounts mention the carriage of materials in the 'King's Barge' or 'Galley', as in 1424 when sand for the castle was carried 'in the King's Barge to the Quay of Carmarthen',[422] presumably referring to its trans-shipment from other, larger vessels. The King's Barge was a permanent chattel annexed to Carmarthen Castle and demesne. It first appeared in the records during the siege of 1233, when one of the defenders, Robert Russell, sought victuals for the castle in 'the king's galley'.[423] The vessel in use in 1394–1401 had at least five oars, while five canvas cables and an iron anchor are listed in the same account;[424] it was repaired with timber from Elfed in 1430–2.[425] As with so much demesne property, the barge was occasionally leased out in the later Middle Ages; it continued to be listed in accounts until 1447–8,[426] after which it was, presumably, permanently alienated from the demesne.

NOTES

1   T. Jones (ed.), *Brut y Tywysogyon: Peniarth MS. 20 Version* (Cardiff: UWP, 1952); T. Jones (ed.), *Brut y Tywysogyon: Red Book of Hergest Version* (Cardiff: UWP, 1955).

2   T. Jones (ed.), *Brenhinedd y Saesson, or The Kings of the Saxons* (Cardiff: UWP, 1971).

3   J. Williams ab Ithel (ed.), *Annales Cambriae*, Rolls Series (London: Longman, Green, Longman and Roberts, 1860).

4   F. Green (ed.), 'Carmarthen Castle: A Collection of Historical Documents relating to Carmarthen Castle from the Earliest Times to the Close of the Reign of Henry VIII', *WWHR*, 3 (1913), 1–72; *WWHR*, 4 (1914), 1–71. Also see G. E. Evans (ed.), 'Carmarthen. Documents relating to the Town from the Earliest Times to the Close of the Reign of Henry VIII', *TCASFC*, 17 (1924), 61–72; *TCASFC*, 18 (1925), 1–22.

5   These include, *inter alia*, N. Fryde (ed.), *List of Welsh Entries in the Memoranda Rolls, 1282–1343* (Cardiff: UWP, 1974); W. Rees (ed.), *Calendar of Ancient Petitions relating to Wales* (Cardiff: UWP, 1975); W. Rees (ed.), 'Ministers' Accounts of West Wales, 1352–3', *BBCS*, 10 (1941), 60–82, 139–55, 256–70; J. G. Edwards (ed.), *Calendar of Ancient Correspondence relating to Wales* (Cardiff: UWP, 1935); M. C. B. Dawes (ed.), *Registers of Edward the Black Prince*, 1–4 (London: HMSO, 1930–3); J. C. Davies (ed.), *Episcopal Acts relating to the Welsh Dioceses 1066–1272*, 1 (Cardiff: Historical Society of the Church in Wales, 1946).

6   NLW, MSS 12364D and 12365D, 'Collectanea concerning Caermarthen', 1 and 2, transcribed by Alcwyn Evans.

7   J. R. Daniel-Tyssen (ed.), *Royal Charters and Historic Documents relating to the Town and County of Carmarthen* (Carmarthen: William Spurrell, 1878), pp. 45–50.

8   H. Pryce (ed.), *The Acts of Welsh Rulers 1120–1283* (Cardiff: UWP, 2005).

9   J. E. Lloyd (ed.), *A History of Carmarthenshire*, 1 (London: London Carmarthenshire Society, 1935).

10 R. A. Griffiths, *The Principality of Wales in the Later Middle Ages: The Structure and Personnel of Government*, 1: *South Wales 1277–1536* (Cardiff: UWP, 1972).

11 These include, *inter alia*, R. R. Davies, *The Revolt of Owain Glyn Dŵr* (OUP, 1995); J. E. Morris, *The Welsh Wars of Edward I* (Oxford: Clarendon Press, 1901); R. A. Griffiths and R. S. Thomas, *The Making of the Tudor Dynasty* (Stroud: Alan Sutton Publishing, 2005); R. Turvey, 'The Defences of Twelfth-century Deheubarth and the Castle Strategy of the Lord Rhys', *Archaeologia Cambrensis*, 144 (1997), 103–32.

12 Jones, *Brut Pen. 20*, pp. 19-20.

13 Ibid.

14 Ibid., p. 24; the account is not given fully in Jones, *Brut Red Book*.

15 Ibid., p. 25.

16 Jones, *Brenhinedd*, p. 97.

17 OS 1" Old Series (Sheet 41), 1831. The tithe schedule records a number of field-names containing the element 'rhyding' around Banc-y-castell (NLW, Llangunnor parish, 1841). However, *rhyd* place-names will naturally occur on both sides of the ford.

18 The location of Rhydygors is discussed in T. James, *Carmarthen: An Archaeological and Topographical Survey*, CAS Monograph 2 (Carmarthen, 1980), pp. 34–5, in which the traditional, east-bank location was preferred. A site to the west of the Tywi is however favoured in a recent paper, which goes so far as to refer to east Dyfed as forming 'effectively, a "county" of Rhydygors' (B. Coplestone-Crow, 'Ystlwyf/Oysterlow: Welsh Commote and Norman Lordship', *Carms. Antiq.*, 46 (2010), 5).

19 E. Armitage, 'Carmarthen Castle', *TCASFC*, 3 (1908), 14. Its defensive capabilities have been

observed by Charles Hill of DAT (pers. comm.), who also suggests another possible candidate in the nearby defended enclosure on Allt-y-cnap (SN 396 187), which, although normally regarded as Iron Age, is undated. The 'ford' and 'marsh' place-name elements may however militate against it. Of course, the possibility exists that another, entirely different site in the region is indicated.

20 King's assumption that Rhydygors represents the present castle site cannot however be entirely ruled out (see King, *Castellarium Anglicanum*, p. 54). But the name 'Carmarthen' would, I suggest, have been applied to the castle from the first (i.e. 'Caer Moridunum'; see below), while the *gors* element is again not particularly applicable.

21 Jones, *Brut Pen. 20*, pp. 25–6.

22 Ibid., pp. 25–7.

23 Including T. James, *Carmarthen Survey*, p. 35.

24 Jones, *Brenhinedd*, p. 109.

25 And other chronicles, probably representing 'purer' texts, suggest that Walter was in Carmarthen on other business – he 'had come to Carmarthen' (Jones, *Brut Pen. 20*, p. 29); he 'happened to come to Carmarthen' (Jones, *Brut Red Book*, p. 59). Also see Jones, *Brenhinedd*, p. 109n (p. 301).

26 R. A. Griffiths, 'The Making of Medieval Carmarthen', *Carms. Antiq.*, 9 (1973), 90.

27 H. James, 'Carmarthen', in E. P. Dennison (ed.) *Conservation and Change in Historic Towns*, CBA Research Report 122 (1999), p. 161.

28 Heather James, pers. comm.

29 Heather James, *Roman Carmarthen: Excavations 1978–1993*, Britannia Monograph Series, 20 (London, 2003), p. 40.

30 Williams ab Ithel, *Annales*, p. 36.

31 Not without interruption, however; Pembroke was confiscated by Henry II in 1171, and remained under Crown control until 1199 (N. D. Ludlow, 'Pembroke Castle and Town Walls', *Fortress*, 8 (1991), 27).

32 Jones, *Brut Red Book*, pp. 86–9.

33 Ibid., pp. 88–9.

34 'Villa combusta' (Williams ab Ithel, *Annales*, p. 36); cf. Jones, *Brenhinedd*, p. 128 n. 17, where the town is termed 'y dref'.

35 Jones, *Brut Pen. 20*, p. 52; Jones, *Brut Red Book*, p. 117.

36 Jones, *Brut Pen. 20*, p. 54.

37 The twelfth-century shift, under the Welsh, from abandonment of castles to their reuse and rebuilding, was not necessarily linear or straightforward. There is no clear evidence that, in west Wales, the Welsh princes left garrisons at any of the castles taken during the 1130s when, according to the chronicles, they returned to their homelands after each campaign. However, we have seen that Hywel ap Gronw was granted, and appears to have occupied, Rhydygors Castle 1102–5 – the earliest recorded Welsh occupation of a castle. And in mid-Wales, the princes had been both reusing castles and building their own since at least 1111 (ibid., p. 35), and possibly as early as 1109 (Jones, *Brenhinedd*, p. 109). Also see D. J. C. King, *The Castle in England and Wales* (London: Croom Helm, 1988), p. 130, and L. Butler, 'The castles of the princes of Gwynedd', in D. M. Williams and J. R. Kenyon (eds), *The Impact of the Edwardian Castles in Wales* (Oxford: Oxbow, 2010), p. 27.

38 Jones, *Brut Pen. 20*, p. 57.

39 Williams ab Ithel, *Annales*, p. 43.

40 Ibid.

41 Roger Turvey, pers. comm.; also see Jones, *Brut Pen. 20*, p. 60. An appreciation of the strategic use of castles by the Lord Rhys is argued in Turvey, 'Defences of Twelfth-century Deheubarth', 103–32. At this early stage of his career, however, Rhys was not in a position to include Carmarthen in his strategy.

42 Green, 'Carmarthen Castle' 3, 26.

43 Jones, *Brut Pen. 20*, p. 61; Jones, *Brut Red Book*, p. 141.

44 Jones, *Brut Pen. 20*, p. 67.

45 Green, 'Carmarthen Castle' 3, 26.

46 Williams ab Ithel, *Annales*, p. 57.

47 Jones, *Brut Pen. 20*, pp. 75–6 and n.

48 Jones, *Brut Red Book*, p. 177.

49 Jones, *Brut Pen. 20*, p. 76; Jones, *Brenhinedd*, p. 191; Williams ab Ithel, *Annales*, p. 60. Thomas Jones, translator of the *Bruts*, was inclined to believe that the former was the case (*Brut Red Book*, p. 190).

50 Roger Turvey suggests that Rhys took and destroyed the castle, adding that his action was incomprehensible and left the Tywi valley open to attack by the royal army (Turvey, 'Defences of Twelfth-century Deheubarth', 122). But it may be that Rhys lacked the resources to repair, garrison and defend Carmarthen. Its destruction may also have been a public display of Welsh power over the English (Roger Turvey, pers. comm.).

51 Jones, *Brut Pen. 20*, pp. 80–1.

52 Green, 'Carmarthen Castle' 3, 27.

53 Williams ab Ithel, *Annales*, p. 71.

54 Jones, *Brut Pen. 20*, p. 91; Jones, *Brut Red Book*, p. 205.

55 Jones, *Brut Pen. 20*, pp. 92, 98.

56 *CPR,* Hen. III, 1216–1225 (London, 1901), pp. 143, 159.

57 Jones, *Brut Pen. 20*, p. 99.

58 Ibid., p. 100; Edwards, *Cal. Anc. Correspondence*, p. 24.

59 *CPR*, 1216–25, pp. 413–14.

60 Ibid., p. 489.

61 With 'thirty sergeants and ten crossbow-men' (Green, 'Carmarthen Castle' 3, 32), while 'divers payments' were made for their keeping and repair (*CLR*, Hen. III, 1, 1226–1240 (London, 1916), p. 17).

62 Evans, 'Carmarthen Documents' 17, 62–3; 6,000 quarrels were also sent to Carmarthen and Cardigan 'for their protection' (Green, 'Carmarthen Castle' 3, 34).

63 Jones, *Brut Pen. 20*, p. 102.

64 Jones, *Brenhinedd*, p. 231; Green, 'Carmarthen Castle' 3, 35–6.

65 *CChR* 1, Hen. III 1226–1257 (London, 1903), p. 189.

66 Griffiths, *Principality*, p. 1.

67 *CCR*, Hen. III 4, 1237–1242 (London, 1911), p. 198.

68 Griffiths, *Principality*, p. 2.

69 According to the 'C' text of the *Annales Cambriae*, thus: *David filius Lewelin combussit Cayrmardyn*. This event is however not recorded in either the 'A' or 'B' texts (Williams ab Ithel, *Annales*, p. 84 n. 8).

70 *CLR*, Hen. III, 3, 1245–1251 (London, 1937), pp. 7, 50.

71 Williams ab Ithel, *Annales*, p. 86.

72 *CLR*, 1245–51, pp. 134–5.

73 Griffiths, *Principality*, p. 2.

74 The fledgeling 'principality' that was formalised under Edward I in 1301.

75 Green, 'Carmarthen Castle', 3, 13 *et al.*

76 *CChR* 6, 5 Hen. VI–8 Hen. VIII, 1427–1516 (London, 1927), Appendix 1215–1288, p. 287.

77 *CChR* 2, Hen. III–Edw. I, 1257–1300 (London, 1906), p. 215.

78 Jones, *Brut Pen. 20*, p. 111 *et al.*

79 The burgesses petitioned that 'there is no truce in their district . . . because the king's enemies and theirs are around them, taking and burning (and they) are so destroyed and impoverished and reduced that some of their neighbours have abandoned the town' (Edwards, *Cal. Anc. Correspondence*, pp. 14–15; TNA: PRO SC 1/3/1).

80 *CLR* 6, 1267–1272 (London, 1964), p. 270.

81 Griffiths, *Principality*, p. 2.

82 W. Rees (ed.), *A Survey of the Duchy of Lancaster Lordships in Wales 1609–1613* (Cardiff: UWP, 1953), p. xv. Maredudd ap Rhys Grug held the commotes of Cetheiniog, Mabudrud, Mabelfyw and Emlyn Uwch Cych, based on Dryslwyn Castle. Rhys Fychan, from Dinefwr Castle, held the commotes of Maenordeilo, Mallaen and Caeo, along with Cantref Bychan. However, both died in 1271 and, under their successors, Cantref Mawr

became gradually subject to English overlordship from Carmarthen; it is apparent from a survey of Carmarthen, undertaken in 1275, that Llywelyn's power was none too firmly fixed in the region (Daniel-Tyssen, *Royal Charters*, pp. 45–50).

83 Along with Chester and Montgomery castles.

84 Griffiths, *Principality*, p. 3.

85 *CCcR*, 1277–1326 (London, 1912), p. 182.

86 Ibid., p. 254.

87 Morris, *Welsh Wars*, p. 166.

88 Rees, *Duchy of Lancaster Lordships*, p. xv.

89 *CFR* 1, Edw. I, 1272–1307 (London, 1911), p. 208 *et al*.

90 Williams ab Ithel, *Annales*, p. 109.

91 The campaign against Rhys, and the siege of Dryslwyn Castle, was undertaken from Carmarthen Castle. A force, drawn from all over England and Wales, was summoned to Carmarthen, including a local contingent (*CCcR*, 1277–1326, p. 314), while arms, with 300lb. of silver to pay the troops, were sent to the castle from Bristol (see M. I. Williams, 'Carmarthenshire's Maritime Trade in the 16th and 17th Centuries', *Carms. Antiq.*, 14 (1978), 61). Dryslwyn Castle fell within three weeks, and Dinefwr and Carreg Cennen were soon recovered.

92 However, Dinefwr Castle was burnt in the rebellion of 1314–16 (S. E. Rees and C. Caple, *Dinefwr Castle/Dryslwyn Castle* (Cardiff: Cadw, 2007), p. 19), when the repair and provisioning of the royal castles of west Wales was ordered (Rees, *Cal. Anc. Petitions*, pp. 76–7 and n.), and the burgesses of Carmarthen petitioned that 'the Welsh greatly threaten to revolt against them' (ibid., pp. 75–6, 80).

93 *CChR* 3, Edw. I, Edw. II, 1300–1326 (London, 1908), p. 6.

94 In February 1319, for instance, Carmarthen was ordered to provide a ship and soldiers for Edward II's Scots war (Rees, *Cal. Anc. Petitions*,

p. 77n), while in 1337, ships from Carmarthen, paid from its exchequer, were again in Scotland 'on the king's service' (Edwards, *Cal. Anc. Correspondence*, pp. 189–90).

95 Rees, *Cal. Anc. Petitions*, pp. 80–1 and n.

96 Lloyd, *History of Carmarthenshire*, p. 243.

97 Green, 'Carmarthen Castle' 3, 52.

98 Rees, *Cal. Anc. Petitions*, pp. 527–8 and n.

99 *Cal. Inq. Misc.* 2, 1307–1349 (London, 1916), p. 242.

100 Rees, *Cal. Anc. Petitions*, pp. 492–3 and n.

101 *CFR* 5, Edw. III, 1337–1347 (London, 1915), p. 263.

102 *CChR* 5, 15 Edw. III–5 Hen. V, 1341–1417 (London, 1916), p. 14.

103 *CPR*, Edw. III 16, 1374–1377 (London, 1916), p. 376.

104 Green, 'Carmarthen Castle' 3, 54, and perhaps as early as 1334, when the royal castles of south Wales were victualled and munitioned 'to the value of £20' (ibid., p. 53).

105 Dawes, *Registers of the Black Prince*, 3, p. 378.

106 In early 1370 the garrison included ten archers with forty bows (Green, 'Carmarthen Castle' 3, 64–5).

107 *CCR*, Rich. II 2, 1381–1385 (London, 1920), p. 549.

108 Green, 'Carmarthen Castle' 3, 65–6.

109 Davies, *Glyn Dŵr*, pp. 105–6.

110 Griffiths, *Principality*, p. 31.

111 Ibid., and pp. 127–8; Davies, *Glyn Dŵr*, p. 113.

112 Griffiths, *Principality*, pp. 123–4; R. Turvey, 'Twelve Days that Shook South-west Wales: The Royal Letters, Owain Glyndŵr and the Campaign of July 1403', *Carms. Antiq.*, 37 (2001), 11. Dryslwyn, Newcastle Emlyn and Llansteffan castles were also taken, and possibly Carreg Cennen. Dinefwr, Llandovery, Laugharne and St Clears however held out. NB: Roger Wigmore was no relation of the Mortimer Earls of Wigmore.

113 Davies, *Glyn Dŵr*, p. 114.

114 It comprised 120 men-at-arms and 500 archers, under the command of John Beaufort, Earl of Somerset (see Chapter 4).

115 Green, 'Carmarthen Castle' 4, 4–7; Lloyd, *History of Carmarthenshire*, pp. 253–5.

116 John Scudamore, or 'Skidmore', of Kentchurch and Ewias Lacy, Herefordshire, had, before 1433, married Glyndŵr's daughter Alice – a marriage which would have been illegal after 1401 (tradition has it that it was in 1395). He was accused, but never charged, with being in league with Glyndŵr in 1405. In fact, he continued serving the Crown against the rebels (Turvey, 'Twelve Days', 10), and although he was named as constable in April 1405, he was also the constable of Grosmont Castle and so may not have been in Carmarthen when it fell (Griffiths, *Principality*, pp. 140, 201). It was not until 1433 that he was decreed, nevertheless, to be 'no longer eligible to hold [office] having married Alice, daughter and heir of the traitor Owain Glyndŵr', and he was replaced (*CPR*, Hen. VI 2, 1429–1436 (London, 1907), p. 286).

117 Davies, *Glyn Dŵr*, p. 295.

118 Ibid., p. 113; Griffiths, *Principality*, pp. 127–8.

119 Davies, *Glyn Dŵr*, p. 279.

120 *CPR*, Hen. V 1, 1413–1416 (London, 1910), p. 308.

121 Lloyd, *History of Carmarthenshire*, p. 256, from Min. Acc. 1165/11.

122 See e.g. Davies, *Glyn Dŵr*, pp. 304–6; Rees, *Cal. Anc. Petitions*, p. 18.

123 Where it is discussed by M. Prestwich, 'Edward I and Wales', in Williams and Kenyon, *Impact of the Edwardian Castles*, p. 7.

124 Fryde, *Memoranda Rolls*, p. xiii.

125 See, *inter alia*, Lloyd, *History of Carmarthenshire*, p. 136; *CPR*, Hen. III, 1225–1232 (London, 1903), p. 58.

126 Ludlow, 'Pembroke Castle', 26–7.

127 J. Hunter (ed.), *The Pipe Roll of 31 Henry I* (London: Record Commission, 1929 edn), pp. 77, 89–90.

128 *Pipe Roll* 24 Hen. II, 1177–1178, Pipe Roll Society, 27 (London, 1906), p. 58.

129 Green, 'Carmarthen Castle' 3, 26.

130 *Pipe Roll* 27 Hen. II, 1180–1181, Pipe Roll Society, 30 (London, 1909), pp. 5, 15. In 1181–3, the work was paid from the exchequers of Somerset, Dorset and Hampshire, all expenditure being sanctioned by Ranulph de Glanville, treasurer and justiciar of England: *Pipe Roll* 28 Hen. II, 1181–1182, Pipe Roll Society, 31 (London, 1910), p. 108; *Pipe Roll* 29 Hen. II, 1182–1183, Pipe Roll Society, 32 (London, 1911), pp. 27, 141. The castle had been munitioned, in 1159, from the issues of the Somerset exchequer (Green, 'Carmarthen Castle' 3, 26). Carmarthen did not initially have its own exchequer or chamberlain.

131 Daniel-Tyssen, *Royal Charters*, p. 46.

132 Ibid.

133 The county court at Carmarthen Castle is first specifically mentioned in 1248: *CCR*, Hen. III 6, 1247–1251 (London, 1922), p. 113; but we are told in 1227 that tenants-in-chief had performed their 'customs and services' at the castle since 'the time of Henry II' at least (Green, 'Carmarthen Castle' 3, 33).

134 Davies, *Episcopal Acts*, p. 281; T. Phillipps (ed.), *Cartularium St Johannis Baptistae de Caermarthen* (Cheltenham: John Lowe, 1865), p. 10). We find the term used again at Carmarthen in 1196 – this time in Welsh, as *kwnstabyl* (Jones, *Brut Pen. 20*, p. 190 n.76) – and in 1234 (Green, 'Carmarthen Castle' 3, 35–6).

135 Cf. sheriffs in England who, after inquiries into their conduct in 1170, were usually recruited from professional administrators rather than local barons.

136 *Pipe Roll* 24 Hen. II, p. 58.

137 *Pipe Roll* 29 Hen. II, p. 27.

138 Green, 'Carmarthen Castle' 3, 26.

139 *Pipe Roll* 45, 1 John, 1199, Pipe Roll Society, 48 (London, 1933), p. 182; *Pipe Roll* 46, 2 John, 1200, Pipe Roll Society, 50 (London, 1934), pp. 226, 230. John of Torrington was

a Devon man (Pryce, *Acts of Welsh Rulers*, p. 176), again demonstrating the close links between west Wales and the West Country during the twelfth and early thirteenth centuries. He was also custodian of Pembroke Castle during its temporary seizure by the Crown.

140 Green, 'Carmarthen Castle' 3, 26–7.

141 *CPR* 1225–32, pp. 276–7; *CChR* 1226–57, p. 100.

142 *CChR* 1226–57, p. 189.

143 See D. J. C. King, 'Pembroke Castle', *Archaeologia Cambrensis*, 127 (1978), 46.

144 Crown custody, between these periods of marcher rule, appears to have become a yearly post, awarded either to aristocrats, or to trusted Crown functionaries like Henry de Audley, sometime sheriff of Shropshire and Staffordshire (*CPR* 1225–32, p. 58). He was followed, in 1227, by John de Braose, Lord of Gower, and then Walter de Clifford, Lord of Llandovery, in 1228 (ibid., pp. 66, 105, 184). After de Burgh's downfall, the king's treasurer Peter des Rivaux was appointed custodian (ibid., p. 501n), succeeded in 1233 by a certain Philip le Bret (Green, 'Carmarthen Castle' 3, 35), the aristocrat Walter de Braose and then, in 1234, Henry III's lieutenant Henry de Turbeville (ibid.).

145 Roger Turvey, pers. comm.

146 Turvey, 'Defences of Twelfth-century Deheubarth', 114.

147 Roger Turvey, pers. comm.

148 Ibid.

149 See Butler, 'Castles of the princes of Gwynedd', pp. 27–36; L. Butler and J. K. Knight, *Dolforwyn Castle/Montgomery Castle* (Cardiff: Cadw, 2004), p. 30.

150 *CPR*, 1216–25, pp. 143, 159.

151 Pryce, *Acts of Welsh Rulers*, p. 399.

152 *CPR*, Hen. III, 1266–1272 (London, 1913), p. 516; Daniel-Tyssen, *Royal Charters*, p. 45; Rees, *Cal. Anc. Petitions*, p. 15.

153 Griffiths, *Principality*, p. 19; Green, 'Carmarthen Castle' 3, 39–40.

154 Daniel-Tyssen, *Royal Charters*, p. 11.

155 See *CLR* 5, 1260–1267 (London, 1961), pp. 40, 43; Jones, *Brut Pen. 20*, pp. 107, 205 *et al.*

156 Griffiths, *Principality*, p. 19.

157 Lloyd, *History of Carmarthenshire*, p. 211 and n. Prof. Ralph Griffiths suggested that the post of sheriff was established before the lordship was reorganised as a feudal county in 1241, yet the only source that he cited is this reference from 1223 (Griffiths, *Principality*, p. 47 n. 3).

158 Daniel-Tyssen, *Royal Charters*, pp. 48–9.

159 *CLR*, 1245–51, p. 7.

160 Ibid., pp. 134–5, 303.

161 The term 'constable' was again used, with reference to the custodian, in 1244 (Evans, 'Carmarthen Documents' 17, 64).

162 For example, TNA: PRO E 372/96, Pipe Roll 36 Hen. III (1251–2); TNA: PRO E 372/104, Pipe Roll 44 Hen. III (1259–60). This continued dependence on Gloucester's exchequer goes unremarked in both Lloyd's *History of Carmarthenshire* and Griffiths's *Principality*.

163 Griffiths, *Principality*, p. 51.

164 As in 1279, for Payn de Chaworth (Griffiths, *Principality*, p. 20), and in the 1240s, when it was applied to deputy custodians (Edwards, *Cal. Anc. Correspondence*, pp. 33, 48). The absence of a steward during this period, and the concentration of power in one office – the custodian's – appears to be acknowledged by Prof. Griffiths (Griffiths, *Principality*, pp. 19–20, 35 and passim), but is later contradicted by the implication that a manorial steward was present from an earlier date (ibid., p. 51) – though no sources for this assertion are cited. Griffiths also acknowledges the continued confusion over terminology in a contemporary description of the first separate castle *constable*, John de Beauchamp, as steward in 1277 (ibid., p. 193).

165 *CPR*, 1216–25, p. 481.

166 Edwards, *Cal. Anc. Correspondence*, pp. 33–4.

167 Ibid., p. 48. As Griffiths notes, these bailiffs were, misleadingly, called 'stewards' by Edwards (Griffiths, *Principality*, p. 19). Richard de Tunderley is termed 'bailiff of Carmarthen', for the custodian Hugh de Turbeville, in 1264 (*CPR*, Hen. III, 1258–1266 (London, 1910), p. 348).

168 Griffiths, *Principality*, p. 4. A confirmation grant of 1268 specifically conferred upon Edmund the right to govern with 'the regality that belongs to the king . . . his writ shall run there as the king's writ' (*CPR* 1266–72, p. 299).

169 Jones, *Brut Red Book*, p. 251.

170 *CPR* 1258–66, p. 275.

171 Ibid., p. 348.

172 Griffiths, *Principality*, p. 20.

173 Green, 'Carmarthen Castle' 3, 41; Griffiths, *Principality*, p. 193.

174 Ibid., p. 19 *et al*.

175 Ibid., p. 22.

176 Ibid. A custodian of the 1220s, Henry de Audley, had also been sheriff of Shropshire, which was a similarly 'marcher' area.

177 Ibid.

178 Lloyd, *History of Carmarthenshire*, p. 211. After 1341 the sheriff was the king's appointment as in England (*Cal. Inq. Misc. 1307–49*, p. 430; Griffiths, *Principality*, p. 49).

179 For example, Pipe Roll 17 Edw. I (in Green, 'Carmarthen Castle' 3, 46–8).

180 *CCcR* 1277–1326, p. 305. An escheat was property that reverted to the Crown on the death, intestate or without heirs, of the owner.

181 Lloyd, *History of Carmarthenshire*, p. 209.

182 Griffiths, *Principality*, p. 23.

183 Tibetot, for example, organised and financed resistance to Llywelyn during the Welsh wars, for which he was rewarded with a grant of all royal castles and revenues in south Wales, which he enjoyed until his death in 1298 (Lloyd, *History of Carmarthenshire*, p. 209). He was also constable of Portchester and Nottingham castles (Fryde, *Memoranda Rolls*, p. 5). Later justiciars were usually also marcher lords in their own right.

184 *CCcR* 1277–1326, p. 328. Similarly William de Camville, Lord of Llansteffan, had been deputy justiciar for Tibetot in 1284 (Rees, *Cal. Anc. Petitions*, pp. 150–1 and n.).

185 Rees, *Cal. Anc. Petitions*, pp. 15–18.

186 Ibid.

187 *CFR* 1272–1307, pp. 344–5.

188 Griffiths, *Principality*, p. 17.

189 Fryde, *Memoranda Rolls*, p. 9.

190 Griffiths, *Principality*, pp. 15–16; Rees, *Cal. Anc. Petitions*, p. 148n. *et al*.

191 The Earls of Pembroke were also subject to the King's County Court at Carmarthen for their lands in these lordships (*CChR* 1257–1300, p. 427), as were the temporal estates of Whitland, Talley and Strata Florida Abbeys, and Carmarthen Priory (*CChR* 4, 1–14 Edw. III, 1327–1341 (London, 1912), p. 385; Griffiths, *Principality*, pp. 13–14). Dubious claims to jurisdiction were also made, but without effect, over the episcopal lordships of Pebidiog and Llawhaden, now Pembrokeshire (ibid., p. 13; *CCcR* 1277–1326, p. 184).

192 Rees, *Duchy of Lancaster Lordships*, p. xiv.

193 *CPR*, Edw. I, 1301–1307 (London, 1898), p. 407; *CChR* 1341–1417, p. 167; Rees, *Cal. Anc. Petitions*, p. 16.

194 Daniel-Tyssen, *Royal Charters*, p. 11.

195 Lloyd, *History of Carmarthenshire*, p. 211, from Min. Acc., 1218/2.

196 Ibid., p. 210.

197 Griffiths, *Principality*, p. 22. It was known as the 'Great Sessions' from *c*.1330 (ibid., p. 24), but the Great Sessions *sensu stricto* were introduced with the Second Act of Union in 1543. As the king's representative the justiciar heard Crown pleas (ibid., p. 22), the fines and other issues from his court forming a high percentage of Carmarthen's profits (Lloyd, *History of Carmarthenshire*, p. 210).

198 Griffiths, *Principality*, p. 22.

199 Ibid., and n. 22.

200 Cardigan was given its own sessions in 1395 (ibid., pp. 26–7), by which time their

concentration at Carmarthen Castle had been a source of grievance for the people of Cardiganshire for over a century (Rees, *Cal. Anc. Petitions*, pp. 33, 124, 156 and n.).

201 Griffiths, *Principality*, pp. 25–6. A separate petty court for Cardiganshire was established in 1349 (ibid.).

202 Ibid., p. 25.

203 Ibid., pp. 47–8. In north Wales, by contrast, the post-1284 sheriffs functioned much as their English counterparts (ibid.). Unlike them, however, the Welsh sheriffs were almost never summoned before the exchequer at Westminster (Fryde, *Memoranda Rolls*, p. xx).

204 Griffiths, *Principality*, pp. 49–50.

205 Ibid.

206 Ibid., p. 25.

207 Ibid., p. 54. Moreover Cardiganshire received its own sheriff in 1386 (ibid., p. 50, from Min. Acc., 1221/14, 1222/2).

208 Ibid., p. 55–7; *CFR* 3, Edward II 1319–1327 (London, 1912), p. 230.

209 Henry II, in his Assize of Clarendon of 1166, ordered every county without a gaol to have one constructed in a castle or borough (R. A., Brown, *English Castles* (London: Batsford, 1976), p. 212). The earliest definite reference to prisoners at the castle however appears to be from 1244 (Evans, 'Carmarthen Documents' 17, 64).

210 Rees, *Cal. Anc. Petitions*, p. 48; Rees, 'Ministers' Accounts', 73.

211 Green, 'Carmarthen Castle' 3, 49.

212 Jones, *Brut Pen. 20*, p. 88 and n.

213 Rees, *Cal. Anc. Petitions*, p. 527.

214 Green, 'Carmarthen Castle' 3, 61, from BL Harl. Roll 7198, wrongly dated therein to 1340 (Stephen Priestley, pers. comm.), see Appendix.

215 Ibid., 70.

216 Ibid., 64.

217 Ibid., 50.

218 Green, 'Carmarthen Castle' 4, 58.

219 Ibid.

220 Green, 'Carmarthen Castle' 3, 17; Rees, *Cal. Anc. Petitions*, p. 431.

221 *CPR* 1374–77, p. 317.

222 *CPR*, Hen. VII 2, 1494–1509 (London, 1916), p. 452.

223 Among the lesser detainees were those awaiting trial, and those held under 'mainprize', i.e. as guarantors for offenders; an account from 1520–1 includes the 'repair of the king's gaol in the castle, and a chamber in the said gaol called "le maynipryce [mainprize] chamber"' (Green, 'Carmarthen Castle' 4, 59).

224 A full list of constables is provided in Griffiths's *Principality*, but a discussion of the office lies beyond the scope of his main text.

225 Griffiths, *Principality*, pp. 91–4. Similarly, in north Wales, the early justiciars could also be the constable, e.g. Sir Otto de Grandison in the late thirteenth century (A. J. Taylor, *Caernarvon Castle and Town Walls* (London: HMSO, 1953), p. 19).

226 See e.g. TNA: PRO SC 6/1220/8, Chamberlain's Account, 1335.

227 For example Rhys ap Gruffudd in the 1330s (Green, 'Carmarthen Castle' 3, 56 *et al.*) and John Scudamore in 1431.

228 Griffiths, *Principality*, pp. 140, 201. Bogo de Knovill had also acted as constable of all other royal castles in south-west Wales in 1280 (Daniel-Tyssen, *Royal Charters*, p. 10).

229 J. Rickard, *The Castle Community: The Personnel of English and Welsh Castles, 1272–1422* (Woodbridge: Boydell Press, 2002), p. 35.

230 Ibid., p. 33.

231 Ibid., pp. 30, 60.

232 Green, 'Carmarthen Castle' 3, 64–5 *et al.*

233 *CFR* 5, Edw. III, 1337–1347 (London, 1915), p. 238.

234 Green, 'Carmarthen Castle' 4, 17.

235 Ibid., 68–9.

236 Ibid., 21; Griffiths, *Principality*, p. 201.

237 Green, 'Carmarthen Castle' 3, 46–8.

238 Rees, *Cal. Anc. Petitions*, p. 134. It is clear that financial administration was more complex,

and formalised, during the period 1280–99
than is suggested in Griffiths's *Principality* (p.
21), from whose list of officials Cressingham is
moreover absent. Cressingham was later treasurer of Scotland, 1296–7.

239 Griffiths, *Principality*, p. 21; cf.
Caernarfon, where a chamberlain had been in
office since the Edwardian conquest of 1284
(Taylor, *Caernarvon Castle*, p. 19).

240 Fryde, *Memoranda Rolls*, p. xxvi; Griffiths,
Principality, pp. 21, 40.

241 Griffiths, *Principality*, p. 35. Cardigan
Castle was given its own exchequer under
in the mid-fourteenth century. However,
Carmarthen was the senior exchequer and was
the only one both receiving and paying monies
(ibid., p. 37).

242 See eg. *CCR*, Edw. II 1, 1307–1313
(London, 1892), p.195.

243 Griffiths, *Principality*, pp. 38–9; Rees, *Cal.
Anc. Petitions*, p. 145. A large chest of Flanders
manufacture, costing 13s. 4d, was purchased
for 'keeping the record rolls and other necessaries' in 1413–14 (Green, 'Carmarthen Castle'
4, 18).

244 Griffiths, *Principality*, p. 40.

245 Green, 'Carmarthen Castle' 3, 53.

246 Edwards, *Cal. Anc. Correspondence*, pp.
189–90; Evans, 'Carmarthen Documents' 17,
71–2.

247 Green, 'Carmarthen Castle' 3, 51, 53,
55–60.

248 Fryde, *Memoranda Rolls*, p. xxvii; Rees,
Cal. Anc. Petitions, pp. 271–2 and n.

249 Green, 'Carmarthen Castle' 3, 67.

250 Griffiths, *Principality*, p. 38.

251 Fryde, *Memoranda Rolls*, p. 62; Green,
'Carmarthen Castle' 4, 18.

252 Dawes, *Registers of the Black Prince*, 1,
p. 54.

253 Griffiths, *Principality*, pp. 40–1. Auditors
are however mentioned in 1306 (Green,
'Carmarthen Castle' 3, 50), presumably under
an *ad hoc* arrangement.

254 *CCR* Ed. II, 1307–13, p. 18.

255 Rees, *Cal. Anc. Petitions*, p. 15 and n.

256 Ibid., pp. 492–3.

257 Ibid., pp. 50–1 and n., pp. 245–7 and n.

258 Ibid., p. 15 and n.

259 Griffiths, *Principality*, p. 24.

260 Lloyd, *History of Carmarthenshire*, p. 209.

261 Griffiths, *Principality*, p. 27.

262 Ibid., pp. 24, 45.

263 Rickard, *Castle Community*, p. 43.

264 Green, 'Carmarthen Castle' 3, 65.

265 *CCR* 1381–5, p. 613.

266 *CCR*, Rich. II 4, 1389–1392 (London, 1922),
p. 212.

267 Griffiths, *Principality*, pp. 51–2.

268 Its duties being undertaken by deputies,
who were usually Welshmen, and who were
– like the thirteenth- and fourteenth-century
stewards – not resident at the castle.

269 Griffiths, *Principality*, p. 143.

270 Ibid., p. 31.

271 *CPR*, Hen. VI 6, 1452–1461 (London,
1910), p. 245.

272 Griffiths and Thomas, *Tudor Dynasty*,
pp. 44–5.

273 *CPR* 1452–61, p. 340.

274 Green, 'Carmarthen Castle' 3, 23.

275 Green, 'Carmarthen Castle' 4, 53.

276 An account of 1461–2 records that '84
soldiers [were] staying in the castle . . . for
the safe-keeping of the castle, town and neighbourhood . . . against the king's adversaries'
(ibid., 54).

277 Ibid., 56.

278 Ibid., 57.

279 Ibid.

280 Green, 'Carmarthen Castle' 3, 24.

281 Green, 'Carmarthen Castle' 4, 70.

282 Green, 'Carmarthen Castle' 3, 24.

283 Lloyd, *History of Carmarthenshire*, p. 261.

284 See Green, 'Carmarthen Castle' 4, 59.

285 Griffiths, *Principality*, p. 31.

286 And this would continue: see J. Davies
(ed.), *The Carmarthen Book of Ordinances*

1569–1606 (Llandybïe: CAS, 1996), pp. vi–viii; E. G. Jones (ed.), *Exchequer Proceedings (Equity) concerning Wales, Henry VIII–Elizabeth* (Cardiff: UWP, 1939), p. ix.

287 C. Drage, 'Urban castles', in J. Schofield and R. Leach (eds), *Urban Archaeology in Britain*, CBA Research Report 61 (1987), p. 117.

288 And may never have been entirely clear-cut: castles were always, to an extent, public spaces, and medieval minds did not readily distinguish between castles and walled towns. See C. Coulson, *Castles in Medieval Society: Fortresses in England, France and Ireland in the Central Middle Ages* (OUP, 2003), pp.179–86 and passim.

289 Edward III's fleet of 1370, for example, was accompanied by a contingent from the borough, which was ordered by the chamberlain 'to cause all ships of 100 tuns burden and upwards . . . to be . . . furnished with seamen, men-at-arms, armed men and archers' (*CCR, Edw. III 8, 1369–1374* (London, 1910), p. 65). A similar order was issued in 1373, as part of a fleet accompanying its new governor, William de Windsor, to Ireland (ibid., p. 520).

290 In spite of the usual conflicts, the exchequer at Caernarfon occupied the town east gate from the first (A. J. Taylor, *Caernarfon Castle and Town Walls* (Cardiff: Cadw, 2008), p. 42). Similarly, Caernarfon's justiciar had, like the courts, moved out from the castle and into the town by at least 1435 (Taylor, *Caernarvon Castle*, p. 42), while other officials may have been quartered in the town from an early date (ibid., p. 19); early post-medieval lodgings outside Warwick Castle appear to have been occupied by castle staff.

291 See Chapter 4. Carmarthen was by no means unusual in this. In fact the envelope was rather more static than at castles such as Ludlow, where a large area of the nascent town was cleared to accommodate the outer ward, and Devizes, where the reverse occurred, the outer ward being given over to the borough for domestic development.

292 J. R. Kenyon, *Kidwelly Castle* (Cardiff: Cadw, 2007), pp. 6, 40.

293 Davies, *Episcopal Acts*, p. 283.

294 Evans, 'Carmarthen Documents' 17, 65.

295 For a full discussion of the medieval town see R. A. Griffiths, 'Carmarthen', in R. A. Griffiths (ed.), *Boroughs of Mediaeval Wales* (Cardiff: UWP, 1978), pp. 130–63; T. James, *Carmarthen Survey*; H. James, 'Carmarthen', pp. 158–68.

296 Lloyd, *History of Carmarthenshire*, p. 313.

297 *CChR 1226–57*, p. 461; also see Griffiths, 'Carmarthen', p. 131.

298 T. James, *Carmarthen Survey*, p. 28; also see T. James, 'Medieval Carmarthen and its Burgesses: A Study of Town Growth and Burgess Families in the Later Thirteenth Century', *Carms. Antiq.* 25 (1989), 14–15.

299 Evans, 'Carmarthen Documents' 17, 65; also see Griffiths, 'Carmarthen', p. 158.

300 Rees, *Cal. Anc. Petitions*, pp. 494–6.

301 Evans, 'Carmarthen Documents' 18, 3–4.

302 *CCR 1369–74*, p. 65.

303 *CChR 1341–1417*, p. 303; Daniel-Tyssen, *Royal Charters*, p. 97; also see Griffiths, 'Carmarthen', pp. 158–9.

304 T. James, 'Medieval Carmarthen', p. 14. The prior and canons were again confirmed in their right to 'enjoy their old-time privileges' in 1330 (Evans, 'Carmarthen Documents' 18, 3–4) while Richard II confirmed market rights of Old Carmarthen, and granted it an annual fair in 1394 (*CChR 1341–1417*, p. 349).

305 Evans, 'Carmarthen Documents' 17, 71.

306 *CCR, Hen. III 2, 1231–1234* (London, 1908), pp. 199, 382. This was the first murage grant for any Welsh town (T. James, *Carmarthen Survey*, p. 27).

307 Daniel-Tyssen, *Royal Charters*, pp. 41–2.

308 Evans, 'Carmarthen Documents' 17, 61–72, 'Carmarthen Documents' 18, 18–22.

309 See, for example, the grant of 1405 made to a Carmarthen burgess in recognition of losses 'sustained by him through the Welsh rebels by the burning of his houses and otherwise, of a tenement with a garden adjoining in Spilman Street' (Evans, 'Carmarthen Documents' 18, 20).

310 In 1415 'the mayor and commonalty of Carmarthen' were granted, for five years, 'the farm of the town, amounting to £20 yearly, in aid of the enclosure of the town; as the king understands that . . . the walls have been razed . . . and the inhabitants are robbed at night for want of enclosure' (*CPR* 1413–6, p. 308).

311 CRO M 420, 'Deeds and documents relating to properties in Carmarthen' (1647–1835), passim; NLW, MS 12358D, 'Records of the Corporate Borough of Carmarthen' (1590–1764), passim. One of the wards was called 'Gely' or 'Gellysland' and appears to have been in the Lammas Street area.

312 O. Creighton and R. Higham, *Medieval Town Walls: An Archaeology and Social History of Urban Defence* (Stroud: Tempus, 2005), pp. 186–7.

313 T. James, *Carmarthen Survey*, p. 53. The gates leading from the bridge and the quay are not shown by Speed and may already have been demolished by 1600.

314 Pryce, *Acts of Welsh Rulers*, pp. 10, 408–9.

315 Jones, *Brut Pen. 20*, p. 103. However there is some confusion in the sources, which suggest that a new bridge may have been built during the siege, and that this was the one destroyed (see ibid. and n.; Jones, *Brenhinedd*, p. 231; Griffiths, 'Carmarthen', p. 141).

316 T. James, *Carmarthen Survey*, p. 27.

317 See e.g. K. Murphy and N. Ludlow, 'Carmarthenshire historic landscape characterisation: Black Mountain and Mynydd Myddfai/Tywi Valley/Dolaucothi/Taf and Tywi Estuary', 1 (unpublished DAT report, 2000), 20–1, and Areas 185 and 244.

318 Comprising *c*.2,270 hectares, the parish also contained a number of other, private holdings. Priory land included two granges. See T. James, *Carmarthen Survey*, pp. 41–4 for a gazetteer of landscape elements.

319 Ibid.

320 Lewis Thorpe (ed.), *Gerald of Wales: The Journey through Wales/The Description of Wales* (Harmondsworth: Penguin, 1978), p. 138–9.

321 Daniel-Tyssen, *Royal Charters*, pp. 4–6.

322 In 1404 it was described as 'a little village' (G. E. Evans, 'Llanllwch: AD 1404–1462', *TCASFC*, 5 (1910), 64, from *CPR* 1401–5). Llanllwch Chapel, dedicated to St Mary, was a chapelry to Carmarthen St Peter's. It is now a parish church, created out of St Peter's in 1843.

323 But provision had been made in 1226 for the sowing of corn in the king's demesnes of Carmarthen and Cardigan, while the keeper of Carmarthen Castle was paid thirty marks towards 'buying oxen for our ploughs there' (Green, 'Carmarthen Castle' 3, 31–2).

324 Daniel-Tyssen, *Royal Charters*, p. 46.

325 Ibid., pp. 51–4.

326 Ibid., pp. 46–7.

327 Lloyd, *History of Carmarthenshire*, p. 321.

328 Ibid., p. 222.

329 The reeve was, after 1299, accountable to the chamberlain whose issues included the farm of the manor (ibid.). As noted above, there is, however, no mention in the sources of an office of manorial steward.

330 This process had begun under Prince Edmund in the mid-thirteenth century, and in 1281 the constable of Carmarthen Castle 'restored thirty-nine acres of land and pasture of the demesnes of the castle of Carmarthen' (Green, 'Carmarthen Castle' 3, 45). The customary tenants, or *gabularii*, paid 6d an acre for their holdings; they were still tied to the castle and could only sub-let on giving due notice (Lloyd, *History of Carmarthenshire*, p. 222). Other tenants included the Prior of Carmarthen who in 1291 was granted all the arable at both Cillefwr and 'Archdeacon's Land', for the rent of 22s. per annum (*CFR*, 1272–1307, p. 297).

331 As in 1404 when it was granted to John Gogh, 'for good service', along with 'all lands, meadows and commodities to the value of £12 yearly' (Evans, 'Llanllwch', 64, from *CPR* 1401–5).

332 *CPR* 1413–16, p. 42; Lloyd, *History of Carmarthenshire*, p. 256, from Min. Acc. 1165/11.

333 Evans, 'Llanllwch', 64, from *CPR* 1461–7; also see Jones, *Exchequer Proceedings*, p. 129.

334 Thorpe, *Gerald of Wales*, p. 139; also see Jones, *Brut Pen. 20*, p. 41 and passim.

335 *CCcR* 1277–1326, pp. 171, 185, 296; cf. the woods around Montgomery Castle, felled for similar reasons in the 1220s (J. K. Knight, 'Excavations at Montgomery Castle, part I', *Archaeologia Cambrensis*, 142 (1992), 100, 108).

336 Along with the smaller, satellite forest of Pennant. See D. Rees, 'The Forest of Glyncothi', *Carms. Antiq.* 31 (1995), 45–55, for a useful summary history.

337 *CPR*, Hen. VII 1, 1485–1494 (London, 1914), p. 28 *et al.*

338 Rees, 'Forest of Glyncothi', 49–50.

339 Murphy and Ludlow, 'Carmarthenshire Historic Landscape Characterisation', 20–1, and Areas 185 and 244.

340 Daniel-Tyssen, *Royal Charters*, pp. 18–23.

341 Rees, *Duchy of Lancaster Lordships*, passim.

342 Jones, *Exchequer Proceedings*, p. 103.

343 Rees, 'Forest of Glyncothi', 51.

344 'Each cow being valued at 5s: and it is the option of the lord or his bailiff to take the cows or for each of them 5s' (Daniel-Tyssen, *Royal Charters*, p. 46). In 1322 the Welsh tenants claimed that the 'constables take their beasts for the king's larder . . . against their will and for half their value' (Rees, *Cal. Anc. Petitions*, p. 246).

345 However, it is apparent that from an early date cash, as opposed to kind, was an important aspect in the provisioning of the castle, and that provisions were obtained over a wide area; in 1227 the custodian John de Braose was granted an allowance to buy corn and other victuals 'wheresoever in the king's land' for the castle (*CPR*, 1225–32, p. 105).

346 Green, 'Carmarthen Castle' 3, 26.

347 Ibid., 36.

348 Ibid., 42.

349 Green, 'Carmarthen Castle' 4, 8–9.

350 Ibid., 13.

351 Green, 'Carmarthen Castle' 3, 46.

352 Williams, 'Carmarthenshire's Maritime Trade', 61.

353 Ibid.

354 Green, 'Carmarthen Castle' 3, 34.

355 Ibid., 46.

356 Ibid., 36.

357 Evans, 'Carmarthen Documents' 17, 63.

358 That is, wine requisitioned for the king's use by his officers, or for the use of his garrisons.

359 Williams, 'Carmarthenshire's Maritime Trade', 61.

360 Lloyd, *History of Carmarthenshire*, p. 311.

361 L. T. Smith (ed.), *The Itinerary in Wales of John Leland in or about the Years 1536–1539* (London: George Bell and Sons, 1906), p. 61. However, in 1751 ships of up to 150 tons could still use Carmarthen Quay, 'as they have eleven feet of water' (J. and V. Lodwick, *The Story of Carmarthen* (Carmarthen: V. G. Lodwick and Sons Ltd, 1972), p. 203).

362 Green, 'Carmarthen Castle' 4, 48.

363 A full analysis of the animal bone assemblage, by Lorrain Higbee of Wessex Archaeology, can be found in the client report on the excavations (D. Schlee, 'Carmarthen Castle: excavations outside the gatehouse, June–August 2003' (unpublished DAT report, 2004), Appendix 3, 99–108).

364 T. James, 'Excavations at Carmarthen Greyfriars, 1983–1990', *Medieval Archaeology*, 41 (1997), 183–4.

365 See K. Murphy and P. Sambrook,

'South-east Dyfed minerals: a survey of the archaeological resource threatened by mineral extraction' (unpublished DAT report, 1994); P. Sambrook, 'Mineral extraction at Pedair Heol, Kidwelly and Llandyfan, Llandybie' (unpublished DAT report, 1995). No stone-quarrying is recorded in an early seventeenth-century survey of the Lancaster lands in Kidwelly and Iscennen, in which coal extraction and other industries (charcoal-burning etc.) are however mentioned (Rees, *Duchy of Lancaster Lordships*). Similarly, George Owen of Henllys recorded lime-burning, but not building stone extraction, during the late sixteenth century (NLW MS 12364D, 502). The earliest reference may come from 1682, when one William Dyer was granted a lease on land near Kidwelly to 'dig lime stones for burning and *selling* [my italics]' (CRO, William Morris Papers, 27/9). Nevertheless, the stone was 'almost too hard for working until the nineteenth century' (T. Lloyd, J. Orbach and R. Scourfield, *The Buildings of Wales: Carmarthenshire and Ceredigion* (New Haven and London: Yale University Press, 2006), p. 7), and workings were presumably localised, and limited. The quarrying industry here was flourishing, and becoming industrialised, by the early nineteenth century (S. Lewis, *A Topographical Dictionary of Wales*, 2 (London: S. Lewis and Co., 1849), p. 35).

366 Murphy and Ludlow, 'Carmarthenshire historic landscape characterisation', 17–18, and Areas 190 and 239.

367 Kenyon, *Kidwelly Castle*, p. 16.

368 John Kenyon, pers. comm.

369 James, 'Carmarthen Greyfriars', 183.

370 Green, 'Carmarthen Castle' 4, 25.

371 Green, 'Carmarthen Castle' 3, 57.

372 Marked on the OS 1" Old Series map (Sheet 41), 1831.

373 See James, 'Carmarthen Greyfriars', 183.

374 Sutton stone, from Glamorgan, was used in Kidwelly Castle gatehouse (Kenyon, *Kidwelly Castle*, pp. 33, 44), but has not certainly been identified at Carmarthen Castle.

375 Green, 'Carmarthen Castle' 4, 51.

376 James, 'Carmarthen Greyfriars', 183.

377 In 1354–5, 15s. 9d. was paid to Philip of St Ismaels for lime, 'together with its carriage from St Ishmaels to Carmarthen Quay, and thence to the castle' (Green, 'Carmarthen Castle' 3, 63).

378 Lloyd, *History of Carmarthenshire*, p. 300.

379 Green, 'Carmarthen Castle' 4, 49.

380 For example, the large quarry at Glogue, with origins in the seventeenth century (A. J. Richards, *A Gazetteer of the Welsh Slate Industry* (Llanrwst: Gwasg Carreg Gwalch, 1991), p. 220).

381 Ibid., pp. 215–26.

382 James, 'Carmarthen Greyfriars', 178–9.

383 Green, 'Carmarthen Castle' 3, 68.

384 See Richards, *Welsh Slate Industry*, pp. 227–8.

385 Ibid. and p. 212.

386 James, 'Carmarthen Greyfriars', 179–81.

387 Lloyd *et al.*, *Buildings of Wales*, passim.

388 J. A. Howe, *The Geology of Building Stones* (London: Edward Arnold, 1910), p. 73.

389 Green, 'Carmarthen Castle' 4, 62.

390 And no known *slate* quarries in south-west Wales possess a similar-sounding name (Richards, *Welsh Slate Industry*, pp. 210–28).

391 While the crests weren't necessarily *manufactured* at 'Laughdony', Llechdwnni also lies within or near the medieval production centre of Carmarthen Bay/Llansteffan Ware. This ware was used extensively in local ridge-tile manufacture, although none has so far been recovered from the castle. It has been suggested that it was produced within the broad area of the Tywi estuary, but no kiln sites have yet been positively identified (Dee Williams, pers. comm.).

392 Green, 'Carmarthen Castle' 4, 49.

393 T. James, 'Where sea meets land: the changing Carmarthenshire coastline', in

H. James (ed.), *Sir Gâr: Studies in Carmarthenshire History* (Carmarthen: CAS, 1991), p. 156 and n. 10.

394 Kenyon, *Kidwelly Castle*, p. 22.

395 James, 'Carmarthen Greyfriars', 179.

396 C. Papazian and E. Campbell, 'Medieval pottery and roof tiles in Wales AD 1100–1600', *Medieval and Later Pottery in Wales*, 13 (1992), 56–9.

397 V. Early and D. Morgan, 'A Medieval Pottery Kiln Site at Newcastle Emlyn', *Archaeology in Wales*, 44 (2004), 97.

398 James, 'Carmarthen Greyfriars', 181–3.

399 Ibid.

400 Daniel-Tyssen, *Royal Charters*, p. 54. In 1328 'the men of . . . Elfed and Widigada' were pardoned their fine of £30 for defaulting this obligation (Green, 'Carmarthen Castle' 3, 53).

401 Phillips, *Cartularium Caermarthen*, 49.

402 Green, 'Carmarthen Castle' 3, 47.

403 Green, 'Carmarthen Castle' 4, 34–40.

404 Green, 'Carmarthen Castle' 3, 50.

405 Green, 'Carmarthen Castle' 4, 25.

406 Ibid., 29–30.

407 Ibid., 53–6.

408 H. Owen (ed.), *The Description of Pembrokeshire by George Owen of Henllys*, 4, Cymmrodorion Record Series, 1 (London, 1936), p. 366 n. 1.

409 W. Rees, *Industry before the Industrial Revolution*, 1 (Cardiff: UWP, 1968), p. 39.

410 Ibid., p. 40.

411 Ibid.

412 Lloyd, *History of Carmarthenshire*, p. 300.

413 TNA: PRO SC 1/11/118, Indenture (*c*.1250).

414 Edwards, *Cal. Anc. Correspondence*, p. 54.

415 *CLR* 4, 1251–1260 (London, 1959), p. 43.

416 TNA: PRO C 47/10/43/14, Indenture, n.d. (*c*.1265–79).

417 Edwards, *Cal. Anc. Correspondence*, p. 158.

418 TNA: PRO E 159/61, Memoranda Roll 16 Edw. I (1287–8).

419 Cf. the 2,504 nails from Carmarthen Friary (James, 'Carmarthen Greyfriars', 186–7).

420 T. James and D. Brennan, 'Excavation at Carmarthen Greyfriars 1983–1990, Topic Report 1: 13th–16th century earthenware and oolitic limestone floor tiles' (unpublished DAT report, 1991), 28.

421 J. Lewis, *The Medieval Tiles of Wales* (Cardiff: National Museum of Wales, 1999), pp. 10, 73–4 (Group 31).

422 Green, 'Carmarthen Castle' 4, 22–3.

423 Green, 'Carmarthen Castle' 3, 35.

424 Ibid., 71 and n.

425 Green, 'Carmarthen Castle' 4, 36–7.

426 Ibid., 51.

CHAPTER THREE

THE PHYSICAL REMAINS

THIS CHAPTER describes the results from the 1993–2006 projects, and all known previous archaeological work. Recent work has inevitably been led by the enhancement programme, although opportunities have arisen for targeted archaeological investigation, including controlled excavation in the bailey in 1980, the evaluations within the shell-keep in 1997–8, and the excavations outside the gatehouse in 2003. However, the work has, by default, focused on the west and south sides of the former inner ward, where the standing remains are concentrated, and has been dominated by the recording of the surviving fabric. Intrusive work has been more limited, and generally associated with the standing structures.

The castle remains break down into five main areas, which are individually described. Within each area, the standing and below-ground evidence, from all periods, is presented chronologically and discussed. The reader may find it useful to refer back to the brief overall description in Chapter 1, and Figure 5.

THE MOTTE AND SHELL-KEEP

The motte, with its shell-keep, occupies the north-west corner of the site (Figures 5 and 13). It is assumed – but not proven – that the motte belongs to the earliest phase of the defences, of which it formed the core, and it still dominates both the castle and town. Its primary-phase superstructures are unknown, but at some period a free-standing structure, probably representing a half-timbered round tower, was erected on the summit. By the mid-thirteenth century a masonry shell-keep had been built, and internal lean-to buildings were afterwards constructed. The shell-keep wall was much altered during the post-medieval period, and was largely rebuilt or replaced in the late eighteenth century. A possible burial suggests that the use of the motte for interment, during the gaol period, cannot be ruled out. However a garden occupied the interior during at least the latter part of this period.

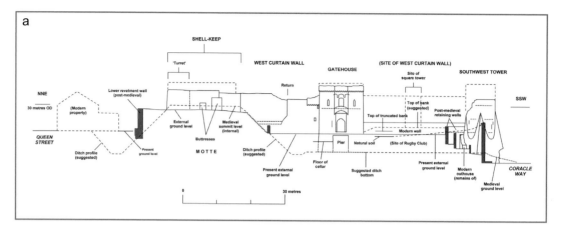

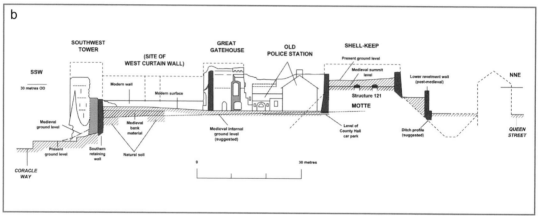

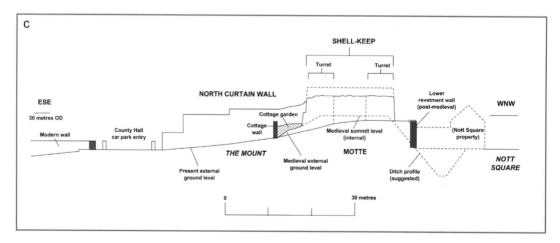

Figure 12 *Profiles across the castle site: a) External elevation of west side of castle; b) Internal elevation of west side of castle; c) External elevation of north side of castle; d) Internal elevation of north side of castle; e) Section WNW-ESE through castle site. See Figure 5 for profile lines.*

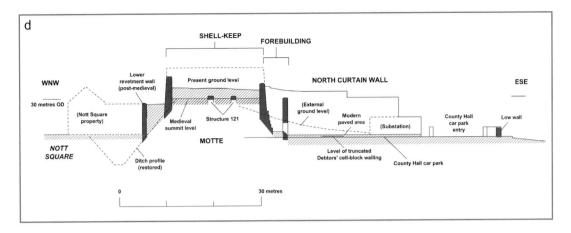

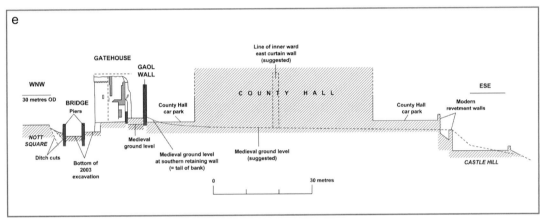

The motte

The motte is an earthen mound, now rising 9 m above internal ground level (i.e. County Hall car park), with a summit diameter averaging 18 m (Figures 13 and 14). A column of its make-up, 7.31 m in depth, was exposed in 1913 when the south-west section of the shell-keep wall collapsed. It was examined by the Carmarthenshire Antiquarian Society, and was considered to be wholly artificial, but to have been 'erected on a natural bank'.[1] Beneath the shell-wall footing, the uppermost 1.52 m was clay, the next 1.22 m gravel, then 1.52 m sand, above 3.05 m of 'black soil on the outer side of the bank, gradually changing to yellow clay towards the interior. However, of the nature of the interior of the mound there is no evidence to show, but probably the yellow clay rises considerably and forms the core for an artificial mound'. The bottom of this exposure appears to have lain some 1.5 m below present internal ground level (see Figure 14).

The motte, as originally constructed, has been considerably altered. It is no longer a 'typical' conical mound, being now almost entirely revetted by two concentric tiers of walling (Figures 13 and 14). The upper tier is a continuous wall which partly revets the top of the motte. This wall largely replaces, but does not always respect, the medieval shell-keep.

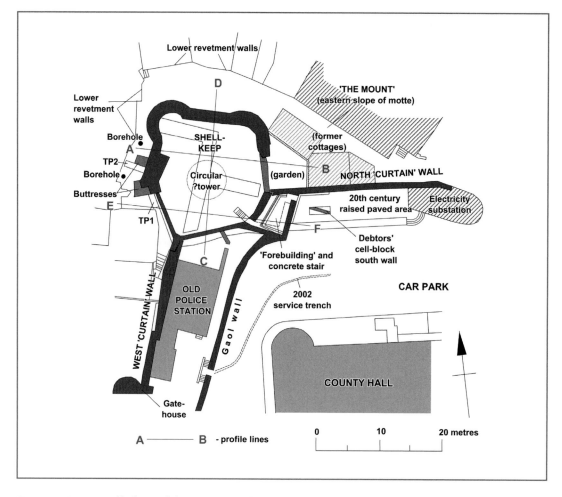

Figure 13 Overall plan of the motte and north curtain wall area

However, the wall descends to present County Hall ground level around the south and south-east sides of the motte, i.e. that part of the motte which lay within the castle interior. This indicates that, at some period, the motte here was cut back flush with the shell-keep, and its ditch presumably infilled.

The north, west and east sides of the motte lay outside the bailey defences. Here, the lower half is revetted by the second tier, a series of walls averaging 6 m in height and lying, on average, 4 m beyond the line of the shell-wall. This revetment walling belongs to the backyards of adjacent properties, along Queen Street and Nott Square, and is probably from many periods. It lies well beyond the projected slope of the motte and appears to have been built as a line of free-standing walls, with little disturbance to the body of the motte itself, after which the space between them and the motte flanks was deliberately infilled. Presumably, then, they were erected as a precautionary measure. A post-medieval context was indicated by a borehole, excavated in 2007 for geotechnical purposes, between the revetment and the shell-wall on the west side of the motte (Figures 13 and 14). The upper-most 5 m of soil was apparently infill, comprising a mixed clay with brick debris. Below lay 2.3 m of clays, which appear to represent the lower flank of the motte, lying above gravels and 'boulders', which were presumably natural, occurring 1.5 m below present ground level, as in 1913.[2] The post-medieval date for the lower revetment walls may be confirmed by their absence in a narrow area to the east of the shell-keep, which slopes gently down towards Spilman Street as a lane called 'The Mount' (Figures 13 and 14). The walls are shown on more or less their present line, along with 'The Mount', on Thomas Lewis's map of Carmarthen, from 1786 (see Figure 111). Later maps show that from the mid-nineteenth century, two cottages and a garden lay at the foot of the shell wall, at its junction with the north curtain wall; the cottages have now been demolished, but the walling enclosing the garden still remains.

The line of 'The Mount' suggests that the motte, as originally constructed, had a basal diameter of approximately 50 m (Figure 5). Queen Street, to the north, follows a curving line which was undoubtedly influenced by the line of the motte ditch, which may have been up to 15 m wide bringing the total basal diameter to 65 m. The ditch has since infilled, and now underlies the backyards of the Queen Street properties. This was probably a piecemeal process resulting, like the lower revetment walls, from infringement and infill by individual properties. Neither process appears to have begun before the

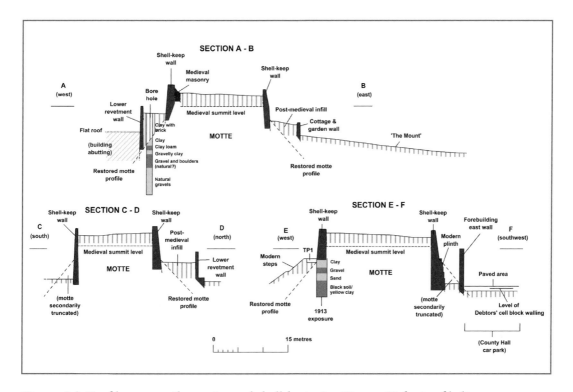

Figure 14 Profiles across the motte and shell-keep. See Figure 13 for profile lines.

post-medieval period, as the south side of Queen Street is empty of properties on John Speed's map of Carmarthen, of *c.*1610 (see Figure 112).

The shell-keep and 'forebuilding'

The shell-keep encloses an area of 280 m² – rather smaller than most medieval shell-keeps – and its perimeter wall now has an external height of 6 m, standing just 1.5 m above the interior. However, little of the fabric that is now visible appears to belong to the medieval shell-wall, which was probably much higher (evidence from the north curtain wall suggests at least 3 m higher). During the post-medieval period, it was largely replaced by the present wall. This process appears to have been largely complete by 1786 when the shell-keep was shown in more or less its present form (Figure 111); it is shown just as today on a plan of *c.*1857.[3]

The present wall averages 1 m in thickness and forms an irregular polygon in plan (Figure 20). The south-west, west, north and east walls now form a revetment to the upper half of the motte, ground level within the shell-keep lying 3.5 m higher than the external footing of the shell-wall (Figure 14). However, this was not so markedly the case in the medieval period when internal ground levels were 1.5 m lower. In contrast, the southern and south-eastern sides of the wall, within the castle bailey, descend to

County Hall ground level, to fully revet the motte where, as we have seen, it was cut away. This probably reflects medieval arrangements, when the motte appears to have been secondarily truncated to provide more space in the bailey (see Chapter 4). Open-backed, semicircular 'lobes' or 'turrets' project from the north-east and north-west angles of the shell-wall and, albeit altered, they may have medieval origins (Figure 15). The 1786 map suggests the presence of a third lobe to the south-west. This had gone by *c.*1857 when the external buttress which now occupies its site was first depicted.[4]

Excavation has shown that the present shell-wall does not always follow the same course as its medieval predecessor, which had therefore, at least in part, collapsed or

Figure 15 External view of the shell-keep from north-east in 2002, showing the two northern lobes

had been destroyed; in the three restricted areas in which the medieval wall was revealed, it lay inside the present wall-line. Nevertheless, much medieval masonry appears to have survived until the 1740s, when the Buck brothers suggested high walling on the motte, and hinted at the lobes (see Figures 126 and 127).

Some investigation, although non-systematic and limited, had occurred before the 1990s. Excavations within the interior, in 1862, apparently revealed a thickness of garden soil above a clay layer which sealed 'a quantity' of loose stones, and a possible mortar floor.[5] When the south-west section of the shell-keep wall collapsed in 1913, the wall here was seen to be '6 to 7 feet thick, faced upon the outside but not on the inside';[6] the account mentions a 'curve' in the lower courses of the wall here, which may indicate that the remains of the third lobe were still visible in the lower courses. The investigators were uncertain of the date of the rest of the wall, which was 'of very inferior masonry, and wretched mortar', but noted that its inner face had been thickened with a drystone rubble wall, '5 to 6 feet high and of uncertain width', which was covered with a metre thickness of stiff blue clay. They inferred that the thickening represented an artillery platform for two or three guns, possibly dating to the Civil War; however, there is no direct documentation to support this. The shell-keep was later examined by David Cathcart King, in 1949 and 1950,[7] and his account is discussed in Chapter 4.

Consolidation of the shell-wall, in 1990 (see Chapter 1), was unfortunately not accompanied by a structured programme of archaeological recording. Sketches and notes were however made by the late Terry James, formerly of DAT.

The 'forebuilding' and stair (Figures 13, 16–18)

The shell-keep is entered through a doorway on its south-east side, 9 m above the level of County Hall car park (Figures 13, 16 and 20). It is approached via a steep, free-standing twentieth-century concrete stairway, which is a replacement of the stairway shown in c.1857;[8] however, it may be the one that was described in 1949 as a 'miserable, degenerate modern stair'.[9] It rises through an open, walled enclosure measuring 7 m north–south by 5 m east–west and defined by the shell-keep, the north 'curtain' wall, and an L-shaped wall, averaging 7 m in height, occupying the angle between them and joined by late eighteenth-century gaol walling to the south (Figure 13).

This enclosure is superficially akin to the forebuildings that house the stairways at a number of other keeps in Britain and beyond, including the shell-keep at Berkeley Castle, Gloucestershire, which also revets the motte. However, the enclosure – with walls constructed from random limestone rubble, and areas of brick facing – cannot now be closely dated. It shows no architectural ornament, nor any evidence for any roof-lines, floors, or openings other than its entrance doorway which, with its segmental brick head, is late eighteenth-/nineteenth-century in character. This is in contrast to the majority of medieval forebuildings which were well lit, roofed and floored.

However, its masonry construction differs from the buildings of the gaol, which largely appear to have been brick-built, and taken along with its relative robustness – its walls are

Figure 16 *External view of the shell-keep from east in 2012, showing the entry, the 'forebuilding' east wall and the north 'curtain' wall to the right*

0.9 m thick – may indicate an earlier rather than later date. It occupies an area of the motte flank that was removed; I suggest in Chapter 4 that this event, if not primary, occurred at some point during the medieval period. A structure here is possibly shown on the Buck prints of 1740 and 1748 (Figures 126 and 127), but the 1786 map omits any internal detail, and its first clear depiction is in *c.*1857.[10] However, the awkward manner in which Nash-phase gaol buildings fitted around it indicates that it was already standing in 1789 (see, for example, Figure 139). Moreover, it is possible that the irregular 'bulges' occurring on the interior face of its east wall, half-way up (Figure 17), may represent the truncated remains of an earlier stair. If so, it may offer further evidence that we are dealing with the core of a medieval forebuilding – as indeed was suggested by King[11] – but much altered and much concealed by later rebuilding and alteration, with the loss of any original detail. Its east wall now butts against the north 'curtain' wall.

In its present form, however, much of the superficial fabric – and particularly in the east wall – is clearly gaol-phase and is associated with the construction of a block of debtors' cells to the east of the forebuilding in 1789–92. These cells have gone, their brickwork footings now lying beneath a twentieth-century paved area (Figures 13 and 131; see below). However, the external face of the 'forebuilding' east wall exhibits four deep, vertical chases which retain the springers for brick arches, 2.2 m above present ground level, which belonged to this block (Figures 16 and 18). The present enclosure

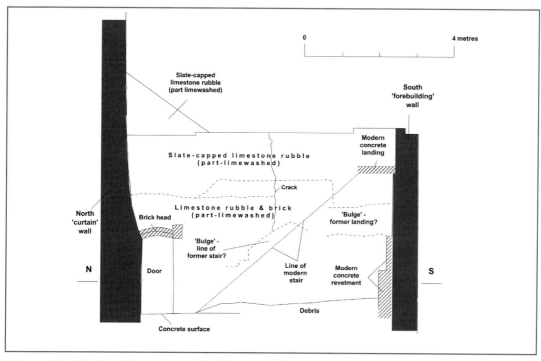

Figure 17 'Forebuilding' east wall: elevation of internal (west) face

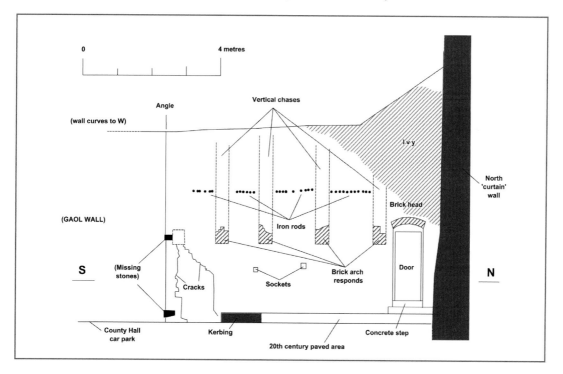

Figure 18 'Forebuilding' east wall: elevation of external (east) face

entrance doorway may be contemporary. Moreover, no joint is now visible between the 'forebuilding' and the gaol perimeter wall, also from 1789–92, which adjoins its south wall (Figures 18 and 106).

The present shell-wall (Figure 20)

Externally, the present shell-wall is slightly battered, is clad with roughly coursed and squared rubble facework, and shows three plain basal offsets to the north-east where ground levels are lower (Figure 15). It averages 1.25 m in thickness, and as we have seen, appears to incorporate at least some earlier masonry including the two northern 'lobes'. Though it had yet to be built in the 1740s, in its general form the present walling appears to be shown in 1786. Interestingly, it is recorded that the 'old castle was repaired' in 1774 (see Chapter 5),[12] which may provide a context for its construction. However, the quality of the facework is inconsistent with such an *ad hoc* repair and it is possible that, though the wall had been built by 1786, it did not receive its present facework until later, perhaps under John Nash, 1789–92; this may be when the last remains of the south-west 'lobe' were removed, as it is not shown on any subsequent plans. The facework had been completed by the 1850s, at least, as it lies beneath the surviving cottage garden wall to the north-east, which is shown on a plan of 1858–66 (Figure 139). Internally, it lies beneath the garden soil mentioned in 1862.[13] Built against the west side are two buttresses. The southern buttress was first depicted in *c*.1857 and may be contemporary with the facework, while the other may be later, being first shown in 1886 (Figure 148). These buttresses are superficial and do not rise to the full height of the wall.

On its south-west side, the shell-wall was entirely rebuilt after the collapse of 1913 in rather more random rubble, while being much slighter with an average thickness of only 0.4 m. The upper part of the south-east section is similar and may have been rebuilt at the same time. The eastern section of the shell-wall was also rebuilt – and its external corework deliberately left exposed, to distinguish it from earlier masonry – in 1990 during a campaign which saw the consolidation of much of the above-ground masonry on the internal face of the shell-wall. Meanwhile the lower half of the south-east side of the shell-wall is encased within a massive, stepped concrete revetment or plinth, presumably from the mid-twentieth century, which may overlie a similar stepped plinth of medieval date; this plinth partly extends around the forebuilding and north 'curtain' walls (Figures 13 and 14).

The level from which the medieval shell-wall was constructed has not been ascertained, and so it is not known how far down the motte it originally extended. The bottom of the *present* shell-wall facework was however observed in two small test-pits (TP), dug for geotechnical purposes in 2004, against the two external buttresses on the west side (Figures 13, 14 and 19, TP 1 and 2). The observations were not altogether conclusive. TP2, to the north, revealed that both the facework and buttress were constructed from just beneath present ground level, and that both overlay a dump of loose rubble which appeared to represent a hard stand for the shell-wall. TP1 was excavated against both the second, earlier buttress and the 1913–14 rebuild of the collapsed south-west section of shell wall, which included

Figure 19 *Test-pit 1 as excavated in 2004, viewed from above (north to right of frame)*

a small area of pre-1913 facework. All masonry overlay a narrow (0.5 m) stretch of walling, possibly truncated, running north-south before disappearing beneath the 1913–14 facework (Figure 19). It does not appear to relate to the shell-keep or to any arrangements shown on historic maps. Neither – significantly – was it recorded in 1913, when it was merely noted that no footing was present, the shell-wall lying directly on the 'black soil'.[14] Its full relationships were not revealed and neither its date nor its function are known.

A further small test-pit was excavated on the east side of the motte, at the foot of the exterior of the section of wall that was consolidated in 1990 (Figure 29). The wall footing lay close to the surface, apparently sitting on redeposited fluvio-glacial deposits including gravels, pebbles, silts and sands. These deposits were investigated to a total depth of 1.5 m. They were entirely sterile, and given their height above the suspected level of the natural soil here, they probably represent the motte. However, the footing level appears only to belong to the 1990 rebuild.

The interior of the shell-keep is now devoid of any structures, as it is in all known historic maps and prints. Some of the earlier maps may however have omitted internal detail. We have seen that it had been laid out as a garden, known as the 'Governor's Garden', by

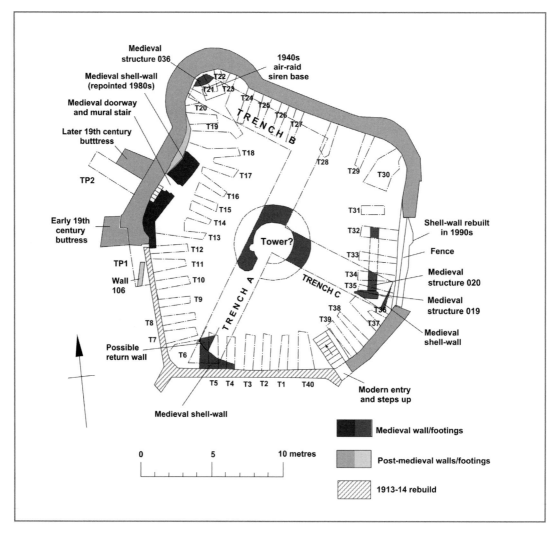

Medieval
structure 036

Medieval shell-wall
(repointed 1980s)

Medieval doorway
and mural stair

Later 19th century
buttttress

TP2

Early 19th
century
buttress

TP1

Wall
106

Possible
return wall

Medieval shell-wall

1940s
air-raid
siren base

Tower?

TRENCH B

TRENCH A

TRENCH C

Shell-wall rebuilt
in 1990s

Fence

Medieval
structure 020

Medieval
structure 019

Medieval
shell-wall

Modern entry
and steps up

0   5   10 metres

Medieval wall/footings

Post-medieval walls/footings

1913-14 rebuild

Figure 20 *Composite plan of the shell-keep at summit level, showing archaeological and construction trenches*

at least 1862. Topsoil was deposited in the interior, to a depth of 1.5 m, which is datable by its finds to the mid-nineteenth century. The interior has now been landscaped. It is entered from the forebuilding stair via a post-medieval doorway in the shell-wall, with a segmental brick head from the late eighteenth or nineteenth century. Its sill lies 1.2 m below the present internal ground level, which is reached via a flight of stone-flagged steps lying in a cutting (Figure 20). Both the doorway, and the level of its threshold, therefore appear to pre-date the dumping of topsoil, while the entry appears to be shown in a plan of 1858–62 (Figure 139). No other openings lie within the present shell-wall, apart from a small, narrow recess, now blind, on the west side (Figure 26); this area was consolidated in 1990 and the original form of the opening is unknown.

The shell-keep interior: excavated features (Figures 20–6)

Three trenches were hand-excavated within the shell-keep (Figure 20, Trenches A–C), by Belinda Allen and Nigel Page of DAT, in 1997[15] and 1998.[16] The erection of a timber deck walkway around the interior of the present shell-wall, in 2002, entailed the further excavation of forty small trenches around the periphery of the motte (Figure 20, T1–T40), but most of these were not deep enough to expose medieval features or deposits. The medieval shell-keep wall was exposed in only four areas, where it was confirmed to have been truncated prior to the construction of the present shell-wall above it.

Medieval features

Medieval contexts were encountered at an average depth of 1.5 m. The lowermost was an arc of truncated walling (121), loosely mortared and forming a circle in plan (Figures 20–4). It occupied the centre of the motte-top and possibly represents the base or sill-wall of a timber-framed tower. The wall was 1.25 m thick, with a projected diameter of 2.9 m internally and some 5.8 m externally. Of medium-sized rubble construction throughout, in Carboniferous limestone with some Old Red Sandstone, it showed well-defined facework and corework. A layer of mortar (040), just within the structure on its east side (Figure 24), may have occupied a construction trench, but the horizon through which it was cut was not investigated. Externally, the walling was followed down to a depth of 1 m, where irregular stonework, possibly representing a footing, was observed. An internal recess towards the south-west may be a deliberate feature or result from missing stones. A gap at the south end may indicate an opening, though it showed no clear facework lining.

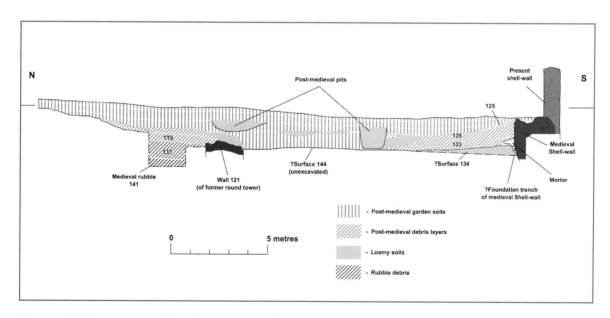

Figure 21 East section of evaluation Trench A

Lying against the external face of 121, on its east side, was a clay deposit containing a sherd of late thirteenth-/early fourteenth-century pottery. This was sealed by charcoal and burnt clay layers (038), (039) and (047), on both sides of the walling (Figures 22 and 24), which may represent demolition debris from a timber superstructure.

A loose rubble deposit, (141), was revealed at the bottom of a deeper area of excavation in Trench A (Figure 21). It was significantly different in character from later spreads of building debris, while mortar was noticeably absent, and was interpreted as a deliberate import. However, its relationship with structure 121 was not clearly demonstrated, and neither was its extent or depth. It may be part of a more extensive deposit – possibly the

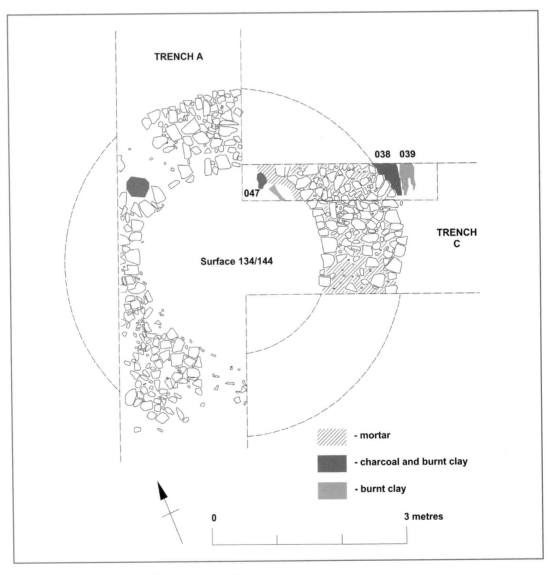

Figure 22 Plan of circular structure 121

Figure 23 *Structure 121 from the north, during excavation, with the medieval shell-wall beyond (post-medieval shell-wall in background)*

'quantity of loose stones' encountered in 1862[17] – and may represent levelling material either pre- or post-dating the structure. However, a well-trodden surface, (134/144), occupied a significantly higher level than rubble 141 and apparently – but not definitely – overlay the truncated structure 121 (Figures 21–2). It may be the clay layer and 'mortar floor' of 1862, which apparently overlay the rubble. The surface was not excavated, only cleaned over, but yielded medieval pottery with a broad date range; one fragment of seventeenth or eighteenth-century pottery may have been derived from the overlying post-medieval deposit 110.

The inner face of the medieval shell-keep was revealed in a number of restricted areas. It ran, at varying distances, inside the line of the present shell-wall – 2.5 m inside, at the southern end of Trench A (Figures 21 and 25). Here, it comprised well-mortared, medium-large limestone and Old Red Sandstone rubble, with definable facework on the exposed face, standing to a height of 0.6 m. Its foundation trench appeared to cut surface 134/144, which also lay beneath its construction debris but above structure 121. However, it must be emphasised that this section of walling is secondary, as the south-east quadrant of the medieval shell-keep was clearly rebuilt, and extended to ground level, when the motte was cut back.

The medieval shell-wall was also exposed on the west side of the motte (Figures 20 and 26), 1.5 m inside the line of the present shell-wall. It incorporated a doorway, and threshold, leading to a truncated, straight mural stair within the thickness of the wall; all were obscured beneath the present shell-wall. Another section, 1 m inside of the line of the north western 'lobe' (Figure 20, Trench B), was rather amorphous but may confirm that the lobes are medieval in origin, if not in their present form.

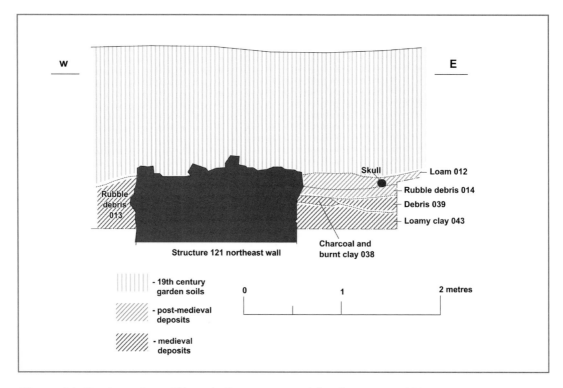

W ——   **E** ——

Skull — Loam 012

Rubble debris 013

Rubble debris 014

Debris 039

Loamy clay 043

Structure 121 northeast wall

Charcoal and burnt clay 038

- 19th century garden soils

- post-medieval deposits

- medieval deposits

0   1   2 metres

Figure 24 North section of Trench C, across east side of structure 121

A further section of medieval shell-wall lay 1 m inside the rebuilt shell-wall along its east side, in Trench C (Figure 20). In addition, a possible medieval internal building was suggested by two conjoining walls, but these were again rather amorphous and slight, being only 0.5 m in width, suggesting that any superstructures were timber-framed or clom-built. One wall (020) ran north–south for at least 4 m; the conjoining limb (019) was exposed running westwards, at right angles, for 2 m, from its south end. Neither showed any direct relationship with the medieval shell-wall, but it was suggested that they were later.[18] A further internal building was suggested by a return wall at the southern end of Trench A, butting against the rebuilt shell-keep walling (Figure 20).

Figure 25 The inner face of the medieval shell-wall on the south side of the motte, during excavation, from northeast. Post-medieval shell-wall to the left

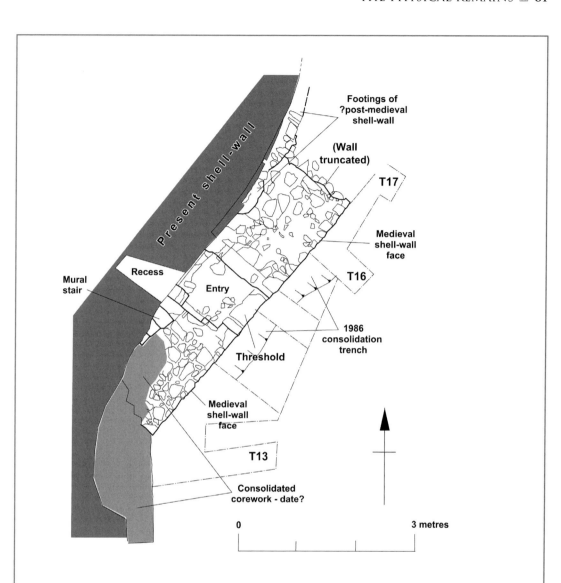

Figure 26 Plan of medieval features on the west side of the motte

Post-medieval features

Medieval deposits were, in the main, directly sealed by the nineteenth-century garden soil, with little intervening material. There were, for example, only limited areas of building debris, concentrated towards – but not confined to – the periphery of the motte (e.g. contexts 119, 125–6, 131 and 133 in Figure 21; contexts 013 and 014 in Figure 24), confirming that the truncation of *all* medieval structures on the motte, through demolition or collapse – and the removal of most of their debris – had occurred before the mid-nineteenth century at the latest.

One of these debris deposits in Trench C was overlaid with a loam layer, (012), containing an almost complete human skull. The accompanying finds were of mid-thirteenth–sixteenth-century date, but could all be residual. Comparison with other sites suggests that the skull may represent the deliberate interment of a gaol-period execution (see Chapter 5) and it is possible that further human remains may be encountered during any future excavation.

This layer was sealed by the garden soils that occupy the entire interior, lying against the present shell-wall.[19] Two phases of soil were identified, both of which contained transfer-printed ware of later mid-nineteenth-century date. There was also evidence for bedding divisions, being defined, in one of the decking trenches, by vertically-set slates. The interior was, until 1997, overgrown with soft vegetation, and an old fruit tree in the centre of the area had been recently removed (see Figure 1). The fruit tree is not visible on an aerial photo of c.1935 (Figure 147) and it may have post-dated the gaol.

An air-raid siren was installed in the north-west corner of the shell-keep during the 1940s. It was dismantled in the 1980s, but its concrete-and-brick base partially survived in Trench B (Figure 20).

Summary

The following developmental sequence is suggested. However, it must be borne in mind that the medieval phases are uncertain and undated. In particular, the relationship between the circular structure and the shell-keep was only observed at one point, where the shell-wall appears to have been a secondary rebuild; there is no stratigraphical evidence that structure 121 predates the construction of the medieval shell-keep. For an interpretation and suggested dating of the medieval phases, see Chapter 4.

1 Initial construction of the motte.
2 Construction of circular structure 121.
3 Construction of the medieval shell-keep wall. (Levelling of the motte top with rubble 141 and establishment of surface 134/144?).
4 Disuse of structure 121. (Levelling of the motte top with rubble 141 and establishment of surface 134/144?).
5 Truncation of the motte south-east quadrant, rebuilding of the shell-keep south-east walls and construction of the forebuilding.
6 Construction of the secondary internal structures.
7 Abandonment of the shell-keep (sixteenth century?), and its subsequent decay.
8 Construction of the lower revetment walls at foot of motte (seventeenth/ eighteenth century, not all one phase?).
9 Construction of the present shell-wall (mid-eighteenth century).
10 Present shell-wall facework (late eighteenth century).
11 Establishment of the garden (mid-nineteenth century).

THE CURTAIN WALLS AND TOWERS

The castle site is still very well defined even though most of the curtain walls have gone. Gone too are the surrounding ditches, although lower levels outside the castle on its west side still indicate the line of the infilled ditch, and the steep scarp slope still defines its southern side. On the north side, moreover, a stretch of high wall leading eastwards from the shell-keep may follow the line of – and perhaps contain fabric from – the medieval north curtain wall. To the west, the wall between the shell-keep and the Great Gatehouse follows the line of the west curtain and exhibits fabric of convincingly medieval date (Figure 5).[20] South of the gatehouse, the west curtain has gone, but a sharp break of slope, and post-medieval walls, define its line. The south curtain wall has also gone but a high revetment wall, of post-medieval date, lies just inside its line and retains something of the flavour of its forebear. All the above wall-lines are thought to relate to the inner ward; nothing survives from the outer ward defences, or from the wall dividing the two baileys.

It is significant that the curtain walling has only survived to the north and west. It may be partly because these walls retain the flanks of the motte where it was cut away in the bailey interior (see above). But more importantly, they were built within the motte ditch (Figures 5 and 13) where they were partly buried, and stabilised during its gradual infill. It is probable – and, in one case, was suggested by the evidence – that the remainder of the curtain walls were constructed, probably without footings, on earthwork banks that were presumably derived from natural fluvio-glacial gravels quarried from the ditches. These natural gravels are very loose, which would make both the banks and the walls above them relatively unstable and vulnerable to collapse – records indicate that the former south curtain, built on and against the natural gravel slope, was similarly always unstable. This hypothesis may also explain why the west curtain is 'staggered' – the southern half, which excavations suggested ran along the top of a bank, was set back 2.5 m east of the northern half, which lay within the motte ditch (see below).

The north 'curtain' wall

A section of high masonry walling runs for 25 m from the east side of the shell-keep towards the County Hall car park entrance (Figures 13, 28–9), which was also the site of the County Gaol entrance from 1792. The wall now represents the northern boundary of the County Hall curtilage. It averages 1 m in thickness, and rises 7.2 m from the interior of the site, but the western half is higher, rising to a height of 10 m where it joins the shell-keep. At its east end, it is butted by a modern electricity substation, while the south face is butted by the forebuilding east wall (Figure 28). The wall is relatively featureless and no evidence of blocked openings is present.

It exhibits evidence for several builds. The lower 7 m is, on both faces, in fairly uniform, random limestone rubble. The top of this work is represented by a chamfer on the north face (Figure 29), which at its west end slopes up towards the shell-keep, at an angle suggesting that the shell-keep wall stood at least 3 m higher than at present when the wall was built. Above this, the west half of the wall has been heightened by an average of 2 m, predominantly in Old Red Sandstone and in at least two successive lifts or phases. The south face lies beneath the remnants of a limewash finish, which appears to pre-date this heightening (Figures 27–8).

The height of the wall and the nature of its construction suggest that it may, at least in part, represent the north curtain wall of the inner ward. Secondary work is predominantly in Old Red Sandstone, so much of the earlier, mainly limestone facework may be medieval, although at 1 m the wall is admittedly rather thin; curtain walling of a similar nature never-theless exists at a number of other sites, for instance around the inner ward of Ogmore Cas-tle, Glamorgan, where, in places, it is rather less than a metre thick. A joint is visible on the north face between the wall and the shell-keep, although this may only relate to the present shell-wall or its facework. A medieval date is also suggested by the fact that it appears to be the primary revetment for the northern half of the motte, where the south-eastern quadrant was cut back during, as I suggest, the later medieval period; the south face is constructed from the level of the castle interior, while the north face appears to follow the downhill slope of the remnant motte (Figure 29). A high wall is apparently shown here on prints from the 1740s (Figures 126 and 127; see Chapter 4), while its present line and extent are shown on the earliest plan, from 1786 (Figure 111); indeed it would be difficult to envisage an entirely new wall-line, in a post-medieval context, before Nash's work of 1789–92. More-over, a test-pit excavated in 2002, at its west end, demonstrated that here, at least, the base of the wall lay c.0.5 m beneath the present surface and was constructed directly, without footings, upon motte material (Figure 29).[21]

Figure 27 The south face of the north 'curtain' wall in 2012

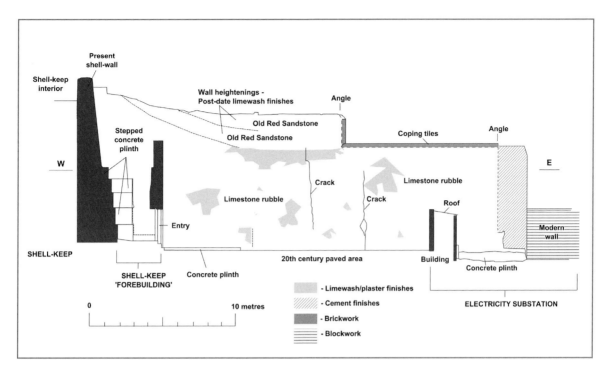

Figure 28 *South elevation of the north 'curtain' wall*

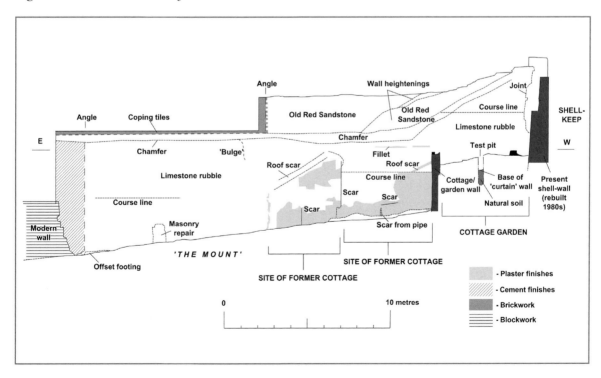

Figure 29 *North elevation of the north 'curtain' wall*

The facework is demonstrably earlier than the 1850s. The north face shows the roof scars, limewash and plaster finishes from two of the three mid-nineteenth-century cottages that formerly lay alongside the lane now called 'The Mount', and butted against it (Figure 29; also see Figure 13); the remains of a walled garden in the angle between the western two still survive. The cottages are not shown on the 1786 map (Figure 111), but were perhaps present in 1834 (Figure 133), and are clearly shown on a map of 1858–66, which depicts the 'curtain' wall as today including the slight southwards turn at its east end (Figure 139).[22]

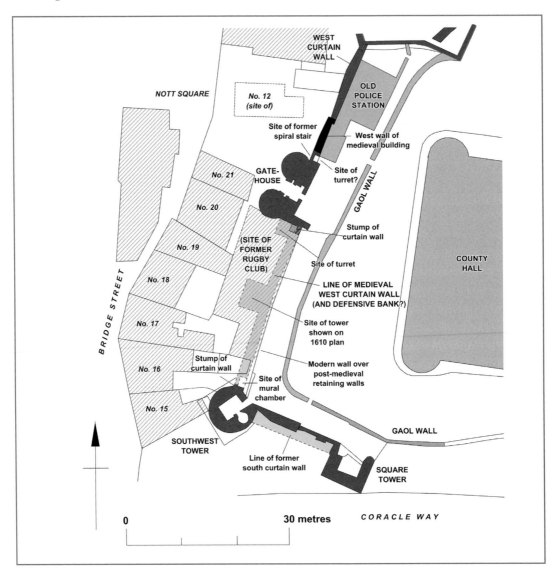

Figure 30 *Overall plan of the western area of the castle showing the line of the medieval west curtain wall*

The west curtain wall: northern section

A second high wall runs southwards from the shell-keep, to join the Great Gatehouse (Figures 30 and 32). Of very mixed construction throughout, but predominantly in random limestone rubble, it is 23.5 m in length and of varying thickness, averaging 2 m. It is now between 9 m and 11 m in height. However, excavation in the area of the gatehouse, described below, demonstrated that the southern half of the wall occupies the infilled motte ditch, in which its lower levels were buried; it was followed down here for another 2.6 m but its base was not revealed (Figures 12 and 67). Externally, the northern half climbs the motte, but internally it descends to present ground level as a revetment of the motte flank where the south eastern quadrant was cut away.

The inner, east face of the wall is largely obscured behind a later building, the Old Police Station, which was built against it in the early 1880s (see Chapter 5; Figures 13, 31 and 33). The full wall thickness of 2.5 m is visible, in section, in the south wall of the Old Police Station annexe. Between this and the gatehouse is a much thinner section, possibly representing the west wall of a former turret; the internal, stepped thickening here appears to be post-medieval (Figures 12b, 33 and 81).

The outer, west face is now free of adjoining buildings and can be seen throughout its length (Figures 31–2). It shows a number of different builds, complicated by areas of secondary facework, and is not easy to 'read'; however, it clearly incorporates elements of the medieval inner ward west curtain. The following account must be regarded as provisional

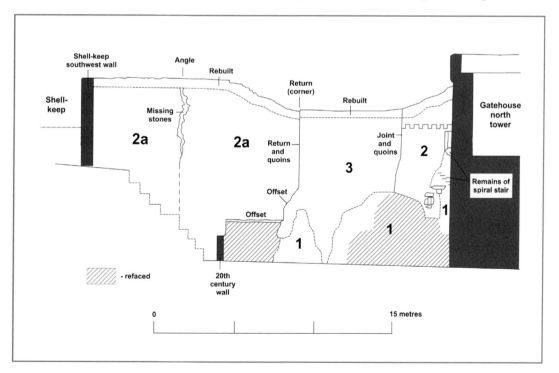

Figure 31 Sketch elevation of the west face of the west 'curtain' wall

only, and may require revision in the light of future study. In particular, a full petrological analysis may do much to clarify its constructional history.

The southern half of the wall is the most complex. Its lower half shows two distinct areas of facework in small limestone rubble (1, Figure 31; also see Figure 32), the southern area partly obscured beneath a later repair. This facework appears be the primary feature, possibly belonging to the early thirteenth-century west curtain. It may be contiguous with an area of irregular masonry that rises to a greater height where the wall joins the gatehouse north tower, and which projects somewhat from the wall-face; the relationship between the two is obscured by the later facework repair. This irregular masonry represents roughly finished corework within which can be discerned at least one diagonal line of slabs, rising to the north; the east face shows two corresponding diagonal lines of corework (Figures 33 and 81) and together they appear to represent the remains of a truncated spiral stair, at the junction between the gate-tower and the curtain, which may have been part of the pre-1409 gatehouse.

The spiral stair remains are fossilised within a short length of wall running northwards for 3 m from the gatehouse north tower, lying above the Phase 1 walling and defined by a prominent corbel table at the summit (2, Figure 31). It is only 0.6 m thick and lacks a parapet walk. Two plain, square-headed openings lie at its junction with the gatehouse, at ground and first floor levels, in the area of the former spiral stair. The former has an Old Red Sandstone surround; the latter is merely a 'cut-out' where the wall abuts a first-floor

Figure 32 The west face of the west 'curtain' wall in 2012

Figure 33 Part of the east face of the west 'curtain' wall in 2012

light in the gatehouse north wall. The corbel table is identical to that in the gatehouse, suggesting that the two are contemporary. The Phase 1 west curtain may therefore have been
truncated when the gatehouse was destroyed during the Glyndŵr rebellion, this Phase 2
walling being constructed, along with the present gatehouse, in 1409–11. Nevertheless, it
may not have formed part of the original design – it appears not to be bonded with the
gatehouse (it must have been higher, if crenellated, but no corresponding toothing is visible
in the gatehouse north wall), and as noted, it interrupts a gatehouse light.

This Phase 2 walling terminates as vertical joint, apparently quoined (Figure 32), suggesting that it may have been a projecting corner when built. It may be that, above the
level to which it survives, the Phase 1 wall was battered back, so that the Phase 2 walling,
as built, projected slightly from the upper half of the wall-face. It may then have formed the
west wall of a shallow turret, possibly rising above the curtain wall. Such an explanation
may account for its slenderness – a more firmly identifiable turret against the south face of
the gatehouse has similarly thin walls (see below). No evidence for a turret now exists on
the east face, but this area was subject to the post-medieval alteration noted above.

The turret no longer projects. Flush with its west face is a third area of walling (3, Figure
31; also see Figure 32) which runs northwards for 6 m and terminates as a second corner,
with good quoins, projecting 0.3 m from the upper two-thirds of the wall-face. It clearly post-
dates wall 2, and overlies truncated walling 1. Walling 3 may then represent the west wall and
north-west corner of a building. An east–west footing, exposed beneath the yard surface to
the east during groundworks in 2002 (Figure 34), corresponds with the corner and possibly
represents the north wall of this building. Only a short length was seen (0.3 m), and was 0.6 m
thick, in Old Red Sandstone rubble. The building thus inferred measured at least 7.5 m
east–west (Figures 30 and 34), but its nature is otherwise unknown. It corresponds with no
known post-1789 gaol building (cf. the infirmary shown in Figures 34 and 101), and moreover its north-west corner was already present by 1786 (Figure 111). Its projecting junction
with the curtain walling to the north is decidedly awkward in a medieval context, and the
building may perhaps be post-medieval, replacing an area of curtain that was slighted after
the Civil War. However, no post-Civil War development is recorded before the late eighteenth century (see Chapter 5), while no building is shown here in either of the Buck prints
from the 1740s (Figures 126 and 127), in which the 1748 view shows the west curtain in
more or less its present form; any post-medieval building here must therefore have been
very short-lived.

It is argued, in any case, that the west curtain survived the slighting (see above and
Chapter 5). The inferred building may therefore have been medieval, and I suggest in Chapter 4 that it represents the Justiciar's Hall that was recorded as having been built between
1409 and 1424. This would make it near-contemporary with the Phase 2 ?turret, but we have
seen above that the design for rebuilding this section of the castle after the Glyndŵr rebellion seems to have been fluid, and liable to change. The physical evidence, too, suggests
that the two phases may have been close together – walling 3 directly overlies walling 1,
and indeed appears partly to replace it in one small area (Figures 31–2).

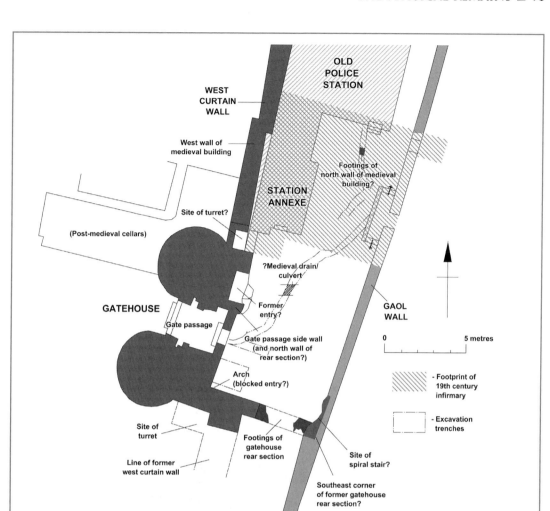

OLD
POLICE
STATION

WEST
CURTAIN
WALL

West wall of
medieval building

STATION
ANNEXE

Footings of
north wall of medieval
building?

Site of turret?

(Post-medieval cellars)

?Medieval drain/
culvert

GATEHOUSE

Former
entry?

GAOL
WALL

Gate passage

Gate passage side wall
(and north wall of
rear section?)

0   5 metres

Arch
(blocked entry?)

Site of
turret

Footings of
gatehouse
rear section

Line of former
west curtain wall

Site of
spiral stair?

Southeast corner
of former gatehouse
rear section?

- Footprint of
19th century
infirmary

- Excavation
trenches

Figure 34 *Plan of the area to the east of the gatehouse after removal of surfaces, showing medieval walling*

The remainder of the west curtain wall, northwards to the shell-keep, may belong to Phase 2, into which walling 3 was inserted (2a, Figure 31; also see Figure 32). The return between the two becomes shallower as it descends the wall face, and where walling 3 overlies walling 1, it is more or less flush. The junction here is however obscured by an area of secondary facework, beneath a horizontal offset, which belongs to later post-medieval domestic development against the castle wall. Moreover this northern half is of rather different construction from the rest of the wall, comprising smaller, very mixed rubble facework, and may be later – a post-medieval date cannot entirely be ruled out. It may not all be of one build: the rubble towards the top is noticeably smaller, and predominantly limestone. Its west face bellies out sharply to a maximum thickness of 3 m where it climbs the motte, and an uneven line of missing stones in this projecting angle appears to represent lost facework (quoin stones?), rather than a joint or the scar from a formerly adjoining structure.

The two areas of later facework repair have been noted. In addition, the uppermost few courses of the wall are clearly rebuilt, as one campaign, throughout its length.

The west curtain wall: southern section and former bank (Figures 30, 35–8)

The southern section of the medieval west curtain, which ran north–south for 30 m between the Great Gatehouse and the South-west Tower, has gone (Figure 30). However, its scar can be seen on the north side of the South-west Tower (Figures 45 and 51), while a stretch of truncated wall, running north from the tower for *c*.4 m, appears to represent its inner face (36, Figures 51 and 96). The scar suggests that the curtain wall was over 3 m thick, but it may have been thicker than elsewhere as it appears to have contained a mural chamber (see below). A similar scar on the south side of the Great Gatehouse is thinner, at 2 m (Figure 79); a turret formerly stood in the angle between the two and the upper half of the scar is only 1 m thick. It is suggested that the west curtain here may, like its counterpart to the north, have been truncated during the Glyndŵr rebellion, and then rebuilt with the gatehouse and turret in 1409–11. The line of the curtain wall was apparently more or less straight, but a square interval tower is shown half-way along its length on John Speed's map of Carmarthen of *c*.1610 (Figure 112).

The curtain wall, along with the interval tower, had gone by 1740; the Buck engraving shows the stump against the gatehouse finished off as today (Figure 126). Later boundaries, belonging to Bridge Street properties, followed its overall line, but lay further east – that is, within the castle curtilage; plans of 1818 and 1819 for instance place the north end of this line at least 5 m further east (Figures 129 and 130). This suggests that any bank formerly present here had entirely gone. By 1845, the line had moved somewhat to the west (Figure 137), but it is clear from subsequent maps that the northern half still lay at least 2 m east of the present western boundary.

The present boundary is a masonry wall, built in 2002 (Figures 12a, 30, 45 and 51), which follows the line of the inner face of the medieval west curtain. To the north, it replaced a brick wall belonging to a mid-twentieth-century building, the Carmarthen Quins Rugby Club, which overlay the castle ditch (Figures 30 and 35). To the south, where external levels are considerably lower as they slope down towards the Tywi, the modern wall overlies two adjoining stretches of post-medieval walling. The southernmost, to the rear of No. 16 Bridge Street, is a high wall retaining the castle interior from the area to the west, which is now 4 m lower (Figures 12a, 30 and 45); it is shown on all maps from 1845 onwards (see Figure 137). A similar wall, also domestic and similarly shown in 1845, continued for 5 m northwards to join the Rugby Club east wall (Figures 30 and 137).

Three east–west trenches (Figure 35, Trenches 1–3) were hand-excavated, by Pete Crane of DAT, across the area of the Rugby Club after its demolition in 2001.[23] In addition, a longitudinal section, measuring 15.7 m north–south, was exposed when the Rugby Club east wall was demolished and replaced (Figures 35–6).[24] This wall had revetted the deposits

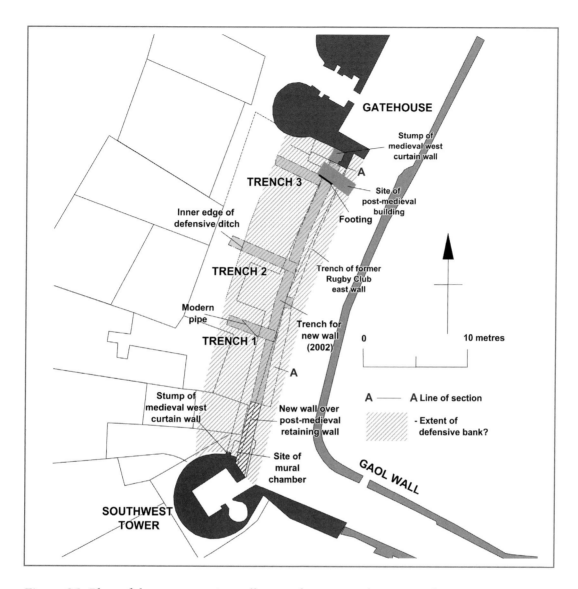

Figure 35 *Plan of the west curtain wall area, showing evaluation and construction trenches*

to the east, where the ground level was 2 m higher. The uppermost metre of the section comprised a featureless soil/debris layer belonging to the nineteenth century. To the north, it overlay the truncated and partly robbed walls of a nineteenth-century building, which had been demolished before the Rugby Club was built in the mid-twentieth century. Elsewhere, the layer overlay a sandy clay deposit, 1 m thick. The latter was entirely sterile and superficially appeared to be natural gravel subsoil, but evidence for stratification indicated that it had been redeposited. Moreover, it was seen to overlay a brown clay loam that appeared to be a buried soil. This in turn overlay natural fluvio-glacial gravels.

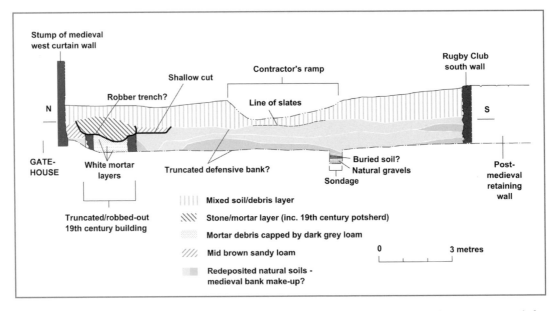

Stump of medieval
west curtain wall

Rugby Club
south wall

Contractor's ramp

Shallow cut

Robber trench?

Line of slates

N

S

GATE-
HOUSE

White mortar
layers

Truncated defensive bank?

Buried soil?
Natural gravels

Sondage

Post-
medieval
retaining
wall

Truncated/robbed-out
19th century building

|||| Mixed soil/debris layer

Stone/mortar layer (inc. 19th century potsherd)

Mortar debris capped by dark grey loam

Mid brown sandy loam

Redeposited natural soils -
medieval bank make-up?

0   3 metres

*Figure 37 Rugby Club evaluation
Trench 2, during excavation, from west*

*Figure 36 (above) West-facing section left
by the removal of the Rugby Club east wall,
showing possible bank deposits*

The absence of any evidence for either
the curtain wall or the tower, even though
a buried soil was revealed, may be due to
the absence of any wall footings, as elsewhere in the castle. However, it is curious
that absolutely no footprint could be discerned. It is therefore more likely that the
redeposited natural gravels represent the
remains of a defensive bank, along the top
of which the curtain wall was built. This
bank was probably thrown up, as part of
the initial castle defences in 1106–9, from
upcast quarried from the castle ditch,
accounting for its composition and steril-
ity. Its truncation during the post-medieval period will have removed all evidence
for the curtain wall, and interval tower,
and tallies with the map evidence, which
suggests that there was no hard boundary
here during the eighteenth and early nineteenth centuries.

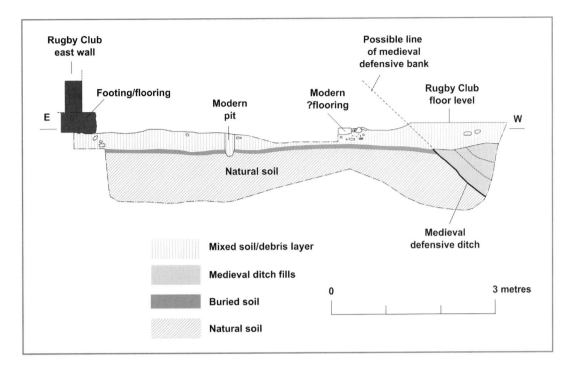

Figure 38 *North-facing section of Rugby Club evaluation Trench 2*

One of the three east–west trenches, Trench 2 (Figures 35, 37–8), revealed the eastern edge of a substantial feature that was cut through the buried soil. It lay 7 m to the west of, and parallel to, the projected line of the medieval west curtain, and probably represents the inner edge of the castle ditch; it may also correspond with the bottom or 'tail' of the defensive bank (unless a berm lay between them). The excavated fills all contained mortar, which would not be inconsistent with late or post-medieval deposits containing collapse or demolition material. Trenches 1 and 3 did not extend as far west, and the ditch edge was not encountered.

The partly robbed walls seen in the north–south trench (and also within Trench 3) belonged to a small nineteenth-century domestic building that straddled the line of the medieval curtain, being cut through the truncated remains of the defensive bank (see Chapter 5). It lay to the south of the former gatehouse turret, no evidence for which was encountered.

Southern revetment wall and former south curtain

The medieval south curtain wall has gone, the southern edge of the inner ward now being represented by post-medieval walling from various periods. Like the curtain, it revets the natural scarp slope, internal levels lying 12 m above the modern Coracle Way, and 8 m above the backyards of the former Bridge Street properties (cleared during enhancement works in 1993; see Figure 39).

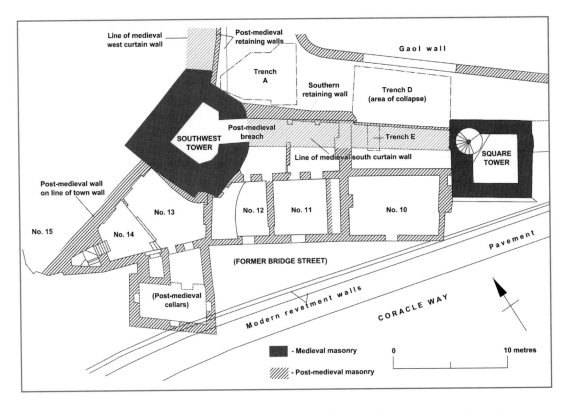

Figure 39 *Plan of the southern retaining wall area showing former properties and archaeological trenches*

The slope represents the natural terrace. Antique pictorial evidence, most notably the Buck prints, show a near-vertical slope suggestive of deliberate scarping during the medieval period (Figures 126–7). It may however have resulted from the collapse of the medieval curtain walls where they revetted the slope. Where exposures have been observed elsewhere in the vicinity, the terrace comprises fluvio-glacial gravels (see Chapter 1), but the Buck prints show it as cliff-like in appearance, without vegetation, suggesting areas of firmer material. In 1805, moreover, Edward Donovan described the scarp as 'a steep, and rather craggy precipice',[25] while in 1917 it could still be termed a 'rocky precipice'.[26] Subsoils, where exposed in the castle, also generally comprised gravels. However occupation deposits immediately north of the present revetment wall were seen to lie directly above the glacial boulder clay, that elsewhere underlies these gravels (Figure 39, Trench D). This clay may therefore be the firmer material suggested by these sources, as nowhere in Carmarthen is the Ordovician shale bedrock known to lie this close to the surface,[27] while the slope was always unstable, as recorded throughout the medieval period.

The medieval south curtain is now represented only by its scars on the South-west Tower and Square Tower (Figures 39, 43 and 61). They show that the curtain was at least 8 m tall, and probably higher, and was substantial – it averaged 2.7 m in thickness, while the lower 3.2 m was battered to a basal thickness of 3.4 m. They also show that it was built from a level that more or less corresponded with the present external ground level. This confirms that it, too, was partly a revetment wall retaining the topmost 3 or 4 m of the natural slope, while its upper 5 m, and probably more, stood proud (see Figures 41, 43 and 61 for these comparative levels). Although no footing or trench was seen in a trial excavation across its line in 1993 (Figure 39, Trench E) it is likely that the wall was constructed – as elsewhere within the castle – without footings; a constant cycle of collapse and repair is a feature of the late medieval documentation.

East of the Square Tower, the south curtain wall has entirely gone, any surviving masonry having been swept away during roadworks for the new Coracle Way in 1963–4. A photograph, taken during the work (Figure 40) shows the wall as it then existed. The upper courses, at least, appear to have been post-medieval, and the lower section had been considerably altered through domestic activity. However, the domestic wall that can be seen inside the wall-line (i.e. to the north) appears to confirm map evidence that the curtain wall turned north *c.*20 m east of the Square Tower (see Chapter 4).

The present retaining wall runs between the South-west Tower and the Square Tower, parallel to, and immediately north of, the line of the medieval curtain. It is entirely post-medieval, but exhibits several builds. It averages 9 m in height, but is only 0.4 m thick

Figure 40 *The demolition of the south 'curtain' wall, east of the Square Tower, in* c.*1964, from south-east* (by courtesy of Martin Walters and Terry James)

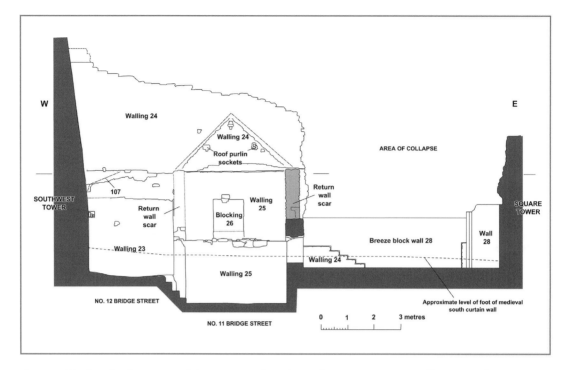

Figure 41 *South elevation of the post-medieval southern retaining wall, in 1996*

where visible (see Figures 98–9) and has a pronounced outward lean (see Figure 43). Its eastern half collapsed, with the partial loss of the deposits behind, in the early 1980s, and was replaced by a lower, thin breeze-block wall (28, Figure 41). This was itself replaced by a new masonry wall in 1996 (not shown in the figures). The surviving half was strengthened in 1995–6.

The medieval curtain seems to have gone by 1740, but the present retaining wall was seemingly yet to be built; the Buck print appears to show the natural slope that it conceals (Figure 126). The earliest element of the retaining wall is moreover represented by the gable end wall, originally free-standing, of a domestic building behind No. 11 Bridge Street (25, Figure 41). Its precise date is unknown. The earliest detailed map of this area – in which the building is present – is from *c*.1860 (Figure 139), but properties are depicted in this general location from the 1740s onwards (Figures 126–7). Its side walls were rebuilt in the nineteenth/twentieth century, in brick, and survived until the clearance work of 1993. This building was later connected to the South-west Tower by a short stretch of wall (23, Figure 41; also see below), which similarly represented the rear wall of a domestic building, behind No. 12 Bridge Street, which was also shown in *c*.1860.

The provision of the retaining wall proper (24, Figure 41) belongs to a subsequent phase. The wall was built on top of the standing walls of both the aforementioned buildings, the gable of No. 11 being rebuilt, and rises 1 m above present internal levels (24, Figure 46). It apparently joined the Square Tower as it continues eastwards for a short distance from No. 11, but this stretch has largely collapsed. It is constructed entirely of uncoursed Carboniferous limestone rubble, with a small amount of Old Red Sandstone, and appears to be of one build, though much repaired and rebuilt.

Retaining wall 24 is first shown for certain on a map of 1845 (Figure 137) but cannot, like the rest of the masonry here, be closely dated. However, on 11 November 1811, it was reported that 'part of Carmarthen Castle fell, burying several cots under its ruin, the cottagers, twenty in number, having fortunately had timely notice of their danger.'[28] This account can only refer to the southern side of the castle, as there is no evidence for a collapse in any other castle wall that still survived during this period, in an area that might affect dwellings. Possibly all walls here post-date this collapse, including the earliest, i.e. those belonging to Nos. 11 and 12. However, it is more likely that only the retaining wall proper, 24, is post-1811, to replace a fallen wall of earlier, eighteenth-century date, while the rebuilding of the gable and side walls of No. 11 suggests that it too may have sustained collapse damage.

The South-west Tower

The South-west Tower (Figure 42) is a substantial, cylindrical tower in the angle between the west and south curtain walls.[29] It now comprises only three storeys, but does not survive complete and it is likely that a fourth was originally present. It was built, mainly without footings, against the southern scarp slope, which turns north-ward beneath the tower to continue as the artificial bank, discussed above, beneath the west curtain. The external ground level at the foot of the tower is therefore 8 m lower than the castle interior. The tower is now 12.5 m high, rising from a massive plinth, approximately 8.5 m square, which continues upwards at the corners to form spur-buttresses; projecting to the south and west, they fade into the former curtains to the north and east where they are incom-plete owing to the collapse of these walls. The external diameter above the spurs is 8 m, and the tower walls have an average

Figure 42 The South-west Tower from south-east, in 2007 (by courtesy of Ken Day)

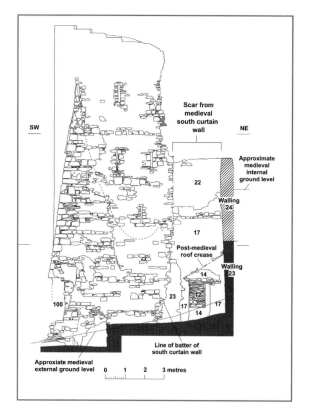

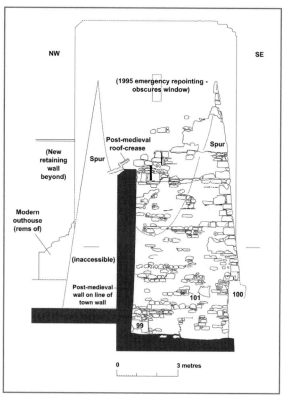

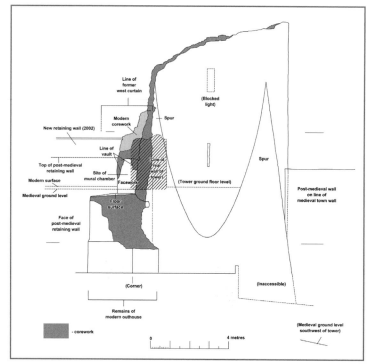

Figure 43 (top left) *South-west Tower: south-east external elevation*

Figure 44 (top right) *South-west Tower: south-west external elevation*

Figure 45 (left) *South-west Tower: north-west external elevation (sketch)*

Figure 46 (opposite left) *South-west Tower: south-east internal elevation*

Figure 47 (opposite right) *South-west Tower: south-west internal elevation*

thickness of 2 m. Facework is all in fairly large Carboniferous Limestone rubble with some Old Red Sandstone, all very roughly squared and coursed, with large squared quoins on the plinth and spur-buttresses. Each of the three surviving stages is occupied by a rectangular chamber, formerly vaulted throughout. The rear wall, against the bailey, has largely gone, as has much of the south-east side of the tower.

The medieval work appears largely to be from a single phase. Stylistically it is characteristic of the late thirteenth century, but the documentary sources suggest that it may be earlier, from the 1230s, and the very similar tower at Cardigan Castle also appears to belong to the mid-thirteenth century; both will be discussed in Chapter 4. However, no direct archaeological dating evidence emerged during the works, while the tower could not be conclusively tied into the stratigraphy of the neighbouring bailey deposits, excavated in 1980 (discussed below).

The lowest stage lies at external ground level, beneath the castle interior, and is hereafter termed the basement. The segmental barrel-vault over the basement chamber survives; those at ground and first-floor level have been cut back to their springers. Surviving openings are generally plain, narrow and square-headed, with lintels; only two of them, on the first floor, have arched embrasures (a third first-floor opening has been damaged). Any dressed stone has been lost, and no evidence for a fireplace or latrine now remains. In the south-east flank of the tower, near – but significantly, not at – the junction with the former south curtain, is a spiral stair which rises throughout. The stair has entries from all three

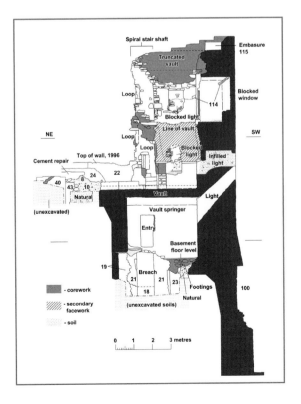

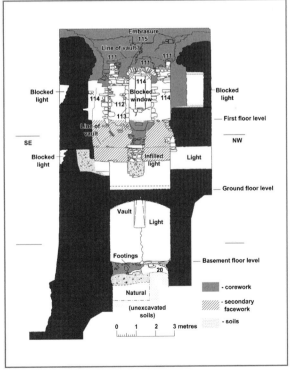

storeys and is lit by small, square-headed single lights. At least some of the sockets in the external wall faces, which have been partly infilled, may represent putlog holes. The high wall that runs north-east from Bridge Street to join the external face of the tower (Figure 39; 116, Figure 44), although largely rebuilt in the eighteenth/nineteenth centuries, follows the line of the medieval town wall.

The South-west Tower was depicted, apparently in good condition, by Speed in c.1610 (Figure 112). Its damage appears to have resulted from slighting of the adjoining curtain walls after the Civil War. It is depicted as today in the Buck prints of 1740 and 1748 (Figures 126–7), which show an empty ruin from which the rear wall, the two upper-floor vaults and any fourth stage have already gone, while the fall of the south curtain had taken the south-east side of the tower with it. The scar left by the curtain is now finished with post-medieval facework which ascends two-thirds of the way up the east face of the tower.

Subsequent use of the tower was continuous, and changing. The basement was undermined by the occupants of the adjoining property, No. 12 Bridge Street, and given over to domestic use. The ground floor was reused in the early or mid-nineteenth century when it was subject to a number of major alterations, before being finally abandoned in c.1900 when it was left empty. It appears not to have been subject to any formal investigation until 1994–6, when it was comprehensively examined and recorded prior to consolidation work.[30]

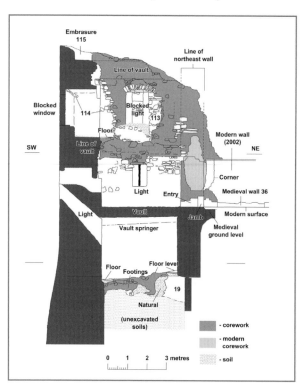

Figure 48 South-west Tower: north-west internal elevation

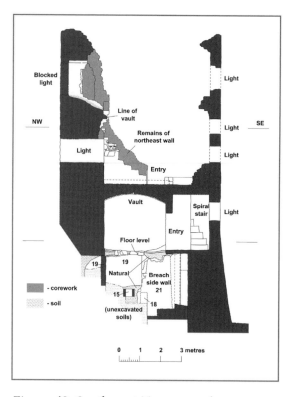

Figure 49 South-west Tower: north-east internal elevation

The basement (Figures 43–50)

The basement chamber was originally accessed only from the spiral stair, and lit by a single loop, with a deep plunging embrasure, in its south-west wall. The medieval floor has gone, having been undermined by at least two phases of post-medieval cellarage that were broken through into the tower, below basement level, from No. 12 Bridge Street to the east.

The chamber measured 3 m by 4 m. Its segmental barrel-vault, which lay on a rebate in both end walls, was 3.25 m high at the apex; the crude nature of the rebate suggests that the vault might be secondary (cf. Cardigan). The chamber was entered, from the spiral stair, via a plain, square-headed doorway, now weathered, in the south-east wall. A lime deposit over the internal walls, at least in part, appeared to be derived from a limewash finish which may have been medieval, as in the ground floor.

Internally, the base of the side walls exhibited a sharp downhill trend from north-east to south-west (Figures 46–8), demonstrating that the tower was constructed directly upon the scarp slope down to the River Tywi. There were shallow footings to the south-west, but no footings at all to the north-east – a remarkable absence given the fact that the terrace is composed of loose fluvio-glacial gravels. To the north and west, the terrace slope continued as the castle ditch and former bank, whose profile was followed by the base of the north-west wall (Figure 48). Externally, the base of the walls lay at a lower level, reflecting the slope.

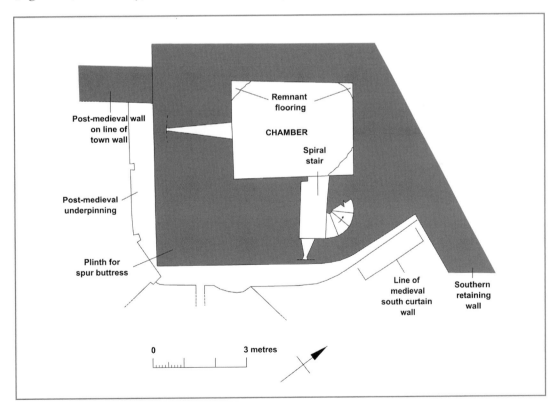

Figure 50 *Plan of the South-west Tower at basement level*

Remnants of the mortar bedding for the medieval floor survived in all four corners, and could be traced along the side walls, just above the wall bases (Figures 46–9). They show that the floor also sloped gently down from north-east to south-west, with a fall of 0.5 m. This too was a reflection of the natural slope, and natural gravel still clung to the underside of the bedding. The relationship of the two floor levels in the south-east wall suggested that here a flight of four or five steps, now gone, led down from the threshold to the lower level, presumably within a 'well' (Figure 46).

The ground floor (Figures 43–9, 51–3)

The ground-floor chamber lay at bailey level, from which it was entered through a doorway in its rear (north-east) wall. It was modified in the early or mid-nineteenth century, when a new floor level was established at a higher level, the upper half of the internal walls being

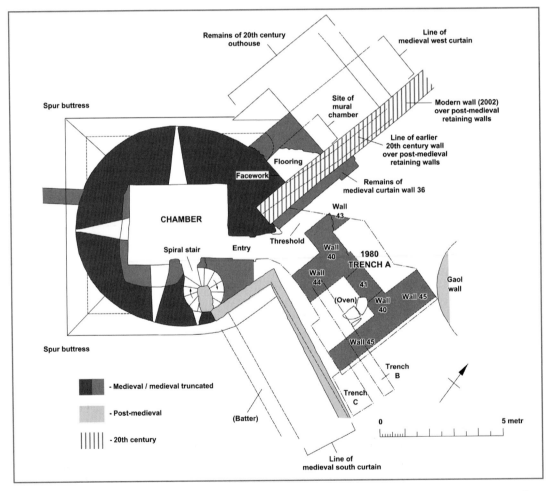

Figure 51 Overall plan of the South-west Tower at ground-floor level, relative to internal buildings

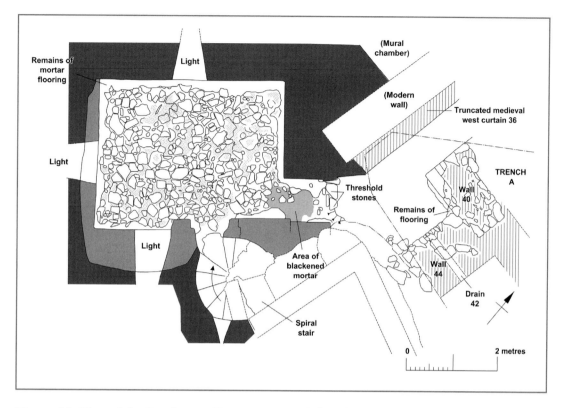

Figure 52 *Plan of the South-west Tower at ground-floor level showing medieval features*

cut back to form a chamber one-third as large again as the old. To accompany the insertion of this higher floor, the former vault was removed and cut right back to its springers.

The original arrangements were similar to those in the basement, comprising a rectangular chamber, originally vaulted, measuring 3 m by 4 m, and 3 m high (Figure 53). The north-east wall survived to a height of 0.35 m above medieval floor level, rising to 3.25 m at its far north-west end, but preserved the entrance which was 0. 8 m wide, its northern jamb partly surviving (Figures 49 and 52). The collapse of the medieval south curtain truncated the adjoining section of the tower's south-east side, but the spiral stair was complete to ground-floor level where it was entered through a doorway, 0.6 m wide (Figures 46 and 52). To the west of this entry, the south-east wall of the chamber was set back 0.3 m via a right-angled rebate. This wall was pierced by a deep slit-light, with a plain square-headed embrasure that was altered in the nineteenth century (101, Figures 46 and 52). The south-west and north-west walls also survived to first-floor level and were pierced by similar lights (Figures 47–8 and 52). All three lights had very narrow embrasures. The vault springers, where they survived on the north-west wall, appeared to rise from a rough rebate and, as in the basement, may be secondary (Figures 47–8). The remains of limewash appeared to pre-date the post-medieval finishes and may therefore be medieval.

The chamber was floored, at medieval bailey level, with angular, medium-large lime-stone flags laid over the basement vault (Figure 52); a line of larger stones running down the long axis may represent the vault keystones. No remains of the medieval surfacing survived, but a 0.3 m-wide strip of white mortar bedding – for tiling? – survived along the foot of the walls. The flags gave directly onto, and were set within, the natural gravels in the area of the threshold, but no medieval occupation deposits survived outside the tower. Two large angular pieces of Old Red Sandstone, lying within in a post-medieval layer over the entry, may represent disturbed threshold stones.

An area of facework is visible, at ground-floor level, within the scar of the former west curtain on the northern flank of the tower (Figures 45, 51 and 54); it was revealed by the demolition of a modern outhouse in 2002. It is 1.7 m high at its apex, and 1.1 m wide, and superficially appears to be a blocked opening; no evidence of a corresponding opening can however be seen within the tower. At its foot was a twentieth-century surface and its brick make-up, lying in the angle between the tower and the post-medieval western revetment wall (Figure 54), removal of which exposed the remains of an earlier slabbed floor measuring 1.9 m north–south and, like the facework, 1.1 m east–west, lying 0.4 m below the level of the tower floor. It therefore appears that the facework belongs to a mural chamber (or

Figure 53 *The South-west Tower from south-east, showing north-west and south-west wall interiors, in 2012*

Figure 54 *The mural chamber against the north side of the South-west Tower, from north, in 2002, before removal of modern surface and make-up*

passage), lying within the thickness of the medieval curtain wall and accessed from the bailey; the earlier surface appears to represent the remains of its floor, overlying the truncated curtain, which is still partly obscured by the remains of the modern building (Figures 45 and 51). No entry is discernible in the curtain (36; see above), but the threshold may have been stepped above ground level, which lay *c.*0.15 m beneath the present surface. The outline of the facework suggests that the mural chamber had a steeply arched, north–south vault.

The first floor (Figures 43–9, 53 and 55)
Internally, the first floor was broadly similar to the ground floor and basement. The remains of the barrel-vault indicated that the first-floor chamber was also 3 m high; on the south-west wall could be seen the sockets for the shuttering used during vault construction (111, Figure 47). The chamber was entered from the spiral stair, but the possibility exists that a second doorway in the truncated northeast wall may have given onto an external timber stair from the bailey.

A finished rebate, just proud of the south-west internal wall (112, Figure 47), suggests that the south-east wall may always have been set back *c.*0.6 m from that in the ground floor, making the first-floor chamber slightly larger. It was also better appointed, and better lit. The south-east wall was pierced by a narrow, splayed loop that was later blocked

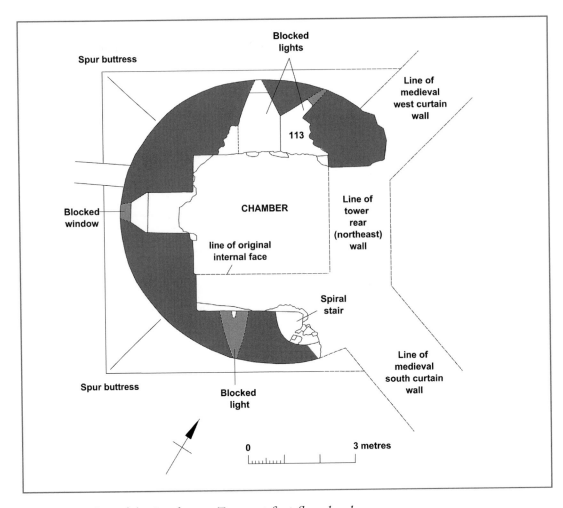

Spur buttress

Blocked
lights

Line of
medieval
west curtain
wall

113

Blocked
window

CHAMBER

Line of
tower
rear
(northeast)
wall

line of original
internal face

Spiral
stair

Line of
medieval
south curtain
wall

Spur buttress

Blocked
light

0   3 metres

Figure 55 Plan of the South-west Tower at first-floor level

and damaged, losing any rear-arch. The south-west wall however was pierced by the fine segmental embrasure – 2.5 m high, with its sill at floor level – for a large, square-headed window, probably of a single light (Figures 47 and 55). This was partly weathered, but it appears that window seats, later altered, may originally have been present. The light itself was later blocked. In the north-west wall was a curious double-light, now unfortunately much weathered. The embrasure is very similar to that in the south-west wall, but without evidence for window seats, and featured a square-headed light of comparable size, also blocked. However, the eastern splay gave onto a loop at right-angles to it (113, Figures 48 and 55); it appears to have been deliberately located to enfilade the medieval west curtain wall. No fireplace was evident, but may have occupied the vanished rear wall of the tower. The remains of the low-pitched mortar roof crease, belonging to the nineteenth-century ground-floor chamber, could be seen half-way up the south-west wall (114, Figures 46–8), extending into the embrasure of the blocked south-west window.

The vault suggests that the first floor may have been overlain by a further storey. Detail at this level is confined to the south-west wall of the tower, where the sill and jambs of an embrasure can be seen (115, Figure 47). While the embrasure may indicate parapet level, it is more likely that it belonged to a window, lighting a second-floor chamber, with a sill at floor level like the one below.

Post-medieval encroachments and alterations (Figures 43–59)

Slighting damage was exacerbated by the numerous alterations that the South-west Tower underwent during the post-medieval period. The earliest of these events for which there is structural evidence occurred after the collapse of the medieval south curtain wall, when the tower was undermined from the adjoining No. 12 Bridge Street, through the scar left by the curtain on the east side of the tower. The breach was excavated at ground level in No. 12, but beneath the base of the tower wall and below its basement level (Figures 43, 46, 49, 56 and 57). It was given masonry side walls (23, Figure 56), to create a passageway 2.1 m wide and at least 3 m high; the northern side wall was a continuation of rear wall 23, of No. 12 Bridge Street, described above. The breach opened out beneath the chamber to undermine the medieval floor. Evidence from the southern retaining wall suggests that this activity occurred before 1811 (see above). The passage was subsequently narrowed with the introduction of secondary side walls (21, Figures 46, 49, 56 and 57) which overlie walling 23.

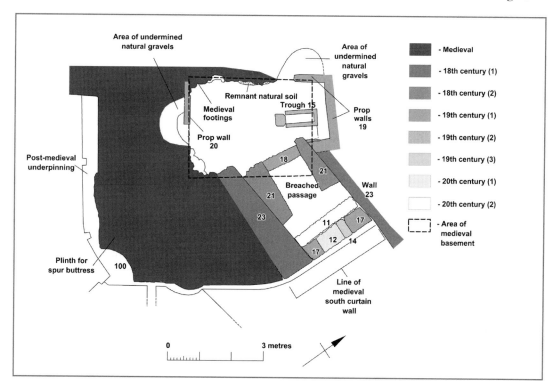

Figure 56 Plan of the South-west Tower at sub-basement level

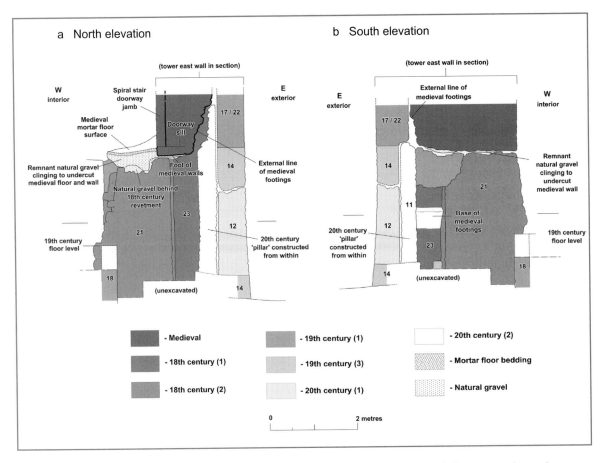

a North elevation

b South elevation

Figure 57 South-west Tower: north and south elevations of the sub-basement breach

A further phase of alteration is represented by two masonry prop walls that were inserted beneath the medieval tower walls (19 and 20, Figures 46–9), as they appear to butt against passage lining 21. Also butting 21 is a low wall inserted in the threshold to retain the natural gravels inside (18, Figures 46, 56 and 57). These features may be associated with works at No. 12 Bridge Street following the partial collapse of the southern retaining wall in 1811, like the facework (22, Figure 43), that was applied over the scar left by the south curtain. Externally, this facework is identical to the ?post-1811 southern revetment wall 24, but within the castle it appears to overlie wall 24 (Figure 46). The two are probably broadly contemporary; the erection of a new retaining wall would provide an opportunity to finish off the scar. However, facework 22 clearly proved unsound and its lower half was replaced (17, Figures 43 and 57), incorporating a narrower – and presumably more stable – entry. This subsequently underwent further narrowing, in brickwork (14, Figures 43 and 57), while a trough, in similar brick but of unknown function, was let into the sub-basement 'floor' (15, Figures 49 and 56) and the south-east spur-buttress was partially robbed to provide access between Nos. 12 and 13 Bridge Street (100, Figure 43; also see Figure 39). At least some of the lower courses on the external faces of the tower may be post-medieval, representing underpinning or infill. There is no documentary or map evidence for any of this domestic activity, but evidence from the upper floors of the tower suggests that it was confined to the nineteenth century.

Tower alterations at ground- and first-floor levels were preceded by the removal of all seventeenth-century demolition debris/collapse, and a lengthy period of subsequent inactivity that was represented by a thin layer of silty organic soil, overlying the medieval flagged surface and representing natural build-up (9, Figure 59). Its datable ceramics were broadly seventeenth-/eighteenth-century; we have seen that the tower had been gutted by the 1740s (Figures 126–7).

A dark, mixed material, (10), overlay 9 in the area of the tower threshold and immediately to the east (Figure 46). It appeared to have been well trodden and contained some clay pipe of possible eighteenth-century date. Overlying this layer was a deep deposit of mortar and building debris, 1.5 m thick and apparently deliberate (8, Figures 46 and 59). It partly lay beneath ?post-1811 retaining wall 24, whilst producing finds no later than very early in the nineteenth century. It may therefore represent a dump/clearance deposit associated with construction of the new gaol in 1789–92 and the demolition of pre-existing buildings.

The ground-floor chamber later received its new floor, 1.3 m above medieval floor level. As a preliminary, the chamber was enlarged by nearly a quarter by cutting back the south-east and south-west walls by 0.9 m and 0.3 m respectively, while the remains

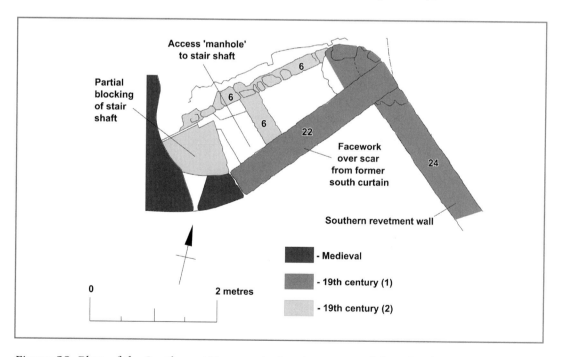

Figure 58 Plan of the South-west Tower spiral stair at ground-floor level

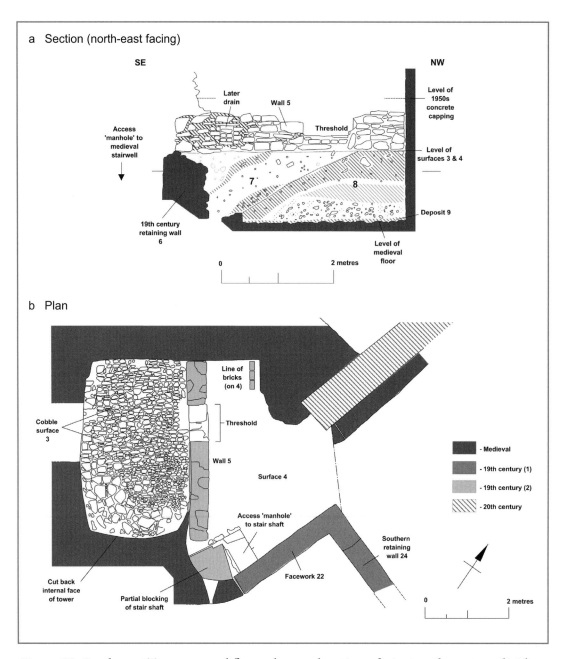

a Section (north-east facing)

SE

NW

Later drain

Wall 5

Threshold

Level of 1950s concrete capping

Access 'manhole' to medieval stairwell

Level of surfaces 3 & 4

7

8

Deposit 9

19th century retaining wall 6

Level of medieval floor

0   2 metres

b Plan

Line of bricks (on 4)

Cobble surface 3

Threshold

Wall 5

Surface 4

Access 'manhole' to stair shaft

Cut back internal face of tower

Partial blocking of stair shaft

Facework 22

Southern retaining wall 24

- Medieval

- 19th century (1)

- 19th century (2)

- 20th century

0   2 metres

Figure 59 *South-west Tower ground floor: plan and section of nineteenth-century dividing wall and floors*

of the vault on the other two walls were finished off (Figures 46–8 and 59). The top of the spiral stairwell was enclosed to form a 'manhole' (6, Figure 58), and the area was levelled, over dumping 8, with a mortar deposit (7, Figure 59); these deposits may have been retained by walling immediately east of the tower (see below). A dividing wall was then built (5, Figure 59), without footings, across the width of the chamber and directly on top of levelling 7. It was of mortared limestone and sandstone, showing the remains of an entry and, though just 0.5 m thick, appears to have risen the full height of the tower. Floor surfaces were then laid down either side of the wall, that to the south-west being cobbled (3, Figure 59), while surface 4 to the north-east was of compacted mortar. The medieval window embrasures on both floors were blocked (Figures 46–8 and 59), and the south-west half of the chamber was roofed at first-floor level (114, Figures 46–8). The walls then received render finishes, now weathered. There are no documentary sources for this reuse, but finds were of broadly nineteenth-century date, and map and print evidence suggests that it may date to the 1830s (see Chapter 5). What happened to the rubble debris from the cut-back walls? Did any contribute to the cobble flooring?

The chamber was finally abandoned in c.1900. Later in the twentieth century, the sub-basement breach was blocked with cemented brickwork (11 and 12, Figures 43, 56 and 57), the basement was infilled with earth, and was sealed beneath a concrete cap at ground-floor level.[31] The fill was removed, and the passage reopened, in 1994 when the tower received emergency underpinning (102, Figure 43).

The Square Tower

The Square Tower (Figure 60) now stands alone and detached, 18 m east of the Southwest Tower, but the stumps of the medieval south curtain, visible on its east and west walls, show that it projected 3.5 m from the wall-face. Like the curtain wall and Southwest Tower, it was built against the southern scarp slope, and excavation suggested that it was constructed directly upon the natural terrace without footings. The tower is now of a single stage, its summit being level with the castle interior. It is 5 m high to the north, and 8 m high to the south where the ground slopes downhill. However, a photograph taken of the south face, in c.1964, shows that the medieval facework – in squared and coursed Old Red Sandstone rubble – formerly terminated as a straight line, 3 m above present external ground level on this downhill slope (Figures 61 and 63). Whilst it is possible that it merely represents the level to which the facework had been robbed, the masonry below this line does not resemble corework and is flush with the tower face, and apparently represents secondary 'underpinning' of post-medieval date; the line may therefore indicate the level from which the tower was built (Figure 63); the internal chamber would then have been partly below ground. The north face of the tower partly revets the natural terrace, but its upper half lies beneath a deep sequence of post-medieval deposits (see below). The walls have an average thickness of 1.7 m, but its lower half is battered, increasing basal thicknesses to 2 m. Square sockets in the west and south faces, which have been partly infilled, may represent putlog holes.

Not quite square in plan (Figure 64), the tower now contains a single chamber, beneath a barrel-vault with a segmental profile. It lies at basement level, relative to the castle interior, and is still accessed via the original spiral stair in the thickness of the north-west corner, at

Figure 60 The Square Tower from south-west, in 2012

the junction with the former south curtain. The chamber averages 3.3 m north–south and 3.2 m east–west, and is 5.15 m high to the vault apex (Figures 62 and 64). The medieval floor has gone, but the stair doorway sill indicates that it lay between 0.25 m and 0.35 m above the modern floor (and c.4.5 m below medieval bailey level). The chamber was lit by simple, rectangular slit-lights in both the south and east walls, with deep plunging splays beneath segmental heads. Their sills lay 2.5 m above medieval floor level. The eastern light has weathered externally, but it appears that a square-headed surround may have been robbed out. The southern light – but not its embrasure – had been blocked prior to 1964 (86, Figure 61; Figure 63), any surround having similarly become weathered or robbed. The tower west face was apparently blind. The spiral stair was markedly wide – 2.25 m – and gave onto the chamber via a segmental-headed doorway at the north end of the west wall; it was carried over the north-west corner, on a segmental arch, as an internal squinch (Figures 62 and 64). The medieval work all appears to be of a single phase, of late medieval character, with no evidence of significant alteration prior to the post-medieval period. As in the South-west Tower, however, there is no direct dating evidence, and no surviving dressings.

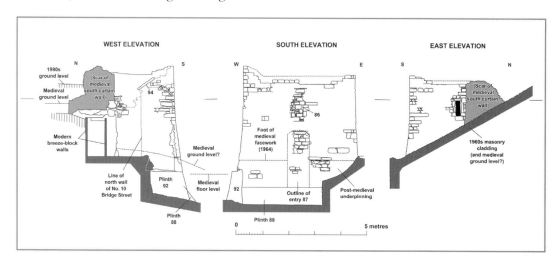

Figure 61 External elevations of the Square Tower

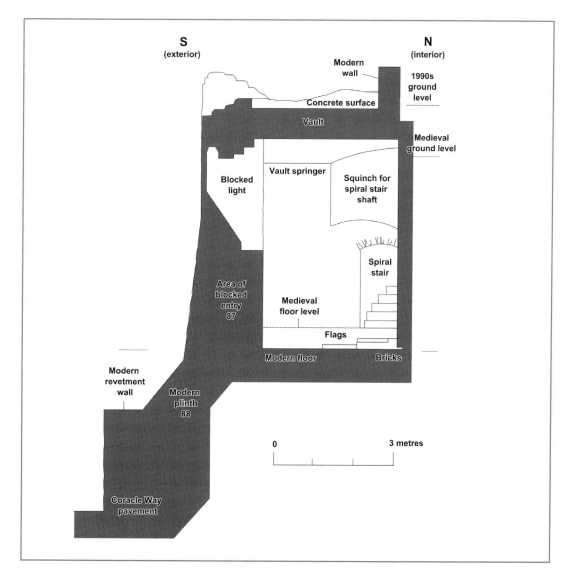

Figure 62 North–south section through the Square Tower, facing west

At least one further storey would be required to bring the tower up to curtain wall parapet level. However, there is no certain evidence for an additional stage, and the antique map and print evidence is not helpful – neither Speed's plan of *c*.1610, nor the Buck prints of the 1740s show the tower (Figures 112 and 126–7). It is probable that, in the Buck views, it was concealed behind Bridge Street housing, suggesting that it was by that time no higher than now.

The tower remained hidden until 1963–4 when, during the construction of Coracle Way, the bulk of these properties were demolished. The roadworks were not accompanied by any formal archaeological work and there appears to have been no structured investigation of the tower until 1993, when it was finally revealed in its entirety through the demolition of Nos. 10–14 Bridge Street, accompanied by an evaluation within the interior.[32] The exterior was partly refaced and entirely repointed in 1995, after the tower had been fully recorded.[33] Some antiquarian notes refer to the tower as the 'Water Tower',[34] but there is no recorded use of this name during the medieval period.

Post-medieval encroachments and alterations

Like the South-west Tower, the Square Tower was subject to post-medieval domestic encroachment from adjoining properties. The 1964 photograph shows a secondary entry in the south face, now blocked, which was of very similar character to that in the South-west Tower (87, Figure 61; Figure 63). It was a rather shapeless breach, between 2 m and 3 m high, cut through from No. 9 Bridge Street to the south (demolished in 1963–4). Its head was represented by unfinished corework, but beneath tower facework level it was lined with the same small, uncoursed rubble that continued onto the outside face as under-pinning. Lying below the suggested medieval ground level, it is unlikely to be an enlarge-ment of an earlier entry or postern.

Corresponding to threshold level in the entry, and perhaps contemporary with it, is a nineteenth-century brick-and-tile floor that was revealed in the northern third of the tower

Figure 63 *The Square Tower in c.1964, showing the former entry in the south wall*
(by courtesy of Martin Walters and Terry James)

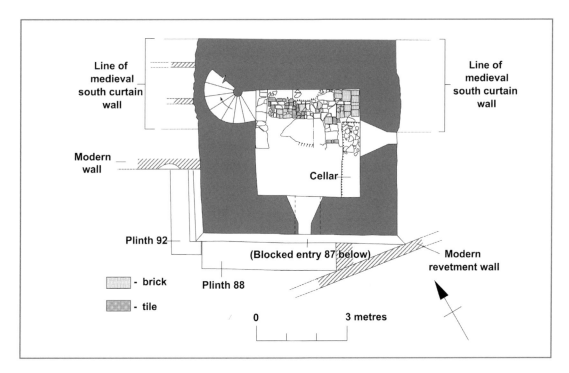

Figure 64 Plan of the Square Tower showing post-medieval flooring

interior in 1993 (Figure 64), and that may formerly have extended throughout. It lay directly upon the natural gravels, beneath medieval floor level – any medieval surfaces having been lost – and featured a step up to the spiral stair doorway (Figure 62). Also perhaps contemporary were the remains of a limewash finish on the internal walls, which terminated around the entry. To the south-east, this flooring was later undermined by part of a cellar belonging to No. 8 Bridge Street to the east (also demolished in 1963–4). It extended, beneath floor level, for 0.5 m into the body of the tower (Figure 64). It was not fully excavated and could not be dated, but a late nineteenth-century context is suggested by the finds.

Superficial alterations, associated with domestic development at No. 10 Bridge Street (demolished in 1993), were also apparent externally, on the west face of the tower. The east side of the property was defined by a sloping plinth built against, and slightly undercutting, the base of the tower (92, Figure 61), and its roof creasing (94, Figure 61). The curtain-wall scar was also considerably undercut.[35]

Post-medieval entry 87 was blocked in 1964, when the tower was refaced with thin, finely cut rectangular sandstone blocks;[36] it is now only distinguishable as an uneven area. The new facework more or less replicated the pre-existing fabric, but could be seen to be recent work where it had weathered away to reveal the cement bonding beneath. The 1964 work also included the finishing of the tower summit, with a concrete screed over the vault – which may conceal medieval flooring – and a 'caphouse' (now removed) over the spiral stair entry.

The southern two-thirds of the tower interior were sealed beneath a concrete 'raft', over 0.30 m thick and filling the cellar, probably representing stabilising work from 1964.[37] A sloping plinth against the south face of the tower (88, Figure 61) appears to be contemporary and overlies both the underpinning shown in c.1964, and nineteenth-century plinth 92. An unknown percentage of the tower east face now lies beneath the massive sloping revetment work over the scarp slope to the east, which is also from 1964.

THE GREAT GATEHOUSE AND BRIDGE

The Great Gatehouse is now the most complete and visible part of the castle, and still dominates the town. As it stands, it is a complex, twin-tower structure from the late medieval period, but it may always have been the site of the main entry to the castle. As in the majority of castle-boroughs – but by no means all of them – it was embraced by the walled town (see Figure 3), and faced west towards the medieval marketplace; a second entrance, originally leading from the field, lay on the north side of the castle. The Great Gatehouse continued as the main entry to the County Gaol until 1789–92 when the axis of the site was changed, a new entry being established on the north side, near the site of the second medieval gate. Nevertheless it was retained, although blocked and apparently unoccupied.

The gatehouse is low, comprising only two storeys. It is now represented by two circular towers flanking a passage, overlain by a single first-floor chamber (Figure 66). It survives to parapet level, with a total height of 12.5 m. However the towers, which show a slight basal batter, lie fully within the ditch around the west side of the castle, into which they extend to an unknown depth; the north tower was followed down for 2.6 m beneath present ground level in 2003, but its base was not revealed (see Figure 67). The towers are each 5 m in diameter, flanking a passage which is 3 m wide, giving a total width of 13 m north–south.

The remains however represent only the western half of the medieval gatehouse, which included a rectangular block to the rear, now gone (Figures 34 and 65).[38] The evidence, discussed below, suggests that this former rear section measured c.7 m north-south and c.7.2 m east–west, giving the gatehouse a total east–west dimension of 14.2 m. In addition, a turret formerly flanked the gatehouse on its south side, possibly mirrored by another on its north side (see above).

The surviving fabric is largely from 1409–11, when the gatehouse was rebuilt following damage sustained during the Glyndŵr rebellion of 1405–6 (see Chapter 4). The fabric is largely in locally quarried Old Red Sandstone, with some limestone, and all detail is consistent with an early fifteenth-century date; where original surrounds survive they are chamfered, are in the four-centred Perpendicular style, and in oolite or red sandstone. However, the gatehouse may incorporate the remains of its pre-1409 precursor. It underwent considerable alteration during the post-medieval period, most of it involving damage and loss of fabric.

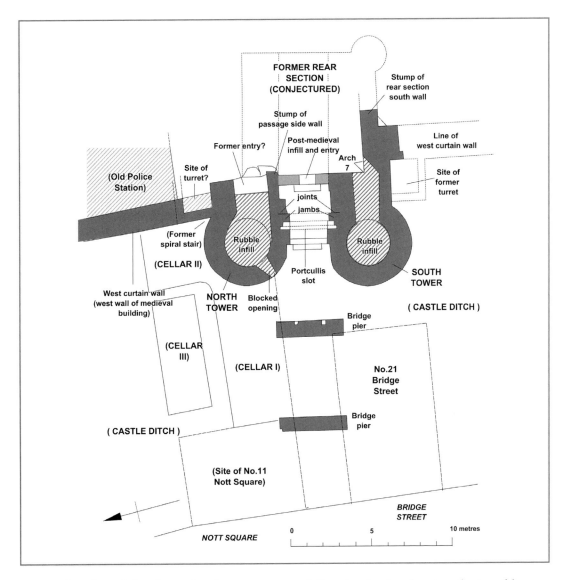

Figure 65 *Plan of the Great Gatehouse at ground-floor level, also showing the possible bridge piers*

The gatehouse was subject to little archaeological investigation prior to 1984, when a photographic record of the exterior was made by DAT, and no intrusive work was undertaken until 2001–3. The upper floor had however been 'repaired' under the direction of the Carmarthenshire Antiquarian Society in 1915–17, including the provision of an asphalt surface over the first floor.[39] The gatehouse was fully recorded before consolidation work in 2001, and an archaeological evaluation was undertaken in the gatehouse passageway. In 2003, full excavation within the castle ditch, in front of the gatehouse, revealed the probable remains of the medieval bridge leading to the gateway.

The ground floor

The entry and gate passage (Figures 65–71)

The entrance façade, facing west towards the medieval marketplace in Nott Square, was very much a 'show' front, as exhibited by the remaining dressings (Figures 66–7). The entry, which is 2.3 m wide and 4 m high, is a plain, four-centred arch, with no surround, lying beneath a similar outer arch (1, Figure 67). A plain offset lies just above (2). A four-centred 'flying' arch (3) is carried between the two towers, just above the offset, and represents the machicolation for a chute (3) emptying over the entry from the first floor (Figure 68;

Figure 66 The Great Gatehouse: the west (entrance) façade in 2012

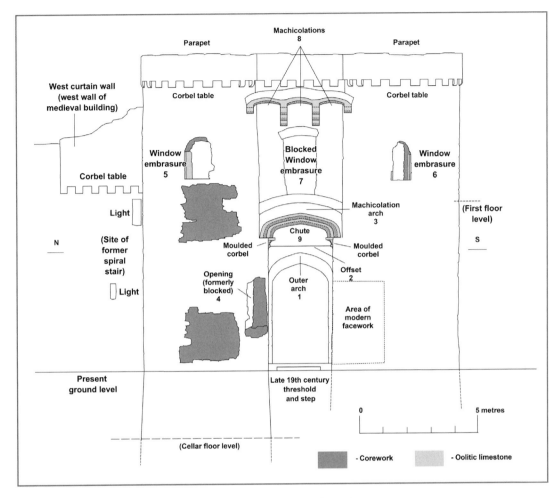

Figure 67 *External elevation of the gatehouse west façade*

see below). It comprises four chamfered orders in imported oolitic limestone, springing from moulded corbels. David Cathcart King regarded this detail as variously 'spurious', 'recooked' and 'phoney'.[40] However, it is all shown in the earliest detailed depiction of the gatehouse, from *c*.1860 (Figure 134) and is here regarded as original.

The surviving gate passage represents only the outer (west) half of the original passage, which continued eastwards through the former rear section (Figures 65, 68–9). It is 4.1 m long, 3 m wide and 4 m high, beneath a segmental barrel-vault which runs throughout. Its approach lay beneath the chute mentioned above, while a portcullis slot still survives. It exhibits the jambs for only one pair of doors, but it is possible that a second pair occupied the former rear section. The east end of the surviving passage was closed off, during the gaol phase, with a wall containing a doorway (1, Figure 81). Further alterations may have occurred when the passage side walls were apparently consolidated. Present floor levels, steps, and the iron railings at the threshold, are from the late nineteenth century at the earliest.

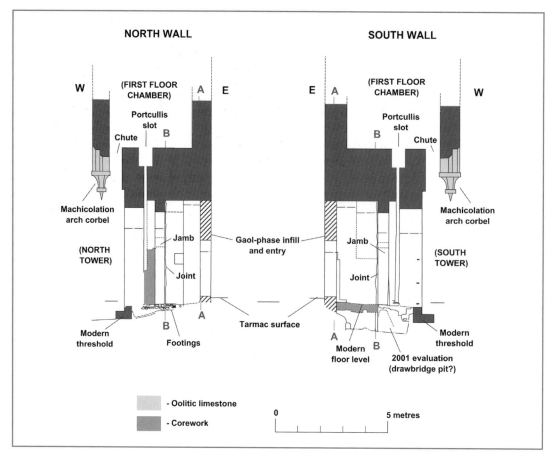

Figure 68 *North and south elevations of the gate passage*

Halfway along the passage, both side walls exhibit a pronounced vertical joint immediately east of the door jambs (Figures 65, 68–9). They rise to the full height of the passage, suggesting that the walls comprise two building phases, and it is possible that the eastern half is a remnant of the pre-1409 gatehouse.

An evaluation was undertaken in the gate passage in 2001 (Figures 70–1), indicating that it formerly featured a drawbridge pit. Removal of the twentieth-century concrete surface revealed a sequence of deposits, which were excavated to an average depth of 0.9 m. They were all post-medieval in character. The east wall of the pit, (531), which was followed to the bottom of the trench, lay 0.5 m west of the present passage east wall. Similar walling continued downward from, but was offset to the north of, the southern side wall but exhibited a vertical butt-joint corresponding with that above, while the two builds (532 and 533) showed different bonding. All walling exhibited good-quality facework, in Old Red Sandstone. The pit was not bottomed and any flooring not revealed, so its depth is unknown. However, the joint in its south wall suggests that it may, like the gate passage, incorporate a pre-1409 feature.

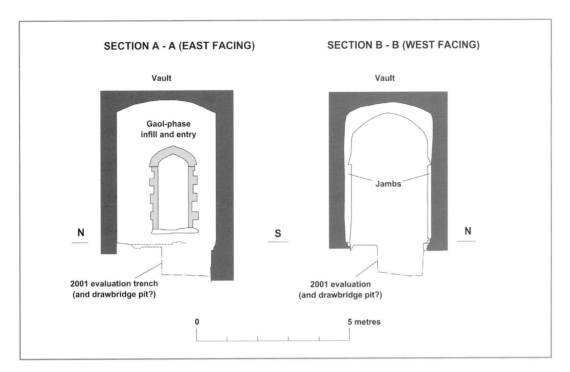

SECTION A - A (EAST FACING)

Vault

Gaol-phase
infill and entry

N

2001 evaluation trench
(and drawbridge pit?)

SECTION B - B (WEST FACING)

Vault

Jambs

S

N

2001 evaluation
(and drawbridge pit?)

0   5 metres

Figure 69 (above) Sections A–A and
B–B through the gate passage

Figure 70 (right) Plan of the gate
passage evaluation trench

The flanking towers

Both gatehouse towers are now solid
at ground-floor level, but originally
were open chambers. They contain a
mortared rubble infill that is clearly secondary, overlying a blocked, damaged
opening in the flank of the north tower
that may represent an arrow-loop covering the gatehouse approach (4, Figure 67; Figure 65). Moreover, the joint
between the infill and the tower walls
was clearly visible, at first floor level, in
the south tower (Figure 72), showing
that the ground floor chambers had an
original diameter of 3 m, with outside

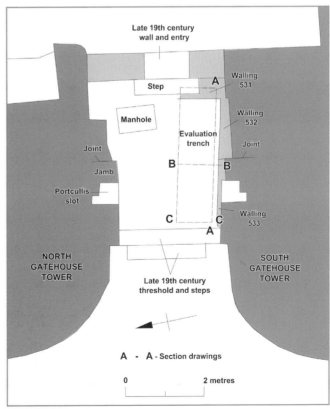

Late 19th century
wall and entry

Step

Manhole

Joint

Jamb

Portcullis
slot

Evaluation
trench

Walling
531

Walling
532

Joint

Walling
533

NORTH
GATEHOUSE
TOWER

Late 19th century
threshold and steps

SOUTH
GATEHOUSE
TOWER

A - A - Section drawings

0   2 metres

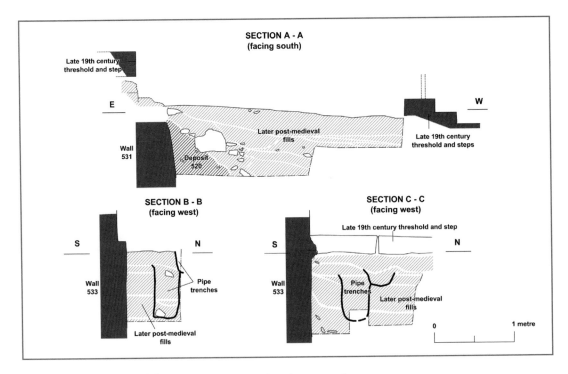

Figure 71 Sections of the gate passage evaluation trench

walls nearly 1.5 m thick. Evidence from the first floor also suggested that both chambers must originally have been accessed from ground floor level, and possible entries are discussed below. There is no trace of any other opening in the south tower and it may have been an unlit chamber.

The first floor and parapet (Figures 72–7)

The first floor of the surviving part of the gatehouse is a single, open chamber overlying the gate-passage and ground-floor chambers (Figure 72). It measures 11 m north–south, averages 4.5 m east–west and is 5 m high to roof-crease level. Its outside walls are 1.2 m thick, i.e. rather thinner than in the ground-floor chambers. Externally, the west front exhibits a series of three machicolations at parapet level, which overlie the entry and are carried on bold, stepped oolite corbels of late medieval form (8, Figure 67; Figure 66). David Cathcart King thought this detail too was spurious, the machicolations being 'too like Kidwelly to be true'.[41] However, it was also shown in c.1860 (Figure 134) and is here also regarded as original. The parapet, which has lost its crenellations, is supported on a narrower corbel table, also of late medieval character.

The entry, at the south end of the east wall (Figures 72 and 73d), is accessed via a short mural passage, 0.8 m wide, in the truncated south wall of the former rear section, leading from a crude, outer entry (3, Figure 83; Figure 72). This outer entry appears to be a secondary breach, of unknown date. However, the passage is clearly an original feature – though much altered – as is the inner entry, which has a segmental head like the other first-floor openings, though missing its voussoirs. It is inferred that the passage may originally have connected the chamber with the spiral stair that is visible, at parapet level, at the junction with the west curtain wall (Figures 72, 77 and 83). The stair appears to have been blocked with masonry at first-floor level, above which an earth fill is visible at parapet level. Its point of origin is therefore unknown, but it may have descended to ground level as the sole original access to the first-floor chamber. In the south wall of the passage can be seen the four-centred surround, in chamfered oolite (Figure 73b), of a blocked entry into the former south turret (5, Figure 79).

The first-floor chamber was lit by three west-facing windows, and a window on each of the north and south sides, all five with splayed embrasures beneath segmental heads. The four tower windows are single lights which have, in the main, lost their oolite dressings; the south-facing light is, however, well-preserved, with a chamfered oolite surround and a

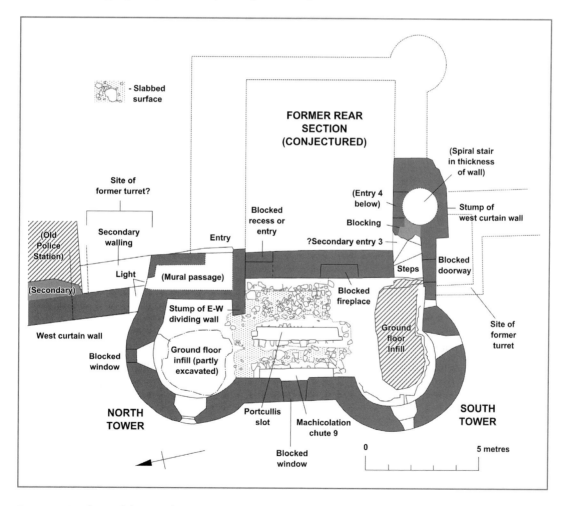

Figure 72 Plan of the gatehouse at first-floor level

sunk-cusped trefoil head of early fifteenth-century character (2, Figure 79; Figure 73b), and the rest may have been similar. The corresponding north-facing light is blocked. The fifth window is central, facing west over the main entrance (Figures 67, 72 and 73a). It has also lost its surround and is blocked. It lies beneath a segmental arch and is somewhat wider than the other four, but it too was probably a single light. A further, smaller single light, with a simple lintel, lies in the angle between the south tower and former turret (3, Figure 79; Figure 73b).

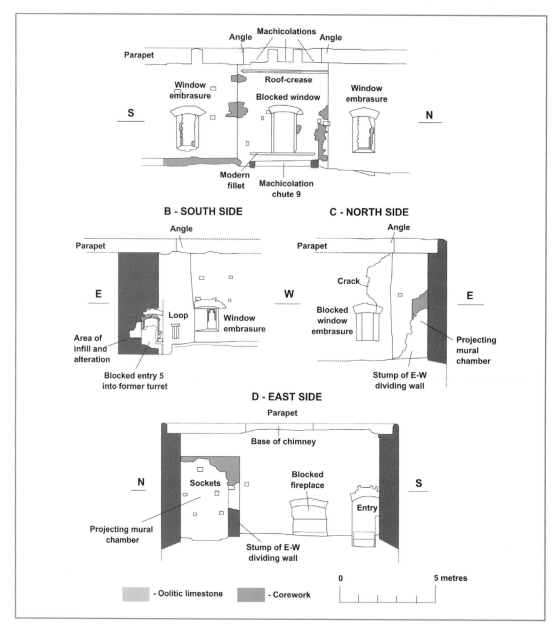

Figure 73 Internal elevations of the gatehouse first floor

Figure 74 Gatehouse, first-floor interior looking north-west, in 2012

Figure 75 Gatehouse, first-floor interior looking south-east, in 2012

In the east wall is a blocked fireplace, 2 m wide and 1.6 m tall, beneath a segmental arch (Figures 72 and 73d). It is not central to the chamber, being offset to the south. This suggests that the possible blocked opening visible in the outside face of this wall (12, Figure 81; see below) may have formerly been an entry that communicated with the rear section, as it would be symmetrical with the present entry either side of the fireplace. However, no trace of an opening is visible from the chamber, whilst the sill of ?opening 12 is nearly 2 m below first-floor level.

The northern third of the east wall is substantially thicker (2 m), where it houses a mural passage. This was accessed from a tall entry in the east face of the wall (4, Figure 81), and terminated after 3 m in the angle with the north wall (Figure 72), where it was lit by a small single-light window, lying within a cut-out in the west curtain, and may be the site of a latrine. The window has a well-preserved surround with a sunk-cusped trefoil head, like that in the south tower (Figure 33). At the southern end of this thicker section of wall is the stump of an east–west internal wall (Figures 72, 73c and 73d). It does not seem to have risen to the full height of the chamber, or to have extended any further west as a dividing wall, and its function is unknown.

A modern concrete floor was removed in 2001,[42] revealing a flagged surface over the gate passage vault – predominantly in Old Red Sandstone slabs – and the top of the infill in the tower ground floors (Figure 72). There were two longitudinal slots in the flagged surface, both 0.5 m wide and occupying the full width of the gate passage. That to the west represents the machicolation chute over the entry (9, Figure 67; Figure 68 and see above), while the eastern slot, which had been later slabbed over, housed the portcullis (Figure 76; also see Figure 68). Both slots were left open in the new flagged surface that was laid in 2002.

There is scant evidence for the roof structure. Surviving creasing is limited to the west wall, between the towers (Figure 73a), and lies just beneath wall-walk level. However, an external opening on the south side of the gatehouse, just above the

Figure 76 *Gatehouse, first-floor interior: the portcullis slot, looking north, as exposed in 2002*

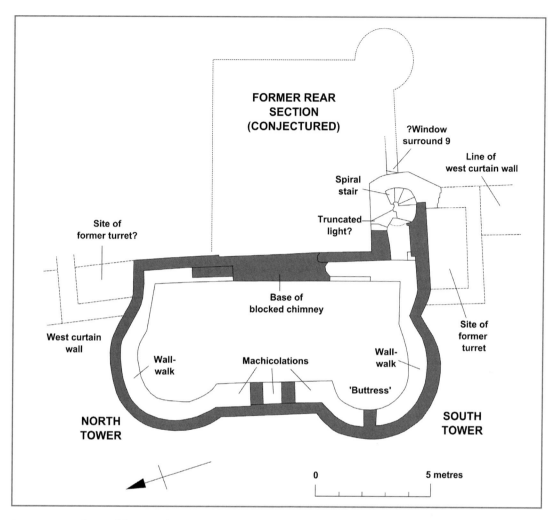

Figure 77 *Plan of the gatehouse at parapet level*

parapet corbel table (see Figure 79), may be a rainwater chute, implying that the eaves lay at wall-walk level (or may even have been carried over the wall-walk). There is no corbelling, or sockets, for any timberwork. Such sockets that exist – concentrated within the south tower, and the east wall of the north tower (Figure 73b and 73c) – do not appear to be structural, but the latter may indicate a superstructure associated with some special use of this 'separate' area.

Parapet level was largely featureless (Figure 77). The parapet itself only stood to an average height of 0.5 m, and had lost its crenellations, but they are shown on the Buck engraving of 1740 (Figure 126). The wall-walk averaged 0.8 m in width, behind a parapet wall that was 0.7 m thick. It oversailed the former rear section, continuing around the east side of the gatehouse where it is interrupted by the chimney leading from the first-floor fireplace. This chimney, which is not shown by the Buck Brothers, has been blocked and truncated, but its base survives and is very wide, measuring 4.5 m north–south. The three openings for the upper tier of machicolations can be seen on the west side (8, Figure 67; Figure 77), separated by low lengths of walling; a similar 'buttress' on the west side of the south tower appears to be bracing for the parapet.

The wall-walk was accessed from the spiral stair in the rear section south wall, described above. This has been truncated, the sill of a slit-light on the north side confirming that it formerly oversailed the parapet as a caphouse or turret.

The southern turret (Figures 78–9)

The stump of the former west curtain wall is clearly visible on the south face of the gate-house (1, Figure 79; Figure 78), which also exhibits clear evidence that a turret formerly lay in the angle between the gatehouse and the curtain. The scar of its west wall (4), 0.6 m

thick, can be seen 2.5 m west of the curtain wall, showing that it rose to the full height of the gatehouse. The gatehouse corbel table does not continue between these two walls, but was carried around the turret at a lower level (14), indicating that turret and gatehouse were coeval. The turret, which was probably square, was occupied by chambers on three levels, ground floor in the gatehouse being represented by two stages in the turret. The two lower chambers were heavily truncated during the post-medieval period, but the remains indicate that they were both a mere c.2.5 m in height and that each was entered, from the east, via a low entry (10) through the west curtain; the upper entry retains its chamfered oolite jamb (8). The entries suggest that the curtain was contemporary with

Figure 78 The south side of the gatehouse showing the site of the turret, and infill, from south (by courtesy of Ken Day)

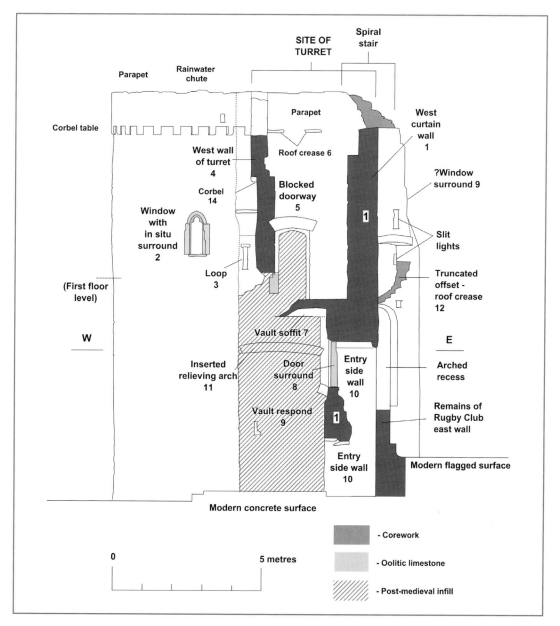

Figure 79 External elevation of the south side of the gatehouse and former turret

the gatehouse and turret, i.e. rebuilt in 1409–11. Both chambers were barrel-vaulted, the lowermost showing the truncated remains of a north–south vault (9), while the respond of an east–west vault (7) can be seen in the one above. The first-floor chamber was taller, and unvaulted; its roof-crease (6) survives on the gatehouse south face and shows that it was 5.5 m high. It was entered from the gatehouse through the doorway, described above, which is visible on this face as a four-centred surround (5) in oolite and red sandstone.

The former rear section

Evidence for the former rear section exists within the standing fabric, as below-ground remains and in map and picture sources. A two-storey structure, tallying with the suggested dimensions of the rear section, is shown to the rear of the gatehouse in the Buck prints of the 1740s (Figures 126–7). Moreover, a substantial rectangular structure is still depicted in this location in a drawing from 1829 (Figure 132). The continuing survival of the rear section may account for a curious feature seen on a plan of 1819 (Figure 130). The two gatehouse towers are shown, but a third tower is marked and labelled immediately behind the gatehouse on the line of the present gaol wall. This tower might be depicted in the 1740 Buck print, in which a very narrow, cylindrical feature appears to be shown at the south-east corner of the rear section (Figure 126), but appears to be a much more substantial feature in the 1829 drawing, possibly representing a spiral stair turret.

The rear section, including any turret, had gone by the 1840s (Figures 136 and 139), although its south wall persisted as a wall-line until the late nineteenth century (see Chapter 5). The truncated western stump of this wall still survives, while its lowermost courses were revealed, just beneath the modern surfacing east of the gatehouse, during groundworks in 2002 (Figure 34). They were of similar fabric to the standing remains, and also 1.2 m wide. Although partly lost to a post-medieval trench, they ran eastwards as far as the nineteenth-century century gaol wall which exhibits, at the junction, an irregular 'bulge'. This section is also of a different build from, and is noticeably thicker than, the remainder of the gaol wall, and may represent the fossilised south-east corner of the rear section. It is moreover possible that a concavity, visible on its west face (Figure 34), confirms the presence of a spiral stair turret here, perhaps belonging to the interior of its shaft. Figure 124 attempts to reconstruct the arrangement of the gatehouse and rear section in the fifteenth century.

Evidence from the gatehouse east face (Figures 80–1)

The east face of the gatehouse is now an outside wall (Figure 80), but was formerly an internal wall dividing the surviving west half from the missing rear section, and is 1.2 m thick. It is a complex piece of masonry and difficult to unravel. Ground-floor arrangements have been much obscured by later alterations including the gaol-period infill of the gate passage (14, Figure 81) where it formerly continued through the rear section. However, the truncated northern side wall of the passage is visible as a strip of corework (2), and as an area of exposed slabbing at its foot, which together show that the wall was 2.5 m thick at ground level. Corework 2 rises, through first-floor level, almost to the parapet where it exhibits, in section, the profile of coping and string-course (6) at the north-east corner of the surviving section. This indicates that both walls were, in this corner, outside walls, and that the gate passage north wall formed the north wall of the rear section, giving it a total north–south dimension of 7 m. Moreover, the corbelled parapet terminates at this wall-line where it is replaced by roof-creasing, (11), belonging to the rear section interior, which continued around the south wall (2, Figure 83; see below), demonstrating that the rear section had a hipped roof. No evidence for a continuation of the gate passage south wall is now

Figure 80 *The east side of the gatehouse, from north-east, in 2012*

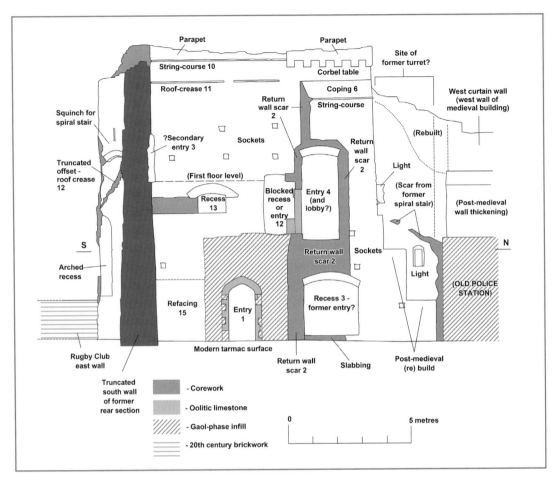

Figure 81 *External elevation of the east side of the gatehouse*

visible, but the surrounding area has been extensively refaced (15, Figures 81 and 83), and may represent ground floor chamber infill.

A recess lies at ground floor level (3, Figure 81), within the junction with the rear section north wall. It is 1 m deep, 2.3 m wide, and 2.2 m high beneath a segmental arch. Although somewhat wide, it may represent a former entry into the gatehouse north tower, possibly blocked when the ground-floor chambers were infilled. Above it is a second entry (4), at first-floor level, also within the thickness of the rear section north wall. Its relationship with ground-floor recess 3 suggests that it was accessed from a stairway that was similarly integral with the rear section north wall, and perhaps carried over recess 3 by an arch (see Figure 124). Corework 2 is thinner above entry 4 (only 0.5 m thick), and the line of coping 6 seems to have continued downward as a lean-to roof over the north wall and entry. The entry, which is tall – 3.5 m high beneath a segmental head – was not fully investigated, but gives onto the mural passage in the east wall of the surviving section, described above, which also lies beneath coping 6.

A blocked opening, 2.5 m high (12, Figure 81), lies next to entry 4, with which it was clearly associated. It has the appearance of a second entry, sharing the remains of an oolite surround, and sill level, with entry 4. However, it cannot be distinguished internally (see above), and its true nature is unknown. A smaller opening (13) appears always to have been a blind recess. It is 0.3 m deep, 1.2 m wide and 0.8 m high beneath a segmental arch, and may have been a cupboard, although it backs onto the fireplace in the first-floor chamber. A regular pattern of square sockets (14) lies higher up in the wall, and these appear to have been structural rather than scaffold sockets. As it is unlikely that a further floor lay at this level, they may have been associated with the roof structure.

The rear section south wall (Figures 78–9, 82–3)
As we have seen, field evidence for the rear section south wall includes both below-ground remains and standing fabric. Its truncated south wall survives as a 3.8 m length of walling, running eastwards from the surviving south-east corner of the gatehouse (Figures 65, 72, 79–83). It has been much altered and the original arrangements are difficult to discern. However, we have also seen that its upper half, at least, contained a spiral stair (see Figures 72 and 77). The upper half of the stair is carried obliquely over the angle between the gatehouse and west curtain by a segmental arch, to form a squinch, and was lit by a small slit-light (Figure 79); a second slit-light lies below the arch, showing that the stair is not confined to the squinched area.

At this level, the south face of the wall was an outside wall. However, a diagonal offset immediately below, sloping down to meet the truncated west curtain at first-floor level (12, Figure 79) apparently received the end of a pitched roof belonging to an adjoining building, lying to the south and against the curtain. Beneath it is a recess, occupying the full height of the suggested building; its arch was also carried over the angle with the curtain.

Figure 82 *The north face of the truncated south wall of the former rear section, in 2002*

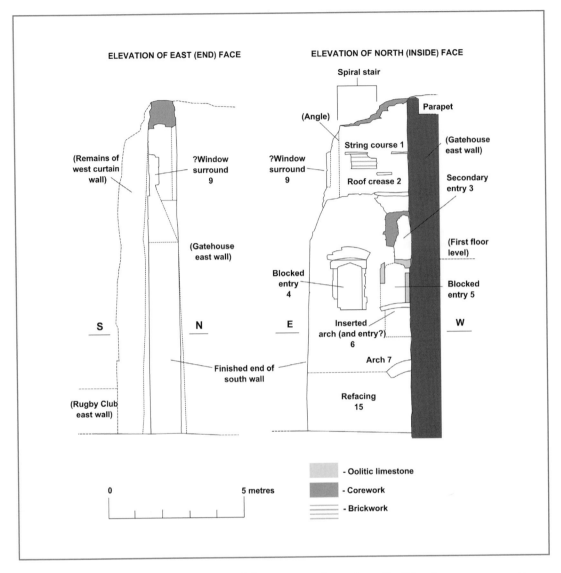

Figure 83 *East and north elevations of the truncated south wall of the former rear section*

In the north (inside) face are two blocked doorways (4 and 5, Figure 83; Figure 82). They lie side by side, some 1.7 m below the present entry to the present first-floor chamber, 3 (see above), and therefore do not correspond with either of the surviving floor levels. Each has a four-centred surround in dressed stone; oolite in entry 5, while the head of entry 4, to the east, has been replaced in cast concrete. Entry 4 lies opposite – and may therefore have led to – the spiral stair. The purpose and destination of entry 5 are unknown however. Its sill was removed by the ?secondary insertion of a crude arch (6), which appears to lie above an area of infill that was rather too small to represent a further entry. The remains of a second arch (7) can be seen in the angle with the present gatehouse east wall, its head lying 2.2 m above ground level. It rises towards the gatehouse east wall, where it apparently terminates. However the rubble fill of the south tower ground floor, visible in the surface of the first-floor chamber, extends up to the east wall (Figure 72; see above), suggesting that an entrance passage from the east was also infilled. The arch may therefore belong to a passage, lying obliquely in the angle between the two walls, which was subsequently infilled and concealed beneath facework 15 (Figures 81 and 83).

The lower half of the truncated east end of the wall has been finished off, but the upper half exhibits some original features, including one jamb of a surround, probably for a window (9, Figures 79 and 83).

Post-medieval alterations

It will have been seen from the description above that the gatehouse sustained considerable damage, and alteration, during the post-medieval period, not least the loss of its rear section. Although these changes belong to a number of periods, and result from a variety of causes, there is no structural evidence either for its gaol-phase usage, or for the kind of domestic encroachment that occurred in the other towers.

It will be argued in Chapter 5 that the ground-floor chambers may have been infilled with rubble as a measure against artillery, possibly during the Civil War of 1642–8. The infill was later partly removed from the north tower, and backfilled with a loose, mortar-rich soil that was excavated in 2002 (Figure 84). It contained stones, brick fragments, some animal bone and one clay pipe bowl of eighteenth-/nineteenth-century date, indicating that this backfill is late eighteenth-century at the earliest and therefore belongs to the post-1789 County Gaol.

The gatehouse appears to have to have suffered from the slighting that occurred, it is suggested, after the Civil War. However, damage was apparently limited to the area of the former west curtain, to the south, and the south turret which lost its vaulted chambers; the lower two-thirds of the gatehouse south wall can be seen to be secondary infill, with a relieving arch half-way up (11, Figure 79; Figure 78). So it is likely that the original walling collapsed when the turret vaults came down. The rear section was not lost until later, map and print evidence suggesting that it survived into the nineteenth century.

Figure 84 The secondary infill in the north gate tower, during excavation in 2002, facing south-west

The gatehouse was blocked when the new County Gaol was built in 1789–92 and was thereafter, apparently, left vacant. The gate passage was brought back into use in the 1870–1880s to provide access to the Old Police Station (see Chapter 5), and the infilled east end, with its entry (1, Figure 81; Figures 68 and 69), probably belongs to this period. The entry has a four-centred surround in yellow oolite, incorporating an iron grille over the doorway like that seen in the Old Police Station, where it is from the early 1880s (see below). The railings and steps at the west end of the passage are probably contemporary; they are shown in a sketch of 1909.[43]

The west ditch, bridge and cellars

The Great Gatehouse was approached, until the 1970s, via a narrow lane running between two properties, No.11 Nott Square to the north and No. 21 Bridge Street to the south (Figure 85; also see Figures 133–4, 148–50 and 153). In general, the lane appeared to follow the line of the medieval bridge across the west ditch, but it will be seen that its alignment gradually swung to the south as the ditch was progressively infilled and built over during the post-medieval development of Nott Square and Bridge Street. Topographic and excavated evidence indicate that the east sides of both streets, which lie between 18 m and 20 m from the west curtain wall, more or less correspond with the western edge of the ditch.

The western (front) half of No. 21 Bridge Street is still standing, and overlies a cellar; the rear half was demolished in 2002. Along with No. 11 Nott Square, the plot appears to have been built over by c.1610 (Figure 112), but was apparently entirely redeveloped after the Civil War; it is clearly built over on all subsequent maps, and the present arrangement – a rectangular building at right angles to Bridge Street, detached from the castle gatehouse – appears to have been in place by 1834 (Figure 133). Historic maps suggest that, during most of the nineteenth century, the property was owned by, and may have formed part of, the public house in No. 20 Bridge Street to the south – the Buffalo Inn (Figures 128–30).

No. 11 Nott Square was formerly an L-shaped property with one limb fronting Nott Square, the other overlying an east–west cellar to the rear, Cellar I (Figure 85; also see Figure 149). A separate, but conjoined building overlay a second cellar (Cellar II), to the northeast, between the gatehouse north tower and the west curtain wall. An open backyard lay between the three buildings, overlying a further cellar (Cellar III). While the excavated evidence suggested that these buildings were no earlier than the eighteenth century, Thomas Lewis's detailed map of Carmarthen, from 1786 (Figure 111), indicates that they were in place by the late eighteenth century, at least. The building was another pub – the 'Swan Inn' – from at least 1818 (Figure 129).

No.11 Nott Square (along with No.12 to the north), was demolished in 1971–2.[44] The underlying cellars were, however, revealed by landscaping works in 2002–3, when they were emptied, recorded and eventually consolidated beneath a new surface. All three cellars had walls of local rubble masonry, and brick vaults (Figures 86, 93–4). They had been closed off and backfilled during the twentieth century, probably when the overlying properties were demolished.

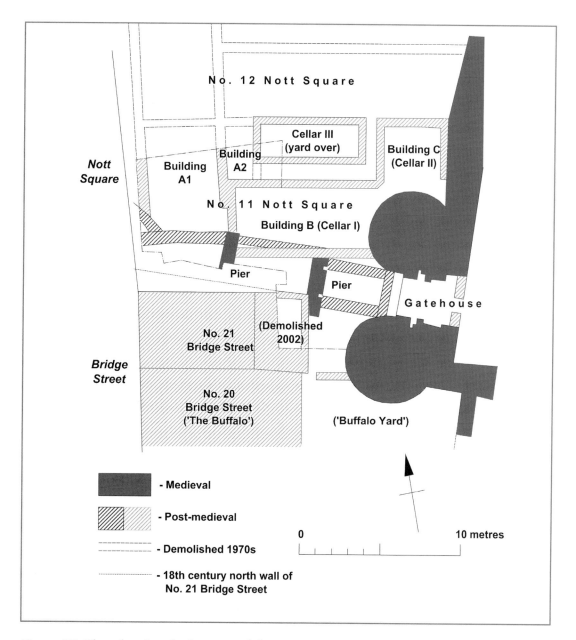

Figure 85 Plan showing the location of the 2003 excavation, cellars, bridge piers etc.,
relative to former buildings

It was seen that the south wall of Cellar I incorporated part of a bridge, of possible
medieval date, that crossed the ditch between the gatehouse and the town (Figures 65
and 85). The bridge appears to have comprised two masonry piers supporting timber
decking. Two parallel alignments of secondary walling, inserted between the piers, initially suggested that the bridge had been converted into a continuous masonry causeway,

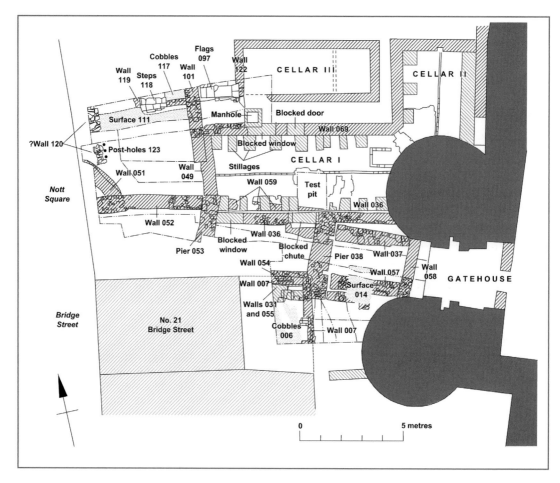

Figure 86 Composite plan of the bridge area showing excavated features

and the clearance work was duly followed by controlled excavation, led by Duncan Schlee of DAT during the summer of 2003.[45] Excavation, however, revealed that this later walling was post-medieval.

The 2003 excavation comprised three main areas, which were separated by walls and could only be partly correlated with each other. The fullest sequence of deposits was revealed beneath No. 11 Nott Square, but practical limitations, and later disturbance, meant that it could not be fully tied in with the more restricted sequences in other parts of the site. Moreover the line of the bridge still represents the lane leading from Nott Square to the gatehouse; as a convenient line for services, it was heavily disturbed by pipe- and cable-trenches – many of them live – and could not be excavated. Similar constraints also meant that Cellar III could not be fully investigated.

The condition of the pottery recovered from the west ditch deposits indicates that the majority of the upper fills were secondary, representing infill that had been imported from elsewhere, perhaps from a rubbish dump (see Chapter 6). The finds are therefore of limited use in dating either the ditch fills, or the structures built upon them; the fills may have been deposited much later than the date of the finds within them.[46] It also means that neither the finds, nor the associated animal bone and plant remains,[47] were necessarily derived from the vicinity of the castle. However, a sequence of deposits lower down in the ditch appeared to be *in situ*. These yielded an important assemblage of leather shoes and wooden bowls, of late medieval date, that were retrieved from a waterlogged context.

The medieval ditch and bridge (Figures 85–90)

The west ditch – which, for practical reasons, could not be bottomed – was at least 5.3 m deep (Figures 87 and 90). Its western, outer edge (085) lay 16 m to the west of the inner edge that was revealed through evaluation trenching in 2001 (see above). It appeared to correspond with the present edge of Nott Square, from which it sloped downwards at roughly 45 degrees. However, it was seen to be cut through a mixed loamy material (087), of a rather different character from the natural fluvio-glacial gravels and boulder clays, and with the appearance of redeposited subsoil. The possibility therefore exists that the ditch cut was secondary, and cut within the (deliberate?) infill of an earlier, wider ditch; there was, however, no dating evidence for the (re-)cut.

Evidence for a possible bridge was first identified in the post-medieval south wall of Cellar I (36; Figure 87), within the fabric of which lay two discrete, narrow pillars of masonry, (038) and (053). Further excavation showed them to be two piers, originally

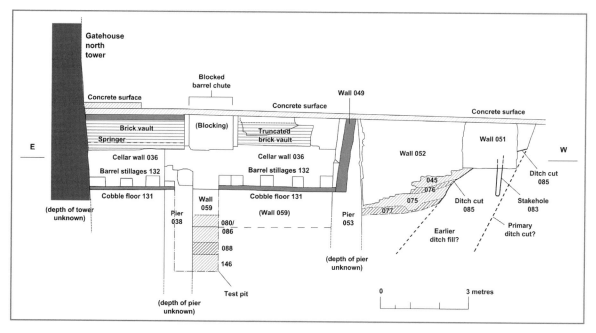

Figure 87 *North elevation of Cellar I south wall showing bridge piers and post-medieval walling*

free-standing, that may have supported a timber bridge of three bays. Both comprised locally quarried rubble, mainly in limestone. The piers, like the ditch, were not bottomed, so their original height is unknown, but was at least 5.3 m.

The eastern pier, 038 (see Figure 89), lay 4.60 m west of the gatehouse threshold, the western pier, 053, lying 5.5 m east of the western edge of the ditch, while they were 4.90 m apart (Figure 86). Pier 038 was 0.92 m thick (east–west) and 4.30 m wide (north–south). Two square-sectioned vertical slots, each 0.24 m wide and 0.30 m deep, with angled bases, ran down its east face, from a point 1.10 m below the top as it survived (Figure 86). In addition, a square-sectioned horizontal slot, 0.20 m wide, ran east–west through the pier, 0.20 m south of the southern slot. A similar horizontal slot may have existed on the north side of the pier, but was obscured by the cellar wall. The western pier, 053, was not fully exposed, but its dimensions were assumed to be similar to those of pier 038. In elevation, however, it was seen to taper markedly towards the top, narrowing to a thickness of 0.50 m, but it showed evidence of a rebuild.

Excavation below the cellar floor revealed evidence for a cut, (145), against the north face of pier 038 (Figure 90). While it may represent a construction trench, the base of the pier was not encountered, and the cut lies at a fairly high level in relation to the angle of ditch edge 085, and so it may represent the trench for repair or rebuilding rather than primary construction. It was cut through an undated deposit, but lay beneath *in situ* contexts (078–080) containing late fifteenth-/early sixteenth-century material. These were the earliest datable fills within the ditch, and very nearly the lowest (Figure 90). They were, moreover, the only deposits that yielded artefacts securely datable to any period earlier than the late seventeenth century. They clearly represent a single depositional event and contained the assemblage of leather shoes and bowls mentioned above. The nature of their other finds, which included cobbler waste, along with large sherds from two medieval pots (a jar and a jug) in 079 and 080, indicate a primary deposit, dumped directly into the ditch as a midden.[48] The shoe styles and pottery fabric, described in Chapter 6, date the dumping event to *c*.1500, or perhaps a little later. It remains unknown whether it relates to the castle, or to domestic development within the castle ditch. Context 080 may be the same as (086) beneath it (Figure 90). The latter overlies a further deposit, (088), lying immediately above trench 145; it was recorded as having contained brick fragments, which would not be altogether inconsistent with a date of 1500+, and so the deposit might be broadly contemporary with 078–080. It is suggested below, however, that the brick may have belonged to a different and later context.

The piers, then, appear to belong to a medieval bridge, but they cannot be closely dated. There are a number of references to 'the castle bridge' during the thirteenth and fourteenth centuries – it was described as 'new' in 1317, which may relate to the construction of the piers in place of an entirely timber structure (see Chapter 4). Any bridge, though, is likely to have been severely damaged – along with the gatehouse – during the Glyndŵr rebellion, so the dates indicated by the finds, and the evidence for rebuilding in both piers, may relate to documented repairs at the gatehouse during the period 1409–11.

Post-medieval structures and features (Figures 86–7, 90 and 92)

Post-medieval Phase 1 (late seventeenth century?)

Also overlying bridge pier 038 (Figure 90), but unfortunately without a direct relationship with 078–080, were four contexts that appeared to represent a single event – (062), (064), (065) and (074). They were of similar character, and dominated by sixteenth- or early seventeenth-century ceramics in a very mixed assemblage of small, highly abraded sherds. This indicates that the deposits were probably secondary – i.e. they had initially been deposited elsewhere, perhaps in a rubbish dump, before being redeposited in the ditch during the late sixteenth century, at the earliest, and possibly much later.[49] Like 078–080, the sequence sloped markedly downhill to the north.

The dumping may have been intended to raise levels in the ditch prior to its development, as a pair of parallel east–west walls was subsequently inserted between the bridge piers, both in the central bay, and in the east bay between pier 038 and the gatehouse (Figures 86 and 90). The central bay north wall, (059), butted against the two piers, flush with their northern faces. Comprising roughly squared sandstone rubble, it was 0.50 m thick, and was exposed immediately beneath cellar floor level, where it was partly overlain by cellar wall 36, suggesting that it had been truncated. Wall 059 was associated with a possible construction trench (081), cutting through midden deposits 078–080, its base lying 3.9 m below present ground level (Figure 90). The possibility exists that the brick fragments recorded in context 088 in fact belong to the fill of this trench.

Lying 2.6 m to the south of 059 was a parallel wall, (054), which was set back 0.50 m from the ends of the piers (Figure 86). It was rather thicker than 059 (0.55 m) and had not been truncated, being exposed just beneath the modern surface. Unlike 059, it was apparently built without a footing or trench, directly upon late sixteenth-century or later deposits 062, 064–5 and 074 (Figure 90). Its base was revealed at a depth of 3 m, which is more or less

Figure 88 *Ditch deposits and wall 049 during excavation, looking east (wall 052 and pier 053 on right; Cellar I beyond)*

the same level – allowing for the downhill slope – from which the suggested construction trench for wall 059 was cut. The two, then, may be contemporary.

East of pier 038 were two parallel walls, (037) to the north and (057) to the south, both also in Old Red Sandstone and the latter continuing the line of wall 054 (Figure 86). They lay just below the modern surface, 1.7 m apart, and were 3.5 m long and 0.65 m thick. They butted against a narrow north–south wall (058) which in turn lay between, and butted, the gate towers. All three walls therefore post-date the gatehouse and while 058 is the earliest, they may be broadly contemporary with each other. The base of wall 057 lay at a slightly higher level than that of wall 054 to the west, but on the same horizon (Figure 90).

Wall 054 was demonstrably of post-medieval date. The others were not bottomed and can only be dated by association. It seems likely, nevertheless, that they are of similar date; they respected the same alignment, were in a similar locally quarried rubble, mainly Old Red Sandstone, and two occupied a similar stratigraphic horizon. Speed's map of c.1610 (Figure 112) shows continuous development along the east side of Nott Square and Bridge Street, suggesting that the ditch had been at least partly backfilled. Some late sixteenth-century leases, discussed in Chapter 5, also relate to domestic plots within the former ditch. However, it is likely that all housing was cleared during the 1650s, when the west curtain was apparently slighted. Moreover, while walls 054 and 057, at least, may be late sixteenth-/

Figure 89 *Bridge pier 038 and post-medieval walls 054 and 057, from southwest*

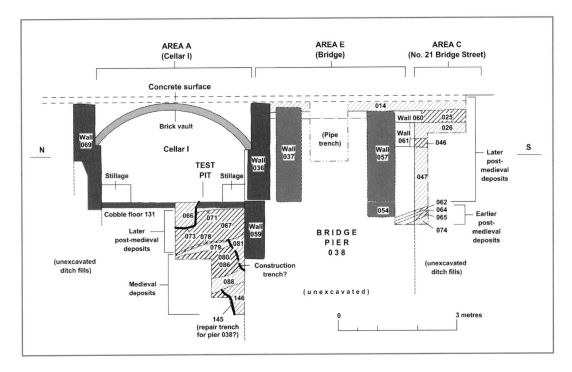

Figure 90 *Composite, transverse section through ditch structures and deposits, facing east*

early seventeenth-century, the nature of the dating evidence indicates that they are more likely to be later, perhaps much later.

So on balance, the evidence suggests that the walls and deposits described above are seventeenth-century at the earliest, and probably from later in the century, but it is uncertain whether they were associated with the castle, or with civil settlement. The walls clearly define the access lane to the main castle entry, which remained in use until the gatehouse was blocked in 1789–92. However, the dating evidence argues against an association with the castle – the Crown had, by the early seventeenth century, disposed of the castle, and from then on it was managed by the county authorities as a gaol, upon which there was very little subsequent expenditure. Similarly, very little outlay was recorded during the late sixteenth century. As a consequence, the evidence also argues against the walls representing a causeway, while northern wall-line 037/059 in any case did not extend the whole length of the access lane.[50]

It is suggested that, instead, the walls belong to post-slighting, domestic redevelopment either side of the castle entrance lane: they also define the edges of the No. 11 Nott Square and No. 21 Bridge Street plots. While it seems that these plots remained largely empty for some time after the Civil War – there are intimations in antique prints that the area was still to be fully redeveloped in the 1740s (Figures 126–7) – a date-stone from 1688, reused in the former No.12 Nott Square, suggests that some building may have begun in the vicinity. Moreover, it will be seen that, by the later eighteenth century, southern wall-line 054/057

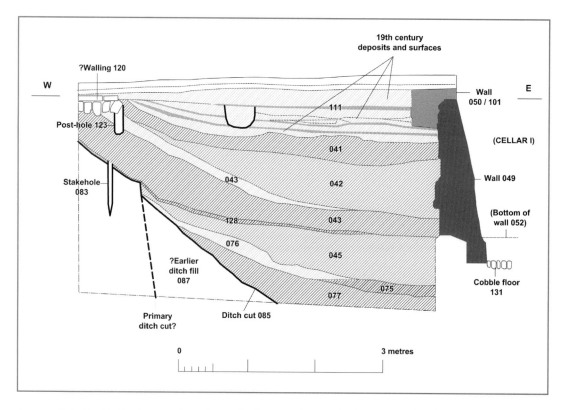

Figure 91 South-facing section through deposits beneath the west side of No. 11 Nott Square

was the north wall of a house occupying No. 21 Bridge Street. But, while the evidence suggests that the walls belonged to the town, rather than the gaol, their exact purpose during Phase 1 is unknown.

Post-medieval Phase 2 (mid-eighteenth-century)
The remainder of the walls and deposits in the excavated area clearly relate the development of the plots as domestic properties. This began shortly after c.1740, was more or less complete by 1786, and was apparently undertaken in two campaigns (Figure 92). Another phase of dumping, again represented by secondary deposits (026, 046–7, 067, 071, 045 and 075–7; Figures 87, 90–1) which yielded seventeenth-century to mid-eighteenth-century pottery, was regarded as a single event.[51] To the west, the sequence was overlain by an east–west wall (052) connecting bridge pier 053 with the edge of the castle ditch. On a different alignment to the Phase 1 walls, it was butted by a roughly contemporary wall (051) which ran diagonally north-west to meet the ditch edge (Figures 86–7). A north–south line of stakeholes to the north (083), may have supported a barrier to stabilise the ditch edge (Figures 87 and 91). Phase 1 walls 037 and 059 appear to have been relatively short-lived. During Phase 2 they were truncated and replaced by a single wall (036), following the alignment of wall 052, although offset 1 m to the south (Figures

86–7); the two walls may therefore be contemporary, and occupy the wall-lines shown on the 1786 map (Figure 111).

The 1786 map also shows that two roofed buildings occupied the No. 11 plot (Buildings A and B, Figures 86 and 92), divided by a north–south wall (049) at the west end of Cellar I (Figures 86–8, 91 and 93), which occupied the same horizon as walls 036 and 052. The cobble floor of Cellar I lay at the same level (131, Figures 87 and 91; Figure 94). However, along with the cellar north wall (069), all are suggested to be secondary to walls 036 and 052. Although these walls stood proud of the ditch bottom when building commenced, Cellar I soon came to lie below-ground, as may have been intended from the first – the construction of wall 049 appears to have been concurrent with dumping against its west side (039 and 041–4, Figure 91). These dumps also contained damaged sixteenth-/

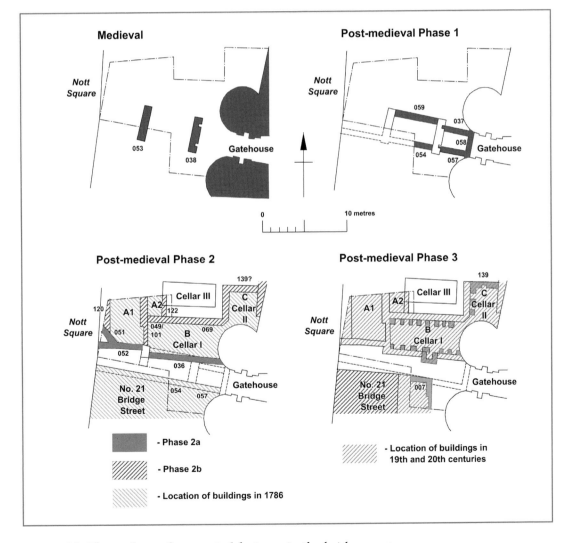

Figure 92 Phase plans of excavated features in the bridge area

seventeenth-century material and clearly represent a third phase of secondary deposition. They were laid down in preparation for the development of the western half of the plot (Building A1), raising it level with Nott Square. A line of slabs along the Nott Square front-age, associated with a line of post-holes, may represent a foundation for the west wall of the plot (120 and 123, Figures 86 and 91), which is shown in 1786 (Figure 111). However, all surfaces excavated in Building A1 appear to be later, belonging to Phase 3.

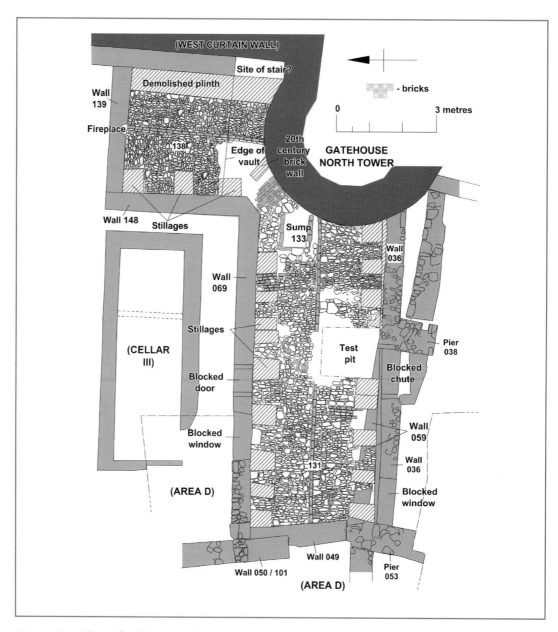

Figure 93 Plan of Cellars I and II

Also shown in 1786 is a narrow ?lean-to (Building A2), adjoining the east side of Building A1. Its east wall, partly rebuilt in Phase 3, was also the west wall of Cellar III (122, Figure 86), suggesting that the cellar was also a product of the eighteenth century. It appears that there never was an overlying building, and the area remained an open yard (Figure 86). A further building is however shown to the north of the yard in 1786 (Building C). It overlay Cellar II, whose west wall was contiguous with Cellar I north wall 069 (148, Figures 86 and 93) and, like Cellar I, was floored with cobbles (138).

Less Phase 2 activity was observed in No. 21 Bridge Street. Walls 054 and 057 persisted rather longer than 037 and 059 in No. 11. They formed the north wall, depicted on the 1786 map, of a building extending all the way from Nott Square to the gatehouse south tower (Figure 111). Layer (025), which appeared to overlie these walls (Figure 90), contained finds of late eighteenth-century date.

Post-medieval Phase 3

A considerable amount of later activity was recognised in the No. 11 Nott Square plot, broadly datable to the late eighteenth/nineteenth century, but was mainly of a minor nature. The east walls of Buildings A1 and A2 were apparently rebuilt; the uppermost courses of wall 049 clearly belonged to a separate build (101, Figures 86 and 91), while wall 122, overlying Cellar III west wall, was also rebuilt, this time in brick (Figures 86 and 94). These rebuilds may be associated with the insertion, in all three cellars, of the present brick vaults, which appear to be secondary. The side walls of Cellars I and II were lined with a series of masonry barrel supports or 'stillages', relating to use as a public house; along with the present brick-lined openings, they are probably contemporary with the vaults (Figures 87 and 93). Cellar II north wall (139), with a brick fireplace, may also have been rebuilt, as it butts against side walls 148 and 140.

The upper levels of Building A1 were much disturbed, and internal features have been lost. However, the remains of its floor surfaces (111 and 117, Figure 86) lay against wall 101 and clearly belong to Phase 3. Building A2 was floored with a cobble surface (098) which lay over Phase 2 surface (108) and against walls 101 and 122; it was sealed beneath a limestone-flagged floor (097), associated with nineteenth-century finds (Figure 86).

Greater change was evident in No. 21 Bridge Street. Its Phase 1 north wall 054/057 was entirely rebuilt, on a different alignment,

Figure 94 Cellar I, under excavation, looking east towards the gatehouse north tower

to define a smaller property, the front half of which still survives; its cellar is assumed to be contemporary. The new building followed the alignment established by walls 052 and 036 during Phase 2 (see Figure 92). Excavation in the rear half of the building (Figure 86) revealed footings (007), a cobble floor (006) and a fireplace (004). Their relationship with the standing front half was not established, but was assumed to be contemporary. The new building can be dated to c.1800, being shown in its present form in 1818 (Figure 129), consistent with the detail shown in Figure 134. East of wall 007 were the fragmentary remains of two external yard surfaces, (014) and (015), disturbed by nineteenth-century features.

THE CASTLE INTERIOR

Archaeological investigation has been more or less confined to the periphery of the castle site, and very little work has taken place within the interior. There are antiquarian records of limited investigations, although they are difficult to interpret. A 'dungeon' was apparently discovered 'in the County Gaol', in 1814, with a 'stout wooden pillar in the middle, to which it is supposed condemned criminals were fastened in feudal times'.[52] This appears to describe an undercroft, though it can be neither located nor dated from the account.

An account in *The Welshman*, from May 1883,[53] relates how drainage works at the gaol revealed

> about twelve or fourteen feet below the surface . . . what appears, at first sight, to be a peat bed but which . . . is evidently only an accumulation of vegetable matter such as might be supposed to form in the eddy of a current. [It] contains what appear to be beech leaves . . . and [animal bone], a piece of thong of primitive manufacture; and some other remains which can only be determined as vegetable. Curiously, the Gaol is on a hill, yet we have here matter that must have been deposited in a water-channel.

The location of these excavations is unknown. However, the account appears to describe the waterlogged fill of a ditch, which can only have been the cross-ditch between the inner and outer wards that was subsumed beneath the post-1869 gaol (Figure 5). A bone stylus was recovered, of uncertain date.

Controlled intrusive work has been limited to the former inner ward. Three areas have been investigated, all occupying the narrow strip lying outside the nineteenth-century gaol wall (Figure 5). Observations east of the Great Gatehouse relate to the gatehouse and the gaol, and are described elsewhere in this chapter. The other two areas both lay immediately north of the southern retaining wall, between the South-west Tower and the Square Tower (Figure 39), where ground levels – unlike in the rest of the castle interior, which is now relatively level – are still higher to the west than to the east, reflecting a historic downhill slope of some 2.5 m (Figure 95). The first of these areas, Trench A, was excavated

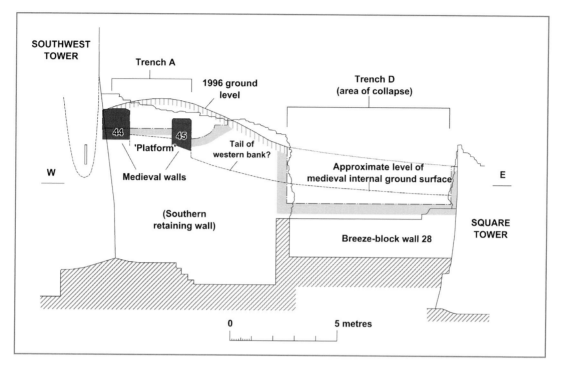

Figure 95 Profile of internal levels between the South-west Tower and Square Tower, facing north

immediately east of the South-west Tower, by Heather James of DAT, in 1980 (see Figures 39 and 51), and was the first modern investigation of the castle site;[54] a complex of internal walls was revealed, now consolidated for display. The second, Trench D, occupied an area of collapse behind the southern revetment wall (Figures 39 and 95); the exposed sections were straightened, cleaned and recorded during groundworks in 1996.[55] At the same time, two small contractor's trenches (Figure 51, Trenches B and C) were excavated within the backfill of Trench A, and confirmed the results from 1980.[56]

Trench A: the 1980 excavation (Figures 39, 51, 95–7)
Trench A occupied the south-west corner of the inner ward, in the angle – formerly just over 90 degrees – between the medieval west and south curtain walls. It averaged 3.7 m north–south by 6.7 m east–west (Figures 39 and 51). The area was shown to have been highly developed. Truncated walling was revealed just beneath the topsoil, associated with floor surfaces. The walls, which survived to an average height of 1 m, were almost entirely in Old Red Sandstone, were well bonded with each other and appeared contemporary. They formed a regular arrangement with the medieval curtain wall-lines, and were substantial, their average thickness of 1 m suggesting that they formerly rose to at least two storeys.

It was not possible to establish any relationships either with the former south curtain, which lay beyond the excavated area, or with the South-west Tower, whose threshold lay

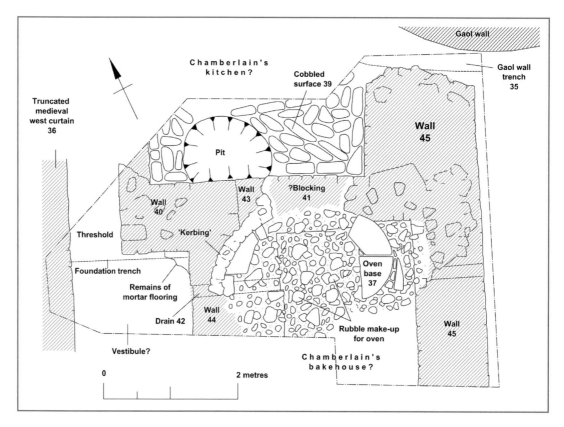

Figure 96 Plan of Trench A

at its south-west edge where medieval occupation deposits had not survived. Moreover, excavation was not total, as some surfaces were retained *in situ* and the full sequence was not exposed. However, the buildings were shown to be secondary to the west curtain. The underlying horizon appeared to be natural, but though hard and clean, it was banded in layers, and may represent spread bank material. Unlike the curtain walls and towers, at least two of the walls occupied deep construction trenches. They were cut directly through this underlying material, and no intervening deposits were recognised.

The buildings appear to have occupied a deliberately terraced area, retained by a north–south wall, (45), east of which the ground sloped down to the Square Tower (Figures 51, 95–7). A second wall (44), 1.3 m wide, ran parallel with 45, 1.9 m to the west. Both presumably ran to the former south curtain, lying just over 1 m to the south and beyond the excavated area. Wall 45 was truncated by the nineteenth-century gaol-wall construction trench (35), and its northern limit is unknown. The north end of wall 44 connected with an east–west wall (40), averaging 1 m in width. This ran eastwards to join wall 45, which decreased in width, from 1.6 m to 1 m, south of this junction. To the west, wall 40 termi-nated at a corner, from which a further length of wall (43) ran northwards for 0.5 m before running under the edge of the excavation.

A narrow gap or passage, 0.8 m wide, lay between wall 43 and the remains of the west curtain wall, 36, described above. The arrangement appears to define a small square area around the South-west Tower entry, possibly representing a vestibule, entered from the north between wall 43 and the west curtain; the foundation trench for wall 40 extended westwards to the curtain – to which it was secondary – suggesting that a threshold was present here. A small area of mortar floor bedding survived in this area, in the angle between walls 43 and 44, at approximately the same level as the South-west Tower ground floor. A narrow, square drain (42), which ran through walls 44 and 45, may have been secondary. Crude, post-medieval 'revetment' walls in this area (not shown in the figures) appear to have been built to retain the nineteenth-century infill deposits in the South-west Tower ground floor.

A second, unexcavated surface (39), of close-set river pebbles, suggests that a chamber lay between walls 40, 43 and 45; the floor was possibly laid directly over the ?bank material. Traces of internal divisions were marked by pitched shale slabs. A spread of charcoal debris was perhaps derived from a fireplace situated to the north of the excavated area. The clean floor surface indicated that, as in the South-west Tower, the chamber had been cleared of all seventeenth-century demolition debris/collapse by the late eighteenth century. The surface was cut by a later pit.

Figure 97 *Trench A from north-west, in 1980, showing all walls and oven base 37*

South of wall 40, lying between walls 44, 45 and the south curtain wall, was a third 'chamber'. It contained a concreted mass of rubble and mortar, representing the base for a slabbed floor in which a few slabs remained, while impressions in the mortar indicated others. However, it was overlain by two very large, rounded limestone blocks (37), each a quarter-segment in plan and up to 0.70 m across, which clearly represent the base of a bread oven. They were 6 cm thick at outer edge and 0.45 cm thick at centre – possibly reused mill-stones? – and some exhibited heat-reddening. They were associated with an area of 'kerbing' to the west, continuing the arc of the circle and possibly representing the bedding for more stones. The whole had an external diameter of nearly 3 m. A slight difference in its masonry suggests that wall 40 featured an opening between the two north–south walls, 1.3 m wide, later blocked (41). It may have represented the access to the oven, from the chamber to the north, whose floor lay 1 m lower than the oven base.

The walls all appear to post-date the west curtain, and the oven can be confidently assigned to the early fourteenth-century chamberlain's bakehouse which, as we shall see in Chapter 4, was located against the south curtain. It was partly rebuilt in 1338–9, including the party wall with an adjoining kitchen (see Appendix) – which may be represented by the chamber to the north – accounting for the secondary character of the excavated oven. The kitchen, and perhaps the oven, may have occupied the ground floor of a two-storey building.

The area had been cleared of any debris prior to the deposition of a layer of rubble (38), which contained eighteenth-century bottle glass and a small amount of pottery. No excavated deposits appear to relate to the known use of the area as a garden during the eighteenth century.

Trench D (Figures 98–9)
Trench D lay within and immediately north of the southern retaining wall, and against the north (i.e. rear) face of the Square Tower. It measured 7.5 m east–west and averaged 4 m north–south, stopping just short of the nineteenth-century gaol wall (see Figure 39). The west section had an average depth of 2.6 m, against the 1.8 m depth of the east section, due to the downhill slope between the two (Figure 95). This partly reflects the slope in the natural soil level, which was 0.35 m lower in the east section (lying at 20.90 m above sea level). Dating evidence from both sections was sparse, and may in any case have been residual.

The east section (Figures 98)
The east section measured 4.2 m north–south. The natural profile was represented by a buried soil horizon, showing some iron-panning, at an average depth of 1.3 m below the existing ground surface. It was level, as were all succeeding deposits, and extended, through 'A', 'B' and 'C' horizons, to the bottom of the trench which lay 0.5 m below. The subsoil was a gravelly boulder clay, rather than the pure gravels seen elsewhere in the castle. There were a number of intrusive features. The construction trench for the Square Tower north wall, (81), appeared to have been cut directly through the natural profile. It was very narrow (0.02 m)

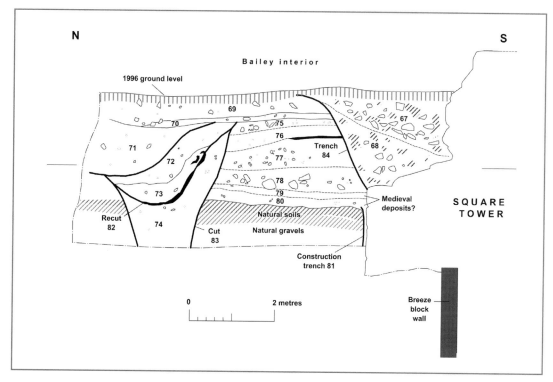

Figure 98 East section of Trench D

and was filled with a mortar-rich soil. It was overlain by two apparent occupation horizons, (79) and (80), of a soily character. The lower, 80, was somewhat gleyed, while 79 showed much charcoal flecking. Layers (77) and (78) above were thick, mixed deposits, containing redeposited fluvio-glacial gravels and waterworn pebbles. Two thin layers of indeterminate nature lay above 77. They were cut by a deep feature, (83), 1.5 m wide and extending beyond the bottom of the section, which appeared to have been successively recut, through a period of time. The fills, which appear to have been truncated, were sealed by (70), which was a layer of black soil, containing brick fragments and nineteenth-century pottery, that extended throughout the section. Like the underlying deposits it was truncated by a trench, (84), cut from just below the surface, which sloped down to the remains of the Square Tower north wall and was clearly associated with intervention at the tower.

The west section (Figures 99)
The west section measured 3.7 m north–south. A level buried soil horizon, as in the east section, lay at an average depth of 1.8 m below the existing ground surface. The overlying sequence was rather different. Immediately overlying the buried soil was stiff yellow-brown loamy clay (66), which rose towards the south. It contained some burnt clay lenses and may represent bank material; if so it may also, as in the west curtain, pre-date the masonry defences. An extensive sequence of deposits lay above, most of them

apparently representing dump layers rather than occupational horizons. They variously contained organic material, burnt material, charcoal spreads, and mortar, which were very mixed and appeared to represent debris layers rather than *in situ* burning. The deposits rose markedly towards the south, following the trend in 66 and perhaps also indicating that they were deposited against a solid boundary. One of them, (64), contained a sherd of Roman *tegula* which was undoubtedly residual and not necessarily from the castle site. Above these layers lay a thick, mixed deposit, (57), similar to 77 and 78 in the east section. It rose up at its southern end, where it had been truncated prior to the formation (or deposition) of the topsoil. The sequence of six deposits above 57 was similar in character to the layers of burning etc. below it. Like 57, they had also been truncated.

Discussion

Context 66 in the west section directly overlay the natural soil and was a homogeneous loamy clay similar to that observed on the west side of the castle, where it was interpreted as medieval bank material. Trench D may therefore occupy the tail of the western bank (possibly truncated and/or spread?), which may even have turned to run along the south side of the site before petering out.

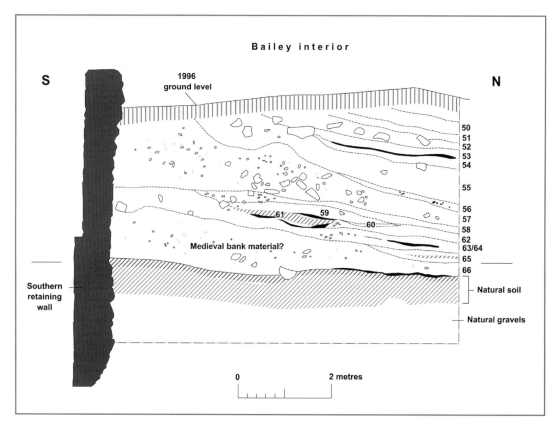

Figure 99 West section of Trench D

The Square Tower construction trench, 81, directly cut the natural. This was unexpected in view of the stylistically late date for the tower, but any intervening contexts may have been truncated. Alternatively, the tower rear wall may have utilised a pre-existing trench that was cut for the earlier south curtain wall. Contexts 79 and 80 in the same section post-dated the Square Tower but appeared to represent occupation deposits, and may be medieval.

However, most of the succeeding layers are much later. In the west section, they comprise a sequence of very similar debris layers, lying either side of redeposited subsoil 57. They appear to represent a single phase of dumping, perhaps of imported soil, while 57 may be the same as 77 and 78 in the east section. This phase cannot be closely dated but is regarded as post-medieval. This suggests that further medieval contexts may have been truncated. For instance, there was no evidence for any masonry structures, yet I will argue in Chapter 4 that domestic buildings, commenced during the mid-thirteenth century, occupied this area.

The north (rear) face of the nineteenth-century retaining wall 24 was very uneven and it may have been built against, i.e. was later than, all these deposits. However, they appeared to have been laid against a solid boundary, perhaps the earlier post-medieval retaining wall that was suggested above.

This area of the castle was used as a garden, from at least the late eighteenth century until 1868, when the construction of the gaol wall left it as a 'waste' area beyond the gaol curtilage (see Chapter 5). However, no garden soils were observed. Contexts 50–7 in the west section had clearly been truncated, and any overlying garden soils may have been removed by the same event. Feature 83 could not be characterised – it may have been a pit or a trench, cut from a high level but similarly truncated. It had clearly been recut at least twice.

All contexts in the east section were truncated by trench 84, which was very late and cut from just below the modern surface. It may be associated with the 1964 consolidation of the Square Tower and the construction of its 'caphouse'.

The remainder of the site

The bulk of the castle interior lies beneath County Hall and its car park, an area which remains more or less unexplored. Groundworks in 2002 however revealed a 3 m length of truncated brick walling, 3 m south of the north curtain wall and between 2.5 m and 5.5 m east of the shell-keep forebuilding (Figure 13). It represents the north wall of the debtors' cell-block, built by John Nash 1789–92, which divided the cells from an open yard at the foot of the curtain (Figures 100, 131 and 139). It ran approximately east–west and was nearly 1 m thick.

The cell-block walling lay 22.65 m above sea level, while medieval deposits in Trench D, described above, lay at 20.92 m – a difference of 1.73 m which would suggest a north–south fall in the medieval horizons of at least 1 m (see Figures 12b and 12e). We have also seen that, along the southern flank of the site at least, there was a gentle west–east fall in the natural profile, enhanced by the spread western bank. The general trend therefore appears to be a natural downhill slope from north-west to south-east, across the entire site.

Figure 100 *The footings of the debtors' cell-block north wall, from the west, in 2002*

However, the cell-block walling lay just beneath the surface of a modern paved area, which is raised 0.5 m above the level of County Hall car park as a strip, 5 m wide, running along the foot of the north curtain wall (Figures 12b and 13–14). South of this strip, the gaol-phase remains – and, possibly, some earlier deposits – were clearly truncated when County Hall and its car park were laid out (see Figure 165). While the downhill slope suggests that any losses may be confined to the north-west of the site, the medieval footings behind the gatehouse – in a similarly higher area west of the gaol wall – lay 0.75 m above car park level, indicating that the truncated area extends south to the gatehouse. In addition, medieval deposits in Trench D, at the southern edge of the site, appear to have suffered some truncation. Moreover, the walls and deposits in Trench A, on the higher ground derived from the suggested western bank material, lie 2 m above the car park – any continuation of these horizons northeastwards into the car park area, at the same level, will have been truncated.

A service trench, also opened in 2002, revealed however that some stratified deposits still survive in the north-west corner of the car park, 0.45 m beneath the present tarmac surface between the gaol wall and car park entry (Figure 13). The small size of the trench meant however that the deposits could not be characterised.

To my knowledge, no further investigation has been undertaken within the castle interior, and none within the area of the outer ward, so other forms of evidence have been used, in Chapters 4 and 5, to suggest the disposition of internal structures and features.

THE GAOL WALL, YARD AND OLD POLICE STATION

A number of other historic features and structures remain, all relating to the late eighteenth-/ nineteenth-century gaol. Of these, the most significant is a section of the perimeter wall, belonging to the rebuilt and enlarged gaol of 1868–72, which ran concentrically within the line of the former curtain walls. It was largely demolished in the 1920s, and now survives only on the west and south-west sides, where it forms the County Hall car park boundary (Figure 5). A very small area of this walling also survives within more recent fabric on the south-east side of the car park.

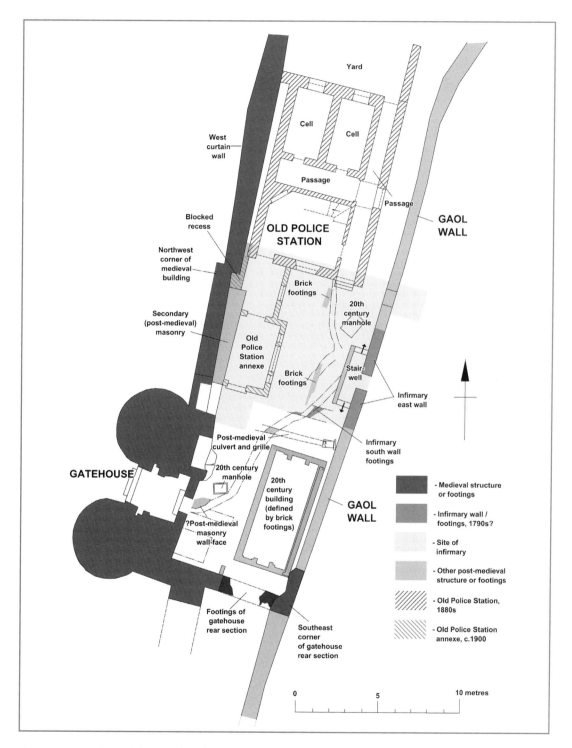

Figure 101 *Plan of the yard to the east of the gatehouse showing the former infirmary, Old Police Station and archaeological features*

The northern half of the gaol wall incorporates pre-existing masonry belonging to John Nash's works of 1789–92, including part of the gaol infirmary (Figure 101). This building was subsequently taken over by the Carmarthenshire County Police, but was demolished in 1880 and replaced by a new station and lock-up, which survives as the Old Police Station (or 'Castle House').

As noted above, the gaol wall also contains part of the former rear section of the medieval Great Gatehouse. Map and print evidence suggests that this was finally demolished between 1829 and the 1840s, when its east wall was replaced by a lower, thinner wall. The area thus defined became an open yard (Figure 101). Its south wall was retained until c.1900, but may have been reduced in height.

The gaol and infirmary walls

The gaol wall, as it survives, runs from north to south c.9 m east of the west curtain wall. It has an overall length of 74.5 m and the east face, where levels are 1.2 m lower than those behind the gatehouse, is on average 6.5 m high. Its average thickness of 0.8 m is fairly consistent throughout. However, it incorporates four distinct sections (Figure 106). From north to south, they are:

1 The northern 16.9 m which, at its north end, curves round to the east to join the shell-keep forebuilding;

2 a length of 11.2 m representing the infirmary east wall, and containing the only current entry;

3 a 12.9 m length of walling leading southwards from the infirmary to incorporate the remains of the south-east corner of the gatehouse rear section;

4 a 33.5 m-long stretch that was newly built in 1868–9. Its southern end curves round to the east, and formerly continued around the gaol to join the main entrance front on the north side of the site.

Section 2: The infirmary east wall (Figures 101–3, 106)

The infirmary lay against the west curtain wall. Its east (gable) wall is defined by two vertical joints in the gaol wall (Figure 103). Both side walls have gone, but a footing in Old Red Sandstone, 0.9 m wide, that was revealed by groundworks in 2002, probably represents its south wall (Figure 101); the north wall lies beneath the Old Police Station. The remains suggest a building measuring 11.2 m north-south by 9 m east-west, which corresponds with the dimensions depicted on plans of c.1860 (Figure 139) and the mid-1870s (Figure 104). The east wall now rises 7.5 m above County Hall car park, 1 m higher than the walling on either side, but has been truncated, having formerly been higher. Facework is predominantly in Old Red Sandstone.

Although the infirmary appears not to have been established until 1838–42 (see Chapter 5), it seems that a pre-existing building, shown on a map of 1834, was adapted (Figure 133). The east wall shows evidence for a number of openings whose detail is stylistically

Figure 102 *The east wall of the gaol infirmary, from east, in 2007* (by courtesy of Ken Day)

consistent with a late eighteenth-/early nineteenth-century date, and the building probably represents original Nash work from 1789–92 (Figure 102). Set high up in the centre
of the wall is a window, 2.2 m tall, but now blocked with masonry (5, Figure 103). Its
graceful, semicircular brick arch – clearly a primary feature – survives on both faces. Just
below the window is a circular, recessed 'medallion' (3), 0.9 m in diameter, with a similar brick surround. It too is visible on both faces, suggesting that it was an open *oculus*.
It was later blocked with masonry, possibly when horizontal chase (4) was cut into the
wall, apparently for a secondary floor. This was also later infilled, this time with brick.
Entry (1), with a brick surround beneath a concrete lintel, is demonstrably secondary and
was not shown in the 1870s (Figure 104), but is present on an aerial photograph from
*c.*1935 (Figure 147). Entry (2), to the north, which is now blocked, evidently led to the
small annexe that is shown in *c.*1860 (Figure 139). It may too have been secondary – its
segmental brick head is in marked contrast to the arched openings in the rest of the wall.
The main entry evidently lay in the former south wall (Figure 104).

There are few other features. A socket (7) on the east (external) face of the wall may
or may not be original, while a horizontal scar (8), halfway up the same face, possibly
belonged to a lean-to building that is now gone, and is not shown on historic maps or

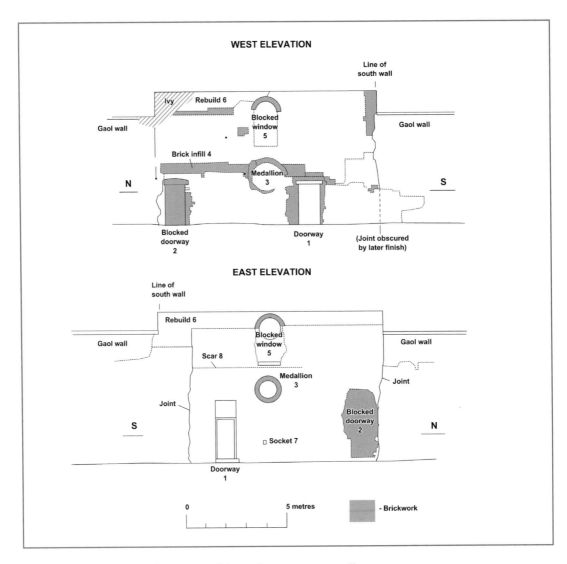

WEST ELEVATION

Line of
south wall

Ivy   Rebuild 6

Gaol wall   Blocked
window
5   Gaol wall

Brick infill 4

Medallion
3

N   S

Blocked
doorway
2   Doorway
1   (Joint obscured
by later finish)

EAST ELEVATION

Line of
south wall

Rebuild 6

Gaol wall   Blocked
window
5   Gaol wall

Scar 8

Medallion
3   Joint

Joint   Blocked
doorway
2

S   N

☐ Socket 7

Doorway
1

0   5 metres   ▨ - Brickwork

Figure 103 Elevation drawings of the infirmary east wall

photographs. The wall was partly rebuilt above window level, in masonry (6), presumably when the gable was truncated.

The evidence suggests that, in its original form, the infirmary was a single, high
chamber, of one storey. By 1851, it had been divided into two storeys for male and female
prisoners,[57] with the insertion of floor line 4. In the mid 1870s, the building was converted
into the County Police Station and lock-up. The accompanying plan shows the proposed
new arrangements (Figure 104), with separate rooms on both floors, including ground-
floor cells, but it is not clear whether all were implemented.[58] However, the first floor is
shown, and like surviving chase 4 it interrupts the *oculus*, along with window 6 and the
main entry.

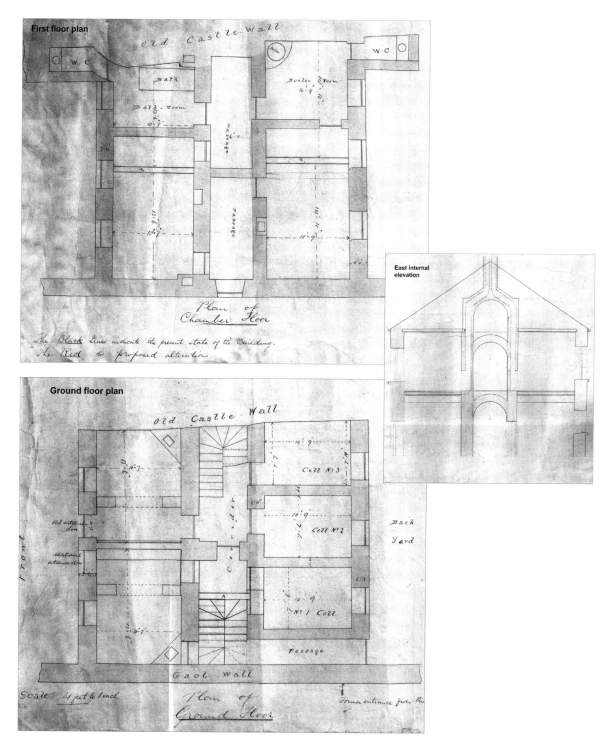

Figure 104 *Plans and east internal elevation of the infirmary/Police Station, 1870s*
(Carmarthenshire Archive Service, CRO Mus. 19, 'New Police Station at Carmarthen', n.d.)

The remainder of the gaol wall (Figures 105–6)

Section 1 of the wall ran north from the infirmary east wall to join the shell-keep forebuilding. Although it butted against the infirmary east wall, it is also suggested to have been part of the 1789–92 campaign – as a necessary element of the new gaol – and it is shown on a map of 1834 (Figure 133). Facework is in limestone and Old Red Sandstone rubble. What appears to be a gabled roof line is visible on the east face, although no building is shown in this location on any historic maps or photographs. The wall also shows evidence of numerous repairs, in brick, and may have been partially rebuilt. A joint is visible half-way up the east face, while the upper third (1.5 m) is secondary, and clearly from 1868–72, as it raises the wall to the same level as Section 4. The present coping, in both sections, may be later still. A blocked doorway with a brick surround – possibly secondary – lies centrally on the east side, and corresponds to a low semicircular arch on the west face, also in brick, lying 1 m above ground level. The entry may be associated with the steps that are shown against the west face in a plan of *c.*1860 (Figure 139).

Gaol wall section 3 connected the infirmary with the remaining south-east corner of the gatehouse rear section; it butts against and post-dates both of these. It may occupy the line of the rear section east wall, but at 0.8 m it is very thin, while it was suggested

Figure 105 *The late nineteenth-century gaol wall, at the south-west corner of the site, from south-west in 2012*

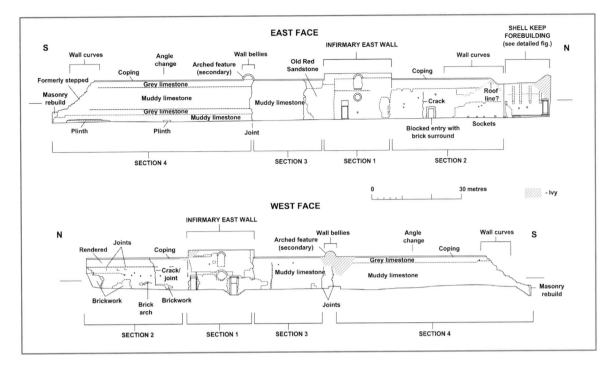

Figure 106 *East and west elevations of the late nineteenth-century gaol wall*

above that the latter wall may have lain slightly to the west. The rear section south wall survived until *c*.1900, when it was truncated and the remains of the south-east corner were finished off. They now form a rather amorphous pillar of predominantly limestone rubble masonry, 2 m wide, which bellies out to a thickness of 1.8 m at this point. It is not visible on the east face where it lies behind nineteenth-century facework.

Section 4, which is external to the Nash-period gaol (see Chapter 5), was newly built in 1868–72 (Figures 105–6). It represents nearly half the length of the surviving gaol wall. Facework is coursed and roughly squared, in alternate bands of grey limestone and muddy limestone rubble. At its south end, the wall curves round to the east where, as a result of demolition in the 1920s, it now descends in steps to form a lower wall which runs eastwards for 25 m.

A small fragment of the gaol wall also survives 70 m to the east, within the present County Hall car park perimeter wall (Figure 5). It comprises mixed random rubble, distinct from the surrounding masonry. Its origins lie in the early nineteenth century, as part of a domestic boundary wall which is shown in a print of 1830 (Figure 135), and a map of 1845 (Figure 137). It was heightened in 1868–72 when it was integrated with the rest of the gaol wall. This island of masonry somehow survived the demolition of the gaol wall in the 1930–1960s, and is Grade II listed. The remainder of the car park perimeter wall is in rock-faced masonry from the late twentieth century.

The Old Police Station and yard (Figures 12b, 101, 108–10)

The open yard, created by the removal of the gatehouse rear section, was extended north-wards in the 1880s, when the infirmary was demolished and replaced by the smaller Old Police Station. The 2002 groundworks in the southern half of the yard revealed a plethora of post-medieval drains, culverts and other service features, some of which cut the infirmary wall-lines. An area of mortared masonry and two lengths of brickwork footing were also exposed (Figures 101 and 107), but cannot be assigned to any known structures. In addition, the truncated brick walls of a long, rectangular building, aligned north–south, were revealed just beneath the surface. It measured 7.5 m by 3.5 m and occupied most of the space between the gatehouse and gaol wall (Figure 107). The bricks were of early twentieth-century manufacture. The building is shown in a photograph taken through the gatehouse entrance passage in the 1920s (Figure 153), in which it appears to be a rendered structure with simple, square window openings; the remains suggest that a fire-place occupied each end wall. Its function is unknown, but it was probably demolished along with the gaol in the 1930s.

The Old Police Station (or 'Castle House') is a two-storey, double-pile gabled build-ing, butting against the west curtain (Figures 12b and 108). Rendered externally and plastered within, construction is, where known, of rubble masonry. Though measuring 10.1 m north–south by 7 m east–west, its roof-line runs east–west. It is shown much as today on the original plan, as proposed, of 1880 (Figure 151), and was complete by 1886 (Figure 148). The annexe to the south, a lean-to building against the west curtain, was also present in 1886 but was rebuilt in its present form, and much enlarged, between 1895 and 1905, when the entire building was shown as it is today in a photograph of the County Constabulary (Figure 152). Used as a police station until 1947, when the Borough and County Police were amalgamated,[59] it was subsequently taken over by the council. Refurbished in 2006–7, it housed Carmarthen's Tourist Information Centre in 2012 and was intended to include an interpretation centre illustrating the town's history.

The internal arrangements in the main block remain more or less as built. The ground floor comprises three bays. The east bay is a narrow through-passage run-ning between entries in each side wall. It is joined by a cross-passage, to the south of which is a single chamber – labelled 'Living Room' in 1880 – with a second entry in the west bay, communicating with the annexe. The two bays north of the cross-passage

Figure 107 *The footings of the twentieth-century building in the yard, from south, in 2002*

Figure 108 (above) *The Old Police Station and annexe, from south, in 2012*

Figure 109 (right) *One of the cells in the Old Police Station, in 2006*

are vaulted cells (Figure 109). Fittings etc. appear to have largely been of local manufacture; the present cell doors, in iron, were retrieved from the old police station at Tumble, Carmarthenshire, in 2005,[60] but the original 'flip-over' prisoner-number plates still survive at the entrances to the cells, while the small observation windows have iron frames stamped 'Carmarthen Foundry'. Other nineteenth-century fittings survive, including gas taps, the alarm bell, and an iron grille over the doorway in the through-passage. The first floor is accessed by an open stair from the living room. It is divided into four bedrooms (labelled as

Figure 110 The Old Police Station annexe: blocked recess in the west curtain, in 2006

such in 1880), all with fire-places; there is a chimney on each gable. A fifth upstairs room, now a bathroom, is labelled 'Weights and Measures' on the 1880 plan. All openings are square-headed; quoins, and Adam surrounds, are in render. The area between the Old Police Station and the shell-keep was an exercise yard, the east side of which is defined by a wall contemporary with the building. It shows the scars from an adjoining building, in the narrow strip between it and the gaol wall, where a small structure is marked in 1895 and 1906 (Figures 149–50). It was probably a WC.[61]

The annexe measures 8 m by 2.5 m and comprises two bays, divided by an internal wall. Materials and treatment are as in the main block, but the openings lack the Adam surrounds. It is entered from the south. The projecting east wall of the southern bay features an arched recess, containing a window, which was flanked by a further window on either side. Removal of the render in the northern bay revealed a blocked recess, with a segmental brick head, in the west curtain wall (Figure 110). This appears to represent the 'Pantry' that is marked and labelled, in the earlier annexe, on the 1880 plan (Figure 151); it was blocked, and concealed beneath a thicker area of walling, when the annexe was rebuilt. However, it was probably modified from an earlier recess, rather than having been a *de novo* breach in the curtain, and may be medieval in origin. The west wall of the main block, in contrast, appears to be free-standing (Figures 101 and 151), with a void between it and the west curtain whose original features may therefore survive unaltered.

The Old Police Station is the sole surviving county lock-up in Wales, and is therefore of national importance, but is only a Listed Building where it joins the medieval curtain wall. Some internal features, moreover, are unusual, for instance the 'flip-over' prisoner-number plates, which were never commonplace.[62] Other features of the interior will, like the window-bars, at least be individual to the site; cells, during this early period, were usually built by local tradesmen and cell doors, for example, were made to fit the size of the room rather than to any general pattern, while embellishments such as door-numbers were in the hands of individual contractors.

NOTES

1   W. L. Morgan, and W. Spurrell, 'Carmarthen Castle Mount', *TCASFC*, 10 (1915), 61–2.

2   The full borehole sequence, recorded by Opus International Consultants UK (formerly Veryards Ltd) was: 0m–5.0m, artificial – clay with brick; 5.0m–5.2m, artificial – light brown clay; 5.2m–6.6m, artificial – brown clayey soil; 6.6m–7.3m, artificial – clay with gravel; 7.3m–10.0m, 'gravel boulder fill' (but occurring well beneath the base of the motte, and therefore probably natural); 10.0m–16.0m, natural gravels (Opus International Consultants UK Ltd, 'Carmarthen Castle phase 4: ground investigation report for base of shell keep walls' (2007), ref. CS7058-01-GIR-1.0). The results may be compared with investigations made in the same overall area, between the two walls on the south-west side, when the collapse occurred in 1913. The made ground comprised 'a 6 foot (1.83 m) layer of ordinary garden soil and debris, next under this about 3 feet (0.91 m) of clay, and lower still a mass of loose, large stones' (Morgan and Spurrell, 'Carmarthen Castle Mount', 62).

3   CRO, Cawdor Maps 41, 'Plan of part of Carmarthen showing County Gaol and premises', (n.d., *c*.1857).

4   Ibid.

5   J. F. Jones, 'Carmarthen "Mount"', *Carms. Antiq.*, 5 (1963), 188.

6   Morgan and Spurrell, 'Carmarthen Castle Mount', 61–2.

7   D. J. C. King, 'Carmarthen Castle', in unpublished field notebooks held in the Society of Antiquaries of London Library, Burlington House, Piccadilly, 1 (1949), 19–20, and 2 (1950), 53.

8   CRO, Cawdor Maps 41.

9   King, 'Carmarthen Castle' 1, 19.

10   CRO, Cawdor Maps 41.

11   King, 'Carmarthen Castle' 1, 20.

12   G. E. Evans, 'Caermarthen, 1764–1797', *TCASFC*, 1 (1906), 101.

13   Jones, 'Carmarthen "Mount"', 188.

14   Morgan and Spurrell, 'Carmarthen Castle Mount', 61–2.

15   N. D. Ludlow and B. Allen, 'Carmarthen Castle: archaeological evaluation within the shell-keep, 1997' (unpublished DAT report, 1997).

16   N. Page, 'Carmarthen Castle shell-keep, archaeological evaluation, 1998' (unpublished DAT report, 1998).

17   Jones, 'Carmarthen Mount', 188.

18   Page, 'Carmarthen Shell-keep', 9.

19   The decking trenches, recorded by Pete Crane of DAT, revealed a series of four masonry buttresses against the present shell-wall interior, in its north-east corner. They were thought to be contemporary with the wall, and similarly lay beneath the garden soil. They were truncated to present ground level, possibly when the garden was laid out.

20   Also see King, 'Carmarthen Castle' 1, 19, and 2, 53, for suggested medieval origins for these walls.

21   N. D. Ludlow, 'Carmarthen Castle: phase 3 archaeological work, 2001–2003' (unpublished DAT report, 2004), 28–32.

22   The cottages were noted in 1908, in rather disparaging terms, by Ella Armitage, who suggested that there may have been more (E. Armitage, 'Carmarthen Castle', *TCASFC*, 3 (1908), 14). Still inhabited in the mid-twentieth century, they had gone by the 1960s (OS 1:2500, plans SN4019 and SN4119, 1969). The date of the heightening of the wall at its west end is unknown, but had occurred by *c*.1935 at least, when an aerial photograph of the gaol shows the wall as today (Figure 147).

23   P. Crane, 'Carmarthen Castle, phase 3 interim report, October 2001' (unpublished DAT report, 2001).

24 Ludlow, 'Carmarthen Castle phase 3', 68–71.

25 E. Donovan, *Descriptive Excursions through South Wales and Monmouthshire in the Year 1804, and the Four Preceding Summers*, 2 (London: Edward Donovan, 1805), pp. 171–2.

26 RCAHMW, *Inventory of Ancient Monuments*, V: *County of Carmarthen* (London: HMSO, 1917), p. 249.

27 Heather James, *Roman Carmarthen: Excavations 1978–1993* (London: Britannia Monograph Series, 20, 2003), p. 4.

28 W. Spurrell, *Carmarthen and its Neighbourhood* (Carmarthen: Spurrell and Co., 1879), p.136.

29 The South-west Tower is misnamed 'Wyrriott's Tower' on the 1895 OS map (1:500, Carmarthenshire Sheet XXIX.7.6); Terry James has shown that this name correctly belongs to a square tower on the town wall (T. James, *Carmarthen: An Archaeological and Topographical Survey*, CAS Monograph 2 (Carmarthen, 1980), p. 33).

30 P. Crane, 'Carmarthen Castle Square Tower: evaluation and watching brief, 1993' (unpublished DAT report, 1994); N. D. Ludlow, 'Carmarthen Castle Southwest Tower: recording and watching brief, 1994' (unpublished DAT report, 1994); N. D. Ludlow, 'Carmarthen Castle: archaeological recording and watching brief 1995–6' (unpublished DAT report, 1996).

31 A layer of soil beneath the cap contained a car number plate from the 1950s and it is possible that this work belongs to the mid-1960s, when many Bridge Street properties were demolished to make way for Coracle Way.

32 Crane, 'Carmarthen Castle Square Tower'.

33 Ludlow, 'Carmarthen Castle 1995–6', 21–9.

34 The name is also used in the Cadw LB database (Cadw, LB No. 9507 (Carmarthen Castle), Cadw LB database accessed via END, July 2006).

35 The breeze-block walls built against the tower here belonged to a building that was abandoned, unfinished, in the early 1980s.

36 Cadw LB database, Carmarthen Castle.

37 The cellar fill produced twentieth-century finds including plastics.

38 Also see King, 'Carmarthen Castle' 1, 19.

39 C. Barnett, 'Carmarthen Castle: The Chamberlain's Hall', *TCASFC*, 26 (1936), 18.

40 King, 'Carmarthen Castle' 1, 19.

41 Ibid. However, the Carmarthen and Kidwelly gatehouses may in fact have been the work of the same master mason, John Hirde of Pembroke (discussed in Chapter 4).

42 Possibly the 'asphalt' surface laid by CAS in 1915–17? It was still 'sound' in 1936 (Barnett, 'Carmarthen Castle', 18).

43 Sketch by A. W. Matthews, *TCASFC*, 5 (1910), opp. 62.

44 Information supplied by John Llewelyn of CCC.

45 D. Schlee, 'Carmarthen Castle: excavations outside the gatehouse, June–August 2003' (unpublished DAT report, 2004).

46 I am much indebted to Paul Courtney and Mark Redknap for their help in interpreting the 2003 excavation results, particularly the former in recognising the significance of the secondary deposition.

47 Schlee, 'Carmarthen Castle', Appendix 3, 99–108.

48 Mark Redknap, pers. comm.; see Chapter 6.

49 Paul Courtney in Schlee, 'Carmarthen Castle', 34, and pers. comm.

50 The possibility that the walls represent a causeway of the Civil War period has been considered, but the other suggested works of this period rendered the gatehouse less accessible, not more. We have seen, moreover, that it would not be a complete span.

51 Paul Courtney, in Schlee 'Carmarthen Castle', 34.

52 Spurrell, *Carmarthen and its Neighbourhood*, p. 137.

53 Reproduced in J. F. Jones, 'Carmarthen Stylus', *Carms. Antiq.*, 2 (1957), 46–7. Also see Anon., 'Long Loans', *TCASFC*, 11 (1917), 82.

54 H. James, 'Carmarthen Castle excavations, September–October 1980: interim excavation report' (unpublished DAT typescript, 1980; see DAT Detailed Record File PRN 57).

55 Ludlow, 'Carmarthen Castle 1995–6', 40–4.

56 Ibid., 38–40.

57 R. W. Ireland, *'A Want of Order and Good Discipline': Rules, Discretion and the Victorian Prison* (Cardiff: UWP, 2007), p. 112 n. 100.

58 There is, for example, no physical evidence for the ground-floor fireplace depicted in the east wall, but it may have been removed by secondary entry 2.

59 Charles Griffiths (curator/archivist, Dyfed-Powys Police Museum), pers. comm.

60 John Llewelyn (CCC), pers. comm.

61 This wall is not shown on the 1880 proposed plan (Figure 151), which instead shows a wall between the police station and the shell-keep, with a WC in the angle with the gaol wall.

62 Charles Griffiths (curator/archivist, Dyfed-Powys Police Museum), pers. comm.

CHAPTER FOUR

RECONSTRUCTING THE CASTLE

RECONSTRUCTING THE medieval castle is not straightforward. It does not occupy a greenfield site, but instead has been extensively damaged and heavily remodelled by later activity. Little standing fabric survives and excavation has been limited. This chapter discusses the archaeological evidence alongside the source material in an attempt to produce a comprehensive reconstruction of the castle. It also examines its changes through time, and the influences on its development that arose from its various roles, military and civil.

Contemporary documentation includes building accounts (reproduced in the Appendix). In general, these relate to those periods when it was under royal control, and during the twelfth and thirteenth centuries are chiefly represented by the Pipe Roll and Liberate Roll accounts. The documentation becomes more extensive during the fourteenth and fifteenth centuries, the Ministers' Accounts and Exchequer Accounts from this period being among the records published by Francis Green, introduced in Chapter 1. They are not quite complete; other entries in the Rolls were found to be relevant, while transcripts of additional, unpublished records in TNA were kindly provided by Stephen Priestley. The latter include Chamberlain's and Ministers' Accounts (TNA: PRO SC 6), Exchequer Accounts (PRO E 101) and Chancery Miscellanea (PRO C 47), and an important account from 1343 (PRO E 163/4/42).

While these records are invaluable as a historical tool in their own right, they can also be used to reconstruct the layout of the castle – particularly, for example, the Chancery Inquisition of 1275 (see Chapter 2).[1] Also of great use is a considerable body of material from the fifteenth century which, although recording little new building work, is very detailed and allows the internal arrangements to be conjectured.[2] It must be recognised, however, that the surviving accounts may be incomplete – the twelfth century is clearly under-represented, while there may be lacunae in, for example, the late thirteenth century, when more work appears to have been undertaken at the castle than the sources suggest.

Contemporary accounts have been analysed alongside the archaeological evidence, the surviving site topography, later maps and prints, antiquarian sources, and comparison with other British castles.

The chapter concludes with a brief discussion of the castle's identity as a residence and its social organisation, and the effect this may have had on its spatial ordering and development.

The earthworks

The castle comprised a motte and two baileys (Figure 113). The basic disposition of its earthworks persisted until 1789 – when it was obscured by Nash's gaol – and it is shown by hachuring on Thomas Lewis's map of 1786 (Figure 111).[3] Physical evidence suggests that the motte was a conical, flat-topped mound, 9 m high from bailey level and with a probable total height of c.15 m, a 45 degree slope and a summit diameter of c.20 m (Renn's type Bd3),[4] occupying approximately 0.2 hectares and surrounded by a 15 m-wide ditch.[5]

To the south lay a bailey, which faced the town and which may have been a separate, inner ward from the first. It was an irregular rectangle in plan, measuring 85 m north–south and averaging 50 m east–west (nearly 0.4 hectares internally, without the motte). Its north, west and east sides were surrounded by a ditch with an average width of 15 m. To the east of this ditch lay the outer ward. This formed a triangle measuring 45 m east–west, and 65 m north–south at its widest point (nearly 0.3 hectares internally). It was defined by a 10–15 m-wide ditch on its north-east side. There was however no ditch around the south and south-east sides of either bailey where, instead, the existing natural scarp slope was enhanced.

The limited investigations within the castle interior suggested that the medieval ground level sloped gently downhill, across both baileys, from north-west to south-east (Figure 12); the slope was enhanced along the south side of the inner ward by the tail of the western defensive bank. The ditch between the two baileys – still called 'Castle Ditch' in 1739[6] – ran out into the scarp slope at its southern end, although its higher, northern end appears to have become infilled by the eighteenth century when it was occupied by a post-medieval thoroughfare, now gone, called 'Castle Green' (Figure 111). The ditch around the west and north sides of the site had become variously built over or infilled, and survived only on the north-east side of the outer ward, where it too was occupied by a routeway, the present Castle Hill.

The excavations of 2003 yielded some evidence for the depth of the west ditch and its rate of infill. A 45 degree profile would give a projected depth of 6 m when the bridge piers were constructed, assuming the bottom to have been both flat and confined between the piers. Its original depth, as dug in the early twelfth century, can only be guessed; a 7 m depth would give a basal width of 2.5 m, and would also coincide with the foot of the scarp slope where the ditch ran out to the south. It appears to have been contiguous with the ditch between the motte and the inner ward; this ditch led off eastwards beneath the gate-house north tower – which lay wholly within it – giving the motte a basal diameter of 65 m. All ditches appear to have normally been dry, but it was seen in the previous chapter that,

Figure 111 *Detail from Thomas Lewis's map of Carmarthen, of 1786, showing the area of the castle* (Carmarthenshire Archive Service, CRO Cawdor Maps 219, Map of Vaughan properties in Carmarthen)

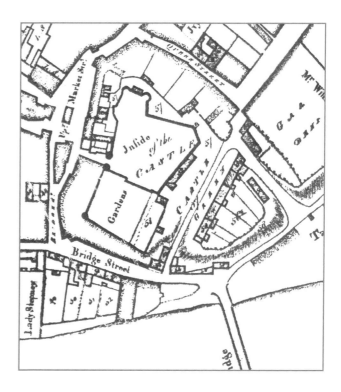

evidently, they could seasonally fill with water – presumably where they were cut through the boulder clay. The west ditch had become infilled and developed with housing by 1610, when the nascent Castle Hill appears to have been established within the outer ward ditch (Figure 112).

The evidence that a defensive bank ran around the west side of the castle, inside the ditch, was presented in Chapter 3, where it was suggested that it was at least 2.5 m high at the south-west corner of the inner ward. It was also suggested that the bank continued around the inner ward, except on the scarped southern side, and that the curtain walls were built on it. It clearly ran out at the gatehouse, which coincides with the motte ditch, while the South-west Tower was built against the natural slope rather than on the bank. Both structures have therefore survived, along with the curtain walls within the motte ditch, while those walls and towers that were built on the bank were naturally less stable, and have gone.

The inner ward

The masonry defences of the inner ward are first described, albeit in outline, in the Chancery Inquisition of 1275.[7] They comprised a 'certain good donjon (*dungeo*) constructed from five small Towers', while 'a certain great Tower [was] there'. Cathcart King identified the 'donjon' as the shell-keep.[8] However, it is clear that 'donjon' here refers to the inner ward, as it did at e.g. Montgomery Castle in 1248–50,[9] Deganwy (Caernarfonshire) and Beeston (Cheshire);[10] the account clearly distinguishes the donjon from the 'great tower', which appears to be supernumerary to the five inner ward towers and is clearly identifiable as the shell-keep in a further account from 1343.[11] The issue is however confused by the description of the towers as 'small', and by the 1343 account which suggests that the shell-keep was also possessed of five turrets.[12] It is however apparent, from a further survey, in 1321,[13] that unlike the shell-keep turrets the five towers of the 'donjon' were sizeable, and fully enclosed. And all sources confirm both that the inner ward followed a basic five-towered plan until the end of the Middle Ages (Figures 117, 119–22), and that the towers were round.

The 1786 map can help us again here (Figure 111). The inner ward appears to have been a straightforward conversion of the timber defences into stone, with no alteration to its basic layout. The South-west Tower, Great Gatehouse and shell-keep are shown, but not the Square Tower which was apparently subsumed beneath the surrounding buildings along Bridge Street. Nor are the internal arrangements within the gaol shown, which was then confined to the northern half of the inner ward. However, the probable north curtain is shown on its present line, while either the south curtain, or its post-medieval replacement, formed the southern edge of the inner ward. It terminated at the cross-ditch between the two baileys, where a wall ran north at 90 degrees, inside the cross-ditch, and eventually joined the north curtain to define the east side of the inner ward. The latter wall was not straight, and comprised two distinct sections. The southern section survived until 1868, as a revetment of the natural slope and its continuation into the cross-ditch (see Figure 139), and so may have occupied the line of – and perhaps contained fabric from – the medieval east curtain. The northern section was offset 8 m towards the interior (i.e. west), and ran at a different angle. Rather than following the curtain wall – which may have been built on a bank, and thus have been lost – it may represent a parallel wall inside the bailey; I will suggest later on that this wall too may have had medieval origins, as the internal wall of a building lying against the curtain (*cf.* Holt Castle, Denbighshire, where the inner walls of the buildings against the curtain wall have survived, while the curtain itself has been lost).

The east–west wall dividing the eighteenth-century gaol from the garden to the south is apparently depicted on Speed's plan of *c.*1610 (Figure 112), and so may have had its origin as a division, possibly secondary, of the inner ward. Speed's plan, however, is not always easy to interpret, and must be used with caution. For example, the cross-ditch is not shown, while the inner ward is confined to the area of the 1786 gaol in a depiction that is at odds with both the map evidence and the medieval building accounts.

The five round towers of 1275 can be inferred as the South-west Tower, the two gatehouse towers (if twin-towered from the 1220s onwards), and two others which have gone. The South-west Tower and gatehouse are clearly shown by Speed (Figure 112), in addition to the shell-keep, while a large tower appears to be depicted on the inner ward east wall. A further tower is shown to the north, just east of the shell-keep, giving

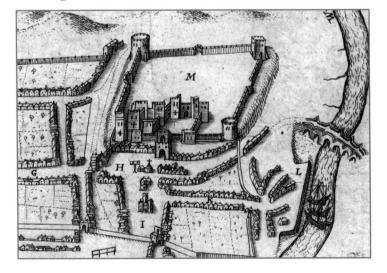

Figure 112 *Detail from John Speed's map of Carmarthen, of c.1610, showing Carmarthen Castle from west* (Carmarthenshire Archive Service, CRO2 (M) 21)

a total of five. A square tower shown between the gatehouse and the South-west Tower was probably a late medieval addition, like the surviving Square Tower – which is not shown and may already have been concealed by housing. However the documented Middle Gate, between the inner and outer wards, can be seen opposite the gatehouse.

The outer ward

Speed's depiction of the outer ward as a regular square, defined by curtain walls and corner towers, is clearly conventionalised and bears no relationship to the physical evidence. Other sources give a clearer idea of the line of its defences. Two accounts, from 1343 and 1464–5, suggest that the outer curtain joined the south-east corner of the inner ward, whence it ran for 30 m to a postern (see Figure 120).[14] The southern end of Castle Green – the post-medieval lane in the cross-ditch – emerged several metres above Bridge Street, from which it was accessed via a steep flight of steps in the nineteenth century (e.g. Figures 133, 139 and 148). The arrangement appears to have been dictated by a pre-existing entry at the bottom of the cross-ditch, where a ruined structure, shown on the Buck print of 1740 and apparently containing an entry (Figure 126), may be the remains of the postern tower mentioned in 1343.[15] The ditch profile is not visible in the print, but may have become heavily silted or infilled.

The remainder of the outer curtain appears to have followed the pre-existing earthworks to define a triangular area (see Figures 120–2). The outer gate was clearly on the north side. It was described as being 'towards the town' in 1338,[16] and Spilman Street doubtless originated as an axial route leading to this entry. It lines up with the cross-ditch, rather than the outer ward itself, but the gateway may have sat at an angle to Spilman Street. The 1786 map shows a curiously offset yard between the two (Figure 111), which may reflect a medieval outwork or barbican.

The Buck prints may locate the other outer ward towers rather more reliably than Speed. They appear to show the truncated side walls of a tower at the southern end of the outer ward, overlooking the town bridge, and a further ruined tower is suggested at the eastern apex (Figures 126 and 127). The site of the eastern tower was known, if not traceable, in 1917, when a plan of the castle marked it as 'site of tower'.[17] The two towers may have been contemporary with the outer curtain, but their shape can only be inferred.

Phasing

It was noted in the previous chapter that there is scant archaeological dating evidence for any of the castle's structures, while no architectural stonework of any kind was recovered during excavation. However, the source material reproduced in the Appendix provides a chronology for many of the buildings, occasionally locates them and, used alongside the map and physical evidence, sometimes allows guesses as to their form and dimensions. The documents suggest seven main building phases (Figures 113, 115, 117 and 119–22). The first represents a castle entirely of timber, in which form it may have largely remained until the second quarter of the thirteenth century. Although the shell-keep may be late twelfth-century, rebuilding in stone was mainly undertaken during the 1230s–40s. Work continued under Henry III, with the addition of a formal range of lodgings, but the outer ward may not have been walled in stone until later in the thirteenth century. Two suites of self-contained chambers – the Justiciar's and Chamberlain's Mansions[18] – were added in the early fourteenth century. The last major campaign was in the early fifteenth century, when substantial rebuilding followed Glyndŵr's attacks. The following sections should be read alongside the Appendix.

A royal castle during most of the Middle Ages, Carmarthen was dependent upon Crown expenditure on its defences – for which there was a great deal of competition, particularly from those sites favoured by individual monarchs such as Henry III's Marlborough (Wiltshire), Edward I's north Wales castles etc. That even basic expenditure, on keeping the castle in good order, was not always forthcoming is demonstrated by the numerous references – throughout the Middle Ages – to its being 'in want of repair' or 'decayed'. This could be exacerbated by negligence on the part of the constables.

Finally, a word about water supply. The castle well, referred to in the sources,[19] may be the same as the gaol well mentioned in the eighteenth century (see Chapter 5), which has not been located. It is not to be confused with the wells belonging to the post-1792 gaol (see e.g. Figure 141), which were brand-new features.

PHASE I: THE TIMBER CASTLE, 1106–1180 (Figure 113)

Carmarthen Castle was a motte-and-bailey from the first, as is made clear in an account from 1116 which distinguishes between the two elements.[20] Its earthworks are fairly unexceptional, both locally and nationally. Carmarthenshire is a county of mottes, with eighteen recorded examples, twelve of them with baileys; in contrast, only five ringworks are known.[21] However, with the exception of St Clears and Llangadog, no fully artificial mottes compare in size with Carmarthen, though at a national level it is only of average size. Rectilinear baileys are not uncommon in Britain – e.g. Lincoln, Warwick, Warkworth (Northumberland), et al. – and that at St Clears appears originally to have been a regular rectangle.[22]

Initially, the motte carried a timber tower (the tŵr of 1116),[23] presumably accessed from the inner ward, via a timber ramp, across the motte ditch. We have seen that the inner ward was apparently defended by steep banks, except to the south, and a timber palisade. The Great Gatehouse represented the main entrance to the masonry castle and it is likely that there was always an entry of some kind here as it faces the town, which was in existence by 1116. The castle was an administrative centre and residence from the first, equipped with a hall and lodgings. No internal buildings are however specifically singled out until the thirteenth century, with the exception of the chapel, which was first mentioned in a confirmation grant of 1158–76;[24] I suggest further on that it lay in the north half of the inner ward.

A number of local earthwork castles may have had two baileys from the first, including Kidwelly, possibly both Llansteffan and Laugharne,[25] and perhaps also Ammanford and Llandovery (all Carmarthenshire). It is not clear, however, whether there were two baileys at Carmarthen during these early years. The outer ward is not specifically mentioned until the fourteenth century, and lies in an unusual position for an urban castle, facing away from the town – and gatehouse – and thus to the 'rear' of the castle. Richmond Castle, Yorkshire, has a small outer ward in a similar position,[26] as Southampton may have done,[27] while one of the two outer wards at Northampton lay to the rear.[28] However, it is an arrangement unknown in any other Welsh castle-boroughs. Whilst it is possible that the castle initially comprised only the inner ward, to which an outer ward was added after town development had begun, the topography suggests otherwise; the site is a self-contained area, more or less level, in which the motte occupies the highest point so that it is the *outer* ward that over-looks the bridge. Perhaps one large bailey was subdivided into two, as possibly occurred at e.g. Kidwelly, Carmarthenshire,[29] and Rochester, Kent.[30] However, until the town wall was extended in the early fifteenth century, the outer ward faced the field. It is possible, therefore, that the main entry was initially from this direction (as at Warkworth, York etc.), and that Spilman Street, which originated as an axial route leading to the outer gate,[31] was a primary feature of the town. If so, the castle was 'turned round' to face west at some point after the town had been established in 1106–16. This process occurred at Usk Castle, Monmouthshire, probably under William Marshal II, who was also active at Carmarthen Castle during the early thirteenth century; the old outer ward at Usk was retained as a purely defensive 'hornwork' when a new outer ward was built towards the town.[32] A similar process has been suggested, albeit tentatively, at Chepstow Castle, Monmouthshire,[33] which was also held by Marshal. However, Carmarthen's outer ward is very small; it was perhaps intended at first to be a defensive hornwork, covering the rear of the castle, as was possibly the case at the nearby castles of Ammanford[34] and Llandovery.[35]

The circular structure 121, excavated on the motte, was too slight to have been the base of a masonry tower and is here interpreted as the sill-wall for a timber tower, round or polygonal. The recess on its internal face may represent a post-setting for the superstructure, while the associated charcoal and burnt clay 038, 039 and 047 may represent debris from its demo-lition. The structure may account for part of the £160 spent by the Crown during the 1180s (see Appendix). Alternatively, it may have been built during one of the episodic

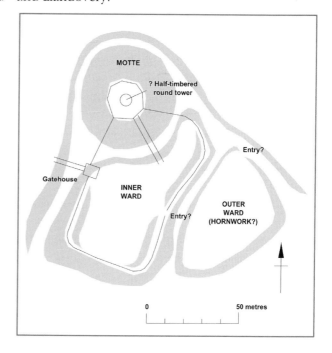

Figure 113 Sketch plan of Carmarthen Castle showing its suggested layout in Phase 1, 1109–80 (assumed internal buildings not shown)

Welsh occupations of the castle after 1146. With an external diameter of only 5.8 m, it was noticeably small – and could only plausibly have functioned as a watchtower, rather than a residential 'keep' – but the similar tower base excavated on the motte at Totnes (Devon), which is dated to the twelfth century, was roughly the same size (Figure 114).[36] However the latter was square, as is still regarded as normal for twelfth-century towers, whether of timber or masonry; I know of no other British examples of free-standing, circular timber towers although circular *interval* towers appear to have been built in timber at Hen Domen, Powys, during the twelfth century.[37] Nor are any free-standing circular keeps known to have been built in masonry by the Welsh princes of Deheubarth, or by the Crown, until the 1220s.[38] The small, free-standing masonry tower recently excavated on the motte at Nevern Castle, Pembrokeshire, shows nevertheless that the cylindrical shape was in use at an early date in west Wales. The castle was abandoned in 1195, suggesting that the tower was built by the Anglo-Norman William FitzMartin, *c*.1171–91; construction by the Lord Rhys during his hold on the castle, 1191–5, is considered less likely.[39] With an external diameter of only 9 m, it is not much larger than structure 121.

It is moreover by no means certain that structure 121 predates the shell-keep, as the only relationship observed was with the rebuilt section of shell-wall. Charcoal and burnt clay layers 038, 039 and 047 moreover sealed a deposit containing a sherd of late thirteenth- or early fourteenth-century pottery. If they do represent its debris, then the tower was not demolished until the late thirteenth century at the earliest, i.e. after the shell-keep had been built. So the two may have coexisted for some time, in a manner now considered to have been widespread in Britain and beyond,[40]

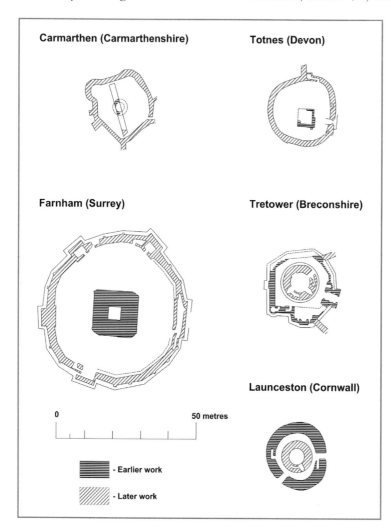

Carmarthen (Carmarthenshire)

Totnes (Devon)

Farnham (Surrey)

Tretower (Breconshire)

Launceston (Cornwall)

0   50 metres

- Earlier work

- Later work

Figure 114 Comparative plans of shell-keeps with associated free-standing towers

and which was recorded at Durham Castle during the 1140s,[41] much as shell-walls coexisted with masonry towers at, for example Tretower Castle, Powys,[42] and Launceston Castle, Cornwall (Figure 114).[43] Structure 121 however was definitely disused when the southern shell-wall was rebuilt during the later Middle Ages.

It is also possible that structure 121 does not represent a tower at all. It may, for example, have been the lining of a well,[44] as at Farnham, Surrey, which was of comparable size, but associated with a masonry tower, and the well recently excavated on the second motte at Lewes Castle, Sussex, which was smaller, being 1.8 m in diameter.[45] Like structure 121, both wells are regarded as belonging to a period when mottes were still expected to provide self-contained defensible accommodation, necessitating a water supply.

PHASE 2: THE SHELL-KEEP, 1181–1222? (Figures 115 and 116)

A timber tower would not by itself account for the 1180s expenditure, which may have included a comprehensive rebuild in timber. However, it might instead be represented by the erection of the masonry shell-keep. The castle withstood a siege in 1189, which is suggested, by the contemporary source,[46] to have been lengthy and perhaps indicates something more substantial than timber defences.

The shell-keep was called the 'Great Tower' in 1275, and again in 1343, when it featured five turrets ('*quinque turrel in magna turr*').[47] Two of these may be represented by the lobes on the north-west and north-east sides, whose possible medieval origins were suggested in Chapter 3 – where it was also observed that a third lobe probably existed on the south-west side (Figure 116).[48] It is possible that the forebuilding, which may be from the early fourteenth century, represented a fourth 'turret'. But there appears to be no room on the perimeter for a fifth. Perhaps it was intramural; the shell-keep appears to be the 'four high towers with the watch-tower (*garit*)' of an account from 1321[49] and the fifth turret may have risen above the shell-wall without projecting from it; cf. the thickened area and mural stair revealed on its west side. Or, of course, the watch-tower may have been the suggested timber tower 121 if it was still standing in 1321.

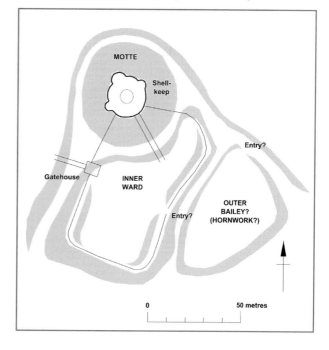

Figure 115 Sketch plan of Carmarthen Castle showing its suggested layout in Phase 2, 1181–1222 (assumed internal buildings not shown)

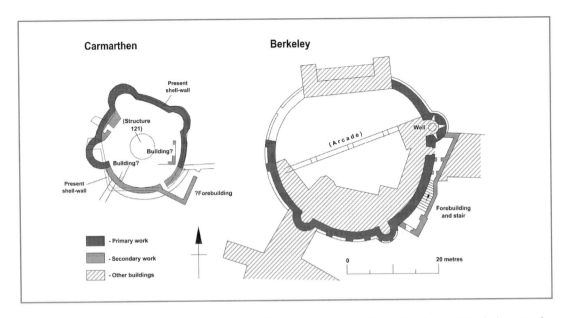

Figure 116 Comparative plans of the shell-keeps at Carmarthen Castle and Berkeley Castle (*Carmarthen conjecturally restored*)

On the face of it, the shell-keep does not appear to have been frequently adopted in south-west Wales – Wiston Castle, Pembrokeshire, represents the only other proven example. However, few local mottes have been investigated and they may have been more widespread in the region than is currently apparent. It is possible, for example, that the motte at St Clears carried a shell-wall.[50]

The evidence suggests that the Carmarthen keep had an original internal diameter of *c*.16 m (Figure 116) – slightly smaller and more circular than today, and smaller than average for Britain. As built, it was a fairly simple structure. The entry appears to have been a plain doorway, with no gate-tower. This need not by itself indicate an early date – the similarly simple entry to the keeps at Wiston and Totnes may be thirteenth-century.[51] Carmarthen's lobate plan is however unusual – most shell-keeps were simple perimeter walls. The nearest parallel is Henry II's keep at Berkeley Castle, in Gloucestershire (Figure 116), the county to whose exchequer Carmarthen Castle was tied during the twelfth century (see Chapter 2). A little over twice as large, with a diameter of 36 m, the Berkeley keep also revets the motte (in this case fully). Its three small, open-backed semicircular turrets reflect Carmarthen's 'lobes', and are contemporary with the shell-wall in an early use of the form.[52] The keep is similarly entered through a simple doorway, leading from a stair housed in a rectangular forebuilding which here too is secondary to the shell-wall, though close in date.

The Berkeley keep can be securely dated to 1153–6, when it was built by King Henry on behalf of the Lord of Berkeley,[53] which would fit in with the construction of the Carmarthen keep during a period of overall Crown control in the 1180s.[54] The expenditure of £160 over three years may be compared with two other royal castles, Berkhamstead,

Hertfordshire, where £114 went towards building the shell-keep in 1157–62, and Peveril, Derbyshire, where the diminutive tower-keep cost £184 in 1175–7.[55] In contrast, the larger tower-keep at Bowes, Yorkshire, cost nearly £600 in 1171–87.[56]

However, there is no dating evidence for the original shell-wall at Carmarthen, while its physical relationship with the adjoining curtain walls was obscured. A date in the 1220–1230s has traditionally been preferred, under the Marshal earls or Hubert de Burgh. But while shell-keep construction was far from over in the thirteenth century, it was in decline and generally confined to rebuilding pre-existing keeps. For instance, the shell-keep at royal Windsor Castle was rebuilt in 1224–5, under the custody of Hubert de Burgh.[57] Nevertheless, the 'great tower' built by Edward I at Builth (Powys), in 1277–80, may have been a shell-wall on the existing motte.[58] Moreover, Wiston's shell-keep may have been built by William Marshal II, on the orders of Henry III,[59] while the vanished keep at Caerleon, Monmouthshire, which may also belong to Marshal's tenure, was possibly of this type.[60] Both Marshal and de Burgh would have been heavily constrained by the existing motte at Carmarthen, which a shell-wall was in many respects the easiest, and cheapest method of fortifying. It may moreover be that the Carmarthen lobes, which, unlike Berkeley's, face the field, were built in the thirteenth-century drum-tower tradition, although there are no close parallels at this date.[61] And in 1215 the castle was 'razed to the ground' by Llywelyn ap Iorwerth, after a five-day siege,[62] suggesting that it was still largely – perhaps entirely – of timber.

PHASE 3: THE MASONRY DEFENCES, 1223–1240 (Figure 117)

Repairs were clearly undertaken by Llywelyn and, although their extent is unknown, Carmarthen Castle was habitable by 1223, when it was surrendered to William Marshal II,[63] whose recovery of the castle is regarded, by most authorities, as marking its conversion into a stone fortress.[64] The *Brut* describes it as having been 'repaired' by Marshal in 1223, on behalf of the Crown, but continues with a fulsome description of Marshal's own castle, under construction at Cilgerran, as 'an ornate castle of mortar and stones'[65] – in marked contrast to the terse Carmarthen entry. Between them, Marshal and the king spent £800 on Carmarthen and Cardigan castles from 1224 to 1226, of which it has been argued that Carmarthen received the greater share.[66] Even so, it would not be sufficient to pay for the completion of an extensive circuit of curtain walling and 'five round towers', even assuming that the shell-keep was already built, and that the outer ward remained of timber. At Montgomery, for example, the masonry inner ward and gatehouse cost the king £3,600 between 1224 and 1228.[67] Nevertheless, Carmarthen's town wall was under construction in 1233,[68] indicating that the curtain walls must have been at least commenced, while in the same year it withstood siege for three months,[69] as against five days in 1215.

Work appears to have been more-or-less complete by 1241, when the castle was taken under direct royal control, as no further expenditure on the inner ward defences was recorded until the later Middle Ages. Only minor 'repairs', in timber, were recorded under

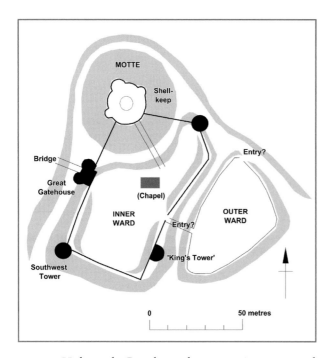

Figure 117 Sketch plan of Carmarthen Castle showing its suggested layout in Phase 3, 1223–1240

Crown control in 1226–8, so the bulk of the masonry may therefore have been the work of Hubert de Burgh and the younger Marshals, who held Carmarthen as Marcher lords between 1228 and 1241 – an independence that would have justified the necessary personal expense, but which unfortunately also means that the relevant accounts do not survive.

Hubert de Burgh and the Marshal earls were among the leading innovators in castle design during the early thirteenth century. The Marshals built extensively, at Chepstow, Pembroke, in Ireland and elsewhere. Hubert de Burgh – who, as acting regent during the minority of Henry III, effectively *was* the Crown – also built on a considerable scale. The work at Carmarthen however stands at an important juncture in British castle development. Hitherto, the great barons had been influential in this development. From the mid-thirteenth century, however, they increasingly looked to the buildings of the Crown – the 'king's works' – for architectural trends and patterns of castle design.[70]

The South-west Tower

The South-west Tower is a large, spurred drum tower of a type generally datable to the last three decades of the thirteenth century, and it is conceivable that the Carmarthen tower is of a similar date. However a very similar, spurred tower at Cardigan Castle appears to belong to the mid-thirteenth century. There is, moreover, no surviving record of the necessary expenditure at Carmarthen during the late thirteenth century, during which the only significant outlay was the £169 spent on a wide range of works in 1288–9 (see below). This may be compared with the £284 that went towards just one storey of the Cardigan tower in 1261.[71]

A tower almost certainly occupied the south-west corner at Carmarthen Castle by 1275, as one of the five towers mentioned in the inquisition;[72] all available evidence suggests that it was the present structure, and that it was built in the 1230–1240s. If so, however, the spur-buttresses require explanation. Spurs are first seen in Britain at Dover Castle, in some of King John's work and in the Constable's Gate and inner ward towers built in the 1220s under Hubert de Burgh's direction.[73] Apparently derived from France, for example Chinon (1180–1200), they are however of a very different form – rarely seen in Wales – in which a square base is chamfered back into a round tower.[74]

An early use of the *pyramidal* spur-buttress, that clasps the tower flanks as at Carmarthen and Cardigan, is in the gatehouse at Tonbridge Castle, Kent, built by Earl Richard de Clare *c.*1250. This building is thought to have been influenced by the 'king's works' in the shape of the former west gatehouse at the Tower of London, built by Henry III in 1238–9.[75] However, such pyramidal spurs were never widespread in England[76] enjoying, instead, great popularity in south Wales and the Marches, where they are characteristic of work, from the 1270s onwards, at Goodrich and Carew castles, Caerphilly's north dam, Kidwelly's Chapel Tower, Chepstow's Marten's Tower and elsewhere.

It is noteworthy that these spurred towers are all at baronial castles. With one exception – the gatehouse at St Briavels Castle[77], built in 1292-4 and more or less a copy of the Tonbridge gatehouse – spurs appear never to have been used by the Crown; they appear at none of Edward I's north Wales castles, for example, and there is no suggestion that the lost Tower of London gatehouse had them.[78] They may therefore not have originated in the king's works. On the other hand, Richard de Clare was a Marcher lord with vast estates in Glamorgan, who knew Wales, and so in this respect his Tonbridge spurs may betray Welsh influence. Almost limited to south Wales and the Marches, and near-absent from royal castles, the origins of the pyramidal spur may therefore lie with the Welsh barons.

The north tower at Cardigan is a near-identical twin of Carmarthen's South-west Tower (Figure 118), with the same prominent spurs. Though somewhat larger – 10.5 m in diameter, against Carmarthen's 8 m – it too contains rectangular chambers, with vaults, openings and internal features mirroring those at Carmarthen.[79] We are told that the 'King's Tower' at Cardigan was under construction in the 1250s. If it can be identified as the north tower[80] – and there is no reason to suppose otherwise – then it may be contemporary with, or possibly earlier than the Tonbridge gatehouse, and therefore the first documented tower with pyramidal spurs in Britain. The tower was perhaps begun by the Crown in 1250[81] – it is first specifically mentioned in 1252[82] – but it may be even earlier. Cathcart King suggested that it was begun on behalf of Earl Gilbert Marshal by his brother Walter, before Crown control resumed in 1241, and represents 'an early example [of the spurred form]'.[83] Its correct dating is crucial. King based his suggestion on entries in the Chronicles recording that, in 1240, 'Walter Marshal came to fortify Cardigan'.[84] The phrasing is vague, and implies that work on the tower continued for a long time. Nevertheless, it does raise the possibility that the Cardigan tower was begun under baronial tenure, if completed by the Crown. The second storey was added in 1261 (see above), but no further expenditure was recorded during the remainder of the thirteenth century.

Gilbert Marshal also held Carmarthen 1234–41, so it is possible that an existing tower there was the model for Cardigan. We know little of other castle-building by Gilbert, although he was probably responsible for the upper barbican at Chepstow, where the cylindrical mural tower is not, however, spurred.[85] Nevertheless, a number of attributes suggest an early date for the South-west Tower. It appears to be conjoined with, or butted, by the town wall (begun by 1233), which may therefore have been still under construction when the work on the tower commenced.[86] The location of the spiral stair within the flank

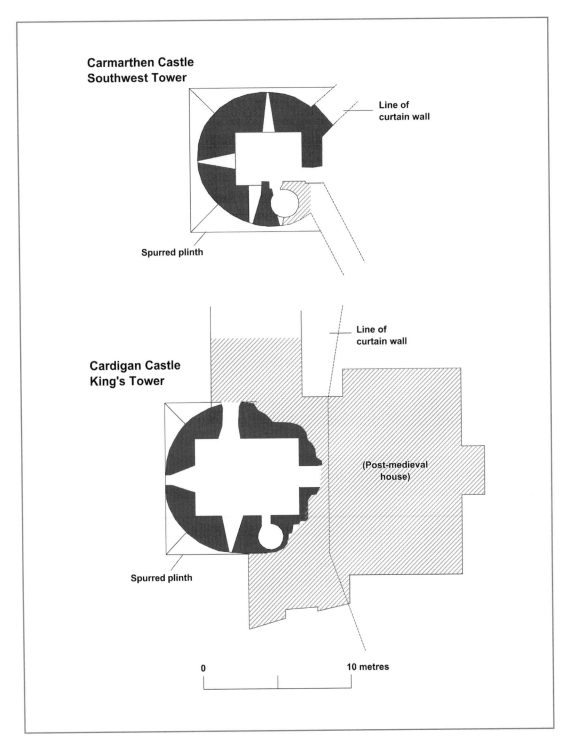

Figure 118 Comparative plans of the spurred towers at Cardigan Castle ('King's Tower') and Carmarthen Castle (South-west Tower)

of the tower, and external to the adjoining curtain, is an unusual and perhaps early feature shared with the Cardigan tower. A stair occupies a similar location in one of the gate-towers at Pevensey Castle, Sussex, dating from the 1190s,[87] while the contemporary gatehouse at Skipton Castle, Yorkshire, features a stair to the front of one of the towers.[88] The rectangular chambers at Carmarthen and Cardigan are also seen at the Skipton gatehouse and, for example, in a cylindrical corner tower at Helmsley Castle, Yorkshire, from 1190–1227,[89] in the Middle Gate (c.1250) of the royal castle at Corfe, Dorset,[90] and a tower at Barnwell Castle, Northamptonshire, from the 1260s.[91]

Simple slit-lights like those in the South-west Tower are seen in the Constable's Gate at Dover, and at Grosmont Castle, Monmouthshire, where they are Hubert de Burgh's work of 1219–32.[92] The Carmarthen openings have very narrow embrasures limiting their usefulness as arrow-loops – itself possibly arguing for an earlier, rather than later date; cf. the narrow embrasures in the West Tower at William Marshal II's Cilgerran, from the 1230–1240s.[93] Moreover, the large first-floor window embrasures, square in plan and with segmental heads, are similar to those at de Burgh's contemporary work at Skenfrith Castle (Monmouthshire), and at Montgomery, also held by de Burgh when under construction between 1228 and 1232.[94] While in marked contrast to the semicircular heads seen in the Marshal-period openings at Chepstow and Cilgerran,[95] the style of the latter, with their double-lights, may imitate those in the great tower of Pembroke Castle in homage to its importance.[96]

In contrast, the South-west Tower has very little in common with Crown work of the later thirteenth century. As well as an absence of spurs, Edward I's north Wales castles for example exhibit a number of motifs neither seen nor suggested at Carmarthen and Cardigan. They show an overall complexity, and fineness of detail, notably absent from the South-west Tower with its simple loops and crude detail. Their openings are characterised by distinctive heads of stylised form, frequently semicircular or square,[97] entirely unlike the Carmarthen openings. These differences extend to Edwardian work outside Wales. The rectangular chambers, at both Carmarthen and Cardigan, are nowhere seen, while stairs normally rise in turrets at the junction of tower and curtain, rather than in the tower flanks. In sum, none of their defining characteristics link the Carmarthen and Cardigan towers with the king's works. None of their openings moreover show the triangular heads characteristic of later thirteenth-century building in south Wales.

The barrel-vaults on all floors of the South-west Tower may be unusual in such an early context. However, the crude rebates for their soffits imply that they may be secondary, and a response to regional styles; the vaulting in the Cardigan tower, too, appears to be secondary.[98] Nevertheless, the gatehouse towers at Pevensey show contemporary barrel-vaults, while the Constable's Gate at Dover was also partly vaulted during the 1220s.[99] Barrel-vaults have a long tradition in the castles of west Wales beginning with the keep at Pembroke, of c.1204,[100] where the vault was copied at Laugharne Castle and Manorbier Castle (Pembroke-shire), in the mid-thirteenth century.[101]

Nevertheless, the Carmarthen spurs are very high, and – unlike the rest of the tower detail – characteristic of the later thirteenth century, so it remains possible that the tower belongs to a bout of unrecorded royal expenditure under Edward I, built to an otherwise 'simple' design influenced by Cardigan Castle.

Its rather basic appointments suggest that the South-west Tower was primarily defensive. It is however incomplete, and it is probable that the first-floor vault carried a fourth storey – the uppermost stage might be expected to be roofed rather than vaulted, while a fourth storey would oversail the curtain walls. The first-floor chamber is better lit than the ground floor, so the fourth stage may have featured further domestic concessions.[102] Nevertheless, the vaulted basement is poorly lit, with a deeply plunging light, and was presumably used as a cellar (the possibility that all inner ward towers could be used for the confinement of prisoners will be discussed later on).

Other towers

The 'King's Tower' of mid-thirteenth-century sources was apparently complete by 1247, when it needed repair. It seems that the castle may have been damaged in the Welsh attacks of 1244 and 1246, as a total of £38 8s. was spent on these repairs and other 'king's works in the castle'.[103] Its name suggests that the King's Tower was larger or more important than the other four. The South-west Tower is possibly meant (cf. the Cardigan tower), or it may have been an alternative name for the shell-keep, as at Pickering Castle, Yorkshire.[104] However, the phrasing of the sources suggests that it was a separate tower, intimately associated with the King's Hall and Chamber – which, I will argue, were located against the inner ward east curtain. It may then have been completed, at least, by the Crown during Phase 4.

A large tower is depicted on the east curtain by Speed (Figure 112). It corresponds with a level area that was shown, projecting into the cross-ditch, in 1786 (Figure 111), and which perhaps represented the site of a tower – either as a platform, or as tumble in the ditch.[105] It lies on the flank of the bailey, rather than the south-east corner where the scarp slope was perhaps just too steep to allow space for a tower. Large D-shaped mural towers were characteristic of the king's works of the mid-thirteenth century,[106] and a single tower of this form similarly flanks the bailey at Montgomery.[107] However, a very similar tower had been built, between 1190 and 1227, at baronial Helmsley.[108] It was clearly designed to be seen and to impress,[109] and a similar tower on Carmarthen's east curtain would dominate the wide views of the castle from the Tywi Valley and the approaches from the Welsh territories.

It is suggested that the third round tower occupied the north-east corner of the inner ward, which is shown as an obtuse angle on the 1786 map (Figure 111). A tower might be expected at this projecting salient, where the ground is level, and indeed seems to be shown on the Speed plan (Figure 112). The 1748 Buck print also appears to show a masonry structure here, in a vague depiction that could conceivably be interpreted as a spurred, round tower (Figure 127).[110] However, no such tower is visible in the 1740 print (Figure 126) and it is more likely that the masonry depicted belongs to the north curtain wall, indicating that the demolition or collapse of both towers was complete, and that they came down comparatively easily. It is likely then that they were, like the interconnecting curtain walls, built on bank material.

It is also likely, for the same reason, that they were neither spurred nor vaulted. Indeed, we are told that the King's Tower was floored in timber in the 1250s,[111] and at least one other inner ward tower carried timber floors in 1321,[112] when it was called the 'Prison Tower' and therefore unlikely to represent the King's Tower. It has not been identified, but may refer to a prison in one of the gatehouse towers, as it appears to have done in 1360–1 (see below).

The thirteenth-century gatehouse and bridge

The eastern half of the present, fifteenth-century gate passage may be a remnant of an earlier gatehouse. It lacks any evidence for jambs or a portcullis slot, implying that, as now, the earlier structure projected westward beyond the line of the curtain. It may then have been twin-towered from the first, accounting for the two remaining towers of the 1275 survey. Twin, rounded gate-towers were employed by William Marshal I in c.1190 at Chepstow, and before 1211 at Kilkenny and Dunamase, in Ireland.[113] Similar gatehouses were built between c.1190 and c.1220 at Helmsley, Skipton, Pevensey and elsewhere,[114] and in the early 1220s at Beeston.[115] A similar gatehouse would not be unexpected at Carmarthen during this period. And while both William Marshal II and Hubert de Burgh chose relatively simple gate-towers at Cilgerran, Grosmont and Skenfrith,[116] the gatehouse built under de Burgh's tenure at Montgomery, between 1223 and 1232, also has round flanking towers, albeit solid at ground-floor level.[117]

It is possible that the gatehouse was already under construction in 1227, when £33 was spent by the Crown on the bridges of Carmarthen and Cardigan castles.[118] This considerable sum may not have been confined to a timber structure, and possibly relates to the two masonry bridge piers. Two such piers were employed at Henry III's Montgomery, where a similar three-span bridge incorporated a drawbridge in the inner bay. The piers were however longer and narrower, measuring 7.5 m by 0.75 m as against Carmarthen's 4.4 m by 0.92 m, and are thought to have been supports for sole-plates and timber trusses; they may represent the bridge that was present by 1250–1 when it was 'renewed'.[119] The ditch at Beeston, contemporary with the gatehouse, was cut through bedrock leaving a similar, central pier, 4 m high but originally higher, which fully supported a timber bridge.[120] In their present form, however, the Carmarthen piers are likely to be the result of repair, or partial rebuilding, after the Glyndŵr rebellion of the early fifteenth century.

PHASE 4: BUILDINGS FOR THE KING, 1241–1278 (Figure 119)

Once the stone defences of the inner ward were essentially complete, work could begin on updating the internal buildings. A full range of domestic and service buildings are assumed from the first, but after the re-establishment of direct royal control in 1241, the castle was equipped with lodgings fit to receive King Henry III. A new 'King's Hall' and 'King's Chamber' were built between c.1250 and 1254, while the King's Tower was repaired and (re-) roofed with lead.[121]

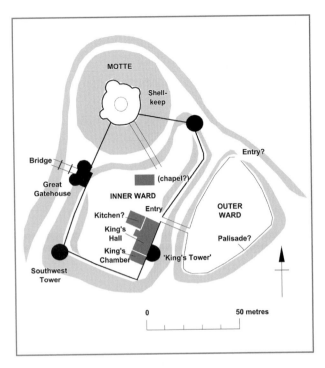

Figure 119 *Sketch plan of Carmarthen Castle showing its suggested layout in Phase 4, 1241–1278*

It is assumed that the hall and chamber at Carmarthen – Henry's main Welsh possession – were of masonry. Costs of at least £160 are recorded, nearly twice as much as the two-storeyed range that was under construction forty years later at Montgomery, where they were light, timber-framed buildings.[122] However, the accounts are not rigidly itemised and are sometimes conflated. For example, the £182 3s. 3d reimbursed to the custodian, Waleran, in 1261, covered additional expenditure at Carmarthen.[123] The King's Hall was probably a ground-floor hall typical of the period, as at e.g. Henry III's Winchester Castle, and his brother Richard of Cornwall's Launceston.[124] Perhaps something akin to the near-contemporary hall block at Hubert de Burgh's Skenfrith – one of the better-preserved domestic ranges of the early/mid-thirteenth century – may be envisaged. This was originally an unaisled ground-floor hall and chamber, in stone but relatively lightly built, with walls averaging 0.75 m in thickness.[125]

The King's Hall is the only hall indicated in the 1275 survey and is therefore probably the 'Great Hall' of later accounts, and the 'Large Hall' whose porch was repaired in 1306.[126] According to an account of 1343,[127] the 'Great Hall' lay 30 m from the castle postern which, I have suggested, was on the south side of the outer ward. This would place it in the southeast quarter of the inner ward. It went up in the same building programme as both the King's Tower, and the 'King's Chamber', which we know from the 1275 survey to have been a conjoining building, as in the Skenfrith range. Hall and chamber were probably, therefore, a unit lying against both the east curtain and the tower. Similar hall–tower associations existed in the mid-thirteenth century at the Tower of London,[128] Deganwy,[129] and Barnard Castle, County Durham.[130] The possibility, raised above, that the east curtain survived here until 1868, suggests that any bank here may have been removed to make way for these developments.

The kitchen is separately listed in the 1275 survey and may have been a separate building, again as at Skenfrith; an associated granary, pantry and buttery building is mentioned in 1338–9.[131] The King's Hall and Chamber may be the 'houses of the castle' that were reroofed with lead in 1287–8;[132] the remaining thatched buildings were roofed with tile-stone or slate in 1289.[133]

PHASE 5: MORE ACCOMMODATION, 1279–1300 (Figure 120)

With its five round towers, including the 'advanced' South-west Tower, Carmarthen Castle was still very much a sophisticated, modern fortress when restored to the Crown in 1279, and very little expenditure was recorded during the late thirteenth century. This has occasioned some surprise, for example from Ella Armitage,[134] representing as it does the period of Edward I's castle-building. However, while this was by no means limited to north Wales, spending at his other properties was modest in comparison.[135] Moreover, while the records are possibly incomplete, it is likely that little work was actually required at Carmarthen during the late thirteenth century.[136] The castles at Caernarfon, Conwy etc. were largely built from scratch; at Carmarthen, Edward was already in possession of a more than adequate building. Nor were all of Caernarfon's administrative buildings initially required at Carmarthen. For although both became the regional heads of the new principality in 1284, this meant rather different things for the two castles. Under the terms of the Statute of Rhuddlan, Caernarfon was to be fully equipped to implement the new regime from the first. At Carmarthen, the administrative changes were introduced more gradually; a justiciar was appointed in 1280, but there is no record of separate Justiciar's Sessions until 1301, and it was not until 1299 that a formal chamberlain – with his own exchequer – was appointed.

It appears nevertheless that some additional domestic buildings were erected. The 'Queen's Chamber', mentioned in an account of 1306, was clearly a pre-existing building, and by definition was unlikely to have been built during the tenure of Edward's son as Prince of Wales, 1301–7. The provision of a private chamber for the queen – often with a

personal chapel attached – is documented at most, but by no means all royal castles (e.g. Winchester and Marlborough), and it is tempting to imagine this chamber being built twenty years previously, for the arrival of Edward I and Queen Eleanor in 1284. Another pre-existing building, the Knights' Chamber, is mentioned in 1309–10.[137] Meanwhile the gatehouse may have been remodelled to meet the needs of the post-1284 constable.

However, there is no record of the construction of any of these buildings. In fact the only significant expenditure recorded during the late thirteenth century was in

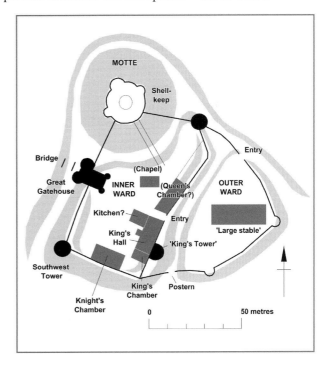

Figure 120 Sketch plan of Carmarthen Castle showing its suggested layout in Phase 5, 1279–1300

1288–9, when the Pipe Rolls tell us that £169 15s. 3d was spent on 'reconditioning' the castle.[138] In the main, moreover, only minor works were undertaken. Although not completely itemised – only £67 is accounted for – the sums are all relatively small, and certainly insufficient for any major projects like, for example, the South-west Tower. In comparison, contemporary operations at Edward's Caernarfon and Conwy annually consumed an average of £1,500, over nine years, with totals between £12,000 and £15,000.[139] Furthermore, the account makes it clear that the inner ward retained its basic five-towered plan, and no further towers are mentioned. However, the Pipe Roll accounts may not be complete – the £30 spent on roofing material in 1289, for instance, was not recorded.

By 1289, at least, the castle walls were whitewashed,[140] in a visual display that was intended to impress and which was kept up; in 1435–6, for instance, lime was bought for whitening the walls.[141] All that was really necessary to bring the castle fully up to date was to rebuild the outer ward defences in stone, and the Pipe Roll does at least confirm that this had begun: the sums include £5 15s. on 'making a new wall below the castle towards the Bridge of Tywi, on both sides of the postern'. However, the sum is too small to represent the construction of the entire circuit. And despite being termed 'new' in 1288–9, the curtain was, only fifty years later, described as 'destroyed on account of its age'.[142] Perhaps it was begun during Phase 4, as part of the king's works of 1241–54; cf. Montgomery, where the outer (or 'middle') ward was walled in 1251–3.[143]

The Knights' Chamber

An account of 1309–10 locates the Knights' Chamber close to the King's Chamber, i.e. in the southern half of the inner ward.[144] It clearly represented additional lodgings for important visitors, comparable with the guest halls and chambers at e.g. Restormel Castle, Cornwall.[145] Such a guest chamber would have been a requirement from an early date, and may have been a rebuild of a pre-existing building. By 1338, a chamber for the esquires appears to have been added, apparently by division of the Knight's Chamber.[146]

I have argued that the south-east side of the inner ward was already occupied by the King's Hall and Chamber. The west side was empty, but we shall see later on that it was soon to be developed. The Knights' Chamber may then have been built against the southern curtain – an available space in another sense, too, as there was no defensive bank to impede development. The excavated evidence showed that the ground level in this area sloped downhill from west to east, implying that the western bank had either been truncated and/ or spread, or that it turned eastwards for just a short distance before petering out. However, no evidence for any subsequent medieval contexts – or masonry structures – was revealed through excavation here, suggesting that the area has been subsequently truncated.

The Queen's Chamber

The Queen's Chamber may have stood apart from the other domestic buildings. A separate chamber in the upper bailey at Chepstow may have been the 'Countess's Chamber' mentioned in 1271–2, for the private use of Earl Roger Bigod's wife.[147] A similar role has been suggested for the Western Hall at Pembroke, from 1219 to 1245, which is likewise set away from the Great Hall, lying next to the possible chapel.[148]

It was suggested above that the eastern boundary wall of the pre-Nash gaol, shown in 1786 (Figure 111), may have belonged to a domestic building lying against the east curtain, as a parallel internal wall. Lying in the northern half of the inner ward, a building here would have been separate from the King's Hall and Knights' Chamber, and may have performed a distinct, perhaps more feminine, role. At *c*.40 m, the wall shown is long, but the Queen's Chamber may have been accompanied by service buildings, and perhaps a private chapel – an adjoining latrine, and 'garret', are mentioned in 1343.[149] It would also occupy the only space that was available in the northern half of the bailey during the late thirteenth century, the remainder being largely taken up by the motte ditch, and perhaps by the castle chapel (see below).

The Great Gatehouse

Early twin-tower gatehouses generally took the form of a short passage between the flanking towers, as at Chepstow and Helmsley.[150] The earliest gate passage flanked by chambers to the rear of the towers, within the bailey, appears to be at baronial Warkworth, from *c*.1200;[151] the form is seen again at de Burgh's Dover and Montgomery. It did not, however, become widespread until the middle of the thirteenth century, simple short passages being used at Beeston in the 1220s, and White Castle, Monmouthshire, in the 1250s.[152] So the rear section at Carmarthen may have been added later in the thirteenth century. The cylindrical stair-turret suggested at its south-east corner, on antique maps and prints (see Chapter 3), is characteristic of Edward I's so-called 'keep-gatehouses' of the 1280–1290s.[153] It may originally have been one of a pair.

The work was possibly undertaken between 1275, when the gatehouse was described as 'decayed',[154] and 1288–9, when it comprised two storeys and was apparently well lit.[155] The south and east walls of the rear section survived to their full height in 1829, when a drawing clearly shows a pair of large arched windows at each level of the south wall (Figure 132); the reveal of one of these windows can still be seen, at first-floor level, on the truncated stump of the south wall (9, Figures 79, 81 and 83). Work on the gatehouse may have been occasioned by the increased status of the castle constable after 1284, and the consequent need for appropriate lodgings. These were probably situated in the gatehouse, as in a number of contemporary castles including Caerphilly; they certainly were by 1354–5, when the 'Constable's Chamber over the large gate' is mentioned in the sources,[156] and we may imagine them lying on the first floor of a purpose-built rear section. The Constable's Kitchen, built for £37 in 1360–1,[157] on the other hand, lay above a 'prison', suggesting that it occupied one of the flanking towers, as it did in the early fifteenth-century gatehouse at Kidwelly.[158] Carmarthen's rear section was apparently remodelled when the gatehouse was rebuilt in the early fifteenth century, but a second spiral stair, fossilised in the angle with the west curtain and described in Chapter 3, may be a further remnant from the earlier arrangements.

The outer curtain wall and stable

While the Pipe Roll indicates that the postern was present by 1288, it is not clear whether the adjoining section of 'new wall' represented the final stage of the outer ward's refortification in stone, or was merely a rebuild of a pre-existing curtain wall. The curtain is likely to have been begun on the north side, which faced level ground and housed the outer gate; the section either side of the postern, on the other hand, occupied the cross-ditch on the south side and may well have been added later, as a spur connecting the inner and outer curtains.

The two towers shown on the Buck prints, on the south and east sides of the outer ward, appear to be semicircular (see Figures 126 and 127). The 1740 print suggests that the southern tower was fully enclosed, rather than an open-backed turret characteristic of the late thirteenth century,[159] but the rear wall (or even the tower itself) may have been a later insertion.

The outer curtain would appear to have been of poor construction and in 1336, it partly collapsed through 'age'.[160] Edward III ordered it to be rebuilt, but it was apparently unfinished several years later and the expenditure of £40 was ordered in 1340.[161] A further tower had been built by 1343, over the postern,[162] probably the square tower shown in 1740 which is comparable to the postern tower in the ditch at Pickering, from 1323–6.[163] Then, in 1338–9, the northern line also had to be 'made anew' at a cost of 66s. over eleven weeks.[164] The outer gate is first mentioned in this account, and by this time at least can be assumed to have been a tower(s); the chamber over the gate passage is mentioned in 1355.[165]

The bulk of the *itemised* expenditure in 1288–9 concerned 'work on the new stable', which accounted for over £10.[166] It was a masonry building, possibly replacing the stable that was 'decayed' in 1275. Clearly sizeable, and probably the 'large stable' of 1338, it may have been located in the outer ward.[167] The usual complement of further ancillary buildings and workshops may be expected within the outer ward, though they receive scant attention in the sources.

PHASE 6: BUILDINGS FOR GOVERNMENT, 1301–1408 (Figure 121)

It was under the future king Edward II, as Prince of Wales 1301–7, that the castle became fully established as a base for the newly reorganised government of south and west Wales, and development continued through Edward's reign, under the pan-Wales justiciars – particularly the Mortimers, who held office from 1308 to 1330. During these three decades, Carmarthen Castle was transformed, with the addition of new administrative buildings and lodgings for the chief officials, the justiciar and chamberlain, along with their deputies, clerks and household staff. Work began with an exchequer which, although first mentioned in 1306,[168] appears to have been a pre-existing building: the justiciar had maintained his own treasury since 1280, but the exchequer may not have been built until the appointment of a chamberlain in 1299.[169] The Justiciar's Kitchen was also repaired in 1306, implying that his lodgings had been commenced. Some of this work may have arisen from a survey

Figure 121 Sketch plan of Carmarthen Castle showing its suggested layout in Phase 6, 1301–1408

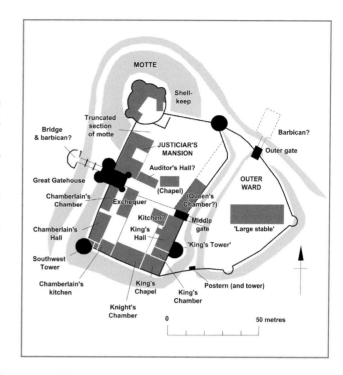

taken in 1303–4,[170] but only £11 appears to have been spent between 1299 and 1306.[171] The bulk of the expenditure followed the appointment of Roger Mortimer in 1308, while lodgings for the chamberlain had been built by 1321. The lodgings of both officers are referred to as 'mansions' in later medieval documents, and represented a tangible expression of their status, power and prestige – and thereby that of the king: they would have been only too visible to suitors at the courts. Apparently comprising ranges of buildings within discrete enclosures, they may be contrasted with Caernarfon, where the justiciar and chamberlain instead occupied towers – the Eagle Tower and the Chamberlain's Tower respectively.[172] These are larger, grander and later towers than those at Carmarthen, which could not have provided the extensive lodgings suggested in the sources.

Remaining expenditure was mainly taken up by upkeep and repair, mainly of the curtain walls and particularly the inner ward south curtain, which needed partial rebuilding in 1338–9. But in general, the castle's development had, as elsewhere in Britain, slowed down by the mid-fourteenth century. Although £192 was spent under the Black Prince, 1343–76, it went towards piecemeal repairs that were a prolonged response to a condition survey commissioned in 1343. And £200 was spent on repairs after the castle reverted to the Crown in 1376, mainly on the troublesome south curtains of both baileys, which appear to have needed continuous work until the end of the century.

However, some further buildings were added including, before 1310, another chapel and, in the 1390s, a tower over the Middle Gate between the two baileys. The well is mentioned in 1348 when a well-house had been built over it.[175] The roofs of most service buildings remained of slate throughout the fourteenth century, although the lead roofs over the towers and Henry III's hall and chambers were presumably maintained; the Chamberlain's Hall also had a lead roof by 1355.[176]

The 'mansions' and exchequer

Itemised expenditure during the first decade of the fourteenth century mainly relates to the lodgings built for Roger Mortimer, justiciar from 1308 until 1311. The 'house newly built' for Mortimer in 1309–10 probably represents the Justiciar's Chamber,[177] although the low cost of 75s. may indicate either a timber building, or perhaps the repair of an exist-ing stone building given that the kitchen had already been built. The dresser, larder and combined bakehouse/brewhouse, which cost £21 and were probably of masonry,[178] were presumably attached to the kitchen. Auditors were appointed for the first time in 1349, and a hall for their use had been built, apparently within the justiciar's complex, by 1418,[179] to which a chamber had been added by 1424.[180] The buildings were situated 'next to the great gate[house]',[181] probably on its northern side, as it will be seen that the chamberlain's lodgings lay to the south.

No separate courthouse is suggested in thirteenth-century building accounts, and it is likely that the King's Hall was used, a dual role served by the halls at many other castles. However, after the old County Court of Carmarthen became divided into separate Welsh and English courts in 1301, and the Justiciar's Sessions became settled at Carmarthen in c.1327 (see Chapter 2), the need for a further administrative hall would have become apparent. And, in the 1330s, the number of courts held at Carmarthen Castle rose to six. A purpose-built courthouse seems to have been built by 1339–40, when it was termed the 'King's County Hall' – as distinct from the 'Great Hall'.[182] It probably formed part of the justiciar's complex, as the 'Justiciar's Hall', which appears to have replaced it in the early fifteenth century, lay north of the gatehouse (see below). Separate courthouses were not widespread in British castles, but a late thirteenth-century chamber next to the hall at Pem-broke, long known as the 'Chancery', is probably the 'County Court' of the sources,[183] while the 'courthouse' recorded at Kidwelly may have occupied a late medieval building in the outer ward,[184] and one of the two thirteenth-century halls at Launceston appears to have fulfilled a similar function.[185] The surviving 'Great Hall' at Monmouth, moreover, may always have been solely administrative.[186]

Over £1,600 was spent on the five royal castles of south-west Wales in 1311–12.[187] Relatively little work has been suggested at the other four,[188] and so at least part of this expenditure may have gone towards the Chamberlain's Mansion at Carmarthen which, like the Justiciar's Mansion, was extensive. The kitchen was built in 1309–10,[189] but the 'Cham-berlain's Hall' is first mentioned in 1321;[190] a chamber had been added by 1355.[191] They demonstrably occupied the south-west corner of the inner ward, lying against both curtain walls: according to later accounts the hall 'faced the town', i.e. adjoining the west curtain,[192] the kitchen and bakehouse overlooked the river,[193] i.e. adjoining the south curtain, while the 'tower next to the [chamberlain's] house', in 1343,[194] was clearly the South-west Tower. The complex may have developed around the pre-existing exchequer, which communi-cated with the Chamberlain's Chamber in 1424.[195] However, the exchequer appears, by this time, to have been rebuilt – it was described as 'new' in 1400–1, at a cost of over £26[196] – and it may therefore have moved.

Excavation in 1980 confirmed the extensive development of this corner of the inner ward, revealing the remains of masonry buildings of at least two storeys, of good quality and clearly of high status. They occupied a deliberately terraced area (the spread western bank?), from which the ground sloped down towards the Square Tower (Figure 95). The remains of the bread oven confirm that the chamberlain's bakehouse was located here. The buildings evidently extended north as far as the gatehouse – a truncated, diagonal offset in the rear section south wall (12, Figure 79), clearly represents the roof-line of an adjoining gabled building lying against the west curtain; it was over 8 m tall and probably represents the chamberlain's hall or chamber, to which the kitchen and bakehouse may have formed an undercroft. The full extent of its roof scar is shown on the 1740 Buck print (Figure 126).

The Justiciar's Mansion had, by 1452, come to occupy a walled enclosure north of the gatehouse.[197] The chamberlain's complex formed a corresponding enclosure, that had been walled by 1338,[198] while a yard was created in front of the Great Hall in 1338–9.[199] Evidence for such enclosed building complexes elsewhere is sparse – and often, by its nature, ephemeral – but the hall range at Stamford Castle, Lincolnshire, was associated with a walled yard or garden in the thirteenth and fourteenth centuries.[200] Carmarthen's 'mansions' do, however, appear to be unusual, particularly in an early fourteenth-century context,[201] although a range of timber-framed buildings at Pickering are arranged around a yard and appear to be the constable's lodging, mentioned in 1441–3, which included a hall, pantry, buttery, cellar, kitchen and storehouses.[202]

The motte and shell-keep

What the accounts do not reveal is the tremendous feat of civil engineering that was apparently undertaken to accommodate the justiciar's lodgings. We have seen that they probably lay north of the gatehouse, but this area was occupied by the motte and its ditch. As the inner ward was otherwise, by this time, fully occupied by buildings, the only way to accommodate the lodgings was to cut back the south-east quadrant of the motte flush with the shell-keep wall, and to backfill its ditch (see Chapter 3). The shell-wall in this section was then extended down to bailey level; its modern concrete finish may overlie a stepped plinth of medieval date, as seen in any number of twelfth-century rectangular keeps, but also in the mid-thirteenth-century outer gate at White Castle.[203] This campaign probably began when the justiciar's lodgings were first built, in c.1308. It was an extreme measure and, to my knowledge, is unparalleled in Britain, although the periphery of the motte at York was also cut back, but to a much lesser extent, in the early nineteenth century to provide extra space for the courts and gaol.[204]

The shell-keep forebuilding also occupies the newly available space, and so may be contemporary with this work. Further modifications to the shell-keep appear to have been undertaken. The demolition of the suggested timber tower 121 – which was inferred, through finds evidence, to have occurred in the late thirteenth/early fourteenth century at the earliest – may have been a stage in this remodelling; an associated surface 134/144 was cut by the new section of the shell-wall.[205] At any rate, the timber-framed buildings inside the shell-keep appear to belong – in their present form at least – to this phase, as their sill-walls butted the shell-wall, including its rebuilt southern section. In 1353, Edward III began a new suite of timber-framed buildings within the shell-keep at Windsor which, though structurally modest, were royal lodgings.[206] Later medieval remodelling of the shell-keep at Cardiff similarly included a new hall and gate tower. However, the main focus at Carmarthen was, by this time, clearly the inner ward, and the new buildings may have been fairly humble in function; none of them can be identified from the sources, suggesting that, as at a number of castles including Carisbrooke (Isle of Wight) and Warwick, they were not of high status.[207]

The inner ward cross-wall

The inner ward was clearly becoming markedly zoned by the mid-fourteenth century, and it was probably at this time that it was divided in half by an east–west cross-wall separating the justiciar's lodgings from the King's Hall and chamberlain's enclosure.[208] This wall was fairly substantial, if not particularly high. It is shown by Speed in c.1610 (Figure 112)[209] and, as a low wall, in 1740 (Figure 126). It survived until 1868, as the southern wall of the gaol, on an earlier nineteenth-century plan of which it is labelled 'ancient wall of the gaol' (Figure 129; also see Figure 130 for an elevation drawing). It ran from the east curtain to the southeast corner of the gatehouse rear section, with a pronounced dog-leg towards its west end (Figure 111), where it incorporated the end wall of a pre-existing building. This building, which probably belonged to the chamberlain's mansion complex – perhaps the exchequer – had gone by 1740, but a doorway and two window openings in its end wall are shown in the Buck print. Similar zoning is seen at e.g. Helmsley, where one of the cross-walls was the remnant of an earlier curtain, retained when the castle was enlarged.[210]

The two chapels

It is likely that the main castle chapel, serving the household, was a masonry building by the fourteenth century, at least, and perhaps much earlier – the chapel was among the first stone buildings at e.g. Pevensey and Pickering.[211] The congestion apparent in the southern half of the inner ward, and the proximity of the possible Queen's Chamber (cf. Pembroke), suggest that it may have occupied the northern half of the bailey. The chapel was appurtenant to St Peter's parish church.[212]

A second chapel, presumably the 'King's Chapel' of later accounts, had been 'newly built' between the King's Chamber and the Knight's Chamber in 1309–10,[213] to form a continuous L-shaped range around the south and east sides of the inner ward (Figure 121).[214] The King's Chapel, which appears to have been dedicated to St Mary and St John the Evangelist, was primarily intended for the private devotions of the king, should he choose to visit, and was reconstituted as a chantry under Edward the Black Prince; the cartulary of Carmarthen Priory records that in 1370 Merthyr Church, Carmarthenshire, was granted to the priory 'so that they shall find, at their own charge', a secular chaplain to perform a daily intercessionary mass at the chapel for the prince and royal family.[215] The King's Chapel was clearly well-appointed, and in 1424–5 John Matthew, the chaplain, purchased a Flemish painting for use as an altarpiece.[216]

It is not always possible to distinguish between the two chapels in the sources. However, the 'big bell', and 'window' that were repaired in 1387–8 are described as belonging to 'the chapel of the castle',[217] rather than the King's Chapel, as was the 'new' porch that was built in 1433–5.[218] By tradition, there was a third chapel in the castle.[219] However, its name is given, in a number of nineteenth-century antiquarian accounts, as 'St Edward's Chapel' or 'Prince Edward's Chapel',[220] clearly meaning the chantry established in the King's Chapel by Edward the Black Prince, and there is no suggestion of a third chapel in contemporary sources.[221] The King's Chapel was dissolved in the 1540s, along with other chantries, to raise revenue for the Crown,[222] but it is possible that the castle chapel survived later into the sixteenth century.

The Middle Gate

There will have been a gateway between the inner and outer wards from the earliest days, presumably the 'Middle Gate' of 1430–2,[223] that had been given a first-floor 'crenellated chamber', in 1394–5, at a cost of just over £6.[224] The gateway is portrayed opposite the Great Gatehouse on the Speed plan (Figure 112), corresponding with the internal angle – and dog-leg – in the east wall of the post-medieval gaol (see Figure 111). It would therefore lie between the suggested King's Hall and Queen's Chamber, and the low cost of its conversion into a tower may indicate that it incorporated their pre-existing end walls. It had apparently gone, along with the bulk of the east curtain, by 1740, but a building shown in 1786, possibly a stable, may have occupied its site.

The bridge and ?barbican

An account of 1318 records that the 'New Bridge' had been recently repaired.[225] It possibly represents a bridge at the Middle Gate, over the cross-ditch. It may however relate to the main entry and the repair – and/or possibly the recent construction – of the masonry piers. The bridge itself had become 'decayed' by 1343, repairs being estimated at £6,[226] a sum suggesting fairly minor work on a structure that was still predominantly of timber.

The 'foundation of an enclosure (wall) opposite the gate', mentioned in 1321,[227] appears to describe a barbican.[228] A similar barbican enclosure, from the 1270s, occupies a similar location at the Tower of London.[229] It was semicircular in plan and may have been the model for the barbican, of c.1300, at Goodrich,[230] and possibly the one at Pembroke.[231] Barbican enclosures also existed at Sandal (Yorkshire) and Oxford castles.[232]

PHASE 7: DAMAGE AND REBUILDING, 1409–c.1550 (Figure 122)

The castle was twice besieged during the Glyndŵr rebellion, when large areas of the town, and its walls, were devastated. It is apparent that the castle also suffered. More than £380 was spent on 'building and repairs' in 1409–11, much of it going towards the reconstruction of the Great Gatehouse, which clearly bore the brunt of the damage, in its present form.[233] In comparison, the contemporary gatehouse at Henry IV's Lancaster Castle, similarly damaged during Scots raids, appears to have taken up the greater part of the £2,500 that was spent at the castle between 1402 and 1422,[234] while the complex North-west Bastion at Rochester Castle,

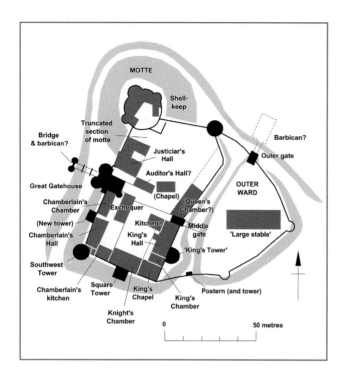

MOTTE

Shell-keep

Truncated
section
of motte

Bridge
& barbican?

Barbican?

Outer gate

Justiciar's
Hall

Auditor's Hall?

Great Gatehouse

OUTER
WARD

(Chapel)

Chamberlain's
Chamber

Exchequer

(Queen's
Chamber?)

(New tower)

Kitchen?

Middle
gate

Chamberlain's
Hall

King's
Hall

'Large stable'

'King's Tower'

Southwest
Tower

Chamberlain's
kitchen

Square
Tower

King's
Chapel

King's
Chamber

Postern (and tower)

Knight's
Chamber

0   50 metres

Figure 122 Sketch plan of Carmarthen Castle showing its suggested layout in Phase 7, 1409–c.1550

Kent, had by itself cost Richard II £350 in 1378–83.[235] Carmarthen's gatehouse – with just two storeys, against the usual three – is however comparatively small, while it is probable that elements of the earlier gatehouse were retained.

The campaign nevertheless represented the largest single building operation at Carmarthen Castle since the thirteenth century and, again, as at Lancaster, Rochester and also Kidwelly – of which more below – was unusually extensive compared with works at the majority of royal castles during this period.[236] The west curtain, to the north, may too have been damaged by Glyndŵr – the physical evidence suggests that it may have been truncated and rebuilt as the west wall of a new building, the Justiciar's Hall. The postern tower in the outer ward also needed repair,[237] while two new square towers may also belong to this phase.

Subsequent entries relate primarily to repairs of existing buildings. However a stable was built 'anew' for the chamberlain in 1418–19,[238] while a second new stable mentioned in 1424 may be the same as the 'Justiciar's Stable' that abutted the Justiciar's Hall in 1435–6,[239] bringing the number of stables in the castle to three.[240] The prison, and the 'new house over', that was built in 1413–14 for £28,[241] seems to have been a new, and separate building. It lay 'near the gate of the castle', as opposed to within the gatehouse, and appears not to denote a tower, as a gable was added in the following year.[242] It may therefore have occupied the justiciar's enclosure.

Both the justiciar's and chamberlain's halls were still heated by open hearths, with roof louvres, in the 1420s–1430s,[243] but their private chambers had fireplaces with chimneys, as did several other buildings. Plumbers' expenses indicate that a number of buildings had lead roofs, though the new Justiciar's Hall was roofed in slate, and some of the 'divers houses, chambers and stables' in the castle still had shingle roofs into the 1490s.[244]

The Great Gatehouse

While referred to as the 'New Gate' in 1411,[245] we have seen that the gatehouse was actually a rebuild of an existing structure, some of which may have been retained, including part of the gate passage, the former rear section and probably the twin-towered footprint. Nevertheless the present towers and first floor are clearly from the early fifteenth century.

Carmarthen

Kidwelly

Llawhaden

Figure 123 The gatehouses at Carmarthen, Kidwelly and Llawhaden castles

Similarities with the nearby gatehouse at Kidwelly Castle have received comment.[246] Begun by the Duchy of Lancaster, under John of Gaunt, in the late fourteenth century, work here progressed until 1422 – as at Lancaster – under his son Henry IV.[247] The two gatehouses are similar in matters of detail, but not in scale (Figure 123). Kidwelly's is much larger, with three storeys over a basement, and was more expensive. But it was entirely new, apparently unrestrained by existing fabric. The basic ground plan, with a rear section and flanking turret(s), is moreover common to both, while the machicolations, window openings and corbel tables are strikingly similar,[248] though Kidwelly lacks the finely dressed outer arch over the entry at Carmarthen. It is worth noting, then, that the master mason employed to oversee the rebuilding of the south curtain wall at Carmarthen, in 1396, was one John Hirde of Pembroke.[249] His name appears on the account book for works at Kidwelly in 1402–3 and it is possible that he was responsible for overseeing

(Justiciar's Hall)

Figure 124 Conjectural reconstruction drawing of the Great Gatehouse during Phase 7, including the former rear section, from the north-east, based on structural, pictorial and map evidence

the construction of both gatehouses.[250] The treatment at both is moreover 'local' in style, suggesting that the masons were drawn from the surrounding region.[251]

All three gatehouses may have been influenced by the earlier Lancastrian example at Dunstanburgh Castle, Northumberland, built c.1313.[252] But these late gatehouses were not exclusively Lancastrian. A third local example, which is very similar, exists at Llawhaden Castle, Pembrokeshire (Figure 123). Built by the bishop of St Davids, it too may belong to the opening decade of the fifteenth century.[253] Like Carmarthen, it comprises only two storeys, has a similar outer arch on moulded corbels, the same large, central first-floor window and the same triple machicolation. Also like Carmarthen, it is flanked by a square turret containing four latrine shafts, but this may be a remnant from an earlier phase, perhaps late thirteenth-century.[254] The towers, moreover, are much larger, D-shaped and spurred, while – like Kidwelly as originally planned – the stair occupies an internal wall, not a turret to the rear. Along with Lancaster, these three were among the last great gatehouses to be built in medieval Britain.[255]

Carmarthen's fifteenth-century gatehouse is reconstructed in Figure 124. The evidence indicates that the rear section had a hipped roof which lay below – and was oversailed by – the surviving eastern parapet. The rear section north wall may have been entirely rebuilt where it conjoined the suggested Justiciar's Hall, which was more or less contemporary (see below). An account of 1409–10 appears to locate the 'Armourer's Tower' or 'Armoury Chamber' within the gatehouse;[256] it had a fireplace with two chimneys in 1424,[257] and may therefore represent the large chamber over the gate passage. Whilst well-appointed, this chamber also housed the portcullis (and drawbridge?) mechanism, which may indicate that the Constable's Hall still occupied the rear section; the latter was heated by an open hearth, with a 'louvre', in 1428–9.[258] The turret between the south face and the west curtain wall may have been newly built in 1409–11 to house latrines, and perhaps other service chambers. The lead roofs in the front half of the gatehouse were completed in 1415, but the Constable's Hall was stone-tiled in 1435–7.[259]

We have seen that the old gatehouse had contained a prison in 1360–1. There is no evidence, however, that the new gatehouse was similarly equipped, either from the sources or in the physical remains, which suggests that both ground-floor chambers had entries to the bailey; a basement chamber in the Kidwelly gatehouse, once thought to represent a prison, has been reinterpreted as a strong-room for valuables.[260]

The bridge and barbican

Whatever form the medieval bridge to the Great Gatehouse took in 1400, it too is likely to have been severely damaged by Glyndŵr. The early fifteenth-century repairs may provide a context for the apparent rebuild of the western pier 053 in its present, tapered form, and the possible construction trench against eastern pier 038 (145, Figure 90).

The eastern bay, in front of the gatehouse, was probably crossed by a 'turning-bridge' that lowered into the gate-passage drawbridge pit. The plank used 'for mending the bridge of the castle', in 1424,[261] may refer to this, but is more likely to have been part of the fixed timber decking over the other two bays. Speed's plan appears to show a twin-towered barbican at the west end of the bridge (Figure 112),[262] and any earlier barbican enclosure may have been destroyed, along with the gatehouse, during the Glyndŵr rising. The 'Middle Tower' barbican at the Tower of London is also twin-towered, but is earlier, belonging to the late thirteenth century,[263] while a castle barbican similarly projects into the marketplace at Alnwick, Northumberland, as it formerly did at Durham.[264] No physical evidence for either barbican was recovered at Carmarthen, but may have lain beyond the excavated area.

The Justiciar's Hall

The Justiciar's Hall was described as 'new' in 1424.[265] Evidently used for judicial purposes, it was called the 'King's Shire Hall' later in the century[266] and clearly replaced, or was a comprehensive rebuild of, the fourteenth-century 'County Hall'. This rebuild may have been one of the 'other divers necessaries' of the 1409–11 campaign, and a further £34 was spent on the hall in 1424–5;[267] it is apparent that work on administrative buildings continued unabated despite the judicial uncertainties of the early and mid-fifteenth century, described in Chapter 2.

The new hall appears to have have occupied the same location as its predecessor and, it was suggested in Chapter 3, lay against the west curtain wall. What is interpreted as its west wall overlies a truncated section of curtain walling which, along with the fourteenth-century hall, may have been another casualty of Glyndŵr's campaign. The body of the suggested building overlies the motte ditch, consistent with an early fourteenth-century date for the ditch infill (see above). It is unlikely to represent a post-Civil War building, overlying seventeenth-century slighting, for the reasons noted in Chapter 3. It is moreover hard to imagine a post-medieval context for the truncation of the motte and the infill of its ditch – with the necessary expenditure – before Nash remodelled the gaol in 1789–92, by which time the building had gone (see Chapter 5).

The towers

The inner ward's basic five-towered plan remained unchanged, but was supplemented by at least two more mural towers, both square, during the later Middle Ages. The surviving Square Tower is stylistically late medieval, but the absence of surviving detail makes precise dating impossible. In addition, its construction trench directly cut the natural soil, and there were few subsequent datable contexts. It was arguably added to the unstable south curtain as much for its buttressing effect as for any defensive considerations, and may therefore belong to one of the rebuilding campaigns of the mid- to late fourteenth century in which its costs could have been met. Square mural towers were used at Pickering in 1323–6; whilst never entirely out of favour in northern England, it was their first use in the king's works since the twelfth century.[268] They became increasingly popular across Britain through the fourteenth century, e.g. at Rochester and Bodiam Castle, Sussex, and became a hallmark of the fifteenth century,[269] both in new foundations and as additions to pre-existing enceintes, as at Coity, Glamorgan, where they may belong to a post-Glyndŵr rebuild.[270]

So the Square Tower may also belong to the fifteenth century. Its facework, while twentieth-century, apparently replicates the original, and is in the same Old Red Sandstone that predominates in the gatehouse, while very similar spiral stair squinches are present in both. Moreover the second, similar square tower, which has now gone but is shown by Speed on the west curtain south of the gatehouse (Figure 112), may have been part of a necessary rebuild of the west curtain after Glyndŵr damage, perhaps also primarily as a buttress.

Later work, 1425–c.1550

By the second quarter of the fifteenth century, Carmarthen Castle was both crowded with buildings and fully developed as a centre of government, and its later structural history is mainly one of repair. The changing political situation in Wales is reflected in the concentration of expenditure on its administrative buildings and official residences. Although its strategic value was still recognised during the Wars of the Roses, there is no record of any spending on defences during this period. A 'gunner' was in the King's service at Carmarthen Castle in 1540, while what was thought to be a 'platform for two or three guns' was apparently revealed within the shell-wall in 1913 (see Chapter 3). However, the observation may relate to the underlying medieval shell-wall where it houses the mural stair, on the west side of the motte, rather than thickening for artillery.

Work at the castle appears mainly to have been confined to existing buildings. Although over £214 was spent between 1425 and 1465, it was mainly on repairs, of which over £97 went towards the troublesome southern curtain of the outer ward, and the postern tower. Subsequent annual expenditure was, until the 1480s, limited to very small sums totalling only £76 (see Appendix).

By the later Middle Ages the Crown had, by various means, acquired more castles than it could reasonably maintain, and many were allowed to slip gradually into decay.[271] The evidence suggests that, by the last decade of the fifteenth century, only Carmarthen's administrative buildings, and its gaol cells, were in regular occupation and properly maintained. Rhys ap Thomas rebuilt part of the Chamberlain's Mansion in 1488–9 at a cost of over £194[272] – a substantial sum – but there appears to have been no corresponding expenditure on the Justiciar's Mansion. Sixteenth-century accounts are limited to just three bouts of spending, totalling just over £46.[273] Nevertheless, according to Leland, the castle in *c.*1534 was 'very fair and double walled',[274] suggesting that it was in reasonable repair and that both baileys were still in active use.

SOCIAL ORGANISATION: THE CASTLE AS A RESIDENCE

Carmarthen, like all castles, was designed to accommodate the seignurial household of a lord and retainers. Whilst it was not a private baronial residence, we have seen that it housed Crown officials of various ranks, on appointments of varying length and with varying degrees of occupancy. Only one household – that of the custodian – is suggested until the 1280s. Subsequently, however, there was a rapid increase in the castle population and the number of resident households rose to three – those of the justiciar, chamberlain and constable, and/or their deputies. This meant a triplication of all the main domestic buildings – three halls, three kitchens etc. – while the king reserved a set of apartments for state use.[275] The supply and provisioning of these households are discussed in Chapter 2.

There is little record of the composition of the household(s), or of the domestic infrastructure generally, during the first 200 years. However, they will, as in all seignurial establishments, have followed a strict social hierarchy, were predominantly male and, in Crown castles particularly, did not include wives.[276] While the resident households may not initially have been large, retainers like the porter, watchmen, pages, grooms – and, for example, the chaplain – will have been permanent occupants from the first, in addition to the domestic staff in the kitchens, bakehouse etc. A *domestic* steward may be implied (as opposed to manorial steward; see Chapter 2), but is absent from the sources. These retainers will have been accompanied by a resident clerical staff – the pre-Edwardian custodians were *de facto* sheriffs, holding the courts of the lordship. And all seignurial households were essentially military institutions, with at least some armed retainers who constituted, in effect, a small permanent 'garrison', as distinct from the garrisons proper who were in the king's service for specific periods of duty (see below).[277] There is no record of any formal 'castle-guard' tenure at Carmarthen, and no associated castle-guard fees. Moreover, the military service owed by the tenants of the Welsh County, and of the Lord of St Clears, was only obliged to be rendered in the field, and during time of war,[278] rather than at the castle, in time of peace.

In addition to its resident community, Carmarthen Castle drew in a large number of visitors. A stream of tenants, bailiffs and litigants passed through its gates, to attend the monthly courts, accompanied by the regular traffic of messengers, artisans, tradesmen and suppliers. Less can be said with any certainty about the household, the domestic and military arrangements, and the visitors, during periods of Welsh rule.

Households, halls and lodgings

A range of domestic buildings – hall(s), kitchen(s), chapel and stable etc. – may be assumed from the first. However, it is not necessarily clear how they functioned during the twelfth and early thirteenth centuries. The Great Hall, for instance, may have been purely ceremonial and/or administrative,[279] the custodian's household possibly occupying a second, smaller hall elsewhere within the castle – perhaps over the gatehouse, like the later constable's lodging.[280]

Something like this appears to have obtained after 1241, at least, when the castle was equipped with a suite of royal lodgings – the King's Hall, chamber and tower. They are a mark of Henry III's kingship, paralleled by similar works elsewhere in England and Wales which reveal his personal tastes and a keen appreciation of the symbols of prestige and authority.[281] Its name suggests that the King's Hall was indeed primarily ceremonial, used for great occasions, and as accommodation for the king's retinue should he visit. The King's Chamber may have been a private apartment for the king; alternatively, it was perhaps an audience chamber, while the King's Tower may have housed the apartments as at London's Wakefield Tower, from the 1220–1230s,[282] and the later Lord's Tower at the marcher Kidwelly Castle.[283]

As we have seen, further high-status buildings, ceremonial and domestic, were added. A chamber for the queen was built, and accommodation for the royal entourage was further upgraded with the construction of the Knight's Chamber. It appears to be the 'hall where the great lords . . . usually stay', mentioned in 1321;[284] these 'great lords' may have included other important guests, such as those local lords – of St Clears, Laugharne etc. – who, as tenants-in-chief, were obliged to attend the county court.

The later households

The King's Hall may have remained primarily non-residential. The households of the post-Edwardian justiciars and chamberlains – or, more normally, their deputies[285] – will have occupied the halls, chambers and offices within their respective 'mansions', both of which were, like the constable's lodging, equipped with their own kitchens. Until 1341, the sheriff was appointed by the justiciar and was included in his household,[286] but afterwards became the king's appointment and perhaps represented a fourth household, although his diminished prestige suggests no more than a few retainers.

In addition to a growing staff to serve in the rising number of households, the clerical staff increased with the multiplication of the courts after 1300. The exchequer, as both treasury and chancery, soon acquired a large secretariat under the chamberlain.[287] The justiciar's household also came to include a number of additional junior posts, assisting the officials described in Chapter 2. They included the narrator, who assisted in the courts from c.1343 onwards,[288] while the post of King's Attorney had been established by 1389.[289] A Marshal of the Court had been appointed by the 1430s, along with the Clerk of the Petty Sessions.[290] The proclamator, also in place by the fifteenth century, assisted in running the courts.[291] Some of these officials, however, were shared with Cardigan (cf. the post-1536 judicial staff described in Chapter 5).[292]

The king's appointments, under the justiciar as his deputy, had by the fifteenth century also swollen to include a number of minor sinecures that were often awarded for military service. Even among these more junior posts we must be careful to distinguish between the office-holder, receiving the privileges that flowed from it – who was possibly an infrequent visitor to the castle, if at all – and the functionary assigned to carry out his duties. For instance, Aeneas Moyle, 'one of the king's bowmen', was granted custody of the king's stores at Carmarthen Castle as a reward for service in Scotland and France.[293] Similarly, the king's sergeant, Geoffrey Williams, 'Page of the Kitchen', was granted the office of chief carpenter, for life, in 1447,[294] while in 1449 the grooms of the king's cellar and chamber were jointly granted the office of Master Mason.[295] However, certain artisans could themselves be awarded long-term contracts and may therefore have been resident at the castle for their duration: a tiler, Adam Scot, was employed, if not continuously, on reroofing projects running from 1318 until the late 1330s,[296] receiving a stipend of 16s. per annum.

Lodgings

Their retainers lived in close attendance on the officials, eating in their respective halls and sleeping where they could, normally in the chambers where they worked.[297] However, the degree of privacy that increased with rank also increased with time, and by 1433 we find references to, for example, the 'Janitor's House' and the 'chamber of Jenkin Maredudd';[298] the Armourer, and his chamber (in the gatehouse?), have been mentioned above. And a chamber, adjoining the King's Chapel, had been allocated to the chaplain by the early fifteenth century.[299]

With these exceptions, there is, however, very little evidence in the sources for additional lodgings over and above those already discussed. Usage of the gatehouse towers and the King's Tower has been suggested above; of the other two original towers, the South-west Tower has features suggesting possible (if limited) domestic use, and it may be that the upper floors of the vanished inner ward north tower could serve as lodgings as and when the need arose. In other castles from the 1220–1230s, mural towers appear primarily to have housed guard chambers, for example Skenfrith and Grosmont, Monmouthshire,[300] and Manorbier.[301] By contrast, all three inner ward towers at Pevensey, from c.1246–54, are equipped with fireplaces and latrines,[302] while early thirteenth-century towers were later converted for domestic use at a number of castles, for example Grosmont and Usk.[303] Even when lacking such apparently basic features as fireplaces, latrines or windows, towers could however be used by more 'junior' staff, while occupation may not have been permanent; it might be, for example, an *ad hoc* response to royal visits or garrisoning requirements which, at Carmarthen, perhaps embraced the two outer ward towers and the outer gate.

The chamber over the Middle Gate mentioned above, and the two square towers added to the inner curtain, may have at least in part been a response to an increased demand for private lodgings in the later Middle Ages, cf. the towers in the outer ward at Pickering.[304] During the early fourteenth century, the South-west Tower was incorporated within the chamberlain's lodgings, and its upper floor(s) may have been used by one of his officers; there is no structural evidence that it fulfilled any other kind of domestic function within the complex, for example as part of the adjoining kitchen/bakehouse. Two towers are given personal names in the sources. 'Skidmore's Tower', which was, along with the 'Armourer's Tower', given gutters in 1409–10,[305] was clearly named after the constable at the time.[306] It almost certainly relates to the new gatehouse, within which he resided, and, as we have seen above, the 'armourer' occupied the same building. 'Greyndour's Tower', mentioned in 1424–32,[307] has not been identified, but its name would appear to be derived from Sir John de Greyndor. Constable of Aberystwyth Castle in 1409–10, Greyndor was prominent in Marcher government and employed after the Glyndŵr rebellion on roving commissions in south Wales,[308] which may have made him a frequent visitor to Carmarthen; the tower may represent his *ad hoc* lodgings.[309]

Zoning

A degree of social organisation, in a hierarchical use of space, is apparent in the physical zoning of the castle. The sources make it clear that the inner ward was, as customary, central to the social life of the castle – no domestic buildings can be positively located within the outer ward – and it appears that its southern half became defined as a 'prestige' core, primarily for state use. Henry III's apartments in the south-east corner were followed by other high-status buildings, mainly for royal use – the King's Chapel, the Knights' Chamber etc. – and we have seen that this half of the bailey was walled off to form a separate area also housing the Chamberlain's Mansion.[310]

It was suggested, however, that the Queen's Chamber occupied the northern half of the inner ward, possibly owing to lack of space, and/or deliberate siting away from the King's Hall and Chamber. The Justiciar's Mansion also lay in the northern half, in an apparent blurring of this division, but that this was also due to lack of space is clear from its location over the truncated motte and its infilled ditch. Zoning was clearly social rather than functional – the same service buildings were replicated in each of the three lodgings, and in the King's Hall complex.

We have also seen that the motte and shell-keep appear always to have been of relatively lowly status, as at many other castles. The buildings revealed inside the shell-keep, probably dating to the early fourteenth century, are of unknown function but, like the towers, represented potential space for accommodation as and when required.

Royal visits: the king's retinue

Suitable accommodation for the king and his extensive household, should he visit, would have been necessary from the first. A royal visit is recorded as early as 1116, when Henry I's son – presumably William 'Adelin' (born 1103) – received the royal lieutenant Gerald de Windsor at Carmarthen.[311] It is likely that Henry II stayed at the castle during his expedition to Deheubarth in 1163,[312] and on his way to Ireland in 1171,[313] while King John may also have stayed *en route* to and from Ireland in 1210.

Despite Henry III's expenditure on the domestic buildings, there is no record of any personal visit, but his son, Prince Edmund, was at Carmarthen Castle during the Welsh war of summer 1277, from where he sent a letter.[314] The first recorded visit by a reigning monarch was in 1284, when Edward I and Queen Eleanor stayed at Carmarthen Castle from 4–6 December[315] – it was tentatively suggested above that the Queen's Chamber may have been built in anticipation of the visit. Edward the Black Prince appears to have visited in 1365,[316] while Richard II stayed at the castle on two or three occasions. He may have been at Carmarthen in 1383 and 1394,[317] while the castle hosted both his entourage, and his army, in 1399 when he stayed at the castle on both legs of his ill-fated Irish campaign. His successor, Henry IV, led the recapture of the castle from Glyndŵr's supporters in September 1403, and stayed there with his army for five days.[318] Henry's son Prince Henry (later Henry V), was – as royal lieutenant in Wales – in charge of the garrison in 1406,[319] and was again at the castle in 1408.[320]

It is not always possible to reconstruct with any certainty the numbers involved, or the composition of the royal entourage. But, even without an accompanying army, it would be large. Wherever the king went, so did his court and government, with a large body of clerks, servants and armed retainers, and also many of the leading barons and great officers of state, each with his own household and clerks; Edward I's retinue could amount to nearly 400 people.[321] Even this pales beside Richard II's 1399 expeditionary force, which comprised at least 4,500 men.[322] While not all of them, clearly, can have been accommodated within Carmarthen Castle, they included a large household element and a number of leading magnates, who probably were. Among them were the Dukes of Aumerle, Exeter and Surrey, the Earls of Salisbury and Worcester, along with six bishops, a host of court chaplains and the staff of the Chapel Royal.[323] Richard's entourage had arrived at Carmarthen by 14 May, when Letters Close were sent from the castle,[324] and did not make the crossing from Milford Haven until 1 June,[325] so a lengthy stay – and a considerable strain on the infrastructure – is implied.[326]

By the early fourteenth century the castle presented a range of accommodation for the higher echelons of the royal entourage – the Knight's Chamber etc. – and there is no reference to the addition of any further high-status lodgings. The remainder of the retinue clearly also made good with the existing accommodation.

Garrisons

While details of numbers and composition are sparse it is clear that, unlike the campaigning armies mentioned above, the standing garrisons at Carmarthen Castle were generally small – in common with other British castles, figures of between twenty and a hundred men are normally given in the sources.[327] In 1226, thirty sergeants and ten crossbowmen were garrisoned at Carmarthen and Cardigan Castles,[328] at that time serving as bases against the threat posed by Llywelyn ap Iorwerth. A garrison was maintained at Carmarthen against Llywelyn in 1231[329] and 1234,[330] and at both castles throughout the uncertainties of 1245–6,[331] but no figures are given. In January 1277, the castle was again garrisoned during the opening stage of the Welsh wars. A larger force, it included forty-seven knights and sixty-six esquires for the customary forty days' knight service; among the knights were a number of leading magnates such as William FitzWarin and John de Beauchamp, the newly appointed constable.[332] Carmarthen was garrisoned several times during the late fourteenth century, in response to the French threat, in similar numbers as before – in 1370, it included ten archers,[333] implying a corresponding number of men-at-arms, and twenty-four bowmen spent a month at the castle in the summer of 1385.[334]

Garrisons during the Glyndŵr rebellion were generally larger. Carmarthen Castle was the base for all armies operating in south Wales and was kept in a state of readiness. Four lords, 17 knights, 91 men-at-arms, 453 archers, and 16 *scutifers* (troopers) were maintained at the castle during 1401,[335] representing an army for mounting offensive operations in the field rather than a purely defensive force.[336] In September 1402 the justiciar, Richard de Grey, was ordered to muster an even larger host of 120 men-at-arms and 600 archers.[337] However, we have seen in Chapter 2 that Henry IV's garrison strategy ultimately failed and the surrounding country was never fully controlled. In September 1403 the king left a force of 120 men-at-arms and 500 archers at the castle, along with spies and scouts, under John Beaufort, Earl of Somerset.[338] Also at the castle were a number of high-ranking nobles including the bishop of Bath and Wells and his retinue, the justiciar Richard de Grey, Thomas Beaufort and Thomas Chaucer (son of Geoffrey Chaucer). The Duke of York subsequently took charge, with the hugely increased force of 250 men-at-arms and 780 archers,[339] while the sheriffs of Somerset, Dorset and Devon were each instructed to send twenty men-at-arms and fifty archers for three months' service.[340] Nevertheless, this figure had dropped to 91 men-at-arms and 240 archers by June 1404.[341] In April 1405 Sir Thomas Beaufort, half-brother of the king, was provided with 120 men-at-arms and 600 archers for a year's garrison duty.[342]

A garrison was maintained at Carmarthen for some time after the rebellion, twenty men-at-arms and forty archers being recorded in 1406.[343] Two men-at-arms and eight bowmen were 'keeping the castle' in 1409–10,[344] while twelve bowmen served, for 132 days, during the following year.[345] Details of garrisons during the Wars of the Roses are sparse, but large garrisons are recorded in 1461–2, with eighty-four 'soldiers' present in October 1461, fifty-eight in November, and thirty-four in early 1462.[346]

Discussing the castle in general, Norman Pounds asked where a garrison knight slept while serving, who was responsible for feeding him, and whether he in any way helped to maintain the castle in a serviceable condition; his own reply was that there were 'no clear answers'.[347] However, the early garrisons at Carmarthen, raised by feudal service, were small, and were both organised and accommodated within the castle according to seignurial household; the concept of segregated, 'barrack'-style quarters for lower ranks had no meaning in medieval society.[348] The existing lodgings may therefore have sufficed. While there was a move towards professional, paid soldiers during the later Middle Ages, the tenurial bond persisted[349] and the household remained the basic unit of campaign.

But the large, offensive field garrisons of the early fifteenth century, like the visiting royal retinues and armies, clearly presented a substantial logistical problem. A view commonly held in the past was that castle outer wards represented defended bases in which these large hosts could camp. Archaeological excavation and geophysical survey have modified this view, demonstrating that the outer wards at many castles could be just as congested with buildings as their inner wards. At White Castle, for example, the large outer ward was suggested to be just such a defended camp,[350] but recent work has shown that it was occupied by a large barn and a number of further buildings, with little empty space.[351] The sources suggest that the outer ward at Carmarthen was similarly developed and Richard II's armies, for example, presumably had to camp out on the demesne lands. Garrisons, by the early fifteenth century, were expected to defend the walled town as well as the castle, and it is possible that some were lodged among the burgesses, as in the seventeenth-century Civil Wars.[352]

Sources of provisions for the extended castle population, when garrisoned, are discussed in Chapter 2, where the difficulties of supply while under siege are illustrated by the use of the king's galley during the siege of 1233.

NOTES

1   J. R. Daniel-Tyssen (ed.), *Royal Charters and Historic Documents relating to the Town and County of Carmarthen* (Carmarthen: William Spurrell, 1878), pp. 45–50.

2   See F. Green (ed.), 'Carmarthen Castle: A Collection of Historical Documents relating to Carmarthen Castle from the Earliest Times to the Close of the Reign of Henry VIII', *WWHR*, 4 (1914), 1–71.

3   Also see L. Austin, C. Hill, H. James, T. James and P. Poucher, 'Carmarthen historic town survey: understanding and protecting the archaeology of Wales' oldest town' (unpublished DAT report, 2005), 15.

4   D. F. Renn, 'Mottes: A Classification', *Antiquity*, 33 (1959), 106–12.

5   The overall area, including the ditch, is 0.4 hectares.

6   CRO, Cawdor 103/8056, schedule of leases in Co. Borough of Carmarthen (*c.*1750), 180.

7   Daniel-Tyssen, *Royal Charters*, p. 45.

8   D. J. C. King, 'Carmarthen Castle', in unpublished field notebooks held in the Society of Antiquaries Library, Burlington House, Piccadilly, 1 (1949), 19.

9   J. K. Knight, 'Excavations at Montgomery Castle, Part I', *Archaeologia Cambrensis*, 142 (1992), 111–12, 133.

10   D. J. C. King, *The Castle in England and Wales* (London: Croom Helm, 1988), p. 78.

11   TNA: PRO E 163/4/42, Survey of Carmarthen Castle (1343).

12   Ibid.

13   F. Green (ed.), 'Carmarthen Castle: A Collection of Historical Documents relating to Carmarthen Castle from the Earliest Times to the close of the Reign of Henry VIII', *WWHR*, 3 (1913), 61, from BL Harl. Roll 7198, wrongly dated therein to 1340 (Stephen Priestley, pers. comm.); see Appendix.

14   In 1343, '6 rods in length . . . of walling between the Postern tower and the great hall'
(TNA: PRO E 163/4/42); in 1464–5 – 'the wall of the said castle . . . between the chapel and the gate there called the Postern' (Green, 'Carmarthen Castle' 4, 56). I argue further on that both hall and chapel were located in the south-east corner of the inner ward.

15   TNA: PRO E 163/4/42.

16   Green, 'Carmarthen Castle' 3, 57; 'Carmarthen Castle' 4, 46.

17   RCAHMW, *Inventory of Ancient Monuments*, V: *County of Carmarthen* (London: HMSO, 1917), p. 250.

18   'Mansion' was the term chosen by Francis Green when translating the records of their construction (Green, 'Carmarthen Castle' 3 and 4, *passim*). It is significant that he did not choose 'house' or 'lodging', both of which are used elsewhere in his text. I have therefore retained his terminology.

19   Green, 'Carmarthen Castle' 3, 62.

20   T. Jones (ed.), *Brut y Tywysogyon: Red Book of Hergest Version* (Cardiff: UWP, 1955), pp. 88–9.

21   D. J. C. King, *Castellarium Anglicanum* (New York: Kraus International, 1983), p. 53.

22   The bailey at St Clears has been obscured by modern dumping, but is shown in its original form in a plan of *c.*1907 (M. H. Jones, 'Report of the First Field Day', *TCASFC*, 2 (1907), 149 and Plate 3, opp. 163).

23   Jones, *Brut Red Book*, pp. 88–9.

24   J. C. Davies (ed.), *Episcopal Acts relating to the Welsh Dioceses 1066–1272*, 1 (Cardiff: Historical Society of the Church in Wales, 1946), p. 283; see Appendix for dating.

25   R. Avent, 'The early development of three coastal castles', in H. James (ed.), *Sir Gâr: Studies in Carmarthenshire History* (Carmarthen: CAS, 1991), pp. 167–88; R. Avent, *Laugharne Castle* (Cardiff: Cadw, 1995), p. 6.

26   J. Goodall, *Richmond Castle/Easby Abbey* (London: English Heritage, 2001), pp. 3–5.

27 J. Oxley (ed.), *Excavations at Southampton Castle* (Stroud: Alan Sutton/ Southampton City Museums, 1986), pp. 114–17.

28 B. L. Giggins, 'Northampton's Forgotten Castle', *Castle Studies Group Bulletin*, 18 (2005), 185–7.

29 J. R. Kenyon, *Kidwelly Castle* (Cardiff: Cadw, 2007), p. 6.

30 H. M. Colvin (ed.), *A History of the King's Works*, 2: *The Middle Ages* (London: HMSO, 1963), p. 808.

31 Terry James suggested instead that Spilman Street originated as a route leading to the bridge, on the evidence that Speed shows a possible gateway, through the later town wall, between Castle Hill and the bridge (T. James, *Carmarthen: An Archaeological and Topographical Survey*, CAS Monograph 2 (Carmarthen, 1980), p. 31). However, no route-way is shown by Speed between Spilman Street and the bridge (Figure 112).

32 J. K. Knight and A. Johnson (eds), *Usk Castle, Priory and Town* (Almeley: Logaston, 2008), p. 57.

33 R. Turner and A. Johnson (eds), *Chepstow Castle; its History and Buildings* (Almeley: Logaston, 2006), p. 20. White Castle, Monmouthshire, a rural site, was also turned round and given a new outer ward – this time under the Crown, 1239–66 – and again the old outer ward or hornwork was retained (J. K. Knight, *The Three Castles: Grosmont Castle/ Skenfrith Castle/White Castle* (Cardiff: Cadw, 2009), p. 12).

34 However, the small crescentic enclosure at Ammanford, which was perhaps a Welsh foundation, may have represented the bailey itself (R. Turvey, 'The Defences of Twelfth-century Deheubarth and the Castle Strategy of the Lord Rhys', *Archaeologia Cambrensis*, 144 (1997), 108).

35 King, *Castellarium Anglicanum*, p. 56; C. J. Spurgeon, 'Llandovery Castle' (unpublished note in NMR record file (NPRN 92751), RCAHMW, Aberystwyth, 1980).

36 S. E. Rigold, *Totnes Castle* (London: HMSO; 1975), p. 6. In the text it is described as 'about 15ft across' (i.e. 4.6 m) but on the plan it appears to be rather larger, at *c*.6 m.

37 P. A. Barker and R. Higham, *Hen Domen, Montgomery: A Timber Castle on the English–Welsh Border: Excavations 1960–1988: A Summary Report* (London: Royal Archaeological Institute, 1988), pp. 8–11.

38 Colvin, *King's Works*, p. 77; C. Caple, *Excavations at Dryslwyn Castle 1980–95*, SMA Monograph 26 (London, 2007), p. 70; S. E. Rees and C. Caple, *Dinefwr Castle/Dryslwyn Castle* (Cardiff: Cadw, 2007), pp. 10–13.

39 C. Caple, 'Nevern Castle: Searching for the First Masonry Castle in Wales', *Medieval Archaeology*, 55 (2011), 330, 332.

40 J. Goodall, *The English Castle 1066-1650* (New Haven and London: Yale University Press, 2011), p. 108; King, *Castle in England and Wales*, p. 64 *et al.*

41 D. F. Renn, *Norman Castles in Britain* (London: John Baker, 1973), p. 179.

42 D. M. Robinson, *Tretower Court and Castle* (Cardiff: Cadw, 2010), pp. 1–2.

43 A. Saunders, *Excavations at Launceston Castle, Cornwall*, SMA Monograph 24 (London, 2006), p. 254.

44 Cf. the similar structure on the motte at Baile Hill, York, interpreted either as the base of a tower or a well (J. R. Kenyon, *Medieval Fortifications* (Leicester University Press, 1990), pp. 15, 17).

45 M. W. Thompson, *Farnham Castle Keep* (London: HMSO, 1961), p. 17; Sussex Archaeological Society, 'Lewes Castle and Brack Mount', *Castle Studies Group Bulletin,* 18 (2005), 163–5.

46 J. Williams ab Ithel (ed.), *Annales Cambriae*, Rolls Series (London: Longman, Green, Longman and Roberts, 1860), p. 57.

47 TNA: PRO E 163/4/42.

48 David Cathcart King argued that the two buttresses on the east side represented a truncated turret (D. J. C. King, 'Carmarthen Castle', in unpublished field notebooks held in the Society of Antiquaries of London Library, Burlington House, Piccadilly, 2 (1950), 53), but excavation confirmed that they were new in the nineteenth century, and the turret suggested by the 1786 map lies a little further south. He also claimed to have seen the traces of a further turret at the junction with the west curtain wall (King, 'Carmarthen Castle' 1, 20), where there is neither physical, pictorial nor map evidence for such a feature.

49 Green, 'Carmarthen Castle' 3, 61 (wrongly dated to 1340).

50 King, *Castellarium Anglicanum*, p. 59; Jones, 'Report of the First Field Day', 149.

51 R. Turner, *Wiston Castle* (Cardiff: Cadw, 1996), p. 5; Rigold, *Totnes Castle*, p. 6; Goodall, *English Castle*, pp. 236–9.

52 Renn, *Norman Castles*, p. 107. The surviving Berkeley turrets however face the bailey interior rather than the exterior, as at Carmarthen. The exterior features, in characteristic twelfth-century fashion, regular pilaster strips, of which there is no evidence at Carmarthen (where, however, the original facework lies beneath various rebuilds).

53 W. St C. Baddeley, 'Berkeley Castle', *Transactions of the Bristol and Gloucestershire Archaeological Society*, 48 (1926), 136; Goodall, *English Castle*, p. 129.

54 The Lord of Berkeley, Robert FitzHarding, had been a merchant in Bristol, which had close contacts with Carmarthen throughout the Middle Ages.

55 Colvin, *King's Works*, pp. 561, 776 n. 6.

56 Ibid., p. 574.

57 Goodall, *English Castle*, p. 177. Cf. the castles of Earl Richard of Cornwall (ibid., pp. 236–9).

58 Ibid., p. 213; Colvin, *King's Works*, pp. 293–6 *et al*.

59 Turner, *Wiston Castle*, p. 5.

60 J. K. Knight, 'The road to Harlech: aspects of some early thirteenth-century Welsh castles', in J. R. Kenyon and R. Avent (eds), *Castles in Wales and the Marches: Essays in Honour of D. J. Cathcart King* (Cardiff: UWP, 1987), p. 79.

61 The towers on the shell-wall at Lewes, Sussex, for instance, are secondary additions of *c*.1202 (Goodall, *English Castle*, p. 183).

62 T. Jones (ed.), *Brut y Tywysogyon: Peniarth MS. 20 Version* (Cardiff: UWP, 1952), p. 91.

63 Ibid., p. 99.

64 T. James, *Carmarthen Survey*, p. 35; King, *Castle in England and Wales*, p. 109 *et al*.

65 Jones, *Brut Pen. 20*, p. 100.

66 King, *Castellarium Anglicanum*, p. 54 n. 14; King, *Castle in England and Wales*, p. 109 n. 5.

67 Knight, 'Excavations at Montgomery Castle', 100.

68 In 1233 the 'good men of [New] Carmarthen' were granted murage 'in aid of enclosing their town' (*CCR*, Hen. III 2, 1231–1234 (London, 1908), p. 199), while a mill had been built 'without the walls of Carmarthen' (*CChR* 1, Hen. III 1226–1257 (London, 1903), p. 182). While this may refer to pre-existing earth-and-timber defences, it is more likely that the masonry walls were under construction.

69 Jones, *Brut Pen. 20*, p. 103.

70 The 'king's works' were the royal masons, who developed an architectural style which grew steadily in importance throughout the thirteenth century (Goodall, *English Castle*, p. 198).

71 Colvin, *King's Works*, p. 590.

72 According to Alcwyn Evans, writing in 1875, the 1275 inquisition mentions a 'western tower' south of the gatehouse (see H. S. Holmes, 'Carmarthen Castle', *TCASFC*, 3 (1908), 21). However, Daniel-Tyssen gave it as 'western *corner*' in both his Latin transcription and English translation (Daniel-Tyssen, *Royal Charters*, p. 45). See Appendix.

73 Goodall, *English Castle*, pp. 171, 173.

74 Ibid., pp. 173, 176–7.

75 Ibid., pp. 190–1; E. Impey and G. Parnell, *The Tower of London: The Official Illustrated History* (London/New York: Merrell, 2011), p. 29.

76 A D-shaped tower at Bramber Castle, Sussex, probably from the 1260s, has deep spurred bases (Goodall, *English Castle*, p. 184). Spurs were also used in fourteenth-century work at Alnwick and Kenilworth (ibid., pp. 242, 248, 344). All three castles were baronial.

77 Where the spurs may also be a response to local fashion; the entire gatehouse shows a mixture of 'royal' and 'local' detail (ibid. p. 236).

78 Impey and Parnell, *Tower of London*, pp. 29–30.

79 K. Murphy and C. O'Mahoney, 'Excavation and Survey at Cardigan Castle', *Ceredigion*, 10/2 (1985), 194–7.

80 As it is in Colvin, *King's Works*, p. 590; King, *Castle in England and Wales*, p. 122 *et al.*

81 Colvin, *King's Works*, p. 590; see also R. A. Griffiths, 'The Making of Medieval Cardigan', *Ceredigion*, 11/2 (1990), 109.

82 King, *Castellarium Anglicanum*, p. 45 and n. 23.

83 King, *Castle in England and Wales*, p. 122.

84 T. Jones (ed.), *Brenhinedd y Saesson, or The Kings of the Saxons* (Cardiff: UWP, 1971), p. 233. See Jones, *Brut Pen. 20*, p. 105, Jones, *Brut Red Book*, p. 237 and Williams ab Ithel, *Annales*, p. 83, for very similar entries.

85 R. Turner, 'The upper barbican', in Turner and Johnson, *Chepstow Castle*, pp. 113–18.

86 It is possible that the town wall was instead levelled here to allow the tower to be inserted.

87 J. Goodall, *Pevensey Castle* (London: English Heritage, 1999), pp. 7–8. The section housing the stair is now butted by the curtain wall of *c.*1250.

88 D. F. Renn, 'An Angevin Gatehouse at Skipton Castle', *Château Gaillard*, 7 (1975), p. 179.

89 J. Clark, *Helmsley Castle* (London: English Heritage, 2004), p. 27.

90 Goodall, *English Castle*, pp. 156, 159.

91 Ibid., pp. 205–6.

92 Knight, 'Road to Harlech', p. 82.

93 J. B. Hilling, *Cilgerran Castle/St Dogmaels Abbey* (Cardiff: Cadw, 1992), pp. 13–14, 19.

94 Knight, 'Excavations at Montgomery Castle', 100, 129.

95 Turner, 'Upper barbican', pp. 113–18; Hilling, *Cilgerran Castle/St Dogmaels Abbey*, pp. 2, 21.

96 Goodall, *English Castle*, pp. 162–4.

97 Ibid., p. 227 *et al.*

98 Murphy and O'Mahoney, 'Cardigan Castle', 196.

99 Goodall, *Pevensey Castle*, pp. 7–8.

100 N. D. Ludlow, 'Pembroke Castle and Town Walls', *Fortress*, 8 (1991), 27–8.

101 Avent, *Laugharne Castle*, pp. 34, 36; King, *Castle in England and Wales*, p. 122 n. 26; Goodall, *English Castle*, pp. 162–4.

102 The Cardigan tower is similarly truncated but may only have comprised three storeys.

103 *CLR* Hen. III, 3, 1245–1251 (London, 1937), pp. 134–5.

104 L. Butler, *Pickering Castle* (London: English Heritage, 1993), p. 5.

105 This platform was occupied by a large building, labelled 'Smith's Shop', which is shown against the east face of the wall on all maps from 1786 through to the 1860s.

106 Goodall, *English Castle*, p. 191.

107 Begun 1223–32, under Hubert de Burgh (L. Butler and J. K. Knight, *Dolforwyn Castle/ Montgomery Castle* (Cardiff: Cadw, 2004), pp. 45–7).

108 Clark, *Helmsley Castle*, p. 12.

109 Ibid.

110 The original drawing for the print is equally vague (Carmarthenshire Museums Service, CAASG 1975/0037).

111 *CLR* Hen. III, 5, 1260–1267 (London, 1961), p. 40.

112   Green, 'Carmarthen Castle' 3, 61 (wrongly dated to 1340).

113   R. Avent, 'William Marshal's castle at Chepstow and its place in military architecture', in Turner and Johnson, *Chepstow Castle*, pp. 86–7.

114   Clark, *Helmsley Castle*, p. 21; Goodall, *Pevensey Castle*, pp. 7–8; Renn, 'Skipton Castle', 173–8.

115   R. Liddiard, and R. McGuicken, *Beeston Castle* (London: English Heritage, 2007), p. 13.

116   Hilling, *Cilgerran Castle/St Dogmaels Abbey*, pp. 12–14; Knight, 'Road to Harlech', 81–4.

117   Knight, 'Excavations at Montgomery Castle', 124–9.

118   *CLR* Hen. III, 1, 1226–1240 (London, 1916), p. 17.

119   Butler and Knight, *Dolforwyn Castle/Montgomery Castle*, p. 41.

120   Liddiard and McGuicken, *Beeston Castle*, p. 11; Kenyon, *Medieval Fortifications*, p. 92.

121   *CLR*, Hen. III, 3, 1245–1251, pp. 303–4; *CLR* Hen. III, 4, 1251–1260 (London, 1959), p. 43. NB: in Colvin, *King's Works*, p. 601, the 'Chamber' is incorrectly identified as the chapel, and the 'Tower' is regarded as the shell-keep.

122   J. D. K. Lloyd and J. K. Knight, *Montgomery Castle* (Cardiff: HMSO, 1981), pp. 10, 21; also see Butler and Knight, *Dolforwyn Castle/Montgomery Castle*, pp. 46–7. Neither campaign by any means approached the cost of, for example, Henry III's magnificent aisled hall at Winchester Castle, upon which £800 was spent in 1222 alone, and which was still un-finished fourteen years later (Colvin, *King's Works*, pp. 858–9). Similarly, the Queen's Chamber at Marlborough cost £235 in 1244–5 (ibid., p. 736). However, these were two cas-tles upon which Henry III lavished particular attention.

123   *CLR* Hen. III, 5, 1260–1267, p. 40.

124   Saunders, *Launceston Castle*, pp. 256–7.

125   O. E. Craster, 'Skenfrith Castle: when was it built?', *Archaeologia Cambrensis*, 116 (1967), 133–58; Knight, *The Three Castles*, pp. 33–4.

126   Green, 'Carmarthen Castle' 3, 49. It may have been renamed 'great' or 'large' in the early fourteenth century to distinguish it from the new 'King's County Hall'.

127   TNA: PRO E 163/4/42.

128   Impey and Parnell, *Tower of London*, p. 26.

129   Kenyon, *Medieval Fortifications*, pp. 54–5.

130   Ibid.; D. Austin, *Acts of Perception: A Study of Barnard Castle in Teesdale*, 1, English Heritage/Architectural and Archaeological Society of Durham and Northumberland Research Report 6 (London: 2007), p. 257.

131   Green, 'Carmarthen Castle' 3, 58. The order and phrasing of the document precludes any confusion with the Chamberlain's Kitchen, which is also mentioned.

132   TNA: PRO E 159/61, Memoranda Roll 16 Edw. I (1287–8).

133   *CCcR*, 1277–1326 (London, 1912), p. 321.

134   E. Armitage, 'Carmarthen Castle', *TCASFC*, 3 (1908), 15.

135   Goodall, *English Castle*, p. 235

136   And no expenditure was recorded during Edward's tenure as Prince of Wales, 1254–65. Indeed, there were complaints that the castle was 'weakened and collapsing' (TNA: PRO SC 1/3/1, Letter to Henry III (n.d., *c*.1257–9)). This may have been protesting rather too much, by burgesses who were understandably feeling threatened, as the 1275 survey costed the necessary repairs at only £66 (Daniel-Tyssen, *Royal Charters*, p. 45). Nevertheless, there is no doubt that the vulnerable south curtain was a concern: it was in a 'ruinous condition and . . . partly fallen down' (ibid.), a condition that it would find itself in again during the following century. The west curtain too was described as ruinous between the gatehouse and the south-west corner, a possible result of its construction on the twelfth-century bank.

137 TNA: PRO E 372/159, Enrolled Account (1309–10).

138 Reproduced in Green, 'Carmarthen Castle' 3, 46–8.

139 Colvin, *King's Works*, pp. 337–54, 372–7.

140 Green, 'Carmarthen Castle' 3, 47.

141 R. A. Griffiths, *The Principality of Wales in the Later Middle Ages: The Structure and Personnel of Government*, 1: *South Wales 1277–1536* (Cardiff: UWP, 1972), p. 38 n. 19 (from Exchequer K. R., Various Acc. 487/27).

142 Green, 'Carmarthen Castle' 3, 57.

143 Knight, 'Excavations at Montgomery Castle', 148; Butler and Knight, *Dolforwyn Castle/Montgomery Castle*, p. 38.

144 TNA: PRO E 372/159.

145 English Heritage, *Restormel Castle* (London: English Heritage, 1996), p. 10.

146 Green, 'Carmarthen Castle' 3, 56, 58.

147 R. Turner, 'The upper bailey', in Turner and Johnson, *Chepstow Castle*, p. 80. However, as Turner points out, the Chepstow chamber may have been the 'Gloriette' of the same account, with a wider function, while such 'ladies chambers' are questioned by Goodall (*English Castle*, p. 28).

148 Ludlow, 'Pembroke Castle', 28 and n. 6.

149 TNA: PRO E 163/4/42.

150 Avent, 'William Marshal's castle at Chepstow', pp. 85–7.

151 Goodall, *English Castle*, p. 165.

152 Liddiard and McGuicken, *Beeston Castle*, p. 13; Knight, *The Three Castles*, pp. 11–12, 40–2.

153 First encountered in the de Clare castles at Tonbridge (*c*.1250) and Caerphilly, Glamorgan (*c*.1268–74), and also at Llansteffan Castle, probably from the 1260s (Goodall, *English Castle*, pp. 191–5). The form may have its origins in the king's works, influenced by Henry III's lost gatehouse at the Tower of London (ibid.).

154 Daniel-Tyssen, *Royal Charters*, p. 45.

155 Green, 'Carmarthen Castle' 3, 47.

156 Ibid., 63. However, the surviving first-floor chamber was traditionally, if erroneously, known as the 'Chamberlain's Hall', while the lane leading to the Great Gatehouse from Nott Square was formerly called 'Chamberlain's Lane' (C. Barnett, 'Carmarthen Castle: The Chamberlain's Hall', *TCASFC*, 26 (1936), 18).

157 Green, 'Carmarthen Castle' 3, 64.

158 Where the constable's kitchen lay on the first floor, below the constable's lodgings (Kenyon, *Kidwelly Castle*, p.30), suggesting that Carmarthen's arrangements may have persisted after its rebuild in 1409-11 (see below).

159 See, for example, Turner, 'Upper barbican', p. 117.

160 TNA: PRO SC 6/1220/10, Chamberlain's Account (1336); Green, 'Carmarthen Castle' 3, 57.

161 Green, 'Carmarthen Castle' 3, 61–2.

162 TNA: PRO E 163/4/42.

163 Butler, *Pickering Castle*, pp. 13–15. It is possible that the Carmarthen postern, which faces the Tywi, is the 'old Water-Gate' of an account from 1691 (NLW, MS 12358D, 'Records of the Corporate Borough of Carmarthen, 1590–1764' (transcribed by Alcwyn Evans, 1851–3), 113).

164 Green, 'Carmarthen Castle' 3, 57.

165 TNA: PRO SC 6/1221/9, Chamberlain's Account (1354–5).

166 Green, 'Carmarthen Castle' 3, 47.

167 One of the two masonry buildings, of late medieval date, in the outer ward at Kidwelly may be the 'great stable' of the sources (Kenyon, *Kidwelly Castle*, pp. 34–5). Both are large, around 20 m by 10 m.

168 Green, 'Carmarthen Castle' 3, 49–50.

169 The exchequer was also a chancery housing the kings' records for south-west Wales, for which a separate area was screened off in 1447 (Griffiths, *Principality*, p. 39).

170 *Cal. Inq. Misc.* 2, 1307–1349 (London, 1916), p. 19.

171 Green, 'Carmarthen Castle' 4, 65.

172   A. J. Taylor, *Caernarvon Castle and Town Walls* (London: HMSO, 1953), pp. 29–34. Also see A. J. Taylor, *Caernarfon Castle and Town Walls* (Cardiff: Cadw, 2008), p. 27.

173   Green, 'Carmarthen Castle' 3, 57.

174   TNA: PRO E 163/4/42.

175   Green, 'Carmarthen Castle' 3, 62.

176   TNA: PRO SC 6/1221/9.

177   TNA: PRO E 372/159.

178   Ibid.

179   Green, 'Carmarthen Castle' 4, 69 n. 2.

180   Ibid., 26. An account from 1452–3 mentions 'the entrance of the ward of the Justiciar and the King's Auditors', making it clear that the Justiciar's Mansion occupied its own discrete enclosure, and that the Auditor's Hall was also situated within it – and not, as might be expected, in the chamberlain's enclosure (ibid., 52).

181   TNA: PRO E 372/159.

182   Green, 'Carmarthen Castle' 3, 60. It was reserved for the trying of pleas, e.g. at the Great Sessions, Petty Sessions and County Courts (Griffiths 1972, 22 n. 24).

183   D. J. C. King, 'Pembroke Castle', *Archaeologia Cambrensis*, 127 (1978), 110.

184   Kenyon, *Kidwelly Castle*, p. 30.

185   Saunders, *Launceston Castle*, p. 256.

186   A. J. Taylor, *Monmouth Castle and Great Castle House* (London: HMSO, 1951), p. 17.

187   N. Fryde (ed.), *List of Welsh Entries in the Memoranda Rolls, 1282–1343* (Cardiff: UWP, 1974), p. 33.

188   For Aberystwyth Castle during this period, see Colvin, *King's Works*, pp. 299–308; for Cardigan, see ibid., pp. 590–1; for Dinefwr and Dryslwyn, see Rees and Caple, *Dinefwr Castle/ Dryslwyn Castle*.

189   TNA: PRO E 372/159.

190   Green, 'Carmarthen Castle' 3, 61 (wrongly dated to 1340).

191   Ibid., 63–4.

192   TNA: PRO SC 6/1221/9.

193   Green, 'Carmarthen Castle' 3, 55–60.

194   TNA: PRO E 163/4/42.

195   Green, 'Carmarthen Castle' 4, 22.

196   Ibid., 1.

197   Green, 'Carmarthen Castle' 4, 52.

198   Green, 'Carmarthen Castle' 3, 57.

199   Ibid.

200   C. Mahany, *Stamford Castle and Town*, South Lincolnshire Archaeology, 2 (Stamford, 1978), pp. 24–6.

201   See Goodall, *English Castle*, p. 233.

202   Butler, *Pickering Castle*, pp. 11–13. An enclosed yard also lay between internal buildings and the defences at Launceston during the twelfth century (Saunders, *Launceston Castle*, p. 109 and 254–5).

203   Knight, *The Three Castles*, p. 38.

204   J. Clark, *Clifford's Tower and the Castle of York* (London: English Heritage, 2010), p. 38.

205   There remains however the possibility that structure 121, demolished before the shell-wall was rebuilt, was the 'watch-tower' mentioned in 1321 (see above), suggesting a later date for the motte remodelling – perhaps as late as the early fifteenth century, when the new Justiciar's Hall was built?

206   Colvin, *King's Works*, p. 876.

207   C. Young, *Carisbrooke Castle* (London: English Heritage, 2003), p. 6; M. W. Thompson, *The Decline of the Castle* (Cambridge University Press, 1987), p. 105. The low status of many mottes is increasingly being recognised (King, *Castle in England and Wales*, pp. 64–5).

208   Heather and Terry James regarded this wall as a curtain, dividing an 'inner ward' to the north from an 'outer ward' to the south, the outer bailey itself being merely referred to as 'Castle Green' (Austin *et al.*, 'Carmarthen historic town survey', 15). However, it was clearly not a defensive wall, unlike the secondary dividing wall at e.g. Rochester Castle, Kent, which was built in 1230–1 across the large pre-existing bailey (Colvin, *King's Works*, p. 808).

209   Although, confusingly, the southern half of the east curtain is not shown.

210 Clark, *Helmsley Castle*, pp. 7–8.

211 Goodall, *Pevensey Castle*, p. 12; Butler, *Pickering Castle*, p. 9.

212 Davies, *Episcopal Acts*, p. 283; Daniel-Tyssen, *Royal Charters*, pp. 4–6. In 1355 it was alleged that the grant of the castle chapel to St Peter's mother-house, Carmarthen Priory, obliged the prior to supply a canon to celebrate divine service daily in the castle. This the prior denied, pointing out that it was annexed to St Peter's in the grant. He asserted that if any canon officiated at the castle it was because the prior had allowed him to, or he had done so at the express wish of the justiciar (J. E. Lloyd (ed.), *A History of Carmarthenshire*, 1 (London: London Carmarthenshire Society, 1935), p. 299).

213 TNA: PRO E 372/159. We are later told that a wall – i.e. the outer curtain – ran from the postern to the chapel (Green, 'Carmarthen Castle' 4, 56), confirming its location in this corner.

214 Again like Skenfrith Castle, where the chapel was built in 1244 to form an L-shape with de Burgh's hall block (Knight, *The Three Castles*, p. 33; also see Colvin, *King's Works*, p. 837).

215 T. Phillips (ed.), *Cartularium St Johannis Baptistae de Caermarthen* (Cheltenham: John Lowe, 1865), pp. 31–2.

216 Colvin, *King's Works*, p. 601. The painting, featuring SS Mary and John, cost 3s. 4d, along with a pax-board featuring the same saints (Green, 'Carmarthen Castle' 4, 30–1). Among the other fittings were a 'red cope with green orphreys, an amice, a gown with a maniple, a silver-gilded chalice and a similar paten, two pewter cups, an iron chandelier with two flowers for holding candles, an altar cover, a crucifix with the images of Holy Mary and St John the Evangelist in gold, and a sacring-bell with a new missal' (ibid.). Two 'stained cloths' for the altar were purchased in 1435–7, 'one above the altar with images of the crucifix, SS Mary and John, and the Apostles Peter and Paul, and the other below before the altar, with the images of Holy Mary, and SS Catherine, Margaret, Cythia and Appolos [SS Sytha and Apollonia, holy virgins?]' (ibid., 47).

217 Green, 'Carmarthen Castle' 3, 68.

218 Green, 'Carmarthen Castle' 4, 41. A 'cope, maniple, stole and complete apparel . . . and a chalice and missal' were purchased for the 'castle chapel' in 1384–5 (Green, 'Carmarthen Castle' 3, 65–6), as were a 'new chasuble with orphreys, and a stole maniple, and seven yards of Brabant linen for an alb' in 1430–2, when 5d was paid to Lleucu [Lucy], daughter of Ieuan ap Henry, 'for making the said vestments' (Green, 'Carmarthen Castle' 4, 38–9). The chapel's 'linen altarcloths, curtains and frontals, curtain-rings and a wax torch' are mentioned in 1433–5 (ibid., 45–6).

219 See e.g. J. and V. Lodwick, *The Story of Carmarthen* (Carmarthen: V. G. Lodwick and Sons Ltd, 1972), p. 19.

220 W. Spurrell, *Carmarthen and its Neighbourhood* (Carmarthen: Spurrell and Co., 1879), pp. 21–2 *et al*.

221 Antiquarian writers associated 'Prince Edward's Chapel' with an undercroft beneath No. 2 Nott Square. This building however lies 40 m west of the castle, on the opposite side of Nott Square. Moreover the Royal Commission, in 1917, stated that the undercroft – like the others in the vicinity – was a post-medieval domestic cellar (RCAHMW, *Inventory*, p. 260). Secondary accounts also mention a chapel for the knights and esquires (e.g. Lloyd, *History of Carmarthenshire*, p. 298), but any primary source for this is unknown to me.

222 Daniel-Tyssen, *Royal Charters*, pp. 37–40, in which it is clear that the King's Chapel is meant. In 1546 it was valued at £5 6s. 8d, of which the tithes constituted 10s. 8d, the remainder being the chaplain's stipend (ibid.). After its dissolution, the Court of Augmentations recorded that the ex-chaplain, John Molde, was still receiving his stipend of £4 16s. 0d per

annum, as a pension (ibid.; also see E. D. Jones (1934), 'Survey of South Wales Chantries, 1546', *Archaeologia Cambrensis*, 89 (1934), 140).

223 Green, 'Carmarthen Castle' 4, 36.

224 Green, 'Carmarthen Castle' 3, 71, in which it is clear that the gate stood between the inner and outer wards.

225 TNA: PRO E 159/92, Memoranda Roll 12 Edw. II (1318–19).

226 TNA: PRO E 163/4/42.

227 Green, 'Carmarthen Castle' 3, 61 (wrongly dated to 1340).

228 The phrasing is however ambiguous and it is possible that the enclosure was *internal*, referring perhaps to the yard in front of the King's Hall which, before the inner ward cross-wall was built, faced the Great Gatehouse.

229 Impey and Parnell, *Tower of London*, pp. 34–8.

230 J. Ashbee, *Goodrich Castle* (London: English Heritage, 2009), p. 5.

231 Ludlow, 'Pembroke Castle', 30.

232 Kenyon, *Medieval Fortifications*, p. 79.

233 The £100 cited by Colvin (*King's Works*, p. 601), appears to have represented only part of the expenditure on the gatehouse (see Green, 'Carmarthen Castle' 4, 16–17).

234 Colvin, *King's Works*, pp. 692–3.

235 Ibid., p. 813.

236 Thompson, *Decline of the Castle*, p. 96.

237 Green, 'Carmarthen Castle' 4, 17.

238 Ibid., 22, 69 n. 2.

239 Ibid., 23, 49.

240 The shared 'Justiciar and Chamberlain's stable' of an account of 1387–8 (Green, 'Carmarthen Castle' 3, 67) may refer to the main, thirteenth-century stable in the outer ward, which was possibly the 'old stable' mentioned in 1343 (TNA: PRO E 163/4/42).

241 Green, 'Carmarthen Castle' 4, 18.

242 Ibid., 19.

243 Ibid., 43, 49.

244 Ibid., 58.

245 Ibid., 17.

246 Kenyon, *Kidwelly Castle*, p. 26.

247 Ibid., pp. 15–17, 20, 30–1. Its design was altered during the later phases, but retaining elements from the original plan.

248 See David Cathcart King's comments, reproduced in Chapter 3.

249 Green, 'Carmarthen Castle' 3, 72.

250 Kenyon, *Kidwelly Castle*, p. 26; Stephen Priestley, pers. comm.

251 Goodall, *English Castle*, p. 343.

252 Ibid., p. 342.

253 R. Turner, *Lamphey Bishop's Palace/ Llawhaden Castle* (Cardiff: Cadw, 2000), p. 33.

254 Ibid., p. 32.

255 A new gatehouse was commenced at royal Monmouth Castle in the fifteenth century, but was not completed. Its form is not known with certainty (Taylor, *Monmouth Castle*, p. 13). Neither is it known whether the 'new hall and chamber' built for the constable at Cardigan, in 1410–11, occupied the gatehouse (see Colvin, *King's Works*, p. 591).

256 Green, 'Carmarthen Castle' 4, 17.

257 Ibid., 25.

258 Ibid., 34.

259 Ibid., 47.

260 Kenyon, *Kidwelly Castle*, p. 27. However, documentary sources also record a prison in the fifteenth-century gatehouse at Monmouth (Taylor, *Monmouth Castle*, p. 13).

261 Green, 'Carmarthen Castle' 4, 24.

262 Also see E. Armitage, 'Carmarthen Castle', *TCASFC*, 2 (1907), 197.

263 Impey and Parnell, *Tower of London*, pp. 34–6.

264 D. Bythell and K. Leyland, *Durham Castle: University College, Durham* (Norwich: University College Durham and Jarrold, 1992), p. i.

265 Green, 'Carmarthen Castle' 4, 26.

266 Ibid., 53.

267 Ibid., 28.

268 Goodall, *English Castle*, pp. 246–7.

269 Ibid.

270 J. R. Kenyon and C. J. Spurgeon, *Coity Castle/Ogmore Castle/Newcastle* (Cardiff: Cadw, 2001), pp. 16, 22–6.

271 Thompson, *Decline of the Castle*, p. 105.

272 Termed the 'new place', it lay on the 'south side' of the castle, so evidently used the existing Chamberlain's Mansion site (Green, 'Carmarthen Castle' 4, 57).

273 Ibid., 59, 71.

274 L. T. Smith (ed.), *The Itinerary in Wales of John Leland in or about the Years 1536–1539* (London: George Bell and Sons, 1906), p. 59.

275 During the later Middle Ages, when the offices were held in plurality, only the main household may have been represented. In the 1390s, for example, all three main posts – justiciar, chamberlain and constable – were held by Roger Mortimer, Earl of March (see Chapter 2), and all deputies would have been his appointments.

276 See C. M. Woolgar, *The Great Household in Late Medieval England* (New Haven and London: Yale University Press, 1999), pp. 18–19, 34–6; Goodall, *English Castle*, p. 21.

277 Woolgar, *Great Household*, pp. 34–6, 103–4; R. A. Brown, *English Castles* (London: Batsford, 1976), p. 185.

278 Daniel-Tyssen, *Royal Charters*, p. 47. And, though not 'castle-guard' as such, the thirteenth-century lords of Narberth were obliged, under the terms of their tenure, to come to Carmarthen's relief in time of siege or attack (H. Owen (ed.), *A Calendar of the Public Records Relating to Pembrokeshire*, 2 (London: Honourable Society of Cymmrodorion, 1914), p. 74).

279 See e.g. Kenyon, *Medieval Fortifications*, p. 97.

280 The excavated evidence suggests that no buildings of suitable status occupied the motte during this period, and indeed appear never to have done.

281 Henry III had a 'highly developed aesthetic sense which he was determined to gratify in a truly royal manner' (Colvin, *King's Works*, p. 94).

282 Impey and Parnell, *Tower of London*, p. 26.

283 Kenyon, *Kidwelly Castle*, p. 39. Alternatively, the tower may have provided service rooms to the King's Chamber, like the King's Tower at Conwy, from the 1280s (J. Ashbee, *Conwy Castle and Town Walls* (Cardiff: Cadw, 2007), pp. 34, 40–1).

284 Green, 'Carmarthen Castle' 3, 61 (wrongly dated to 1340).

285 With the possible exception of Rhys ap Thomas, who appears to have been personally resident and made the castle his main seat, spending his own money on the chamberlain's lodgings.

286 Lloyd, *History of Carmarthenshire*, p. 211.

287 A chest for the 'Record Rolls', ministers' accounts etc. was purchased for the 'Treasury', i.e. the exchequer, in 1413–14 (Green, 'Carmarthen Castle' 4, 18; see Appendix), and a second was acquired in 1443–5 (ibid., 44). This is clearly distinguished from the chest provided for the castle chapel, which was for keeping 'the ornaments of the said chapel' (ibid.), rather than the king's records as suggested by Griffiths (*Principality*, p. 39 and n. 22), from the same source.

288 Griffiths, *Principality*, p. 34.

289 W. Rees (ed.), *Calendar of Ancient Petitions relating to Wales* (Cardiff: UWP, 1975), p. 424.

290 *CPR*, Hen. VI 3, 1436–1441 (London, 1907), pp. 233, 400.

291 Griffiths, *Principality*, p. 34.

292 And as we have seen, it is possible that by the late medieval period, at least, not all staff were resident in the castle.

293 *CFR* 5, Edw. III, 1337–1347 (London, 1915), p. 155.

294 *CPR*, Hen. VI 5, 1446–1452 (London, 1909), p. 44.

295   Ibid., p. 246.

296   TNA: PRO SC 6/1219/9, Chamberlain's Account (1318–19); TNA: PRO E 101/683/54, Letter of Adam Scot, tiler (1336).

297   Goodall, *English Castle*, p. 23.

298   Green, 'Carmarthen Castle' 4, 40–1.

299   Ibid., 46; RCAHMW, *Inventory*, p. 250.

300   Knight, *The Three Castles*, pp. 21, 29.

301   D. J. C. King and J. C. Perks, 'Manorbier Castle, Pembrokeshire', *Archaeologia Cambrensis*, 119 (1970), 107–8.

302   Goodall, *Pevensey Castle*, pp. 11, 23.

303   Knight, *The Three Castles*, p. 21; Knight and Johnson, *Usk Castle*, pp. 69–70.

304   Butler, *Pickering Castle*, pp. 13–17.

305   Green, 'Carmarthen Castle' 4, 17. See Chapter 2 for Skidmore/Scudamore.

306   Cf. Pickering's 'Coleman Tower' (Butler, *Pickering Castle*, p. 7).

307   All we are told in the sources is that its roof was leaded in 1430–2 (Green, 'Carmarthen Castle' 4, 23, 34–5).

308   Griffiths, *Principality*, pp. 235–7.

309   The tower's construction may instead have been ordered by Greyndor, receiving his name accordingly; cf. 'Giffard's Tower', one of the gatehouses at Caerphilly, which was built on the orders of the royal administrator John Giffard (Renn, *Caerphilly Castle*, p. 33). If so, one of the square towers may be indicated.

310   A social distinction between the upper and lower halves of the bailey, separated by a hard boundary, is also suggested at Hen Domen, where the division may also have been a defensive line (R. Higham and P. Barker, *Timber Castles* (London: Batsford, 1992), p. 335).

311   Jones, *Brenhinedd*, p. 135; Jones, *Brut Pen. 20*, pp. 44–5.

312   Jones, *Brut Pen. 20*, p. 62.

313   Ibid., pp. 65–8. His meeting with the Lord Rhys however took place at Pembroke Castle, which had been temporarily seized from Earl Richard 'Strongbow' de Clare.

314   J. G. Edwards (ed.), *Calendar of Ancient Correspondence relating to Wales* (Cardiff: UWP, 1935), p. 158.

315   *CFR* I, Edw. I, 1272–1307 (London, 1911), p. 208 *et al.*

316   A letter from the prince, or his chief minister, was sent from Carmarthen on 25 September (M. C. B. Dawes (ed.), *Registers of Edward the Black Prince, 3: 1351–1365* (London: HMSO, 1932), p. 483).

317   A letter patent was dated 30 September 1383, at Carmarthen, 'with the king's seal which he uses in Wales' (*CPR*, Rich. II 3, 1385–1389 (London, 1900), p. 206). It appears however that Richard II was at Westminster around that date. The letter may therefore have been issued by Simon de Burley, who was justiciar and constable in 1383 (see Chapter 2) and entitled to use his seal. Carmarthen probably also hosted Richard's 1394 expeditionary force, which sailed from Milford Haven to Ireland in October of that year (N. Saul, *Richard II* (New Haven and London: Yale University Press, 1997), p. 279).

318   R. R. Davies, *The Revolt of Owain Glyn Dŵr* (OUP, 1995), p. 114.

319   Griffiths, *Principality*, p. 31.

320   Where he awarded a grant (Daniel-Tyssen, *Royal Charters*, pp. 28–9).

321   Ashbee, *Goodrich Castle*, p. 35.

322   Saul, *Richard II*, p. 289.

323   Ibid. While it is difficult to be sure of the exact size of Richard's army in 1394, it was exceptionally large and well equipped – perhaps 7,000–8,000 men (ibid., p. 279). At its core was a household contingent of 4,000–5,000, including the Earls of Rutland, Huntingdon (Chamberlain of the Household), Thomas Despenser, Thomas Percy (Steward of the Household) and William Scrope (Vice-chamberlain of the Household).

324   *CCR*, Rich. II 6, 1396–1399 (London, 1927), p. 502.

325   Saul, *Richard II*, p. 289.

326 Richard II's return visit, in July 1399, was in straitened circumstances, and with a much smaller retinue. It was at Carmarthen that he learnt of Bolingbroke's successes, and he fled at midnight, attended by only fifteen companions (ibid., p. 411).

327 These figures are normally restricted to the armed men – the knights, men-at-arms, crossbowmen and archers. Support staff such as smiths, porters and carpenters generally go unrecorded.

328 Green, 'Carmarthen Castle' 3, 32.

329 G. E. Evans, 'Carmarthen. Documents relating to the Town from the Earliest Times to the Close of the Reign of Henry VIII', *TCASFC*, 17 (1924), 62.

330 Green, 'Carmarthen Castle' 3, 37.

331 *CLR* Hen. III, 3, 1245–1251, pp. 7, 50.

332 Green, 'Carmarthen Castle' 3, 42–4.

333 Ibid., 64.

334 Ibid., 66.

335 Lloyd, *History of Carmarthenshire*, p. 303.

336 And it had been reduced to twenty men-at-arms and forty archers by the beginning of 1402 (H. Nicolas (ed.), *Proceedings and Ordinances of the Privy Council of England*, I: *1386–1410* (London: Record Commission/Eyre and Spottiswoode, 1834), p. 174).

337 Green, 'Carmarthen Castle' 4, 2–3.

338 Ibid., 4–6; Davies, *Glyn Dŵr*, p. 114.

339 Lloyd, *History of Carmarthenshire*, pp. 254–5.

340 Green, 'Carmarthen Castle' 4, 7.

341 Ibid., 9.

342 Ibid., 15; J. L. Kirby (ed.), *Calendar of Signet Letters of Henry IV and Henry V, 1399–1422* (London: HMSO, 1978), pp. 81–2.

343 Green, 'Carmarthen Castle' 3, 22.

344 Green, 'Carmarthen Castle' 4, 17.

345 Ibid. One man-at-arms and twelve bowmen were serving in 1413–14 (ibid., 18), in response to the threat posed by the Lollards under Sir John Oldcastle, a former royal favourite who had served at Carmarthen in 1407, during the Glyndŵr rebellion (Green, 'Carmarthen Castle' 3, 22).

346 Green, 'Carmarthen Castle' 4, 54.

347 N. J. G. Pounds, *The Medieval Castle in England and Wales: A Social and Political History* (Cambridge University Press, 1990), p. 49.

348 See Brown, *English Castles*, p. 186.

349 See e.g. King, *Castle in England and Wales*, pp. 192–3.

350 C. A. R. Radford, *White Castle* (London: HMSO, 1962), p. 16.

351 Knight, *The Three Castles*, p. 39. Nevertheless, some form of temporary accommodation for troops is still considered possible at White Castle: Knight suggests that a late thirteenth-century flanking tower, with a small lodging containing a fireplace and latrine, may have housed a quartermaster responsible for troops and supplies while they were occupying the outer ward (ibid.).

352 In 1403, for example, men-at-arms and archers were mustered for 'keeping the town and castle of Carmarthen' (Green, 'Carmarthen Castle' 4, 4), and troops from the West Country were in the king's service in 'the town and castle of Carmarthen' (ibid., 7).

CHAPTER FIVE

DIVISION, DEMOLITION AND DEVELOPMENT: THE POST-MEDIEVAL CASTLE

THE POST-MEDIEVAL history of the site begins with sixteenth-century decline, leading to its near-total abandonment as a residence and judicial centre, probably before the century was out, and its disposal by the Crown. This was followed by a period of military reuse during the Civil War and Commonwealth and, it is suggested, its deliberate slighting around the late 1650s. However, prisoners were kept at the castle throughout this period, after which its remains continued to be used as a gaol. The abandoned outer ward meanwhile was given over to domestic development. Some new gaol buildings are recorded in the 1770s, and in 1789–92 an entirely new gaol was built within the old site. This was largely removed to make way for a larger gaol, occupying the whole of the castle site, in 1868–72. This in turn was demolished in the late 1930s to make way for the present County Hall.

A considerable body of new research was undertaken, primarily focusing on the period before the commencement of Nash's gaol, in 1789, which had hitherto received little attention. Until the early seventeenth century, the castle remained within Crown administration and features in the Exchequer Accounts and Calendars of Patent Rolls, Letters and Papers, State Papers *(CSPD)* etc. and also, for example, the seventeenth-century Treasury Books,[1] while the late sixteenth-/early seventeenth-century administrative machinery was described in 1630.[2] Nevertheless, much county material, taking in the castle, has been lost, and records held by the Carmarthenshire Archive Service at CRO, for example, mainly relate to the borough. However, they include the important Cawdor collection of papers, many of which relate to the castle site and contain leases, and sometimes plans, from the early seventeenth century until the mid-nineteenth century. CRO also holds the sixteenth-/seventeenth-century borough Corporation Order Books, selected entries from which have been published;[3] a number were also transcribed in the nineteenth century as part of the extensive Alcwyn Evans MSS deposit at NLW.[4] Other records examined at the NLW include selected entries in the 'Gaol Files' or records of the Great Sessions.[5]

For the Civil War and interregnum, J. R. Phillips's *Memoirs of the Civil War in Wales* is still an important source and contains transcripts of contemporary correspondence, pamphlets etc.[6] The schedule of the 'Thomason Tracts'[7] – a collection of over 22,000 Civil War and Commonwealth pamphlets, papers, parliamentary reports, letters and newsletters – was examined, along with further contemporary literature including John Vicars's account of the conflict;[8] material relating to west Wales is, however, scant. Published parliamentary acts and ordinances for the period 1642–60 were examined,[9] along with the *Journals of the House of Commons* (*JHC*) for the same period.[10] Much useful discussion of Carmarthen's Civil War fortifications was published by Terry James, building on the work of Bryan O'Neil.[11] No private papers, diaries etc. relating to this period came to light.

The Cawdor papers (CRO) remain the most important source for the late seventeenth/eighteenth century. Others include the reformer John Howard's report on the pre-Nash gaol[12] (cf. James Neild's account of Nash's replacement[13]). Otherwise, there are few documentary sources for this period. Written descriptions had, in the main, to wait until the 'Age of the Travellers' of the late eighteenth and early nineteenth centuries, and relate to the Nash gaol rather than its predecessor. Earlier writers, such as Daniel Defoe and Thomas Dineley,[14] unfortunately tell us little about the form and condition of the site. However, a handful of map and picture sources exists. Speed's map of *c*.1610 was looked at in Chapter 4, along with Thomas Lewis's 1786 map of which there are two versions, showing separate property ownerships.[15] The two Buck prints, of 1740 and 1748 (Figures 126 and 127), are almost the only illustrations of the castle before the construction of Nash's gaol in 1789–92; the 1740 view from the south was slavishly copied by artists and engravers well into the early nineteenth century, and a host of these secondary versions exist in NLW and other collections.[16] Interestingly, no depictions of Carmarthen by Richard Wilson – otherwise prolific in west Wales – are known.[17] Although there are a number of nineteenth-century views of the quay, including the castle site (e.g. Figures 135–6 and 138), few pictures specifically feature Nash's gaol.[18]

The post-1792 gaol was only mentioned in passing, if at all, by contemporary travellers such as Nicholas Carlisle, Sir Richard Colt Hoare, Richard Fenton and Benjamin Heath Malkin;[19] Edward Donovan described it in brief, while, somewhat later on, Samuel Lewis accorded it a comprehensive entry in his *Topographical Dictionary*.[20] A detailed social history of the nineteenth-century gaol has recently been published by Richard Ireland,[21] who very kindly provided pre-publication proofs, while a short description of the Nash gaol – with a reconstructed plan – has been produced by Richard Suggett.[22] These sources were augmented by examination of further documents at CRO, including an extensive archive of plans of the gaol from the mid-/late nineteenth century,[23] and other map sources including John Wood's map of Carmarthen, from 1834,[24] and nineteenth-century OS maps, in addition to nineteenth-/early twentieth-century pictures and photographs of the gaol held by the Carmarthenshire Museums Service and the NMR.[25]

Transcripts of a number of primary and manuscript sources can be found within local antiquarian journals,[26] while further source material was collected and published by

Carmarthen's remembrancer, William Spurrell, in 1879.[27] Occasional reports from the gaol appeared in the *Carmarthen Journal* and other newspapers. Additional information was kindly provided by Charles Griffiths, curator of Dyfed-Powys Police Museum. Secondary sources were also examined for background material relating to the Cawdor (Golden Grove) estate, castle officials and lessees, and especially for comparisons with other sites.[28]

DECLINE: THE LATE SIXTEENTH/MID-SEVENTEENTH CENTURY

It is not known exactly how Carmarthen Castle was used after *c.*1540. Nationally, castles were in decline; Michael Thompson considers that only a third of the castles described in the 1530s, by Leland, were in normal use, but over a third of those, which included Carmarthen, were in Wales, suggesting that they retained a greater importance here.[29] However, baronial castles became largely irrelevant as a result of the Acts of Union of 1536 and 1543, the impact of which was also felt by castles of the Crown: Carmarthen's importance as a judicial and administrative centre was much diminished. Its military significance similarly declined in the social changes of Tudor Britain. The 'gunner' at Carmarthen Castle in 1540, mentioned in Chapter 4, suggests that its strategic use continued into the middle of the century, but a combination of circumstances was slowly bringing its active life to an end.

The sparse documentary evidence for the form and condition of the castle tells us little about how it was affected during this important time of transition. As Crown property, the castle was administered by the officials of the County of Carmarthen; the borough had no control over it. But records of post-medieval Carmarthen at CRO, while extensive, represent those kept by the borough and are largely confined to borough affairs.[30] Diminishing royal interest in the castle is reflected in an overall decrease in Crown (and county) records, which become progressively limited to court proceedings. It is not until the acquisition of the site by the Golden Grove estate in the seventeenth century that the documentation resumes. Borough and county administration remained separate until the Municipal Corporations Act of 1835.

So there are three key questions concerning both the role and the nature of Carmarthen Castle during this period:

- When did it cease to be an administrative centre?
- When was it effectively 'abandoned', losing its medieval household(s) and staff?
- And when was it finally disposed of by the Crown?

Gradual abandonment: the late sixteenth century

Rhys ap Thomas, justiciar and chamberlain, died in 1525 (see Chapter 2). The two appointments were subsequently granted to Walter Devereux, Lord Ferrers,[31] who was in office when the Acts of Union were passed in 1536 and 1543. He found his powers much reduced. Under the acts the County of Carmarthen became a civil shire, united with the lordships of Kidwelly, St Clears, Cantref Bychan and Laugharne (Figure 125), that was effectively

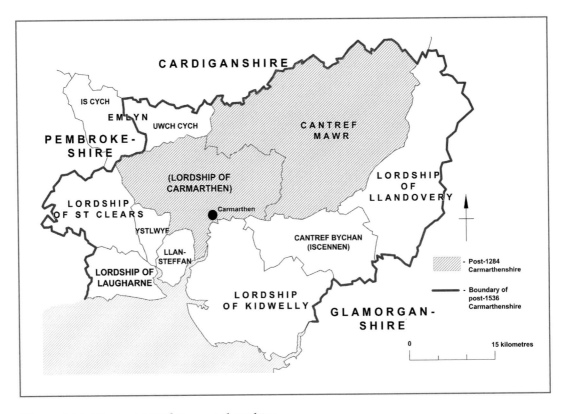

Figure 125 *The post-1536 Carmarthenshire*

governed from Westminster and Ludlow. Judicially, Wales was divided into four circuits, each with a justice (later two) appointed by the king. Carmarthen was the centre for the south Wales circuit – Carmarthenshire, Cardiganshire and Pembrokeshire – and its justice was based at the castle. However, twice a year he was itinerant, presiding over the Great Sessions 'in each shire at the appointed place for six days',[32] formalising the intermittent 'tourns' that were introduced in the fifteenth century.[33] In addition, County Quarter Sessions were established.[34]

The sixteenth-century justices were equipped with a staff of officials that were initially also based at the castle. They included the sheriff, the steward of the commotes, an auditor, coroners and an escheator, as well as clerks and notaries.[35] The issues of the courts were paid into the exchequer of Carmarthen, administered as before by the chamberlain, or 'Treasurer of the Circuit', as he also became known. The castle therefore remained an administrative centre, but with reduced powers. Feudal government was being replaced by civil government.

Continued administrative and penal demands contributed to the survival of castles as institutions, at Carmarthen and elsewhere, but made them increasingly unpleasant to live in; many had been abandoned as residences by the mid-sixteenth century.[36] Moreover, the Crown had virtually ended expenditure on its castles – the last recorded works at

Carmarthen were in 1546, when a mere £7 16s. was spent.[37] So while the circuit officers for south Wales may have been based at Carmarthen Castle there is evidence that, increasingly, neither they nor their deputies were necessarily ever resident there. Moreover; they were still often aristocrats and clearly absentee, like Ferrers and his successor Sir Rhys Mansel of Oxwich Castle, Glamorgan, who became chamberlain, for life, in 1554.[38]

The sixteenth-century constables were similarly drawn from the aristocracy, like William Herbert, later Earl of Pembroke, appointed in 1543;[39] they continued to be absentee, as they had been during the later Middle Ages, though their deputies were resident in the castle. For instance, we are told that Ferrers's grandson Walter (later Earl of Essex, d. 1576) was granted the office of constable, for life, in the 1570s, on condition that his deputy be permanently resident, and the castle repaired and maintained.[40] The recommended repairs, which were estimated at over £233, were however confined to the Justiciar's Hall and lodgings – along with the Auditor's Chamber – the gatehouse and the exchequer.[41] Maintenance costs at royal castles throughout Wales, moreover, were increasingly falling to local officers, who spared themselves expense by neglecting it.[42]

Meanwhile, we know from the Corporation Order Books that the Borough Guildhall was also being called the 'Shire Hall' by 1581,[43] indicating that county business – in the form of the Great and Quarter Sessions – had begun to be held there instead of the castle. As we hear no more of the castle being in regular administrative use, it is likely that the move out was permanent; the Guildhall still hosts the County Court and Magistrates' Court, and is regarded as a Crown Court. Launceston Castle, Cornwall, also lost its courts in around 1610, whilst similarly being retained as the County Gaol.[44]

The castle had therefore lost anything resembling its resident medieval household by the end of the sixteenth century. However, the constable may have maintained a lodging until the Civil War, as it was only due to the slighting of the castle that his post was finally abolished (see below).[45] And prisoners, if not under a resident gaoler, were kept at the castle throughout the sixteenth century and beyond.[46] We saw in Chapter 4 that the King's Chapel, as a chantry, had been dissolved in the 1540s, but it is possible that the main castle chapel may, for a while, have served the diminishing sixteenth-century community.

The castle in the early seventeenth century

Speed's drawing of *c.*1610 may be misleading. It shows the castle as substantially intact (Figure 112), but many castles similarly depicted by Speed are known to have been ruinous.[47] And when, in 1630, an inquest was held at Carmarthen Castle to assess its value, only 'two several chambers, Castle Green and ditches' were mentioned, valued at 20s. p.a..[48] This deceptively terse account is informative. The fact that only two chambers are singled out for mention implies that they alone were in regular use and maintenance. Disuse of the Justiciar's Hall as a courtroom may be confirmed by the Buck prints which show that its internal walls had gone by 1740 (Figure 126), suggesting that it had been slighted; it would probably, however, have been both retained and maintained if had been reserved for civil use, much as the administrative halls at e.g. Monmouth, Lancaster and Winchester were spared when the rest of the castle was demolished.[49] So the inquest may instead refer to the chamber in the gatehouse – still, presumably, the constable's residence – and the prison. Also recommended for repair in 1578,[50] the gatehouse, significantly, was retained in its entirety after the Civil War.

The 'Castle Green' of the 1630 valuation clearly refers to the outer ward, in an early use of the name by which it was always later known. The 'green' element does not by itself imply that the bailey had become disused, or empty of buildings – the baileys at Monmouth and York castles were similarly called 'Greens' during a period of at least partial use.[51] The castle 'ditches' of the 1630 account were apparently still claimed as parcel of the castle curtilage, but excavation, documentary and map evidence suggest that this was not always followed in practice. Considerable encroachments had been made by c.1610, when Speed depicted the western ditch as almost entirely occupied by housing (Figure 112); indeed the borough appears to have claimed formal ownership of some of these properties – in 1576 a lease was granted by the corporation on a 'piece of commons, adjoining the Castle Ditch, on the north side . . . and the Castle Gate on the east', which clearly lay within the line of the ditch.[52] However, no record of any contemporary sale or lease of the ditches has survived – unlike, for instance, Lincoln Castle under Charles I [53] – and the encroachments may have been unauthorised, as at Monmouth Castle,[54] but difficult to reverse by the early seventeenth century. The development did not, apparently, fully extend around the north side of the castle; only one side of the nascent routeway (the later Castle Hill), within the outer ward ditch, is shown by Speed as developed (Figure 112).

Figure 126 Carmarthen Castle from south, by S. and N. Buck, 1740 (Carmarthenshire Museums Service, CAASG 1976/1964)

Disposal: 1620–40

It would appear that the castle was disposed of by the Crown during the 1620s. It had been acquired, before 1630, by the Phillips family of Cwmgwili and consequently became attached to the lordship of Elfed (part of the old County of Carmarthen).[55] The Phillipses may have acquired the lease of the lordship, with the castle, in 1628–30,[56] as a deed of 1639[57] confirms that it had been leased out in 1628, and again in 1630. In 1634 it was granted to Sir Henry Browne and John Cliffe, along with the 'Manors and Commotes of Elfed and Widigada, with their appurtenances, to be held of the Crown in free and common socage, and not in chief, for an annual rent of £3 6s. 8d'.[58] Browne and Cliffe were prominent in the acquisition of Crown land, doubtless profiting from the Commission for the Sale of the King's Lands through which the early Stuarts reduced the disproportionately large number of royal castles and manors. In 1631–2 we find them acquiring Crown land in London, Middlesex, Surrey and Oxfordshire,[59] and also Cambridge Castle, which they held in trust for the county so that the sessions could continue to be held in the otherwise ruinous castle.[60] There is no record of such an arrangement at Carmarthen, which may confirm that the courts had permanently moved out of the castle. The lease appears to have passed to the Vaughans of Golden Grove in 1639.[61] However, the castle's prisoners were kept by the county authorities, on behalf of the Crown.

SLIGHTING: FROM CIVIL WAR TO RESTORATION, 1642–60

Very few contemporary sources relate directly to the castle during either the Civil War or its aftermath. It was garrisoned, so was clearly in sufficient repair to be both defensible and habitable, though not necessarily roofed throughout. Governors were appointed, both during and after the war, who presumably took over the constable's lodgings and were responsible for any prisoners as, for example, at Lancaster Castle.[62] Beyond this, however, the sources tell us very little about the nature of the castle. During the war, the majority of newsletters were Parliamentarian in sympathy – particularly after 1649 – so we know rather less about Royalist activity in Wales. Moreover, the campaigns in Pembrokeshire were well documented, while those in Carmarthenshire were not. And the sources, in general, are much fuller for England than Wales. The same limitations continue through the interregnum.

The Civil War

The castle appears still to have been under lease to the Vaughans at the outbreak of the war in 1642. The leading political figures in Carmarthenshire, they virtually controlled both the county and the borough.[63] In 1642 Richard Vaughan of Golden Grove, Earl of Carbery and twice MP for Carmarthen, joined the Royalist cause, along with the most influential borough and county gentry. Carmarthen Castle was selected as the headquarters of the Royalist Association for the three western counties.[64] Vaughan was subsequently appointed Commander-in-Chief for the king in south Wales,[65] and Parliamentary forces, under Major-General

Rowland Laugharne, were initially confined to Pembrokeshire, but took Carmarthen in April 1644,[66] 'together with a great store of prisoners, many arms and ammunition'.[67] They apparently met little resistance, and there is no suggestion of any formal attack on the castle; the burgesses declared for 'King and Parliament', forcing the garrison to withdraw, and Vaughan subsequently relinquished his command. Carmarthen was recaptured in June 1644 by his replacement, Colonel Charles Gerard, and its garrison was put under the command of Colonel Francis Lovelace, as Governor of Carmarthen Castle.[68] Increasing Parliamentary sympathy in the locality saw the desertion of many former Royalists, and Carmarthen's loyalties were split between the castle garrison, under Lovelace, and the local gentry under the Vaughans, who were beginning to waver in their support.[69] While 'the garrison of Carmarthen required 1,200 men to keep it' in September 1645, only 700 could be mustered in the entire district[70] and, with the support of Parliamentary sympathisers, Carmarthen finally capitulated to Laugharne's forces, without opposition, on 12 October 1645.[71]

It was apparently recorded that when first attacked by Parliament in 1644, Carmarthen was 'fortified with a mud wall around it', but the relevant source has been lost and only exists in secondary form.[72] It may have referred to the unfinished, poorly designed and possibly hurried ditch system investigated by Terry James, south of Lammas Street, in the 1980s, which may have been dug under Vaughan's command.[73] Whether the castle was strengthened at the same time is unknown. However, the masonry infill of the gatehouse towers may have been a Civil War measure against artillery, though earth was the normal choice of fill in such circumstances, as at Chepstow Castle, Monmouthshire.[74] The deep sequence of post-medieval dump layers, recorded in the trenches along the southern edge of the inner ward, was perhaps laid down as a defensive bank behind the southern curtain. It may moreover be that the castle, while primarily a base for local forces, was also used as a gun platform to cover the bridge and quay;[75] doubts regarding the 'platform for two or three guns' in the shell-keep, apparently observed in 1913–14, were raised in Chapter 4, but it may be noted that upon the castle's surrender in 1645 'eight pieces of ordnance' were apparently found, along with 'about fifteen hundred arms'.[76] What may have been done with the prisoners at the castle during this period is unknown, but those at Lincoln Castle, for example, were moved out when it was fortified in 1643.[77]

It is more likely that any defensive works at the castle were ordered by Col. Gerard – who unlike Vaughan was a professional soldier – later in 1644. It is clear that he intended the castle to be the nucleus of Royalist defences within the town, confirmed when loyalties were divided in 1645:[78] Gerard was described as 'fortifying [Carmarthen] for the king' in a contemporary pamphlet.[79] He had trained as a soldier in the Netherlands, and is thought to have been responsible for the surviving Civil War defences, 'The Bulwarks', at the west end of the town.[80] They comprise a rampart, bastion and a demi-bastion, and are the only British example of an earthen town defence that survives in anything like its original condition.[81] A further bastion has recently been identified to the north-east,[82] proving that the rampart – as long suspected – originally extended eastwards to join the Roman town defences to form a continuous line (Figure 3). So it may be that Gerard's work included some (re)construction at the castle, but it is equally possible that parts of the castle may have been demolished for masonry to create the new defensive line.

Slighting was initially contemplated in 1645. Before their final capitulation, the townsmen had submitted a draft agreement that 'the workes and all fortifications about the Towne and Castle be utterly demolished', along with all other garrisons in the county,[83] but Parliament hesitated on the grounds that quarters would be needed for its troops.[84] The castle was still garrisoned in 1647, but in March the Commons ordered that, along with many other castles throughout Britain, it should be 'disgarrisoned, slighted, and made untenable'.[85] However, the order was rescinded in July, the Commons instead proposing to keep a garrison of one hundred men.[86] The widespread slightings of 1647 were, in any case, normally confined to new defensive works, erected specifically during the war, rather than castles, many of which, like Carmarthen, performed civil functions as gaols etc.[87] The Bulwarks may then have been destroyed at this time.

Although Carmarthen was again a military centre during the Second Civil War in 1648, there is no clear indication that the town itself was the scene of any action; it did not stand a siege, nor is there any mention of fortifications,[88] although some other strongholds in west Wales were apparently 'fortified'.[89] While the Carmarthen garrison declared for the rebels in March,[90] and were joined by the local leaders, Cols. Poyer and Powell,[91] the sporadic engagements took place outside the town, which was not itself attacked. Support for the insurrection was far from universal in west Wales, and Richard Vaughan was influential in preventing many of the gentry from joining it.[92] Moreover the rebel garrison, on hearing of Cromwell's arrival in Wales in May, withdrew from the town,[93] allowing Cromwell to pass through without resistance on his way to reduce Pembroke.[94]

Aftermath

Parliament appointed its own governor to Carmarthen Castle, a Colonel Rowland Dawkins of Kilvrough, Glam.. A Baptist from a prominent Glamorgan family, Dawkins was an up-and-coming official in the new administration. He had been a local commissioner for a number of Acts of the Commonwealth,[95] and became one of the leading political figures in Wales during the interregnum. He was appointed both governor and Captain of Military in 1648,[96] and was in office when Cromwell stopped at Carmarthen, in July 1649, on his way to Ireland.[97] Dawkins also took over as Governor of Tenby Castle, where a garrison had been retained for fear of foreign or Irish invasion.[98]

A garrison is recorded at Carmarthen in October 1651,[99] and it is possible, if perhaps unlikely, that some defensive works at the castle belong to this period, as they may have done e.g. Chepstow.[100] Royalist sympathies remained strong in west Wales and conflict continued into the 1650s. In June 1651, for example, Governor Dawkins 'marched from Carmarthen to Cardigan', to suppress a Royalist uprising in which twenty-eight rebels were killed and sixty prisoners taken, and took part in the subsequent trials.[101] Dawkins was reappointed head of militia in March 1655, when the Commonwealth scaled up security measures,[102] and military rule was effectively imposed. Dawkins was, moreover, deputy in west Wales to James Berry, Major-General of Wales and the Marches – one of the twelve Major-Generals who more or less ruled as dictators in England and Wales between 1655 and 1657.[103] He was also elected joint MP for Carmarthen in 1654 and 1656; his third victory in 1659 was however contested, costing him the seat,[104] and his association with Carmarthen came to an end with the Restoration in early 1660.

Slighting

Carmarthen Castle was still 'defensible and strong' in 1652, according to the poet John Taylor, who visited the town in that year,[105] while the town wall is mentioned, apparently still intact, in an account from 1654.[106] Moreover, the castle may still have been in active use in October 1656, when Major-General Berry was at Carmarthen with Dawkins and a number of other parliamentary commissioners.[107] But by December 1660 it was reported to be 'now quite demolished',[108] while in 1673 the castle and town wall were described by the cartographer Richard Blome as 'long since reduced to ruin'.[109] It is clear therefore that both were deliberately slighted.

An exhaustive search of the 'Thomason Tracts', *CSPD, JHC* and *Acts and Ordinances*,[110] as well as manuscript sources in NLW and CRO, yielded no documentation relating to its slighting. But as Michael Thompson has pointed out, the post-1648 demolitions were usually undertaken by county committees or deputy lieutenants whose records, like other county material, have not survived.[111] They were occasionally recorded by local diarists, as at Monmouth Castle – where the demolition was unauthorised[112] – or in private papers, like those in the Powis Castle Estate collection which record the demolition of Montgomery Castle.[113] However, slighting at the nearby castles of Laugharne and Newcastle Emlyn similarly went unrecorded.[114]

A presentment of 1657 mentions the 'houses under the castle walls';[115] as it is likely that any such housing – including that in the west ditch – would have to be cleared to facilitate demolition of the curtain walls above, I suggest that the slighting occurred between 1657 and December 1660.[116] Carmarthen may therefore have been among the spate of slightings that followed Cromwell's death in 1658 and were partly triggered by the brief rising in the north-west of England in July–August 1659. Parliament once again ordered the demolition, by local officers, governors and private owners, of a number of 'inland garrisons and castles'.[117] There was often a marked reluctance to comply, particularly from those governors who wished to preserve their castles as administrative and penal centres; this was the case at Lancaster,[118] and it may be significant that prisoners were kept at Carmarthen Castle until at least 1658.[119]

Carmarthen Castle, however, had clearly proved to be of use to the Commonwealth, and so it may not have been demolished until the Restoration, which precipitated another bout of slighting – as late as 1662 at Northampton Castle.[120] The wording of the December account, in which the castle was '*now* quite demolished [my italics]', implies moreover that its demolition was a recent event. An act for the disbanding of garrisons was passed on 15 September 1660,[121] but demolition at Carmarthen was clearly well advanced (if not

Figure 127 *Detail from 'The south-east view of Carmarthen', by S. and N. Buck, 1748*
(Carmarthenshire Museums Service, CAASG 1976/1695)

complete) by December and may have already begun by September; it had been ordered in March–May 1660 at three other Welsh castles, Caernarfon, Chepstow and Denbigh.[122]

Further evidence that the castle was slighted is indirect, but compelling, and can be read by comparing those sections of the castle that survived into the following century – or were allowed to remain – and those which had gone (see Figures 126 and 127). It was suggested in Chapter 3 that the castle walls, with the exception of the north curtain, and the west curtain north of the gatehouse, were built on unstable slopes, or bank material, and would have come down easily. It may also be that it was the curtain walls that were targeted, rather than the towers, whose damage may have been incidental. The South-west Tower may have been saved by its spurs (as at Cardigan), but may also have been deliberately retained as a revetment of the south-west corner against the development beneath it. However, it appears to have lost its rear wall and vaults when the adjoining curtain walls came down. The Square Tower may, by contrast, have been saved by its vault, though losing its upper stage(s), while it too revets the southern side of the site. The other inner ward towers, like the curtains, may have occupied banks. The 1740 print shows the shell-keep as ruinous and incomplete (Figure 126). The vestigial outer ward curtain and towers shown by the Bucks suggest that they were also slighted, though the postern gate on the southern side seems to have survived. Damage to the gatehouse was minimal, being confined to the junction with the west curtain, which took the southern turret with it when it fell, and the putative barbican. Whilst this may in part have been due to its physical resistance to demolition, through its masonry infill and the stabilising effect of the ditch deposits around it, the gatehouse may have been intentionally spared.

THE LATE SEVENTEENTH AND EIGHTEENTH CENTURIES

The lease of the castle was, after the Restoration, restored to the Vaughans of Golden Grove, and it is clear that it applied to the entire site – in 1669, the 'Castle of Carmarthen and Ye Green' was included in a valuation of the lordship of Elfed and Widigada.[123] Crown interest continued nonetheless: county prisoners were still kept within the slighted ruins, while the gatehouse may have been intended to house the constable (or his deputy) as it had probably done before war intervened. However, the office of constable was subject to a treasury review in December 1660, which resulted in its abolition owing to the otherwise ruinous state of the castle.[124] By this act, Carmarthen Castle now existed solely as a gaol, ceasing to be an official residence for good. In 1669 we find the gaol under the control of a formal keeper, working alongside the sheriff, but he likewise was not necessarily resident.[125]

The gaol occupied less than half the castle site; the remainder was put to other uses, including domestic development. At some point during the late seventeenth or early eighteenth century, the Golden Grove estate both relinquished its claim on the former inner ward and acquired outright possession of the outer ward. The castle was henceforth divided into three discrete parcels – the gaol, i.e. the northern half of the inner ward, held by the county authorities; the southern half of the inner ward, the bulk of which was also held by the county and which became a garden for the Clerk of the Sessions (termed 'Cursitor' at Carmarthen); and the outer ward and cross-ditch, which was owned by Golden Grove.

This division, and the apparent exchange, probably occurred in 1713, when the Vaughan lineage became extinct and the heiress, Lady Anne Vaughan, married Charles Paulet, Marquis of Winchester and later Duke of Bolton. In 1753, shortly after Lady Anne's death, the estate finally passed out of the direct line and fell to a distant cousin, John Vaughan. The castle, however, was treated as an escheat, a Grand Jury finding that the entire site was the 'right and property of the Crown and [belonged] to His Majesty, his heirs and successors'.[126] Golden Grove was obliged to forfeit its parcel to the Crown.[127] However, the forfeiture proved temporary and the land was soon back in Vaughan hands. John Vaughan's grandson died without issue in 1804 and demised the Golden Grove estate – without any further complication – to his friend John Campbell, Lord Cawdor. Administratively, however, the outer ward remained part of the county rather than the borough. As tenants of the lordship of Elfed and Widigada, moreover, the Castle Green householders were answerable to the court leet of Elfed and were parishioners of Newchurch, in Elfed, rather than St Peter's in the borough.[128]

The County Gaol (Figure 128)

The castle had become a 'county' gaol with the Act of Union, as distinct from the borough which had a gaol of its own, over one of the medieval town gates, called the 'Upper House' (Figure 128).[129] Like other county gaols it was under the jurisdiction of the county authorities through their justices, its administration being executed through discussion at the Quarter Sessions.[130] From the sixteenth century onwards, its records were kept with the records of the sessions, but these mainly relate to court proceedings (e.g. the Gaol Delivery Rolls, which begin in the 1650s, and prisoners' lists beginning in 1675), rather than any discussion of the castle fabric.[131]

So there are few written sources for the nature of the post-slighting castle, while archaeological evidence is also scant, and we must turn to pictorial and map sources. Very little standing fabric was shown by the Bucks in the 1740s – little more than exists

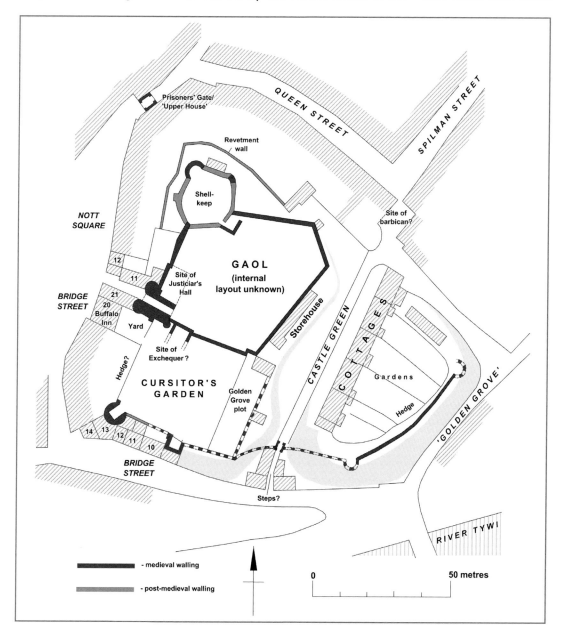

Figure 128 *Plan of the entire castle site in the mid-eighteenth century (reconstructed)*

today (Figures 126–7). The north curtain and the west curtain north of the gatehouse, the inner ward cross-wall, and a wall on the east side – which, I have suggested, may have been the internal wall of a medieval building – remained to define the gaol enclosure or 'courtyard' (see Figures 111, 126–8). The gatehouse, otherwise as today, retained its rear section in which the medieval hipped roof had been replaced by a north–south running gable, with chimneys of post-medieval form. The medieval shell-keep and forebuilding were ruinous. The South-west Tower was also ruinous, as today, having lost its roof, rear wall and upper floors, while the Square Tower was concealed behind housing on Bridge Street and is not shown. All other medieval buildings had gone, and they may too have been victims of slighting, but it is possible that they were already in decay before the Civil War. There appears to have been very little accommodation for prisoners (as at e.g. Launceston Castle),[132] and it was limited to the gatehouse. No post-medieval gaol buildings are discernible on the Buck prints.[133]

However, the prison population may always have been relatively small. There were twenty-six inmates when the reformer John Howard visited the gaol in 1774, and only eleven on his second visit in 1776.[134] He nevertheless found it cramped, and 'offensive', and indeed the figures appear to indicate its maximum capacity – it was reported to be 'crowded with prisoners' in 1787,[135] yet only fourteen inmates were present on Howard's third visit the following year.[136] Prisoners were divided almost equally between felons and debtors, while the gaol also housed the House of Correction (or 'Bridewell') for the county's petty offenders.[137] Howard found that

> The old apartments are too close, and so are the new cells for criminals. These are about 7ft by 6ft, apertures in the doors are only about 9" square; earth floors. The Day-Room is used as a chapel. Over it is a free ward, and over that, a room for the sick. One court-yard, but it is spacious.[138]

Some new building had clearly been undertaken since the 1740s. Howard's description suggests a building of three storeys, while the gatehouse comprised only two, although it is possible that an attic floor is indicated. Nevertheless, Howard also distinguishes between 'the old apartments' and 'the new cells'. We are told that the 'castle' had been 'repaired' in 1774, when a pump was also installed.[139] This may relate to a limited campaign of new building. Howard moreover reported that a 'house for the gaoler' had been 'lately built in the yard' and there were 'convenient rooms for Masters' Sidedebtors'; the newly installed pump however was clearly a failure, as there was 'no water', the well being 'useless'.[140] The location of these new buildings is unknown; the interior of the gaol is left blank on Thomas Lewis's map of 1786 (Figure 111), which also omits the gatehouse rear section, and the shell-keep forebuilding, in what may be a conventionalised depiction. However, the present shell-wall appears to have been built between 1740 and 1786, and is shown on Lewis's map; could it have been one of the 'repairs' of 1774? Otherwise very little archaeological or structural evidence for this period has been revealed.

Political clashes in 1755, between Whig and Tory supporters, apparently saw both the county and borough gaols being 'fortified' by the Tory faction, who 'made port-holes etc. and supplied themselves with great guns and small arms'.[141] An 'attack was made on the gaol, and pieces of cannon were brought into the town with the declared intent of battering it down'. The extent of neither the 'fortification' nor the damage is known, but the artillery was apparently not brought into play.

The 'Cursitor's Garden'

The Cursitor's Garden, in the southern half of the inner ward, belonged to the county, but the eastern third was retained by the Golden Grove estate and was leased to a succession of individuals (see Figures 129–30). The garden is not clearly shown in either Buck print but is labelled on maps from 1786 onwards.

The west ditch alongside Nott Square and Bridge Street was gradually redeveloped after the Civil War (see Chapter 3), but the Buck prints suggest that the process was not fully under way until after the 1740s (Figures 126 and 127). The medieval west curtain, where it fronted Bridge Street, had largely disappeared and a boundary hedge had been established along its line by c.1800 (shown in 1819; Figure 130). However, the two stretches of wall occupying the southern third of the medieval wall-line retain ground levels which, to the east, are up to 3 m higher than the Bridge Street backyards – by whose tenants they were presumably built. Both are shown on a map of 1845 (Figure 137), and may have been built, out of necessity, fairly soon after the curtain was slighted. The hedge was progressively replaced by further domestic walls through the nineteenth century.

The 1740 Buck print does however appear to show the medieval southern curtain, in truncated form. It may also be the solid boundary that is shown on the 1786 map, although the section west of the Square Tower may have already been replaced by the rear walls of Nos. 11–12 Bridge Street (see Figure 128). The 1786 map also shows a solid boundary on the east side of the garden, revetting the steep slope down to the cross-ditch between the inner and outer wards, which may similarly represent the truncated medieval east curtain.

'Castle Green': the outer ward

By 1725, the outer ward and cross-ditch – as 'Castle Green and Castle Ditch' – was being leased by the Golden Grove estate to a number of individuals.[142] Described as 'a waste piece of ground', it was presumably then empty, but the establishment of a roadway in the ditch, also called 'Castle Green', and the development of its east side with housing, began soon afterwards. A row of cottages had been built by 1740 (Figures 126 and 127), and survived until 1868, although they may have been rebuilt in or after 1789–92, when the gaol was extended eastwards and the roadway was widened (compare Figures 111 and 129).[143] The road became a popular public meeting place – in 1744, the Methodist Howell Harris preached there,[144] as did John Wesley in 1763 and 1767.[145]

The remains of the medieval outer ward curtain and towers, with the postern tower, were depicted by the Bucks in the 1740s (Figures 126 and 127). The southern scarp slope is shown as a high, vertical cliff – much higher than in later pictures (e.g. Figure 132) – which was described as a 'steep, and rather craggy precipice' in 1805 (see Chapter 3), although a degree of licence may be inferred. Castle Green appears to have been a cul-de-sac in the 1740s, terminating at the edge of the scarp, but by 1786 a connection to Bridge Street had been made, with the removal of the postern tower. This lane – known as 'Castle Ditch' well into the nineteenth century[146] – is straight in Figure 111, but all later maps show a staggered flight of steep, narrow steps, leading up from Bridge Street to the cross-ditch and former postern (Figures 133 and 137), perhaps reflecting medieval arrangements. A complex of domestic properties had developed either side of the steps by the mid-nineteenth century,[147] but a section of 'cliff' remained to define the southern end of the cross-ditch, on its eastern side, as late as 1845 (labelled 'Mount' on Figure 137).

The remains of the outer ward curtain had largely disappeared by 1786 when a hedge is shown running along the top of the scarp slope (Figure 111). The lower half of Castle Hill was widened in 1804,[148] and it is clear from map evidence that it was at the castle's expense, some 8 m of the south-eastern periphery of the outer ward being lost.[149] The loss may however have been largely external to the curtain wall-line, as the site of the east tower was apparently still identifiable in 1917.[150] A new wall was built to retain the truncated slope, and a second was built around the summit, just inside the line of the earlier hedge (Figures 129 and 132). Little change subsequently occurred within the former outer ward until 1868–72, when it became incorporated within the enlarged gaol.

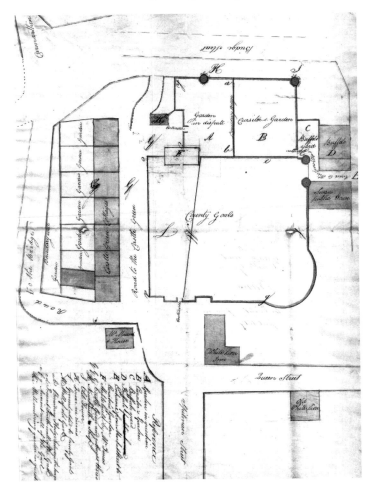

Figure 129 Plan of Carmarthen Gaol in 1818. NB: north at bottom of frame (Carmarthenshire Archive Service, CRO Cawdor Maps 43, 'Plan of County Gaol and premises', 1818)

THE NEW COUNTY GAOL, 1789–1868

Following the publication of the Howard report, a new gaol was proposed in 1783.[151] John Nash, who had relaunched his career in Carmarthen and was later to design similar gaols at Cardigan and Hereford, was appointed as its architect. Work began in 1789 and the new gaol opened in 1792. It served the borough, too, the prisoners in the 'Upper House' or Prisoner's Gate being transferred in 1792.[152]

Like its predecessor, the new gaol occupied the northern half of the inner ward, but was extended eastwards up to the Castle Green thoroughfare, on land acquired from the Golden Grove estate (Figure 129), increasing the enclosed area by a quarter (from 0.28 to 0.34 hectares). This entailed the demolition of the old eastern gaol wall which, as we have seen, may have been medieval in origin,

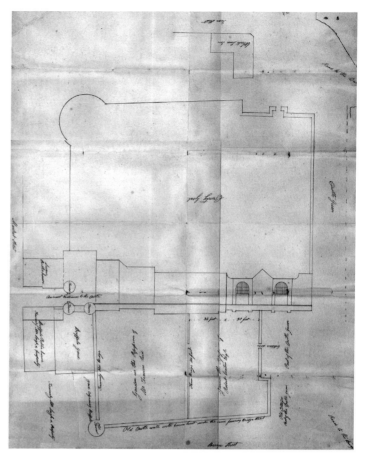

Figure 130 *Plan of Carmarthen Gaol in 1819* (Carmarthenshire Archive Service, CRO Cawdor 2/112, 'Plan of the County Gaol etc.', 24 August 1819)

and the erection of a new east wall, but no other surviving medieval fabric appears to have been affected. A detailed plan from 1858–66 (Figure 139) shows the gaol before it was rebuilt in 1868–72, which, viewed alongside John Wood's map of Carmarthen, of 1834 (Figure 133), allows the plan of the 1790s gaol to be reconstructed (see Figure 131).[153]

John Nash's gaol (Figure 131)
The north and west curtains, which had assumed their present form by at least 1786, continued in use as perimeter walls, while the inner ward cross-wall was extended eastwards, for *c*.35 m, to meet the new east wall, and may also have been heightened (cf. Figures 126 and 130). The medieval gatehouse rear section was retained and, with the south-east stair turret, is clearly shown in a drawing from 1829 (Figure 132; also see Figure 130). However, although apparently still standing to its full height, and retaining its medieval

windows, it appears to have become an open, roofless yard. Map and print evidence suggests that it was finally demolished between 1829 and *c*.1840 (Figure 136), when its north wall was lost and its east wall may have been (re)built as the lower, thinner wall which still survives as part of the gaol wall. Its south wall was however retained (Figures 133, 137 and 139).

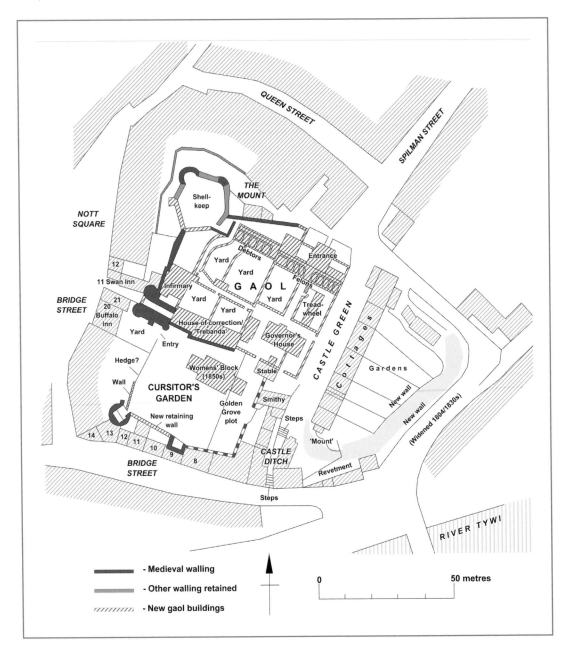

Figure 131 *Plan of the entire castle site in the early nineteenth century (reconstructed)*

Figure 132 Carmarthen Castle from south in 1829 (NLW, Drawing Vol. 404, p. 21, PG 321, 'Carmarthen Castle' by the Rev. E. Edwards, 1829: by permission of Llyfrgell Genedlaethol Cymru/ The National Library of Wales)

The cells in the castle gatehouse, and any accommodation added in the 1770s, were replaced by an ordered complex of new cell-blocks and associated buildings. These occupied nearly a third of the compound, arranged around a subdivided open space. The cell-blocks were brick-built, well ventilated and possibly arcaded,[154] comprising two storeys beneath hipped roofs (see Figures 132 and 136). Prisoners were segregated into three groups – felons, debtors and petty offenders – who each occupied a separate block, with its own 'airing yard'. The gaol was 'Howardian' in layout, with individual cells, and was generally well regarded; it won the cautious approval of the reformer James Neild,[155] while in 1796, the traveller Sir Christopher Sykes described it as 'convenient, clean and airy'.[156] It accommodated twenty-six inmates, or sixty 'by placing more than one [prisoner] in the same cell'.[157]

The axis of the castle was turned through 90 degrees, the new gaol being entered from the north. The medieval gatehouse was blocked by a wall between the towers and stayed that way until the gaol was rebuilt in 1868–72 (Figures 129 and 134). The new entry, facing Spilman Street, was central to an elaborate façade block. Of two storeys and three bays, it was in a strict Classical idiom with ashlar facework, rusticated below, and a cornice at

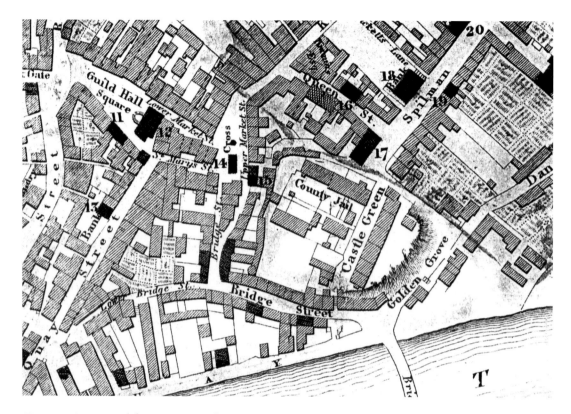

Figure 133 *Detail from a map of Carmarthen of 1834* (Carmarthenshire Archive Service, CRO (M) 786, Map of Carmarthen by John Wood, 1834)

roof level (Figures 139 and 145). The central bay comprised a projecting portico containing the entrance lobby, over which lay the gaoler's lodgings.[158] The segmental doorway, approached by a low flight of steps, was set in a full-height, semicircular-headed recess, with bold voussoirs, containing a grille above string-course level (cf. Hereford Gaol). A plaque, at cornice level, carried the inscription 'The Gaol. County of Carmarthen'. The flanking bays contained open yards, each with a semicircular-headed opening, like the entry in the façade. Integral to the façade block was the prison chapel, which occupied the first floor of a fourth bay to the west. It too was segregated, by partitions,[159] and was approached from the western yard by separate flights of steps.

The interior was divided into four quadrants, one for each class of inmate and a fourth for domestic use. The first three quadrants were largely taken up by their airing yards, each of which was enclosed by a high wall 'surmounted by a *chevaux-de-frise*, giving it an air of security', and was surfaced with large, heavy flagstones.[160] The north-east quadrant was occupied by the Felon's Block, an east–west range joining the rear of the entrance façade, from which it was separated by a corridor. It comprised a row of nine day-rooms, with twelve night cells above.[161] A central cross-passage led south from the main entry and continued between the two associated airing yards. Each cell and day-room was lit by a small,

Figure 134 *The Great Gatehouse from west, in c.1860, by Mary Ellen Bagnall Oakley*
(reproduced by kind permission of Mrs Suzanne Hayes)

glazed, south-facing window (Figure 147), while floors were of brick.[162] The Felons' Block also housed the new well, which had been sunk by 1803 along with 'a reservoir prepared to supply the prison with water'.[163] Although replacing the well that had been described as 'useless' by Howard, and in a virgin location, it too apparently furnished 'an insufficient supply of water'.[164] Intriguingly, beneath basement level were 'two dark cells measuring 7' 3" and 7' in height without any warmth or even a hole for the admission of air',[165] but there is no good reason to suppose that these originated as medieval cellars or undercrofts. A treadwheel, containing '16 divisions for prisoners, immediately partitioned from one another', was erected in the eastern airing yard in 1833 (Figure 139).[166]

In the north-west quadrant was the similar Debtors' Block, which joined the Felons' Block to form a long, east–west range. The brick foundations of its north wall were uncovered in 2002, separated from the north curtain by an open area or yard. The block comprised a row of five day-rooms, also linked by a corridor and with night cells above,[167] with windows like the Felons' Block (Figures 144 and 147). A cross-passage occupied the junction between the block and the shell-keep forebuilding, whose east wall shows the remains of its vault springers. The Debtors' Block also faced two airing yards, of which the larger of the two, to the east, had become a garden by 1858–66 (Figure 139). The west wall of the second yard survives in the present gaol wall.

The south-west quadrant was occupied by the House of Correction, which had been completed by 1796.[168] A large, detached, east–west building, it was also of two storeys, and similarly faced two airing yards which were divided from the debtors' yards by a passage. It had an unusual plan, lying at an angle to the main axis of the new buildings, and with a kink in the south wall; both attributes were derived from the medieval inner ward cross-wall, against which it was built and which its south wall incorporated. The eastern half, with its associated yard, was called 'The Trebanda', in which three first-floor cells for temporary remand prisoners overlay a ground-floor cell and a day-room.[169] The western half, for petty offenders, contained a day-room and five cells, one of which was used as an isolation ward for prisoners with scabies.[170] The ground-floor rooms in both halves were stone-flagged, each day-room had a fireplace, and windows were glazed.[171] The House of Correction can be seen in views from 1829 and 1830, with small, rather severe square openings, and a low-pitched gable roof through which rise three chimneys (Figures 132 and 135); it was faced with bricks, along with the chapel, during the 1840–1850s.[172]

The south-east quadrant was set aside for the Governor's House (Figure 133),[173] which occupied a square enclosure with entries from Castle Green and the Cursitor's Garden; these two entries, in the new section of cross-wall, are depicted as semicircular arches with 'portcullises' in a drawing of 1819 (Figure 130). The Governor's House was enlarged in 1857–8, when a further building, shown in 1834, was converted into a kitchen.[174]

Peel's Gaol Act of 1823 provided for the office of surgeon, but there appears to have been no provision for sick prisoners until an infirmary was established in 1838–42.[175] It occupied a pre-existing building that was shown, between the gaol proper and the west curtain, in 1834 (Figure 133) and may hitherto have housed a lunatic ward.[176] It was a high, single-storey chamber with a flagged floor, well lit and ventilated, and probably subdivided into wards;[177] the surviving architectural detail suggests that it was a Nash design. It was clearly not adapted from the earlier building on the same site, interpreted here as the medieval Justiciar's Hall, which was ruinous by 1740 (Figure 126). It appears that this building had already gone, and its north-west corner, fossilised in the west curtain wall, does not correspond with any of the infirmary wall-lines and was in any case already present by 1786 (Figures 101 and 111). Nor does the infirmary appear to have extended as far south as the gatehouse rear section north wall, and neither did it incorporate it. The yard behind the gatehouse, and the enclosed area south of the shell-keep, were used as infirmary airing yards.[178]

Nash's three gaols represent 'an interesting group in terms of their plans and façades'.[179] Carmarthen was unusual in being contained within the castle, unlike Cardigan and Hereford, which occupied new sites and were inspired by the radial plan promoted by William Blackburn, a prominent prison builder and friend of Nash. However, all three were essentially similar in layout. The slightly later gaol at Hereford, built 1792–6, was a two-storey cruciform building within a rectangular walled enclosure.[180] Three of the arms housed cell-blocks and were ranged around a central observation hall; the fourth arm led to the entrance lobby, which, like Carmarthen, housed the gaoler's lodgings. The airing yards lay between the arms.

As a piece of architecture, Carmarthen Gaol was generally admired.[181] Edward Donovan, in 1805, described it as a 'handsome building',[182] and it was still favourably spoken of towards the middle of the century, for example by Samuel Lewis who called it 'appropriately

Figure 135 *Carmarthen Castle from south-west, by Henri Gastineau, 1830* (NLW, Carm. Top. A5 A007: by permission of Llyfrgell Genedlaethol Cymru/The National Library of Wales)

Figure 136 *'Carmarthen Quay and Castle', by Alfred Keene, 1840s* (Carmarthenshire Museums Service, CAASG 2006/0332)

massive, without any unnecessary heaviness'.[183] These judgements relate primarily to the façade, which was very similar to that at Hereford, and like that building was a smaller version of Newgate Gaol.[184] These façades were, however, primarily meant to deter – garlands of manacles were hung over the entrances at all three.[185] And sensibilities had changed by 1867, when Carmarthen was described as a 'repulsive looking building', the manacles, in their 'sombre festoons', receiving particular opprobrium.[186] Nevertheless, despite minor alteration, the façade was retained until the demolition of the gaol in the 1930s, including the chapel, which in 1859 was altered, and extended, with the addition of a schoolroom, by the local architect J. L. Collard.[187]

Although Nash's gaol lacked the visual dominance of either the castle, the later nineteenth-century gaol or the present County Hall – contemporary pictures show that its walls and buildings were relatively 'low-rise' affairs (see Figures 132, 136 and 138) – its prominent site could still be exploited. It was reported, in 1833, that minor miscreants were escorted 'out of town, with . . . a distant view of the treadwheel in full operation'.[188] Above the east wall could apparently be seen the 'metal figure of a man in prison garb, which was mechanically connected with the treadwheel and was automatically set in motion when [it] was being worked'.[189]

County executions had traditionally taken place at Pensarn, just to the south of the town, but after 1817 they were carried out in the gaol.[190] And the Death Sentence Reform Act, of 1820, specifically required victims to be buried in their place of imprisonment. During the late nineteenth century, Carmarthen's executions were apparently buried in the new, extended yard around the 1868 gaol,[191] but it is not known exactly where. Burials however can be expected somewhere within the castle curtilage and their potential for discovery should be taken into account during any future work. The human skull, revealed during excavation within the shell-keep in 1997, was not associated with a recognisable grave-cut, and no other human remains were encountered, but the motte at e.g. Lincoln Castle was used for gaol burials during the nineteenth century, and a similar context may be suggested for the Carmarthen skull.[192] That the shell-keep was at least in active use is indicated by its refacing which, as we saw in Chapter 3, may belong to the Nash reconstruction. The interior had, however, been laid out as a second garden some years prior to 1862,[193] and a stairway up to the summit is shown on its present line in the forebuilding on a plan of 1857 (Figure 139; also see CRO, Cawdor Maps 41). It apparently continued to be used as a garden into the twentieth century (see Figure 147).

The Cursitor's Garden

By 1818, at least, the Cursitor's Garden proper had been divided from the Golden Grove plot to the east by a thorn hedge, shown in 1818–19 when both plots were under lease to private individuals (Figures 129 and 130). The entire area had, however, been laid out as a formal garden, with paths, by 1845 (Figure 137).[194] It was entered, by 1818 if not before, through a gap in the western boundary hedge immediately south of the blocked gatehouse (Figure 129). There were also two entries from the gaol (see above), and one from the east, where the suggested remnant medieval curtain appears to have been partly rebuilt with an inturn either side of the entry (Figures 129 and 130).

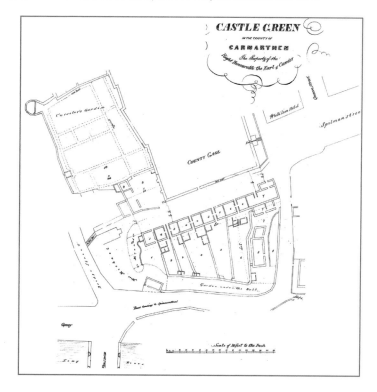

Figure 137 *Plan of Castle Green and the Cursitor's Garden, 1845. NB: north at right of frame* (Carmarthenshire Archive Service, CRO Cawdor Maps 38, 'Plan of the Castle Green in Carmarthen, 20 August 1845')

The South-west Tower had been a neglected corner of the garden until it was brought back into service with the new floor and internal wall that were revealed in 1994. The wall is shown in 1845 (Figure 137) and appears to be contemporary with the blocking of the windows. The latter, however, are shown as open in a print from 1830 (Figure 135), perhaps furnishing a date in the 1830s for the conversion; the sketch for the print may of course have been somewhat earlier. It is significant that the reused section of the tower is depicted as lying outside the county property boundary on contemporary maps (e.g. Figure 139), and it may have belonged to the same kind of private enterprise that was making claims to the tower basement. It was still in use later in the nineteenth century, and the hatching shown in 1895 confirms that it was the south-west, 'outside' half that was a roofed chamber while the 'inside' was open (Figure 149), but had evidently become disused by 1906 before the closure of the gaol (Figure 150). The new chamber was of a single storey, and unless there was a window in the dividing wall, was unlit. It appears to have been deliberately tailored to a specific function. A gunpowder magazine, for '300 barrels', was apparently a feature of the Nash gaol until 1811 when it was moved to a new location in the town.[195] The magazine is not shown on any maps or plans of the gaol, but the South-west Tower chamber – thick-walled, dark and above ground – would be an ideal candidate. However, we have seen that the evidence,

Figure 138 Carmarthen Castle and bridge from south-east, attributed to Hugh Hughes, c.*1850* (Carmarthenshire Museums Service, CAASG 1976/1864)

albeit slender, suggests a later date for the conversion, while the magazine was, unlike the chamber, county property. And why was so much medieval walling cut back?

It was suggested in Chapter 3 that the 'castle wall' which fell in 1811 may instead have been a post-medieval retaining wall between the South-west Tower and Square Tower (24, Figure 41). East of the Square Tower, however, the medieval south curtain was apparently still recognisable in 1819, if truncated; it is labelled 'old Castle Wall with houses built under' on Figure 130. It survived until the 1960s.

The new Women's Block, 1857–8

The disposition of the gaol buildings remained more or less unchanged until the 1850s. However, there had been significant changes of use (see Figure 139). An inspection in 1851 noted that petty offenders were now housed in the Felons' Block, which had become termed the House of Correction (or 'Correction Ward').[196] It was not in good con-

dition; its day-room, while used by prisoners under summary conviction, was also a work-room for picking oakum, and the remaining cells on the ground floor were, 'owing to their dampness', used chiefly for lumber.[197] However, one of these cells had, since 1840, been used as a refractory cell with a harsher regime (and its own yard), with the consequent disuse of the underground cells.[198] The old House of Correction was split between untried and convicted prisoners, and the entire building had become known as the Trebanda.[199] Debt remained punishable by imprisonment until 1869,[200] and Nash's debtors' cells were used for that purpose until the gaol was rebuilt (Figure 139).

But accommodation for female prisoners had been limited since the stipulation, in the 1823 Gaol Act, that sexes must be segregated.[201] And so by 1851 part of the Debtors' Block may have been taken over as a female wing; the infirmary

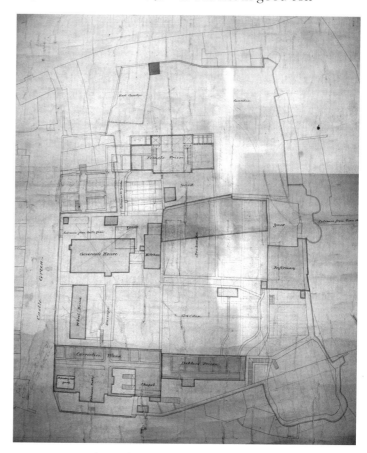

Figure 139 Plan of Carmarthen Gaol, c.1858–66. *NB: north at bottom of frame* (Carmarthenshire Archive Service, CRO MS 19, 'Plan showing boundary of Carmarthen Gaol and land belonging to the County', n.d.)

meanwhile had been divided into two storeys to accommodate prisoners of both sexes, 'carefully separated from one another and approached by separate staircases'.[202]

A new Women's Block was built in 1857–8.[203] It occupied the north-east corner of the Cursitor's Garden, outside Nash's gaol precinct (Figures 131 and 139), and lay partly within the Golden Grove plot, half of which was purchased from the estate for £30.[204] The design, originally by R. Kyrke Penson,[205] had been commissioned by the county magistrates in contravention of the new 'separate system' of solitary confinement approved by the Prison Inspector.[206] It was a rectangular, east–west block of three bays, intended for sixteen prisoners and comprising six dormitories, two punishment cells and a separate laundry.[207] Short-lived, it was demolished in 1868.

Domestic encroachments

Domestic properties were recorded on Bridge Street, south of the castle, as early as 1268,[208] but Speed suggests that in c.1610 they were confined to the southern side of the road (Figure 112). Development along the north side had begun by 1740 (Figure 126), and had extended east to the bridge by 1786 (Figure 111). What is not depicted on the historic maps is the intrusion of these properties into the body of the South-west Tower and Square Tower, to create additional domestic space, described in Chapter 3.

By the late eighteenth century the western ditch, in front of the gatehouse, had been fully redeveloped with domestic buildings. They extended right round the west and north sides of the castle, along Bridge Street, Nott Square and Queen Street (Figure 111), running up to the west curtain and the flanks of the motte. The motte had received its lower revetment wall by 1786, creating the lane called The Mount, which continued along the foot of the north curtain and, with its cottages, was under Golden Grove ownership (Figure 139; also see Figure 13).

Immediately south of the gatehouse, the medieval west curtain had ceased to be any kind of hard boundary. The hedge here appears to have joined the south-east (stair) turret of the gatehouse rear section (shown in 1819; Figure 130), several metres to the east of the medieval wall-line, confirming that all standing masonry – and bank material? – had gone, while demonstrating just how far into the castle interior the Bridge Street properties had been permitted to encroach. By 1761, No. 20 Bridge Street was an inn called The Buffalo.[209] Its yard extended into the castle site, while one of its outbuildings, revealed through excavation in 2001, overlay both the truncated gatehouse south turret and the 1818 entry to the Cursitor's Garden (Figure 139),[210] which had clearly become disused by the 1850s. The Buffalo remained in business until at least 1906 (Figure 150).

We also saw in Chapter 3 that these properties also took full advantage of the castle ditch as a convenient space for their cellars. Two of these cellars were given fireplaces in the late nineteenth/early twentieth century and were apparently used as additional living space – testimony to the overcrowding that was rife even in country towns.[211]

Castle Hill (as 'Golden Grove Street' – see Figure 133), had been extended around the east side of the site, south to the bridge, by 1740 (Figure 126). Limited development along its north-east side is suggested in 1786 (Figure 111) and was complete by 1834 (Figure 133).

THE LATE NINETEENTH-CENTURY GAOL AND COUNTY HALL, 1868–1993

A new Gaol Act, passed in 1865, called for the separation of prisoners, abolished the distinction between gaols and 'Houses of Correction', and promoted severity and uniformity in prison regimes. To comply with the Act, Carmarthen Gaol would have to be rebuilt to provide at least forty cells, with larger exercise yards.[212] Plans were initially submitted, in June 1866, for a major rebuild within the confines of the Nash gaol.[213] However, it was decided instead to extend the gaol over the entire medieval castle site, including the Cursitor's Garden and Castle Green.[214] After some controversy over the necessary removal of the Castle Green thoroughfare and the eviction of the cottagers, Castle Green was purchased from the Golden Grove estate, and the Birmingham architect William Martin was appointed to design the new gaol for a cost of £17,700.[215]

The new gaol (Figure 140)
Work commenced in October 1868, and the new gaol, described as a 'substantial and well-finished structure' containing forty-eight cells, was complete in 1872.[216] No record of the groundworks was kept, but two gold half-nobles of Edward III were found, 'in mint condition'.[217] The gaol occupied a large, open enclosure, with a new perimeter wall, covering some 80 per cent of the medieval castle site – and the long-standing division between inner and outer wards was finally lost. In addition, the medieval cross-wall in the inner ward was demolished. These appear, however, to have been the only medieval casualties. Nash's buildings were largely demolished, but the entrance façade was retained, along with the conjoining felons' and debtors' cell-blocks.

The main block, for male prisoners, was entirely new. Like the present County Hall, it was a massive, free-standing building, of three storeys, lying centrally within the old castle site (Figures 140 and 141) and dominating the town. It was an unequal cruciform in plan. 'A Wing' and 'B Wing', in the east and west arms respectively, were larger and divided into six bays. 'C Wing', the northern cross-wing, was smaller, comprising three bays, while the southern cross-wing was a single bay. The building was of starkly institutional appearance (Figures 142–3 and 147).[218] Facework was in snecked rubble. All three storeys were lit by single-light windows, simply arched, with prominent surrounds in plain ashlar. However, the gable-wall of A Wing exhibited a three-light, Gothic window of plain lancets, beneath a pointed outer arch and hoodmould, at first-floor level; it lit the main east–west corridor (see below and Figures 142–3). The main entry was from the north, in C Wing, and faced a rectangular yard behind Nash's entrance portico, while the gable wall of the southern cross-wing was pierced by a number of windows at both upper levels, flanking a small, two-storeyed annexe with a half-hipped, lean-to roof. Otherwise roofs were low-pitched, slated gables, on dentillated eaves-cornices, with ventilators on the ridges and a low, octagonal cupola and lantern over the central 'crossing'. A massive, square, stepped chimney-stack rose through the eastern gable, above the Gothic window, providing a landmark visible for miles around and prominent in old photographs of the town (Fig. 143). Smaller chimneys occupied the gable wall of the southern cross-wing and the east wall of C wing. The ground floor was a basement. Cells occupied the two upper floors, arranged either side of broad corridors running centrally along the two main axes (Figures 142 and 144), the upper corridors lying either side of an open well, in standard pattern. The arched roof trusses were decorative, of timber, and supported on corbels along the corridor walls. The interior was whitewashed.[219]

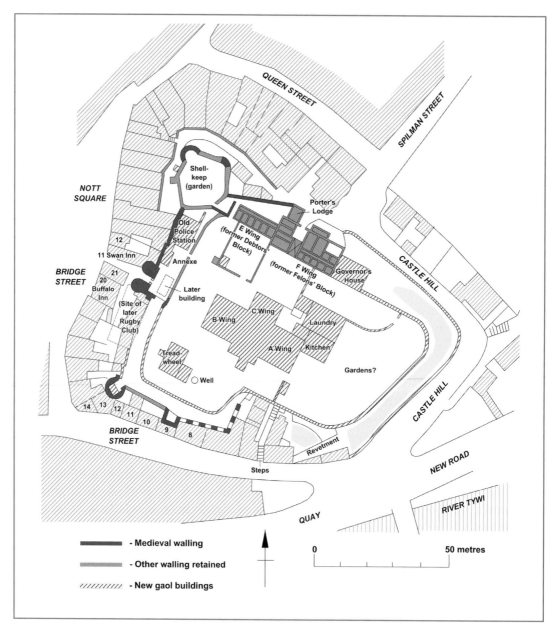

Figure 140 Plan of the entire castle site in the late nineteenth century (reconstructed)

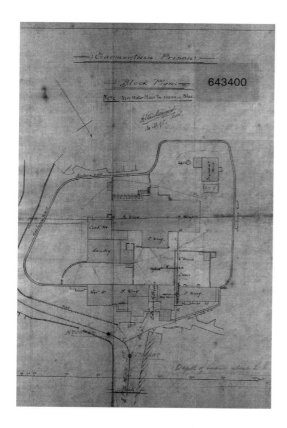

An annexe, housing the kitchen and laundry, joined the north-east corner of the main block (Figure 141). It was of a single stage, with similar detail to the main block and a complex of low-pitched gable roofs.[220] The treadwheel occupied a third new building, with a steep hipped roof, lying detached in the south-west corner of the site – the former Cursitor's Garden (Figures 140 and 141). The wheel was used to draw water from the gaol well,[221] immediately to the east, which was also an entirely new feature 'perhaps necessitated by cases of cholera for which the cesspool had been blamed'.[222]

Figure 141 (left) Plan of Carmarthen Gaol in 1898. NB: north at bottom of frame (Carmarthenshire Archive Service, CRO Acc. 7812, Block plan of gaol, 1898)

Figure 142 (right and below) Sections through the late nineteenth-century gaol, 1937 (Carmarthenshire Archive Service, CRO CAC/PL/11)

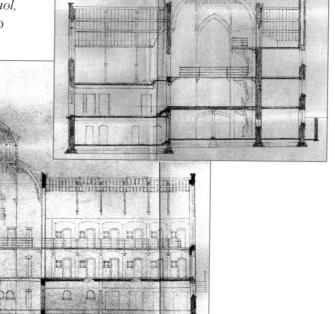

Facing southeast

Facing southwest

Figure 143 *The late nineteenth-century gaol block from southeast, in 1931* (Carmarthenshire Archive Service, CRO Mus. Vol. 36, 'CAS Scrapbook', 124)

Nash's debtors' and felons' cell-blocks were remodelled, as 'E Wing' and 'F Wing' respectively, to house women prisoners (Figures 141 and 144),[223] but their yards, to the south, were entirely new. The Governor's House was relocated and built anew, against the east end of the Felons' Block, facing Spilman Street (Figure 146); double-pile, and of three bays, it featured steep gabled roofs and neo-Gothic detail. The gaol entrance façade was also remodelled. The main entry was blocked, and converted into a window; the former lobby was given over to domestic use and a further window was inserted in the overlying arch, replacing the grille. An entirely new entry was formed in the bay to the west, beneath Nash's arch, leading into the yard (Figure 145). The four western felons' cells were remodelled to include a wide entrance passage emerging as a large, segmental archway into the interior (Figure 147). The chapel was again altered and given a pyramidal roof,[224] while a new Porter's Lodge, with a low, hipped roof, was built immediately to the west of the entry, facing Spilman Street (Figure 145).

The high perimeter wall around the new gaol, which partly survives at the west end of the site (see Figures 5 and 105–6), ran concentrically inside the line of the medieval curtain walls to create a *cordon sanitaire, c.*9 m wide. It was a solid boundary within which, apart from the main gaol entrance, there were originally no doorways (Figure 141); the present entry was a later insertion. The wall ran south-eastwards from the Governor's House to incorporate the early nineteenth-century retaining wall around Castle Green, which was heightened; a small section of this earlier wall is still preserved in the present County Hall boundary. It continued to join the east wall of the former gatehouse rear section which, with the east walls of the former infirmary and debtor's yard, was also incorporated (Figure

Figure 144 *The former debtors' block ('E Wing') from south-east, in the 1930s*
(© Crown Copyright: Royal Commission on the Ancient and Historical Monuments of Wales, B42/1502)

Figure 145 *Carmarthen Gaol: John Nash's entrance front in 1922* (Carmarthenshire Museums Service, CAASG 2005/0817/2)

Figure 146 The new Governor's House, looking down Spilman Street from north-east, n.d. (Carmarthenshire Museums Service, CAASG 1976/2394)

141). The lines, at least, of two or three of Nash's airing yard walls were also retained in the internal divisons of the new enclosure, the eastern half of which was apparently occupied by the gaol gardens.[225]

Lying externally to the new perimeter wall were the surviving north and west curtain walls and the southern retaining wall, which, like the eastern boundary of the former Cursitor's Garden, were retained. The latter was extended eastwards, around the north side of the Bridge Street properties, to join the lower, existing retaining wall around Castle Green. Where it ran above the cliff outcrop at the south-east extremity of the site, it was supported by a sloping revetment, forming a 'glacis' wall (Figure 148). All these walls survived until the 1960s.

Figure 147 Aerial photograph of the gaol, from south-east, c.1935 (Carmarthenshire Museums Service, CAASG 1987/0074)

Figure 148 (top right) Detail from Ordnance Survey 1:2500, first edition, Carmarthenshire Sheet XXIX.7, 1886 (© Crown copyright, 1886)

Figure 149 (centre right) Detail from Ordnance Survey 1:500, Carmarthenshire Sheet XXIX.7.6, 1895 (© Crown copyright, 1895)

Figure 150 (bottom right) Detail from Ordnance Survey 1:2500, second edition, Carmarthenshire Sheet XXIX.7, 1906 (© Crown copyright, 1906)

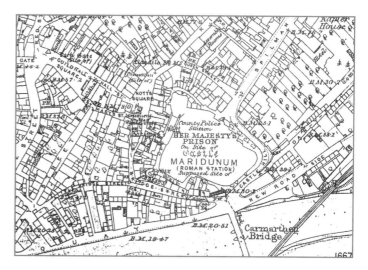

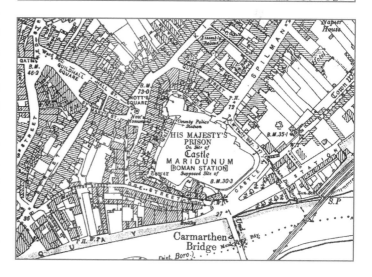

The Old Police Station and gatehouse

Carmarthenshire County Police had been established in 1843,[226] but the location of its headquarters during its early years is unknown.[227] Nash's infirmary building, which had survived the rebuild, was converted during the 1870s for combined use as a lock-up and County Police Station, with the division of the ground floor into cells and the insertion of first-floor chambers (Figure 104). The infirmary was finally demolished and replaced, between 1880 and 1886, by a new Police Station and lock-up (Figures 151, 108–10), which partly overlies its footprint (cf. Figures 139 and 148).

This area lay outside the perimeter wall and could not be accessed from the gaol. The reopening of the medieval gatehouse, to allow access to this area and the Police Station, must therefore be contemporary with the gaol wall.[228] We have seen that the

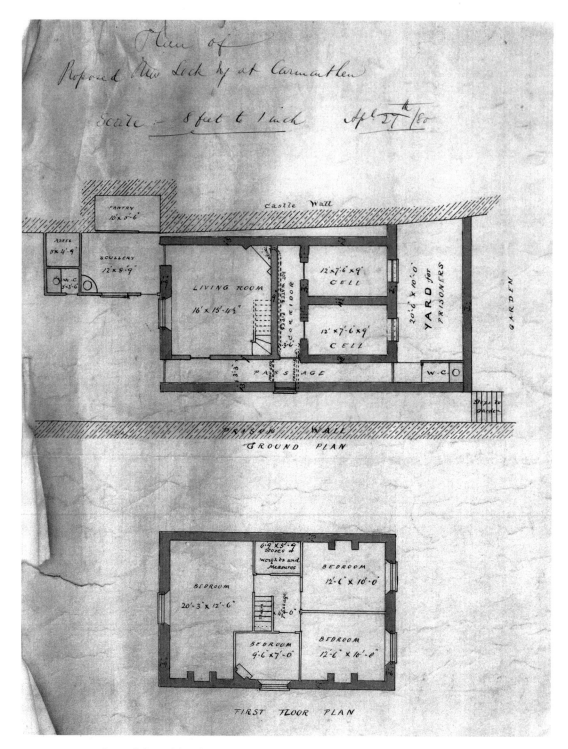

Figure 151 *Plan of the Old Police Station as proposed, 1880* (Carmarthenshire Archive Service, CRO MS 19, 'Plan of proposed new lock-up at Carmarthen, 27 April 1880')

gatehouse rear section had been removed by 1834; its south wall was now truncated to its present length, and a new, smaller entry was inserted at the east end of the passage. This has a 'neo-Perpendicular' four-centred surround (Figure 81), in sharp contrast with Nash's neo-Classical work. The partial removal of the blocking from the gatehouse north tower, described in Chapter 3, may be contemporary, but for reasons unknown.

The brick building revealed in the yard behind the gatehouse in 2002 is early twentieth century, but is of unknown function.

Figure 152 *(above) The Old Police Station from south, in 1905* (by kind permission of Dyfed-Powys Police Museum)

OLD CARMARTHEN CASTLE GATEWAY.
CHAMBERLAIN YARD.
30587

Figure 153 *(left) View looking east through the gatehouse passage, showing former yard building,* c.*1920* (Carmarthenshire Museums Service, CAASG 2003/0069)

It is not shown in maps and photos from 1905–6 (Figures 150 and 152), but had been built by the 1920s (Figure 153) and appears to have still been standing in c.1935 (Figure 147). It was probably demolished, along with the gaol, in 1937–9.

Closure and demolition, 1924–39
Britain's gaols were nationalised in 1877, and their management taken out of the hands of the county authorities.[229] Many closures followed, including Cardigan and Haverfordwest, whose prisoners were moved to Carmarthen,

causing extreme overcrowding. However, by the early twentieth century the gaol had become restricted to male prisoners only.[230] Some small ancillary buildings were added, and are shown on later plans, but no major alterations or building works were undertaken after 1872. According to a report from the early 1920s, Carmarthen was 'not a good prison for carrying out the modern treatment of prisoners [and] a small place with no industrial possibilities',[231] with a staff of only twelve warders and a governor.[232] And so it fell victim to the infamous 'Geddes Axe' in 1922, when the Geddes report recommended its closure on cost-cutting grounds.[233] Closure was finally ordered in September 1924.[234] The inmates were moved to Swansea Gaol, whose female prisoners were moved to Cardiff to make way for them.

As the former prison authority, the County Council was invited to purchase the property for £3249,[235] the sale going ahead later in 1924. Demolition was proposed as early as 1931,[236] but various plans for conversion were subsequently put forward, including county offices, a museum and library.[237] Finally, in 1934, it was decided to demolish the gaol to make way for a new County Council building.[238] The contract for demolition was apparently awarded in 1937,[239] but work had already begun in 1935[240] with the dismantling of the gaol perimeter wall (see Figure 147).

Efforts were made to save the Nash entrance façade and portico which apparently was carefully dismantled for re-erection. Its subsequent fate is unclear: one account has it that the stones were mislaid during the Second World War,[241] others claim that the portico was, in fact, broken up.[242] In the event, the only gaol-phase building to be retained, apart from the surviving stretch of gaol wall, was the Old Police Station and lock-up, which remained in use until 1947, continuing the castle's penal role for a little longer. However, an interesting nod to the castle's defensive role was given in the Second World War by the installation of the air-raid siren in the north-west corner of the shell-keep.

Demolition of the gaol coincided with the dismantling of the medieval town bridge, and its replacement with the present structure, in 1936–7. At the same time, Castle Hill was widened, with profound implications for the castle site. The east and south-east flanks of the former outer ward, which had already lost around 7 m to road widening in c.1804, were further cut back by between 3 m and 10 m (see Figure 165); altogether, over 10 per cent of the castle interior was lost. The early nineteenth-century retaining wall around Castle Green, and the slightly later lower wall, were removed,[243] and a new retaining wall was built. An informal 'watching brief' on the works, and a photographic record, were maintained by George Eyre Evans of CAS.[244]

County Hall (Figure 154)

County Hall, Carmarthenshire's administrative headquarters, was eventually commenced in 1939. It was designed in 1935 by Sir Percy Thomas, who was also responsible for the acclaimed Swansea Guildhall, built in 1934, the Temple of Peace and Health in Cathays Park, Cardiff, from 1938, and a large part of the Aberystwyth University campus at Penglais.[245] He was later knighted for his services to architecture.

Figure 154 County Hall in 2007, and the castle remains, from south-west (by courtesy of Ken Day)

Construction work, undertaken by W. T. Nicholls of Gloucester,[246] was interrupted by the war and was not completed until 1955; the official opening was in 1956.[247] It is a large building with two high storeys over a basement. A quadrangular block in plan, it comprises four office ranges around a central yard, which is divided by a cross-wing containing the council chamber.[248] The style throughout is that of a French *château*, presumably in acknowledgement of the historic origins of the site. It is massive in form, faced in plain, rock-faced grey Forest of Dean stone, and external detail – in white Portland stone – is pared to a minimum. The main north and south fronts are of thirteen bays, those at the ends being curved projections or *tourelles*; the sides comprise twelve bays. Each bay is lit by a window in all three storeys. The tall rectangular cross-windows in the upper floors are lengthened as French windows, with balconies, in the projecting end bays and in the central bays of the main fronts; the basement features small casement pairs. The basement storey forms a projecting plinth and there is a cornice at the eaves. Roofs are steeply pitched and in green Pembrokeshire slate, creating a handsome effect, and two massive stone chimney-stacks rise through the roof ridge in both main fronts. The main entrance, in the north front, has a Portland stone surround featuring reliefs, by the sculptor David Evans, showing the council's various activities. It is reached by a broad flight of steps. The third bay from each end features a smaller doorway, also in Portland stone. The interior is functional, with terrazzo floors and stairs. The council chamber is in modern historicist style, with an ornate coffered ceiling carried on Gothic corbelled arcading. County Hall is one of the most notable mid-twentieth-century public buildings in Wales, by a leading Welsh architect, and the dominant building of the town.

Groundworks for its construction were not accompanied by any archaeological record, and their impact, and the nature of the underlying levels are unknown. We can be sure, however, that a considerable loss of deposits occurred. But apart from a small electricity substation built against the north curtain wall, County Hall is still the only new building in the castle site.

NOTES

1   W. A. Shaw (ed.), *Calendar of Treasury Books*, 1–26 (London: Institute of Historical Research, 1904–54).

2   J. Dodridge, *An Historical Account of the Ancient and Modern State of the Principality of Wales, Duchy of Cornwall and Earldom of Chester* (London: J. Roberts, 1630, second print, 1714).

3   J. Davies (ed.), *The Carmarthen Book of Ordinances 1569–1606* (Llandybïe: CAS, 1996). This is a transcription, by John Davies of Carmarthenshire Archive Service, of one of the two Corporation Order Books, CRO (M) 156 and 156a, the entries in which run from 1569 until 1606. Extracts from the second book, CRO (M) 155, can be found in NLW, MS 12358D, 'Records of the Corporate Borough of Carmarthen, 1590–1764' (transcribed by Alcwyn Evans, 1851–3); it is also undergoing further transcription by John Davies. Both books relate to the borough rather than the county.

4   For example NLW, MS 12358D; NLW, MSS 12364D and 12365D, 'Collectanea concerning Caermarthen', 1 and 2 (transcribed by Alcwyn Evans); NLW, MS 12367D, 'Carmarthen borough records, charters etc. 1581–1610, 1738–1835' (transcribed by Alcwyn Evans).

5   See G. Parry, 'A guide to the records of the Great Sessions in Wales' (Aberystwyth: NLW, 1995).

6   J. R. Phillips, *Memoirs of the Civil War in Wales and the Marches 1642–1649*, 1 and 2 (London: Longmans, Green and Co., 1874).

7   Early English Books Online, Thomason Tracts.

8   J. Vicars, *God in the Mount or, England's Parliamentary Chronicle*, 1 and 2; *God's Arke overtopping the World's Waves or, the Third Part of the Parliamentary Chronicle*; *The Burning-bush not Consumed or, the Fourth and Last Part of the Parliamentarie-Chronicle* (London: J. Rothwell and T. Underhill, 1644–6).

9   C. H. Firth, and R. S. Rait (eds), *Acts and Ordinances of the Interregnum, 1642–1660* (London: History of Parliament Trust, 1911).

10   Some of the *JHC* entries were published by Michael Thompson, including a number relevant to Carmarthen Castle – see M. W. Thompson, *The Decline of the Castle* (Cambridge University Press, 1987).

11   T. James, 'Carmarthen's Civil War Defences', *Carms. Antiq.*, 27 (1991), 21–30; B. H. St J. O'Neil, 'The Bulwarks, Carmarthen', *Archaeologia Cambrensis*, 93 (1938), 126–30.

12   J. Howard, *The State of the Prisons in England and Wales, with Preliminary Observations, and an Account of some Foreign Prisons* (Warrington: William Eyres, 1777), pp. 467–8. Extracts of an account from his second visit in 1788 can be found in G. J. Thomas, 'Carmarthen Gaols, 1774, 1788', *TCASFC*, 29 (1939), 104–5.

13   J. Neild, *An Account of the Rise, Progress and Present State, of the Society for the Discharge and Relief of Persons Imprisoned for Small Debts throughout England and Wales* (London: John Nichols and Son, 1808), pp. 72–3.

14   D. Defoe, *A Tour through the Whole Island of Great Britain* (London: Longman, 1962 edn.); T. Dineley, *The Account of the Official Progress of His Grace Henry the first Duke of Beaufort through Wales in 1684* (London: Blades and Blades, 1888 facsimile edn).

15   CRO, Cawdor Maps 219 (see Figure 111), and CRO (M) 459a. A third map, CRO2 (M) 5, is identical to the latter. The depiction of the castle area is the same in all three.

16   For instance NLW, Carm. Top. A5, A011, 'Carmarthen Castle, Metcalf sculpt.', *c.*1785; NLW, Carm. Top. A5, A013, 'South view of Carmarthen Castle and Town', *c.*1820; and many others. There are some original views (e.g. NLW, Carm. Top. A5, A009, 'Carmarthen

Castle, South Wales', 1792), but few show the castle clearly. Pictorial sources for the castle area are discussed in A. Dorsett, 'Artist's depictions of Carmarthen Quay', in H. James and P. Moore (eds), *Carmarthenshire and Beyond: Studies in History and Archaeology in Memory of Terry James* (Carmarthen: CAS, 2009), pp. 61–6.

17 P. Lord, 'Artisan Painters in Carmarthen', *Carms. Antiq.*, 27 (1991), 48.

18 And the early nineteenth-century artist Charles Norris, of Tenby, appears not to have chosen it as a subject.

19 N. Carlisle, *A Topographical Dictionary of the Dominion of Wales* (London: Nicholas Carlisle, 1811); M. W. Thompson (ed.), *The Journeys of Sir Richard Colt Hoare through Wales and England, 1793-1810* (Gloucester: Sutton Publishing Ltd, 1983); J. Fisher (ed.), *Tours in Wales (1804–1813) by Richard Fenton* (London: Bedford Press, 1917); B. H. Malkin, *The Scenery, Antiquities and Biography of South Wales*, 2 (London: Longman and Rees, 1807).

20 E. Donovan, *Descriptive Excursions through South Wales and Monmouthshire in the Year 1804, and the Four Preceding Summers*, 2 (London: Edward Donovan, 1805), pp. 171–2; S. Lewis, *A Topographical Dictionary of Wales*, 1 (London: S. Lewis and Co., 1849), pp. 180–6.

21 R. W. Ireland, *'A Want of Order and Good Discipline': Rules, Discretion and the Victorian Prison* (Cardiff: UWP, 2007). Although primarily a social history, drawing on the gaoler's journals and Quarter Sessions records, it includes a valuable account of the gaol buildings and their function.

22 R. Suggett, *John Nash, Architect in Wales* (Aberystwyth: RCAHMW/NLW, 1995), pp. 25–30.

23 CRO, MS 19.

24 CRO (M) 786.

25 Curated by RCAHMW (NPRN 100074).

26 Notably George Eyre Evans's notes from the seventeenth-/eighteenth-century MSS of the Phillipses of Cwmgwili (G. E. Evans, 'The Cwmgwili Manuscripts', *TCASFC*, 23 (1932), 90–3, *TCASFC*, 26 (1936), 26–31), which were transcribed from the Cwmgwili MSS at CRO, and his copies of the MS diary, from 1764–97, of John Vaughan of Golden Grove (G. E. Evans, 'Caermarthen, 1764–1797', *TCASFC*, 1 (1906), 101–2).

27 W. Spurrell, *Carmarthen and its Neighbourhood* (Carmarthen: Spurrell and Co., 1879).

28 The schedules of the Alcwyn Evans and George Eyre Evans deposits at NLW were also looked through for further relevant material.

29 Thompson, *Decline of the Castle*, pp. 105–8.

30 The 'County' is not to be confused with the 'County Borough' of Carmarthen, which was established in 1604 (*CSPD*, James I, 1603–1610 (London, 1857), p. 117).

31 R. A. Griffiths, *The Principality of Wales in the Later Middle Ages: The Structure and Personnel of Government*, 1:, *South Wales 1277–1536* (Cardiff: UWP, 1972), pp. 162, 189.

32 Dodridge, *Historical Account*, p. 42.

33 Griffiths, *Principality*, p. 30.

34 Davies, *Carmarthen Book of Ordinances*, pp. vi–viii.

35 *CPR*, Elizabeth I 2, 1560–1563 (London, 1948), p. 120; *CPR*, Elizabeth I, 3, 1563–1566 (London, 1960), passim; Dodridge, *Historical Account*, p. 60; Parry, 'Records of the Great Sessions', iv–v. Cf. Chapter 2.

36 Thompson, *Decline of the Castle*, p. 12.

37 F. Green (ed.), 'Carmarthen Castle: A Collection of Historical Documents relating to Carmarthen Castle from the Earliest Times to the Close of the Reign of Henry VIII', *WWHR*, 4 (1914), 71.

38 *CPR*, Philip and Mary, 1, 1553–1554 (London, 1937), p. 270. Admiral Sir Rhys Mansel, *c*.1487–1554, had been sheriff of Glamorgan and chamberlain of Chester under Henry VIII. However, there was a subsequent

shift towards the appointment of professional civil servants, like John Walsh, justice during the 1550s (ibid., p. 269), and his successors John Restall and the highly regarded George Fettiplace of Berkshire, justice between 1574 and 1577 (see A. L. Browne, 'George Phetiplace, Justice of South Wales, 1574–1577', *TCASFC*, 24 (1933), 38–42, for a brief biography).

39 Green, 'Carmarthen Castle' 4, 60.

40 Ibid., 60–1, where the account is wrongly dated to 1578, two years after Essex's death. Another condition of the grant was that 'the Auditor and Receiver may have place when they come to the country, and the Justice in circuit time'.

41 Ibid., 62–4. Cf. Monmouth Castle, where completion of the gatehouse, left unfinished in the mid-fifteenth century, was recommended in *c.*1550 so that the exchequer, held in the town, could move back into the castle (A. J. Taylor, *Monmouth Castle and Great Castle House* (London: HMSO, 1951), p. 13).

42 J. Goodall, *The English Castle 1066-1650* (New Haven and London: Yale University Press, 2011), p. 470.

43 When it may also have been rebuilt (Davies, *Carmarthen Book of Ordinances*, p. iv). It occupied the site of the present building, in the middle of the town, and was possibly the same Guildhall that had been established by 1313–18 (W. Rees (ed.), *Calendar of Ancient Petitions relating to Wales* (Cardiff: UWP, 1975), p.495). It was again rebuilt in 1767–77.

44 A. Saunders, *Excavations at Launceston Castle, Cornwall*, SMA Monograph 24 (London, 2006), pp. 41–2. This process had its origins in the Middle Ages, e.g. at Caernarfon Castle where the courthouse had moved into the town by the fifteenth century, to be followed by the justiciar's lodging (A. J. Taylor, *Caernarvon Castle and Town Walls* (London: HMSO, 1953), p. 42).

45 The 'Constable and Usher of Carmarthen Castle' still represented part of the court apparatus in 1630 (Dodridge, *Historical Account*, p. 60).

46 Green, 'Carmarthen Castle' 4, 60; *CPR 1560–63*, p. 604.

47 Goodall, *English Castle*, p. 470.

48 Evans, 'Cwmgwili Manuscripts' 23, 92–3.

49 See Taylor, *Monmouth Castle*, p. 21; J. Champness, *Lancaster Castle: A Brief History* (Preston: Lancashire County Books, 1993), pp. 11–13.

50 Green, 'Carmarthen Castle' 4, 63–4.

51 W. Rees (ed.), *A Survey of the Duchy of Lancaster Lordships in Wales 1609–1613* (Cardiff: UWP, 1953), pp. 10–11; D. F. Renn, *Clifford's Tower and the Castles of York* (London: HMSO, 1971), pp. 18–22.

52 NLW, MS 12358D, 60.

53 M. Darwen, *Lincoln Castle* (Lincoln: Lincolnshire County Council, n.d.), p. 4.

54 Rees, *Duchy of Lancaster Lordships*, p. 11.

55 Evans, 'Cwmgwili Manuscripts' 23, 92–3.

56 It may, however, already have been in private hands; James I had, before his death in 1625, disposed of many ruined properties to raise funds, including Pembroke and York castles (J. Clark, *Clifford's Tower and the Castle of York* (London: English Heritage, 2010), p. 33).

57 CRO, Cawdor 21/613, Inspeximus of deeds (1639), 163.

58 Ibid.

59 A. Crossley and C. R. Elrington (eds), *A History of the County of Oxford*, 12 (OUP, 1990), pp. 82–4; H. E Malden (ed.), *A History of the County of Surrey*, 3 (London: Constable, 1911), pp. 467–75; W. Page, *A History of the County of Middlesex*, 2 (London: Constable, 1911), pp. 314–19.

60 R. B. Harraden, *History of the University of Cambridge* (Cambridge: Harraden and Son, 1814), pp. 252–3.

61 CRO, Cawdor 21/613, 163.

62 Champness, *Lancaster Castle*, p. 13.

63 J. E. Lloyd (ed.), *A History of Carmarthenshire*, 2 (London: London Carmarthenshire Society, 1939), p. 25.

64 A. L. Leach, *The History of the Civil War (1642–1649) in Pembrokeshire and on its Borders* (London: H. F. and G. Witherby, 1937), p. 40.

65 Ibid., p. 31.

66 Phillips, *Memoirs of the Civil War*, p. 215.

67 Vicars, *God's Arke*, p. 224. The exact date that Carmarthen was taken is not known. Most contemporary accounts place the action in May (see e.g. ibid.; Thomason 669, f.10, Lists of Parliamentary victories by Joseph Ricraft, 1646), but letters telling of the event had arrived in London by 3 May (Thomason E46.8, *The Parliament Scout*, by John Dillingham (1643–5), 383), placing it in late April (as suggested by James, 'Carmarthen's Civil War Defences', 25–6).

68 Phillips, *Memoirs of the Civil War*, p. 232

69 Ibid., pp. 274–6; Thomason E307.15, Letter from Maj.-Gen. Laugharne to the House of Commons, 28 October 1645. Also see James, 'Carmarthen's Civil War Defences', 27.

70 Letter from George, Lord Digby (G. E. Evans, 'Carmarthen Castle', *TCASFC*, 1 (1906), 27).

71 Thomason E307.25, Journal of Matthew Walbancke (1644–6), 5–6; Phillips, *Memoirs of the Civil War*, p. 337; Vicars, *Burning-bush*, p. 302.

72 A note to this effect was apparently pinned in one of the Borough Corporation Order Books, and was seen during the nineteenth century (NLW, MS 12364D, 518). A number of pin-holes are all that remain (as discussed in James, 'Carmarthen's Civil War Defences', 25–6); there are altogether very few entries relating to the Civil War in the order books.

73 James, 'Carmarthen's Civil War Defences', 29.

74 G. Geear, S. Priestley and R. Turner, 'After the Restoration', in R. Turner and A.

Johnson (eds), *Chepstow Castle; Its History and Buildings* (Almeley: Logaston, 2006), pp. 235–8.

75 Heather James, pers. comm.

76 Thomason E307.25, 5–6.

77 Thomason E84.34, Declaration by Parliament concerning Lincolnshire, 9 January 1643.

78 James, 'Carmarthen's Civil War Defences', 27.

79 Phillips, *Memoirs of the Civil War*, p. 233 (from *The Weekly Account*, No. 42, 18 June 1644).

80 O'Neil, 'The Bulwarks', 128–30.

81 Ibid.; James, 'Carmarthen's Civil War Defences', 28–9. Parliamentary origins have not, so far, been suggested for any of the defensive works at Carmarthen. It is of interest that one of the best surviving Civil War defence systems in Britain has no documentary record.

82 E. Rae, 'Archaeological investigations at the former Cattle Market, Carmarthen, Carmarthenshire, October 2007–May 2008' (unpublished report by Northamptonshire Archaeology, 2009, copy held in DAT HER), 8, 24–5.

83 Thomason E307.15.

84 See James, 'Carmarthen's Civil War Defences', 28.

85 *JHC 5, 1646–1648* (London, 1802), pp. 123–5.

86 Ibid., 249–51; also see Thompson, *Decline of the Castle*, p. 180.

87 Thompson, *Decline of the Castle*, p. 143.

88 James, 'Carmarthen's Civil War Defences', 28; O'Neil, 'The Bulwarks', 127.

89 Thomason E442.11, Declaration of Maj.-Gen. Laugharne and Col. Rice Powell, 15 May 1648, 5.

90 Leach, *Civil War in Pembrokeshire*, pp. 149, 155, 160. Cols. Poyer and Culpepper of the garrison wrote a declaration in support of the king, at Carmarthen (Thomason E435.9, Declaration of Col. Poyer, 10 April 1648).

91 Phillips, *Memoirs of the Civil War*, p. 400; Thomason E441.6, 'The particular relation of

another great fight in south Wales', by Thomas Hill, Cornet, 3 May 1648.

92 Phillips, *Memoirs of the Civil War*, p. 398.

93 Ibid., p. 406.

94 The Corporation Order Books apparently recorded – on another pinned slip of paper – that quarters for 160 men were found in Carmarthen, possibly for Cromwell's troops (G. E. Evans, 'Carmarthen Local Events AD 1547–1836', *Yr Encilion*, 1/1 (1912), 13).

95 Firth and Rait, *Acts and Ordinances*, pp. 14–16, 24–57.

96 Ibid., pp. 24–57; S. K. Roberts, 'Dawkins, Rowland (1618–1691)', *Oxford Dictionary of National Biography* (OUP: 2004; online edn 2008, accessed September 2012).

97 B. S. Capp, *The World of John Taylor the Water Poet, 1578–1653* (OUP, 1994), p. 161; NLW, MS 12364D 1, 518.

98 Roberts, 'Dawkins, Rowland'; also see Thompson, *Decline of the Castle*, pp. 153–4.

99 *JHC 7, 1651–1660* (London, 1802), pp. 25–6.

100 Where work on the defences continued after the Restoration (Geear *et al.*, 'After the Restoration', pp. 229–42; J. Knight, 'Civil War and Commonwealth', in Turner and Johnson, *Chepstow Castle*, p. 227).

101 Spurrell, *Carmarthen*, p. 117, from a letter sent by Dawkins.

102 Roberts, 'Dawkins, Rowland'.

103 Ibid.

104 *JHC 7, 1651–1660* (London, 1802), p. 617.

105 Thomason E1432.2, Account of a journey through Wales by John Taylor in 1652, 18 (for Taylor see Capp, *World of John Taylor*). Moreover Dawkins was still titled 'Governor of Carmarthen Castle' in that year (Green, 'Carmarthen Castle' 4, 72).

106 NLW, MS 12358D, 67.

107 R. Mathias, 'The Second Civil War and Interregnum', in B. Howells (ed.), *Pembrokeshire County History, 3: Early Modern Pembrokeshire 1536–1815* (Haverfordwest: Pembrokeshire Historical Society, 1987), p. 221.

108 W. A. Shaw (ed.), *Calendar of Treasury Books*, 1, 1660–1667 (London: Institute of Historical Research, 1904), p. 101.

109 R. Blome, 1673 *Britannia or, A Geographical Description of the Kingdoms of England, Scotland and Ireland, with the Isles and Territories thereto Belonging* (London: Thomas Roycroft for Richard Blome, 1673), pp. 269–70.

110 Firth and Rait, *Acts and Ordinances*.

111 Thompson 1987, 142. No county records exist, at CRO or NLW, beyond the NLW 'Gaol Files' i.e. the records of the sessions. What are normally preserved are the orders for demolition that were recorded, as at Carmarthen in 1647, in *JHC* and *CSPD*.

112 Taylor, *Monmouth Castle*, p. 8; Thompson, *Decline of the Castle*, p. 183.

113 J. K. Knight, 'Excavations at Montgomery Castle, part I', *Archaeologia Cambrensis*, 142 (1992), 119–21.

114 R. Avent, *Laugharne Castle* (Cardiff: Cadw, 1995), p. 21; C. Parry, 'Survey and Excavation at Newcastle Emlyn Castle', *Carms. Antiq.*, 23 (1987), 11.

115 CRO, (M) 49, Presentment on properties within Carmarthen (1657).

116 It was suggested by the local historian William Spurrell that 'the castle was dismantled by Cromwell in 1648' (Spurrell, *Carmarthen*, p. 116). However, we have seen that it was in use for some time afterwards.

117 Thomason E993.33, *The Weekly Post*, by D. Border, 1659–1660, 144; *JHC 7*, pp. 769–70.

118 Champness, *Lancaster Castle*, p. 13.

119 The disruptions of the Civil War mean that for many Welsh counties there are large gaps in the records of the sessions during the 1640s and, to a lesser extent, the 1650s. Carmarthenshire is fortunate in that records, although in the main patchy, include deposits from 1653–8 (J. F. Jones, 'Common Law Records: Carmarthenshire', *TCASFC*, 24 (1933), 37–8, from the 'First report of the Deputy Keeper of the Public Records',

1840; Parry, 'Guide to the records of the Great Sessions'). What may have been done with the prisoners during slighting is, as during fortification, unknown.

120   N. Guy (ed.), 'News: Northampton Castle', *Castle Studies Group Bulletin*, 18 (2005), 99.

121   Thomason E1075.13, 'An act for the speedy disbanding of the army and garrisons of this kingdome', 15 September 1660. Also see *JHC 8, 1660–1667* (London, 1802), pp. 142–3. *JHC*, sadly, is incomplete for the crucial period of September–October 1660.

122   Chepstow's slighting was ordered on 21 May 1660 (*JHC 8, 1660–1667* (London, 1802), pp. 38–40), but was not carried out (Geear *et al.*, 'After the Restoration', pp. 229–42). For Caernarfon and Denbigh see Thompson, *Decline of the Castle*, p. 156.

123   CRO, Cawdor 112/8400, Rental of Vaughan properties in the Borough of Carmarthen etc. (1669), 501.

124   Shaw, *Calendar of Treasury Books* 1, p. 101.

125   CRO, Cawdor 2/54, Writ to the keeper of the gaol (1669), 464.

126   CRO, Cawdor 125/8647, Notebook including transcription of presentments of Grand Jury of Carmarthen re. boundaries of the liberties of Carmarthen Castle (1753), 1141.

127   Which was, tellingly, described as lying within 'the liberty of the County Gaol' (CRO, Cawdor 22/659, 'Specification of the manors and lordships of the late Lady Anne Vaughan' (1753), 493). The county authorities pursued the claim still further, suggesting – with little success – that the outer ward belonged to the office of the 'Chamberlain of the Sessions' (CRO, Cawdor 103/8056, Schedule of leases in Co. Borough of Carmarthen (*c*.1750), 180).

128   See CRO, Cawdor Papers Vol. IV, Manorial records (1275–1814). Castle Green was eventually declared extra-parochial in 1835 (G. E. Evans, 'Carmarthen: Castle Green',

TCASFC, 24 (1933), 9, from the MS diary of C. D. Williams, 1835).

129   This gatehouse, which formerly stood between King Street and Nott Square, had become the borough gaol by 1581 (Davies, *Carmarthen Book of Ordinances*, p. 14). It was called the 'Upper House' from the sixteenth to the eighteenth century (ibid.; *The Gentleman's Magazine*, 24 November 1755, p. 570) and, occasionally, the 'Prisoner's Gate' (Evans, 'Carmarthen Local Events', 15). It had become a debtors' gaol by the time of its demolition in 1792 (T. James, *Carmarthen: An Archaeological and Topographical Survey*, CAS Monograph 2 (Carmarthen, 1980), p. 53).

130   Ireland, *A Want of Order*, passim.

131   See Parry, 'Records of the Great Sessions' (some of these records are catalogued in NLW, 'Handlist of MSS at NLW, 8 - MSS acquired 1981–1991').

132   Saunders, *Launceston Castle*, pp. 44, 259.

133   Map evidence indicates that the buildings shown by the Bucks all belong to post-Civil War domestic development on Castle Green. The medieval towers had to suffice for prisoner accommodation, until new building in the eighteenth century at a number of other castles, e.g. York (Clark, *Clifford's Tower*, p. 36).

134   Howard, *State of the Prisons*, pp. 467–8.

135   Evans, 'Cwmgwili Manuscripts' 26, 28.

136   Thomas, 'Carmarthen Gaols', 105.

137   Howard, *State of the Prisons*, pp. 467–8.

138   Ibid.

139   Evans, 'Caermarthen, 1764–1797', 101; Evans, 'Cwmgwili Manuscripts' 26, 28.

140   Howard, *State of the Prisons*, p. 468.

141   *The Gentleman's Magazine*, 24 November 1755, p. 570.

142   CRO, Cawdor 103/8056, 180.

143   'Upwards of seventeen' cottages are mentioned in the 1750s (ibid.), but only ten are shown on all maps from 1786 onwards.

144   Spurrell, *Carmarthen*, p. 122.

145   RCAHMW, *Inventory of Ancient Monuments*, V: *County of Carmarthen* (London: HMSO, 1917), p. 251n.

146   CRO, Cawdor 2/71, Rental of Vaughan properties (1819).

147   See CRO, Cawdor Maps 40, 'Plan of part of Carmarthen (Bridge Street – Gaol), 5 April 1858', etc.

148   Spurrell, *Carmarthen*, p. 134.

149   John Wood's map of 1834 appears to indicate Castle Hill *before* any widening (Figure 133). Nevertheless, earlier prints and pictures clearly show the widened road with its new retaining wall (see Figure 132).

150   RCAHMW, *Inventory*, p. 250.

151   It had been successfully voted in 1783 (CRO, Mus. 693, 'Vote in House of Commons re. building of Carmarthen Gaol, 1783'). A site on Royal Oak Common, Johnstown, was initially suggested by the county, but was rejected on the grounds of expense. John Nash, who had already been appointed, preferred the castle site, which was eventually chosen in 1788 (Evans, 'Cwmgwili manuscripts' 26, 30).

152   Evans, 'Caermarthen, 1764–1797', 101. Another gaol was however built for the borough, in 1810, on a new site.

153   And see Richard Suggett's published plan (Suggett, *John Nash*, p. 25). Few pictures of Nash's gaol have been located, though there are a relatively large number of maps and plans.

154   Ibid., p. 27.

155   Neild, *Rise, Progress and Present State*, pp. 72–3.

156   NLW, MS 2258C, 'A journal of a tour in Wales', by Sir Christopher Sykes, Bart.' (typescript copy).

157   Lewis, *Topographical Dictionary* 1, 184 (the 1833 edition is identical).

158   Evans, 'Caermarthen, 1764–1797', 101.

159   Suggett, *John Nash*, p. 28.

160   *CarmJ*, 25 April 1851.

161   Each measuring '9' 10" by 7' 2", and 9' in height' (ibid.).

162   Ibid.

163   Neild, *Rise, Progress and Present State*, pp. 72–3.

164   *CarmJ*, 25 April 1851.

165   Ibid. Two more solitary cells apparently lay beneath the House of Correction, on the ground floor of which was a separate refractory cell (Ireland, *A Want of Order*, pp. 197–8).

166   Ibid., p. 92; *CarmJ*, 25 April 1851. The treadwheel was introduced to the prison system in 1818. Under the terms of the 1865 Gaol Act, male prisoners were obliged to spend three months of their sentence on the wheel.

167   Each of which was 'about 12ft by 9, with fireplaces' (Neild, *Rise, Progress and Present State*, pp. 72–3; cf. Evans, 'Caermarthen, 1764–1797', 101).

168   NLW MS 2258C.

169   Ireland, *A Want of Order*, pp. 111–12 and n. 97, p. 160; *CarmJ*, 25 April 1851.

170   *CarmJ*, 25 April 1851.

171   Ibid.

172   Ireland, *A Want of Order*, p. 191.

173   The Governor's House was part of Nash's original plans, as at e.g. Hereford Gaol (Ireland, *A Want of Order*, p. 115; Suggett, *John Nash*, p. 28).

174   Ireland, *A Want of Order*, pp. 113, 115.

175   Ibid., pp. 112 and n. 98, p. 113 n. 104. However, a surgeon had been appointed in 1823, one John Jenkins who had previously been surgeon to the Borough Gaol (ibid., p. 137).

176   Ibid., p. 113 n. 104.

177   Ibid., p. 191.

178   *CarmJ*, 25 April 1851.

179   Suggett, *John Nash*, p. 27.

180   Ibid., p. 28.

181   But even though it was 'virtually the only large, neo-Classical building in the vicinity' (ibid., p. 29), it was only mentioned in passing by contemporary travellers.

182 Donovan, *Descriptive Excursions*, p. 171.

183 Lewis, *Topographical Dictionary*, p. 184.

184 Suggett, *John Nash*, pp. 28–30. It has been said that the design was also influenced by the stables built for the great country houses of England by Robert Taylor, with whom Nash had trained (D. L. Baker-Jones, 'John Nash, architect and builder', *Carms. Antiq.*, 3 (1961), 157), and who had designed Carmarthen Guildhall in 1765–77 (T. Lloyd, J. Orbach and R. Scourfield, *The Buildings of Wales: Carmarthenshire and Ceredigion* (New Haven and London: Yale University Press, 2006), p. 140).

185 Suggett, *John Nash*, pp. 28–30.

186 *CarmJ*, 6 December 1867.

187 CRO, Misc. Maps 1, 'Plans, elevations, agreement etc. for building a new chapel in the gaol' (1859); also see Ireland, *A Want of Order*, pp. 115–16. James Collard, of Queen Street, Carmarthen, was responsible for a number of churches in Carmarthenshire and some commercial buildings in Carmarthen town (Lloyd *et al.*, *Buildings of Wales*, pp. 41, 95, 148). He emerged as the leading Carmarthen town architect of the 1840–1850s.

188 *CarmJ*, 16 August 1833. Richard Ireland notes that it is difficult to see how much of it would be visible from outside (Ireland, *A Want of Order*, p. 92).

189 *CarmJ*, 26 December 1924, from the reminiscences of T. E. Brigstocke.

190 P. J. R. Goodall, *The Black Flag over Carmarthen: over Three Centuries of Barbarism, Crime, Murder, Punishment and Executions* (Llanrwst: Gwasg Carreg Gwalch, 2005), p. 15. An account of the last public execution at the gaol, in 1829, can be found in Anon. (ed.), 'A Carmarthenshire Diary, AD 1829, 1830', *TCASFC*, 9 (1914), 17. The last execution was in 1894 (Goodall, *Black Flag*, p. 43).

191 *Daily Express*, 30 May 1931.

192 Darwen, *Lincoln Castle*, p. 10. The skull has not been dated; the possibility exists that it is earlier, and was residual in a post-medieval context.

193 J. F. Jones, 'Carmarthen "Mount"', *Carms. Antiq.*, 5 (1963), 188. It is not however labelled 'garden' on the 1858–66 plan (Figure 139).

194 But ownership of the Golden Grove plot, in dispute in 1818–19, had been resolved in favour of the estate by 1846 (CRO, Cawdor Maps 39, 'Plan of Carmarthen showing County Gaol (Castle Green)', 1846).

195 Spurrell, *Carmarthen*, p. 136.

196 *CarmJ*, 25 April 1851.

197 Ibid.

198 Ireland, *A Want of Order*, pp. 197–8; see Figure 139.

199 *CarmJ*, 25 April 1851.

200 Ireland, *A Want of Order*, pp. 152–3. Eighteen prisoners were however still in Carmarthen Gaol for debt in 1877.

201 Ibid., pp. 113–14.

202 *CarmJ*, 25 April 1851.

203 Ireland, *A Want of Order*, pp. 113–14.

204 Ibid.; also see CRO, Cawdor Maps 41, 'Plan of part of Carmarthen showing County Gaol and premises' (n.d., *c*.1857) and Cawdor Maps 42, 'Plan of part of Carmarthen showing property belonging to the Earl of Cawdor' (*c*.1867).

205 Ireland, *A Want of Order*, pp. 114–15. Penson may have been replaced by W. H. Lindsay of Haverfordwest (ibid., n. 110), who also reroofed Carmarthen St Peter, 1860–1, and removed the outside stairs from Carmarthen Guildhall (Lloyd *et al.*, *Buildings of Wales*, pp. 43, 129 and 141).

206 Ireland, *A Want of Order*, pp. 114–15 and n. 112.

207 Ibid. and n. 111.

208 James, *Carmarthen Survey*, p. 28.

209 CRO, Cawdor 63/6602, Letter dated 26 January 1761.

210 Also see CRO, Cawdor Maps 41. The overlying building is clearly shown as an annexe of the Buffalo Inn in a drawing of 1857

(NLW, Drawing Vol. 64, 9a, 'Carmarthen Castle (rear view of tower)', 1857).

211　The cellars gave rise to spurious tales of 'passages' to and from the castle, whilst others were thought to represent the crypts of medieval chapels.

212　Ireland, *A Want of Order*, pp. 116–18.

213　CRO, MS 19, 'Plan showing proposed alteration at Carmarthen County Gaol, 30 June 1866'.

214　Map evidence shows that there was very little open space on Castle Green from the mid-eighteenth century onwards (see Figures 129, 133 and 137). However, early twentieth-century accounts appear to take the name 'Castle Green' at face value, with claims that it included, until 1868, a large public open space for recreation, and gatherings as for the Wesley sermon. In particular, see the reminiscences of T. E. Brigstocke in *CarmJ*, 26 December 1924; Brigstocke however had his own reasons for making the claim: to 'restore' the area as a public open space, after the closure of the gaol and acquisition of the site by the council in 1924.

215　Ireland, *A Want of Order*, pp. 116–20. William Martin (1829–1900), was, along with his partner J. H. Chamberlain, chiefly known for public buildings such as police stations, baths, libraries and, especially, schools. Neither had much experience of gaol design, despite a report in *CarmJ* insisting that Martin gave 'the whole of his time and attention to gaols'. However, he had also been approached concerning Cardigan Gaol (ibid., 119 and n. 137).

216　Ibid., pp. 120–2; Spurrell, *Carmarthen*, p. 163.

217　RCAHMW, *Inventory*, p. 251. The inmates themselves apparently contributed to the construction work, following standard practice (Ireland, *A Want of Order*, p. 191).

218　A photograph held by Carmarthenshire Museums Service claims to show the interior of the new gaol (Ireland, *A Want of Order*, Plate 3). However, it is clearly not Carmarthen Gaol.

The arrangement of the two wings differs from the Carmarthen layout, while the architectural detail is also very different.

219　Ibid., p. 191.

220　Photograph in *CarmJ*, 30 January 1935.

221　Ireland, *A Want of Order*, p. 187. Water had been drawn from the earlier well via a hand-pump.

222　Ibid., p. 122. It was opened up during excavations for County Hall in 1939 and found to be circular, brick-lined and much choked up with debris (J. F. Jones, 'Carmarthen Gaol, 1808', *Carms. Antiq.*, 4 (1962), 88).

223　Ireland, *A Want of Order*, p. 122.

224　See CRO, MS 19, Plan of proposed alterations to frontage of Carmarthen Gaol (n.d.).

225　*CarmJ*, 26 December 1924.

226　Spurrell, *Carmarthen*, p. 150 n. 34.

227　Charles Griffiths (curator/archivist, Dyfed-Powys Police Museum), pers. comm.

228　The access lane from Nott Square to the gatehouse is labelled 'entrance from Town Hall' on the 1858–66 plan (Figure 139), but the gatehouse is clearly depicted with a wall across the entry in M. E. Bagnall Oakley's painting of *c.*1860 (Figure 134), in which all windows in the west face are also blocked.

229　Ireland, *A Want of Order*, p. 116.

230　Ibid., p. 221.

231　Ibid. and n.1.

232　*CarmJ*, 13 February 1922.

233　Ibid. Sir Eric Geddes headed a committee to investigate cuts in all government departments throughout England and Wales, including Docks, Board of Health, Mines, Police and Prisons. Eight other prisons, including Caernarfon and Usk, were also closed, leaving only two in Wales, at Swansea and Cardiff.

234　The closure was a blow to Carmarthen's pride, despite assurances that its status as an assize venue would be unaffected (Ireland, *A Want of Order*, p. 221).

235　Ibid.

236　*Daily Express*, 30 May 1931.

237   Anon., 'County Council action', *TCASFC*, 18 (1925), 47.

238   Cadw, LB No. 82151 (County Hall), Cadw LB database accessed via END, July 2006.

239   Ireland, *A Want of Order*, p. 221.

240   Lloyd *et al.*, *Buildings of Wales*, p. 139.

241   Cadw LB database, County Hall.

242   Ireland, *A Want of Order*, p. 221 and n. 2. Another claim is that the Nash chapel, much altered during the nineteenth century, was also dismantled and re-erected, 'stone by stone', at Lime Grove Girl's School, Carmarthen, in 1938 (J. and V. Lodwick, *The Story of Carmarthen* (Carmarthen: V. G. Lodwick and Sons Ltd, 1972), p.79). The plans and elevation drawings for the new chapel make it clear, however, that it was an entirely new build (CRO, Carmarthen Borough, 331, Acc. 5570, Lime Grove Chapel 1938), but using materials recovered from the gaol chapel (Lloyd *et al.*, *Buildings of Wales*, p. 155). The chapel, renamed All Saints Church, is now a chapel to St David's Church, Carmarthen, but is derelict.

243   Apart from a small, Grade II listed section, defined in Chapter 7.

244   CRO, Mus. Vol. A4, 'Carmarthen: book of the bridge'. See also G. E. Evans, 'Castle Hill and Carmarthen Bridge Works', *TCASFC*, 27 (1937), 43.

245   J. B. Hilling, *The Historic Architecture of Wales* (Cardiff: UWP, 1976), pp. 196–8.

246   Cadw LB database, County Hall.

247   CRO, CAC/CL/32 (file relating to the completion and opening of County Hall).

248   This description is largely drawn from the Cadw LB database and Lloyd *et al.*, *Buildings of Wales*, p. 140.

CHAPTER SIX

POTTERY AND OTHER FINDS

ALTHOUGH BELOW-GROUND investigation has been limited, it has produced a large assemblage of artefacts. This chapter is confined to those that were recovered from the five structured investigations, i.e. to securely stratified material that has been subject to specialist analysis. It is arranged according to material category, and each category is subdivided by area (and author) – namely the shell-keep, the gatehouse passage, the South-west Tower, the Square Tower cellar, and the west ditch. Material from other areas was in the main scanty, and largely confined to the overburden.

The evidence from the finds must be assessed with caution. The majority of them, from all areas, may be from secondary dump deposits. Only a very small percentage of the site has moreover been investigated, and those areas were, in the main, peripheral, while the largest excavation – from which the vast majority of the finds were recovered – was external to the castle, in the west ditch outside the gatehouse. Medieval material from the castle interior is almost confined to pottery from the shell-keep evaluation, where it is mainly local and comparable, overall, with the assemblages excavated from the castles at Carew, Dryslwyn and Wiston.[1] However, it may not be particularly diagnostic as much of it was residual within later contexts, and was possibly imported within garden soil and dump material; where *in situ*, it is largely late medieval and may belong to a period of decline in the status of this part of the castle (see Chapter 4).

Finds from the shell-keep were however mainly later post-medieval in date, from the garden deposits. There was very little material from the earlier post-medieval period, and none from the sixteenth and seventeenth centuries including the Civil War period, when we know the castle was garrisoned. This may confirm other evidence that shell-keep deposits, including collapse/demolition debris, were truncated and removed when the garden was laid out. Perhaps the greatest interest comes from the human skull recovered from a probable gaol-phase context.

Deposits within the South-west Tower were either secondary, or unstratified. Little pre-eighteenth-century material was present, all of it residual. Finds from the gate passage evaluation were also probably residual. The only finds recovered from excavation in the Square Tower came from the nineteenth-century cellar belonging to the adjoining domestic property. They were entirely eighteenth–twentieth-century. The garden soils in the shell-keep decking trenches, excavated in 2002, produced mid-/late nineteenth-century material including transfer-printed ware, but in small quantities; no finds were recovered from the shell-keep test pits. Material from excavations on the line of the western defensive bank was confined to the modern overburden. Trench E, beneath the line of the south curtain, was entirely sterile and no finds were recovered. Excavation of the secondary fill of the north gatehouse tower produced brick fragments, some animal bone and one clay pipe bowl of eighteenth-/nineteenth-century date. A single sherd of eighteenth-century bottle glass from Trench C in the castle interior, and a fragment of Roman roofing tile from the adjacent Trench D, were residual, or from secondary deposits of unknown source. None of this material was subject to professional study, while a full specialist report was not produced on the finds from the 1980 excavations in the castle interior.

The remainder of the finds came from excavations outside the curtilage proper. The finds evidence suggests that only three deposits in the west ditch are of medieval date (contexts 078, 079 and 080/086), probably from c.1500, with material probably derived from manufacturing and domestic activity outside the castle. The nature and preservation of the finds in the overlying fills suggests that they were secondary deposits, from an unknown source (see Chapter 3).

The leather and wood assemblages from west ditch contexts 078–080 are of national importance. The wood includes a small group of vessels, which is significant for its rarity and good state of preservation. Groups of wooden vessels are not commonly found, while wooden bowls from Wales are rare. Though small by UK standards, the leather assemblage is also significant for Wales.

Although a quantity of slate was recovered, from all areas, it was in the main very fragmentary. Little of it could be positively identified as roofing material, and most was discarded. In general, the slate observed was a greenish phyllite, characteristic of the Preseli and lower Teifi Valley areas. See Chapter 2 for a discussion of the roofing slate.

The vast majority of the animal bone came from the west ditch, the largest stratified collection being from eighteenth-century deposits, most of which were secondary. A full analysis of the animal bone assemblage from this excavation, by Lorrain Higbee of Wessex Archaeology, can be found in the client report.[2] The relatively small amount of mollusc shell was mostly discarded and is not described here.

POTTERY AND GLASS (PAUL COURTNEY AND DEE WILLIAMS)

An attempt was made by both authors to correlate the ceramic fabric series with that established by O'Mahoney[3] for the Carmarthen Friary excavations (see Figure 155 and Table 1). Unfortunately this proved especially difficult for the local wares, subdivided into eighteen fabrics, without an available type-series. A simplified fabric series was therefore established. The glass was all post-medieval, but included one residual sherd of appliqué glass, of possible sixteenth-century date, from a late eighteenth-century (or later) fill of the west ditch.

The medieval pottery from all excavations mainly comprised small body sherds and little is illustrated here. Pottery from the west ditch was generally in poor condition and, moreover, largely from the secondary deposits; however, five items are illustrated in Figure 158.

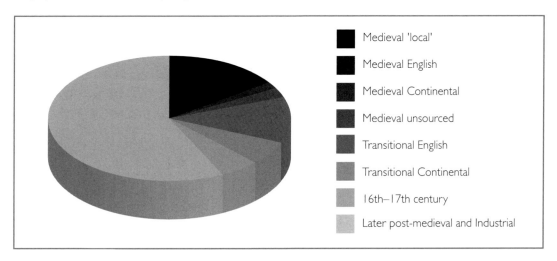

Figure 155 *Pottery fabric types from all excavations at Carmarthen Castle*

Medieval: local wares

LCP. Local medieval cooking pots (O'Mahoney, A2). Mostly oxidised unglazed sherd fabric with abundant rounded quartz (up to 0.5 mm) and sparse to abundant large siltstone inclusions (Dyfed gravel-tempered ware).[4] A kiln site for this ware has been discovered recently near Newcastle Emlyn; it is the first unquestionably medieval kiln to be found west of Caerleon and only the sixth in Wales.[5]

LGW. Local glazed wares (A3 and A4). Glazed jugs and internally glazed vessels in hard fabric (some individual sherds are unglazed) with moderate to abundant fine quartz inclusions (up to 0.5 mm) and occasional siltstone fragments. Mostly oxidised surfaces and reduced core.

The two above wares probably date to the thirteenth and fourteenth centuries but could extend later. They are petrologically similar to other wares from southwest Wales (broadly under the term 'Dyfed gravel-tempered ware') but are most likely dominated by local

Table 1 Occurrence of ceramic types by individual area (figures rounded for clarity)

Fabric	Shell-keep	SW Tower	Square Tower cellar	Gate passage	West ditch
Medieval local	70	1		5	312
Medieval English	15				11
Medieval Continental	20	1			19
Medieval unsourced	69				
Medieval ridge tile	(4)	(1)		(1)	(101)
Medieval floor tile					(1)
Total medieval	**174**	**2**	**0**	**5**	**342**
Transitional English					312
Transitional Continental	5	1			158
Transitional ridge tile					(13)
Transitional floor tile	(1)				(5)
Total Transitional	**5**	**1**	**0**	**0**	**470**
16th–17th century					137
16th–17th century ridge tile		(1)			(4)
Total 16th–17th century	**0**	**0**	**0**	**0**	**137**
Later post-medieval	206	189		1	246
Industrial	327	193	195	4	136
Total later post-medieval	**533**	**382**	**195**	**5**	**382**
TOTAL ALL FABRICS	**712**	**385**	**195**	**10**	**1331**

products. There is no typological sequence and so vessels are normally dated by association with other wares.

Llansteffan jugs (B11). Wheel-thrown, thin-walled, glazed jugs with small voids from calcareous inclusions from the Carmarthen Bay area, probably thirteenth–fifteenth-century. No known kiln sites.

LMW. Local late medieval wares (A8–9? and 13–14). Mostly thick-walled vessels though thinner-walled vessels occur. They have sparse to abundant ill-sorted and coarse (up to 1 mm) quartz temper and sparse to moderate siltstone inclusions. Usually entirely oxidised orange to red in colour, they sometimes have a reduced grey inner surface. Glazes are often thin and patchy, green to brown in colour or else a thick olive-green, pitted with brown centres to the pits. These wares are similar to those produced by the Newport kiln (Pembrokeshire), of probable early post-medieval date, though are likely to be mostly products of a local kiln. They also have broad parallels with the 'orange wares' of the west Midlands. They can be dated to the around the fifteenth century though exact dating is uncertain. It remains uncertain if production extended into the sixteenth century.

Medieval: English imports
Ham Green jugs (O'Mahoney, B5). Handmade jugs in pale fabric with dull green glaze from Ham Green near Bristol. Late twelfth century–*c*.1300.

Bristol Redcliffe jugs (B16). Wheel-thrown jugs in light fabric similar to Ham Green with bright green glaze. Mid-thirteenth century–*c*.1500.

Minety tripod pitchers (B2). Reduced hand-made, grey fabric with dull green glaze and calcareous inclusions or voids. Single sherd has characteristic combed decoration. Probably late twelfth/early thirteenth century, from Wiltshire.

Misc.A. Pale-firing, partly reduced, glazed jugs in sandy fabric (possibly south-west Wales Coal Measures), two sherds with siltstone temper. Thin yellowish glazes. Medieval.

Medieval English. English, unsourced. A number of green- and yellow-glazed sherds remain unclassified. The sandier fabrics are probably English imports. They include sherds from painted jugs.

Medieval: continental imports
Saint.Green (O'Mahoney, C2). Green-glazed jugs from Saintonge, south-west France, 1250–fifteenth century. Mottled green glazes predominated, but all-over green glazes were also represented. The main period of import of both types was 1250–1350, although smaller quantities were imported throughout the medieval period.

Saint.Poly (C2). Saintonge polychrome jugs, *c*.1250–1320.

Medieval: unsourced imports
Medieval English?, medieval English/French? and medieval unsourced. Uncertain imports. A number of green- and yellow-glazed sherds remain unclassified. The sandier fabrics are probably English imports, while the finer fabrics may be from Saintonge, in south-west France (see below). They include sherds from painted jugs.

Transitional: English imports, late fifteenth–mid-sixteenth century
Cistercian ware (O'Mahoney B36). Brown-to-black glazed redwares, sometimes reduced with green glaze on grey body. Dominated by globular cups with flared rims. Also of note: one sherd copying a straight sided Raeren-type mug neck, one similar rim sherd with angular carination below rim, one body sherd from a ridged cup (Brears Type 13), one pedestal base (possibly a jug) and six sherds with applied white pads, one of which was stamped with a simple radiating pattern. Late fifteenth/sixteenth century. Source(s) uncertain.

Malvernian ware (B32). Hard red fabric with occasional Malvernian rock fragments, sparse, often brownish glazes. Mostly unglazed jugs but also internally glazed bowls and glazed cups. The jugs may be as early as the late fourteenth century, though Bristol and Monmouthshire evidence points to the late fifteenth–early sixteenth century as main period of importation along the Severn.[6]

North Devon med? (B6). An unglazed bowl or pancheon rim from the west ditch, with coarse angular quartz temper, is probably a North Devon product. It does not fit into the normal post-medieval typologies and therefore is perhaps late medieval/transitional in date.

Misc. B. Fine pink fabric with a few red iron mineral inclusions and very fine quartz with external and internal glossy orange-yellow glaze, probably jars. Possibly sixteenth century. This resembles post-medieval Fabric A from Usk, Monmouthshire.[7] Possibly a Somerset or other West Country product.

Tudor Green (B28). Green-glazed whiteware from the Surrey/Hampshire border, late fifteenth–sixteenth century.

Transitional: continental imports, late fifteenth–mid-sixteenth century
The vast majority of continental imports came from the 2003 west ditch excavation. See Hurst *et al.* for type definitions.[8]

Merida (C5). Micaceous unglazed orange fabric. Forms include flasks, handled jars, lids and bowls, probably from Portugal, fifteenth/sixteenth century.

Saint. Unglazed. Unglazed ware in Saintonge fabric (probably later medieval–sixteenth century). Unglazed types are found with glazed wares at the kiln sites and would appear to have been made from the start of production.[9]

Saint. post-med (C2). Saintonge post-medieval ware. Two sherds of Saintonge ware recovered from the west ditch, from a worn lobed cup and polychrome decorated bowl, are both of sixteenth-century date.

Raeren (C11). Stoneware mugs with dark grey fabric and light grey to brown surfaces, mugs, *c.*1500–50.

Cologne-type SW (C13). Stoneware in light grey fabric with a light-grey surface (patchy brown surface in parts, but not mottled like later Frechen), from Cologne or possibly early Frechen,[10] *c.*1500–50.

Beauvais SW (C15). Off-white stoneware, with grey to brown surfaces, from Picardy/east Normandy. Probably two mugs and a jug represented, *c.*1500–50.

Beauvais Sgraf (C16). Whiteware, with red slip and sgraffito decoration, from Picardy or east Normandy, *c.*1500–50. One dish rim.

Beauvais Double Slip (C16). Whiteware with red and white slips, presumably from sgraffito flatware vessel, *c*.1500–50.

Beauvais Green (C18). Bright green-glazed whiteware mugs, *c*.1500–50.

Beauvais Yellow (C17). Yellow-glazed whiteware mugs, *c*.1500–50.

MWW (C3). Miscellaneous whitewares, possibly from northern France. They are mostly green-glazed jugs, with off-white micaceous fabrics, probably from various sources in northern France, though English copies can be deceptively similar. Thirteenth–sixteenth century.

Seville Maiolica (C10). Sevillian maiolica bowls with white glaze over pink fabric, sometimes with traces of green glaze on back. Gutiérez dates plain white forms to *c*.1480–1650 and half-dipped green and white to the fifteenth century.[11] Probably late fifteenth–early sixteenth century in a Welsh context.

Isabella Polychrome (C9). Pink fabric, with white maiolica glaze, and decoration in blue and purple, *c*.1500–50. Manufactured in the Seville region, *c*.1450–1550 but most likely to be early sixteenth century in south-west Wales.[12] The eight sherds recovered, all from context (046) in the west ditch, are probably from a single jug.

Montelupo (C26). Italian maiolica ware from the late fifteenth–sixteenth century (redefined as Italo-Dutch by Hurst, as some was produced by emigrant Italian potters). The single sherd, from the west ditch, is from a dish or bowl with painted bright polychrome decoration.

Italo-Netherlands Flower vase (C30). A sherd from a blue-decorated flower vase, recovered from the west ditch, is probably a southern Dutch product though similar ceramics were produced in Italy from where potters emigrated to the Low Countries. Dated *c*.1500–75.

Martincamp I (C21). Sherds in unglazed off-white to pink hard, thin-walled earthenware from flasks. Late fifteenth–sixteenth century. Produced probably in the Beauvais region of Picardy, and east Normandy.[13]

Late sixteenth- and seventeenth-century wares
Somerset wares (B37). Hard-fired dense fabric with very fine quartz inclusions, smooth surfaces. The fabric is partially or wholly oxidised with white slip being common. Glazes vary from even to patchy and are often an olive-green. External grooves are common. Mostly jars, also some jugs and mugs and a single pancheon from 046. The identification of Somerset wares to kiln site is notoriously difficult. However, the bulk of the Carmarthen wares probably derive from the Nether Stowey kilns in north Somerset on comparison with published forms from Bristol.[14] At Bristol, the main period for importation of Nether Stowey (and Wanstrow) products was the late sixteenth/seventeenth century. They appear to have been largely pushed out of the Severn trade by North Devon products which become more widespread after the mid-seventeenth century. The dominance of Somerset and North Devon wares would argue against any significant local production in the late sixteenth/seventeenth century at least.

Frechen SW (C12). Stoneware mugs in grey fabric with mottled brown surfaces from late Cologne potters or more likely Frechen. Late sixteenth/seventeenth century.

N. Italian Marbled ware. A sherd of red earthenware, with polychrome marbled glaze on the interior and a glazed exterior, was recovered from the west ditch. Probably from Pisa, seventeenth/eighteenth century.

French Redware (C20). Highly fired fine redware, post-medieval. One sherd from the west ditch, a hooked bowl rim, is possibly in this fabric, Similar earthenwares were produced in Normandy for purely local use or might be an underfired (eastern) Normandy stoneware.

Later post-medieval wares, post-1650

NDGT (B39). North Devon gravel-tempered ware, glazed coarsewares. Sixteenth–nineteenth century; but the main period of importation into south-west Wales was seventeenth/early eighteenth century, especially after *c*.1650. Vessel shapes underwent little change during a long period of production making close dating difficult. These kitchen/dairy wares are extremely common on sites in south and west Wales.

NDGF (B41). North Devon gravel-free, variant of normal gravel-tempered ware used for jars and jugs.

ND Sgraf. (B43). North Devon sgraffito wares. Most common in the second half of the seventeenth century though examples, with a running S-shaped scroll, from sites of *c*.1625 onwards found in Virginia, USA.[15]

ND Slip (B44). North Devon slip-coated wares. All dishes, some may be from sgraffito vessels. Late seventeenth/eighteenth century.

B/S YW (B58). Bristol/Staffordshire type yellow-slipped wares, white fabric, mugs dated to *c*.1680–1760.

B/S slipped (B57). Bristol/Staffordshire-type press-moulded dishes, in white to buff fabric, with slip decoration. *c*.1680–1760.

B/S glazed. As B/S slipped, but without slip decoration, glazed. Late seventeenth/early eighteenth century.

B/S mottled (B59). Bristol/Staffordshire-type brown mottled wares, white to buff fabric, tankards. *c*.1680–1760.

Whieldon ware. Buff earthenware, glazed inside and out, with mottled tortoiseshell patterns. Staffordshire, early/mid-eighteenth century.

Blackware (B55) Blackware drinking vessels with black glaze on red earthenware fabric. Seventeenth–early eighteenth century.

LRE (B46 and B56). Lead glazed red earthenwares, utilitarian wares, plain or with trailed slip decoration. Seventeenth–nineteenth century? Possibly several sources including Glamorgan and Somerset.

TGE. Tin-glazed earthenware. English, seventeenth–mid-eighteenth century.

Westerwald ware. Imported German stoneware, seventeenth–early eighteenth century.

Buckley ware. Red earthenware with 'black' glaze inside and out. North-east Wales. Eighteenth/nineteenth century.

Unclassified post-med. Post-medieval pottery of uncertain form and source.

Industrial wares, eighteenth–twentieth century
RE. Mass-produced red utility ware of the nineteenth and twentieth centuries.

BE. Plain buff utility ware, otherwise unclassified, nineteenth century.

Creamware. Off-white glazed earthenware, *c.*1740s–1800.

Banded creamware. Earthenware body, glazed. Zonal banding in white and dark brown on a buff ground, often with 'Mocha' decoration. Utility wares with this type of decoration are common and were produced on a large scale at many of the potteries. Late eighteenth–twentieth century.

Pearlware. Blue tinted whiteware, *c.*1770s–1830s.

IYW. Industrial yellow-ware, yellow-glazed white fabric. Early nineteenth century.

IBW. Industrial black earthenware, nineteenth century.

SGSW. Saltglazed stoneware, 1720s–*c.*1800.

ESW. English stoneware, mostly with brown wash or glaze. Eighteenth/nineteenth century.

Eng. porcelain. English porcelain, late eighteenth–twentieth century.

Copper lustre ware. Late nineteenth century.

Marbled ware. Nineteenth/twentieth century.

DWW. Developed whiteware. Industrially produced whitewares, early nineteenth century–present. Produced on a large scale at many of the potteries. Variety of treatments including the widespread blue-and-white transfer-print. Ubiquitous across the castle site.

Building ceramics
LRT. Local glazed ridge-tiles in fabrics similar to the medieval jugs (LGW) but sometimes with more siltstone inclusions. Simple cut crests. Presumably thirteenth century–post-medieval period.

Malvernian RT. Ridge-tiles in Malvernian red fabric with sparse or no glaze. Fifteenth/sixteenth century.

NDGT RT. North Devon gravel-tempered green-glazed ridge-tile. Sixteenth/seventeenth century.

LFT. Local floor tile. A sherd in reduced, siltstone-tempered fabric with no trace of glaze surviving, recovered from context (041) in the west ditch, may be local. Straight sides. Uncertain date.

Normandy FT. Normandy-type floor tiles, straight-sided floor tiles in buff to pink fabrics with worn green or yellow glazes. Early sixteenth-century imports from Seine Valley region of Normandy. Their export from Normandy and Le Havre is documented.[16] Cf. similar Normandy-type floor tiles from Carmarthen Friary, for which no date-range was suggested.[17]

Micaceous medieval tile? An applied glazed pyramid, from a jug or roof furniture, from context (026) in the west ditch. Micaceous fabric suggests an Old Red Sandstone source. Typical of Herefordshire/Monmouthshire.

Unclassified RT. A sherd of unsourced ridge-tile, recovered from context (008) in shell-keep Trench B/C. Probably fifteenth/sixteenth century.

The building ceramics are discussed in Chapter 2.

Shell-keep Trench A, 1997 (by Dee Williams)

A total of 323 sherds of pottery was recovered from Trench A, the north–south trench in the shell-keep interior (Figure 156; Table 2). Of these, only thirty sherds were medieval (9.3%), all of them small body sherds without diagnostic features and therefore of little use for accurate dating. However, of these medieval sherds, sixteen were thought to be 'local' (53.3%, i.e. 5% of the total sherd count from the castle), one sherd was thought to be from an English import (3.3%, i.e. 0.3% of total), six sherds were from continental imports (20%, i.e. 1.9% of total) and seven were from unsourced/unclassified imports (23.4%, i.e. 2.1% of total).

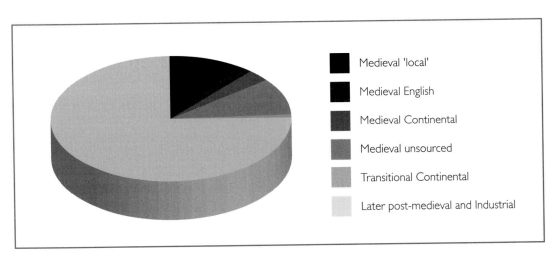

Figure 156 Pottery fabric types from excavations in the shell-keep, 1997–8

Table 2 *Shell-keep Trench A ceramics and glass: catalogue by context (in all tables in this chapter, DV = drinking vessel, FW = flat ware and HW = hollow ware)*

Fabric	Sherd Count	Comments
Context [101] – 19th century or later		
Ceramic		
RE	1	
Banded creamware	2	HW
DWW	7	HW. Transfer.
Total	**10**	
Context [102] – 20th century		
Ceramic		
Medieval; unsourced	1	Jug. Ext. olive-green glaze
NDGT	13	Int. glaze
B/S mottled	1	Tankard
RE	8	Jars. Int. glaze
RE	2	Int. black and brown glaze
ESW	1	Tankard. Glazed. Staffs.
BE	1	Chamber-pot. Clear glaze
DWW	56	Transfer. Prob. Staffs.
Eng. Porcelain	1	Saucer, miniature. Glazed
Clay pipe	(30)	
Electrical fitting	(1)	20th century
Total	**84**	
Glass		
Wine bottle; free-blown	1	Olive green. English; Bristol? 18th century
Jug or bowl	2	White. 20th century
Indeterminate	1	Pink. 20th century
Total	**4**	
Context [103] – 19th century or later		
Ceramic		
Saint. Green	2	Jugs. Ext. glaze
Medieval; unsourced	1	Jug. English. Ext. green glaze
Medieval; unsourced	1	Jug. English? Yellow-green glaze
Medieval; unsourced	1	Jug. Dark green ext. glaze. Late medieval
LGW?	1	Jug? Ext. Green glaze. Llansteffan?
NDGT	26	Jars and bowls. Glazed
ND Slip	2	

Table 2 *(continued)*

Fabric	Sherd Count	Comments
RE	10	Jars and bowls. Int. glaze
B/S slipped	5	HW and FW. Brown slip
ESW	4	Tankard and jars. Salt-glazed
DWW	29	HW and FW. Painted and transfer
Clay pipe	(37)	
Misc. red tile/brick	(1)	
Total	**82**	
Glass		
Wine bottle; free-blown	1	Olive green. English; Bristol? Late 18th/19th century
Total	**1**	

Context [104] – 19th century or later

Ceramic

Fabric	Sherd Count	Comments
DWW	1	Transfer. Staffs?
Clay pipe	(1)	
Total	**1**	

Context [106] – 19th century or later

Ceramic

Fabric	Sherd Count	Comments
RE	4	Int. brown glaze
DWW	4	HW and FW. Plain and transfer
Clay pipe	(2)	
Total	**8**	

Context [107] – 19th century or later

Ceramic

Fabric	Sherd Count	Comments
NDGT	6	Int. glazes
Westerwald Ware	1	Tankard. Glaze and ext. decoration
BE	1	Lustre. Staffs?
DWW	1	FW. Glazed
LRT	(1)	
Total	**9**	
Glass		
Wine bottle; free-blown	1	Olive green. English; Bristol? Late 18th/19th century
Total	**1**	

Context [109] – 19th century or later

Ceramic

Fabric	Sherd Count	Comments
NDGT	13	Int. glazes

Fabric	Sherd Count	Comments
RE	4	Jar. Glazed
B/S slipped	3	FW. Brown slip
ESW	2	Salt-glazed
DWW	12	Painted; transfer; plain
Clay pipe	(10)	
Total	**44**	
Glass		
Indeterminate	2	Colourless. English. Late 19th/20th century
Total	**2**	

Context [110] – 19th century or later

Ceramic

Fabric	Sherd Count	Comments
Medieval; English?	1	Jug. Grooved. Ext. green glaze with darker bands
Saint. Green	2	Jug(s). Ext. glaze
Medieval; English?	1	Jug? Yellow-green glaze
LCP	1	Grooved. Unglazed
Llansteffan	2	Jug(s), reduced. Ext. green glaze
LMW	8	Jugs. Patchy brown and green glazes
NDGT	42	Jars, bowls and jugs. Int. glazes
NDGF	3	Jug and bowl. Glazed
ND Sgraf	1	Jug. Ext. white slip and glaze
RE	18	HW and FW. Int. glazes, some slip dec.
B/S slipped	5	DV.
Whieldon Ware	2	
ESW	4	Tankards. Salt-glaze
DWW	16	HW and FW. Painted; transfer; plain
Clay pipe	(27)	
Total	**106**	
Glass		
Wine bottles; free-blown	2	Olive green. English; Bristol? 'Onion'. Late 18th century
Total	**2**	

Context [114] – 19th century or later

Ceramic

Fabric	Sherd Count	Comments
Saint. Green	1	Jug. All-over ext. glaze
NDGT	1	Jars. Int. green glaze
Buckley Ware?	2	Jar(s). Unsourced though of Buckley type
ESW	3	Inkpot

Table 2 *(continued)*

Fabric	Sherd Count	Comments
BE	1	Bowl/basin. Clear glaze
DWW	5	HW and FW. Painted; transfer
Total	**13**	
Glass		
Water bottle	1	Natural. English. Late 19th/20th century
Total	**1**	

Context [115] – 19th century or later

Ceramic		
Medieval; English	1	Jug? Dark green ext. glaze
RE	2	Glazed. 1 with cordon dec.
Clay pipe	(1)	
Total	**3**	

Context [116] – 19th century or later

Ceramic		
NDGT	2	HW. Int. glaze
RE	1	FW. Glaze and slip-trail dec.
DWW	2	FW. Transfer; plain
Clay pipe	(1)	
Total	**5**	

Context [118] – 19th century or later

Ceramic		
Medieval: English?	1	Jug? Dark green ext. glaze
NDGT	9	HW. Int. glaze
NDGF	1	Jug. Glazed; ext. slip
RE	4	HW. Int. glaze
RE	2	Jar. Int. black glaze
RE	2	Plant-pot
B/S glazed	2	HW and FW with pie-crust rim. Int. glaze
ESW	3	HW. Impressed dec., and stamp.
DWW	30	HW and FW. Moulded; painted; transfer
Clay pipe	(4)	
Misc. red tile/brick	(2)	
Total	**54**	
Glass		
Window; bottle; tumbler	6	Natural. English. 19th century
Total	**6**	

Fabric	Sherd Count	Comments
Context [119] – 18th century or later		
Ceramic		
Clay pipe	(1)	
Total	**0**	
Glass		
Wine bottle; free-blown	2	Olive green. English. 'Onion'. 18th century
Total	**2**	
Context [122] – 18th century or later		
Ceramic		
NDGT	1	Int. green glaze
Clay pipe	(1)	
Total	**1**	
Context [125] – Medieval or later		
Ceramic		
Medieval: English?	1	Jug. Yellow-green glaze
Total	**1**	
Context [126] – 18th century or later		
Ceramic		
RE	1	FW. Int. glaze; slip-trail
Total	**1**	
Context [137] – Medieval or later		
Ceramic		
LRT	(1)	
Total	**0**	
Context [144] – Late 17th century or later		
Ceramic		
Saint. Green	1	Jug. Ext. glaze
LCP	1	Unglazed
LMW?	3	Jug. Ext. brown glaze. Late medieval. Newport?
B/S slipped	1	FW with pie-crust rim. Int. glaze
Total	**5**	

The majority of medieval sherds were from thirteenth/fourteenth-century green-glazed jugs of French and probable English make. The French vessels were from the Saintonge region of south-west France (mainly Saint. Green), whilst the English examples largely remain unclassified. 'Local' material was present in small quantities. It comprised sherds from unglazed cooking pots in a distinctive gravel-tempered fabric (LCP), sherds from jugs of Llansteffan type (Carmarthen estuarine) and possible late medieval material from the Newport area (LMW). There was no 'transitional' pottery (late fifteenth/early sixteenth century), or any material from the early post-medieval period.

Two fragments of locally produced medieval ridge-tile were found (LRT). These were in a gravel-tempered fabric similar to that used for 'local' pottery.

Shell-keep Trenches B and C, 1998 (by Dee Williams)

A total of 312 sherds of pottery was recovered from Trenches B and C, the east–west trenches in the shell-keep interior (Figure 156; Table 3). Of these, 153 sherds were medieval (49.1%) – a much higher percentage than in Trench A – and of these, fifty-eight sherds were 'local' (37.9%, i.e. 18.6% of the total sherd count from the castle), fifty-nine sherds were English imports (38.6%, i.e. 18.9% of total), thirteen sherds were continental imports (8.5%, i.e. 4.2% of total) and twenty-three were unsourced/unclassified imports (15%, i.e. 7.4% of total).

Medieval pottery comprised 'local' wares, English imports, unclassified French or English imports, and Saintonge ware from south-west France. The 'local' wares mainly comprised sparsely glazed jugs (LGW), and a very small number of sherds from glazed jars and cooking pots (LCP), in the distinctive 'local' gravel-tempered fabric. Vessels in a calcareous, slightly vesicular fabric are identified as being of Llansteffan type (Carmarthen Bay). The suggested date range is mid-/late thirteenth century–fifteenth century. Later, or early post-medieval wares (LMW) included possible products from Newport (Pembrokeshire). English imports included a handful of sherds from Ham Green jugs, with an accepted date range of late twelfth century–c.1300. A larger number of sherds were from unclassified English and French imports. Saintonge fabric types represented included Saint. Green in both mottled green and all-over green glazes. There were also five or six sherds of Saint. unglazed, and one sherd was tentatively identified as early Saint. Polychrome (context 043), with a suggested date of c.1280–1320.

The post-medieval material comprises the usual range of fabrics found in Carmarthen ceramic assemblages, with nothing of particular note. However, there was very little 'Transitional' pottery (late fifteenth/early sixteenth century) and, as in Trench A, no material from the early post-medieval period.

The South-west Tower, 1994 (by Dee Williams)

A total of 385 sherds of pottery was recovered from the South-west Tower and the area of the castle interior lying immediately adjacent (Table 4). Those from contexts (007–010) are from the excavation within the ground floor of the tower, and around its entry, and

Table 3 *Shell-keep Trenches B and C ceramics and glass: catalogue by context*

Fabric	Sherd Count	Comments
Context [003] – 19th century or later		
Ceramic		
NDGT	12	Jars and jugs. Int. glaze
RE	11	HW and FW. Glazed/unglazed; 1 with slip-trail dec.
ESW	3	HW. Glazed
Banded creamware	4	1 with 'Mocha' dec.
DWW	10	HW and FW. Transfer
DWW	11	HW and FW. Sprigged; painted; sponged
Clay pipe	(11)	
Misc. red tile/brick	(3)	
Total	**51**	
Glass		
Phial	1	Blue-green. 18th century
Total	**1**	
Context [008] – 20th century		
Ceramic		
Saint. Green	3	Jug(s). Ext. glaze. Applied vertical strip dec.
Saintonge?	6	Jugs. French. 4 unglazed; 2 with yellow-green glaze
Saintonge?	2	Jug. All-over ext. glaze
Medieval; English	3	Jug. Ext. green glaze over orange slip
Medieval; English?	2	Jug. Grooved. Ext. green glaze with darker bands
Medieval; English	3	Jug. Ext. brown glaze. 15th century? Malvernian?
LMW	4	Jugs. Ext. green/brown glaze
LCP?	1	Unglazed. Late medieval?
NDGT	10	Jars. Int. glaze; 1 with ext. glaze over slip
ND Sgraf	1	Bowl. Int. glaze over slip
Unclassified RE	4	Jar? Int. glaze. Post medieval
Unsourced slip	4	Dish/bowl. Int. glaze with slip-trail dec. Welsh?
Blackware	1	Tankard?
B/S slipped	3	Dishes. Pie-crust rim
BE	1	Glazed utility ware
DWW	2	FW. Transfer
Clay pipe	(4)	
Unclassified RT	(1)	Unsourced ridge tile. 15th/16th century?
Misc. red tile/brick	(3)	
Total	**50**	

Table 3 *(continued)*

Fabric	Sherd Count	Comments
Glass		
Bottle	1	Olive green. 20th century
Total	**1**	

Context [011] – 19th century or later

Fabric	Sherd Count	Comments
Ceramic		
NDGT	1	Int. glaze
Banded creamware	1	'Mocha' dec.
Total	**2**	
Glass		
Stopper	2	Blue-green. Late 19th/20th century
Total	**2**	

Context [012] – 16th century or later

Fabric	Sherd Count	Comments
Ceramic		
Saintonge?	2	Jug(s). Ext. glaze
Medieval; French?	8	Jugs? 5 unglazed; 3 with ext. yellow glaze
Medieval; English?	20	Jug. Grooved. Ext. yellow glaze with brown bands
Medieval; English?	4	Jug. Grooved. Poorly-fired ext. glaze
Medieval; English?	10	Jug(s). Grooved. Ext. green glaze with yellow band
Medieval; Eng/French?	2	Jug. Ext. yellow glaze
Medieval; Eng/French?	1	Jug. Strap handle. Clear glaze
Ham Green	2	Jugs. Grooved. Ext. green glaze
Ham Green?	2	Jugs. Ext. green glaze
Llansteffan	7	Jug. Grooved. Ext. green glaze
Llansteffan	4	Jug. Cordon. Ext. green glaze
Llansteffan?	3	Jug. Ext. dark green glaze
LCP	11	Unglazed
LGW	10	Jug. Ext. dark green glaze
LGW	5	Jugs. Ext green/brown glazes. Late medieval/Transitional
LGW?	6	Jugs. Ext. thin brown glazes. Late medieval/Transitional
LRT	(1)	
Normandy FT?	(1)	French. Bright copper-green glaze. 15th/16th century
Misc. red tile/brick	(2)	
Total	**97**	

Fabric	Sherd Count	Comments
Context [013] – Late medieval or later		
Ceramic		
Saint. Green	1	Jug. Ext. glaze
Medieval; English	1	Jug. Ext. green glaze
Medieval; English	1	Jug. Ext. green glaze
Medieval; Eng/French?	1	Jug? Ext. yellow-green glaze
Llansteffan	3	Jugs. Grooved. Ext. green glaze
LGW	2	Jug. Ext. green glaze. Late medieval/Transitional
LCP	1	Unglazed. Late medieval?
Misc. red tile/brick	(1)	Undated
Total	**10**	

Fabric	Sherd Count	Comments
Context [016] – 18th/19th century or later		
Ceramic		
Misc. red tile/brick	(1)	18th/19th century?
Total	**0**	

Fabric	Sherd Count	Comments
Context [018] – 18th/19th century or later		
Ceramic		
Saint. Green	3	Jug(s). Ext. glaze
Saint. Unglazed	2	Jug
Saint. Unglazed?	1	Jug
Ham Green?	1	Jug. Ext. green glaze
Llansteffan?	1	Jug. Grooved. Ext green-brown glaze
Medieval; English?	1	Jug. Ext. dark green glaze. Late medieval/Transitional
Medieval; English?	1	Jug. Ext. dark olive green glaze. Late medieval/Transitional
Medieval; unclassified	6	Jugs. Shoulder grooves. Ext. brown glaze. Transitional
Post-medieval; unclassified	1	Jar? Girth grooves. Int. brown glaze. 18th/19th century
LRT	(1)	Newport? Late medieval-16th century
Total	**17**	

Fabric	Sherd Count	Comments
Context [026] – Late medieval or later		
Ceramic		
Medieval; English?	1	Jug. Ext. dark green glaze. Late medieval/Transitional
Total	**1**	

Table 3 *(continued)*

Fabric	Sherd Count	Comments
Context [032] – 19th century or later		
Ceramic		
Ham Green	1	Jug. Vertical grooves. Ext. green glaze
NDGT	7	Jars. Glazed and unglazed
Unclassified RE	4	Glazed and unglazed. Post medieval
ESW	1	Bottle. Grey ESW. Salt-glazed. 19th/early 20th century
DWW	11	FW and HW. Transfer; painted; lustre; plain
Clay pipe	(2)	
Total	**24**	
Glass		
Bottle	1	Natural. 18th/19th century
Total	**1**	
Context [033] – Late medieval or later		
Ceramic		
Saint. Green	1	Jug. Ext. glaze
Saint. Green	1	Jug. Ext. glaze
LGW?	1	Jug. Ext. thin green glaze. Late medieval/Transitional
Medieval; English	1	Jug. Ext. green glaze
Medieval; Eng/French?	1	Jug? Ext. bright yellow glaze
Medieval; unclassified	3	Jugs. 1 grooved. Ext. brown glaze. Late medieval/ Transitional
Total	**8**	
Context [035] – 20th century		
Ceramic		
NDGT	12	HW. Int. glaze
Unclassified RE	5	FW. Glazed/unglazed. 1 slip. Post medieval/19th century
Blackware	1	Tankard. Staffs.
B/S mottled	1	HW. Int. glaze
TGE	1	Bristol?
SGSW	1	Staffs.
ESW	1	Bottle. Grey ESW. Fulham?
DWW	26	HW and FW. Transfer; painted; plain
Clay pipe	(14)	
Misc. red tile/brick	(20)	Local?
Total	**48**	

Fabric	Sherd Count	Comments
Glass		
Medicine bottle	1	Colourless. Entire. Embossed. 19th/early 20th century
Wine bottle	2	Dark green. Bristol? Cylindrical
Total	**3**	
Context [043] – Post-medieval		
Ceramic		
Saint. Poly	1	Jug. Ext. yellow-green glaze; brown ?painted dec.
Misc. red tile/brick	(2)	
Total	**1**	

are stratified. However, the contexts represent dump layers and are probably secondary deposits; very little medieval material was present – three pottery sherds and a ridge-tile fragment – and was all residual. The unstratified material, which is entirely post-medieval, is from the fill of the tower basement, which accumulated over many years and was much disturbed; it similarly represents a secondary deposit. Of local interest however are the two nineteenth-century miniature promotional sample bricks, from Thomas Morgan's brickyard, Carmarthen, and the fragment of a jug/jar bearing his stamp.

One sherd of North Devon gravel-tempered green-glazed ridge-tile, sixteenth/seventeenth century, came from context (007). A dump layer, of probable secondary origin, it cannot be taken to indicate any post-medieval building activity here (although works on the adjoining Chamberlain's Mansion are recorded in the early sixteenth century; see Chapter 4).

The Square Tower cellar (by Dee Williams)

A total of 195 sherds was recovered from the three fills, contexts (006) – (008), of the nineteenth-century cellar belonging to No. 8 Bridge Street, which extended beneath the level of the tower ground floor (Table 5). All finds were later post-medieval (eighteenth century onwards), and all contexts contained twentieth-century material. The nineteenth-century finewares (DWW) nevertheless represent a good regional assemblage, with a number of Llanelli products. Cf. published assemblages from Carmarthen excavations, 1976–90.[18]

The gate passage evaluation, 2001 (by Dee Williams)

Only ten sherds of pottery were recovered from the evaluation trench within the probable drawbridge pit in the gatehouse passage (Table 6). Five of the sherds (50 per cent) were late medieval wares, of local manufacture, including one from the earliest deposit (520) overlying the pit floor; in addition there was a fragment of local ridge-tile, but both may be residual. The deposits were all post-medieval in character and contained much building debris, including handmade brick fragments, and may therefore be secondary.

Table 4 South-west Tower ceramics and glass: catalogue by context

Fabric	Sherd Count	Comments
U/S fill of tower – 19th/20th century		
Ceramic		
NDGT	4	HW. Int. glaze
IBW	3	HW
RE	2	HW. Glazed. 19th century
RE	1	Plant-pot
ESW	1	Jar/jug. Impressed 'T Morgan, Dark Gate, Carmarthen'
ESW	1	Tankard
ESW	4	HW
Banded creamware	2	HW. Mocha dec.
Marbled ware	1	HW
DWW	65	HW and FW. Transfer; painted; plain; dec.
Misc. red tile/brick	(2)	2 miniature sample bricks. Local
Total	**84**	
Glass		
Wine bottle	2	Olive green. 18th/early 19th century
Phial	1	Colourless. Entire. Chemist's phial
Medicine/tonic bottle	1	Blue-green. Moulded
Glue bottle	1	Blue-green. Entire. Moulded
Total	**5**	
Context [007] – 19th century or later		
Ceramic		
NDGT	115	HW. Int. glaze
ND Sgraf	2	
B/S slipped	6	FW. Varying design
B/S mottled	8	Tankards
RE	34	Slip-decorated
Buckley Ware	2	
Westerwald Ware	1	
SGSW	9	
ESW	19	HW
TGE	1	Painted design
Creamware	25	HW
Eng. Porcelain	5	Painted design
DWW	3	HW. Transfer; plain

Fabric	Sherd Count	Comments
Clay pipe	(25)	
LRT	(1)	
NDGT RT	(1)	
Total	**230**	
Glass		
Wine bottles	9	Olive green. 18th century
Wine bottles	11	Olive green. 18th/19th century. Cylindrical
Wine bottles	103	Green
Phial	2	Natural. 18th century
Jug	1	Blue. Handle. 'Bristol Blue'
Total	**126**	

Context [008] – Early 19th century or later

Fabric	Sherd Count	Comments
Ceramic		
Saint. Green	1	Handle
Merida	1	
NDGT	44	
ND Sgraf	1	
B/S slipped	1	FW. Pie-crust rim
RE	13	Slip-decorated
TGE	1	
ESW	1	
Creamware	3	
Eng. Porcelain	1	Underglaze 'chinoiserie' design
Clay pipe	(9)	
Misc. red tile/brick	(1)	19th/20th century
Total	**67**	
Glass		
Wine bottles	18	Olive green. 18th century
Wine bottles	71	Green. Late 18th/early 19th century
Total	**89**	

Context [009] – 17th century or later

Fabric	Sherd Count	Comments
Ceramic		
NDGT	2	
Total	**2**	

Table 4 (continued)

Fabric	Sherd Count	Comments
Context [010] – post-medieval		
Ceramic		
LGW	I	Ext. glaze
Post-medieval; unclassified	I	Ext. brown glaze.
Clay pipe	(3)	
Total	**2**	

Table 5 *Square Tower cellar ceramics and glass: catalogue by context*

Fabric	Sherd Count	Comments
Context [006] – 20th century		
Ceramic		
RE	4	Pancheon. Black-glazed
RE	29	Crocks/jars. Int. brown glaze
RE	7	Jug. Double-glaze
Banded creamware	I7	Chamber-pot
Copper lustre ware	I	Jug
ESW	3	Jar
DWW	35	HW and FW. Transfer; painted; moulded
Clay pipe	(I)	
Total	**96**	
Glass		
Wine bottle; cylindrical	I	Dark green. Late 19th century
Bottle	I	Colourless. Late 19th/20th century
Wine bottles; machine	3	Pale green. 20th century
Total	**5**	
Context [007] – 20th century		
Ceramic		
RE	I3	Pancheons. Int. brown glaze
RE	5	Jug. Int. double-glaze
ESW	I	Entire. Ink-bottle
Banded creamware	3	Chamber-pot
Copper lustre ware	I	Jug
DWW	I4	HW and FW. Transfer; painted; moulded
Total	**37**	

Fabric	Sherd Count	Comments
Glass		
Wine bottle; machine	I	Pale green. 20th century
Total	**I**	

Context [008] – 20th century		
Ceramic		
RE	I	Pancheon. Black-glazed
RE	8	Jar/jug. Int. brown glaze
RE	I	Plant-pot holder. Unglazed
ESW	I	Tankard/mug. Glazed, with banded dec.
Copper lustre ware	3	Jug(s)
DWW	48	HW and FW. Transfer; painted; plain; moulded
Total	**62**	
Glass		
Wine bottle	I	Green. Embossed 'X', ie. 1868
Wine bottle; cylindrical	3	Pale green. 20th century
Codd Bottle	I	Blue-green. 20th century
Total	**5**	

Table 6 Gate passage ceramics and glass: catalogue by context

Fabric	Sherd Count	Comments
Context [507] – 19th/20th century		
Ceramic		
DWW	4	Tableware. Int. and ext. blue glaze
Total	**4**	
Context [510] – Post-medieval		
Ceramic		
Misc. red tile/brick	(4)	Handmade bricks. Post-medieval
Total	**0**	
Context [516] – Post-medieval		
Ceramic		
Misc. red tile/brick	(I)	Handmade bricks. Post-medieval
Total	**0**	

Table 6 (continued)

Fabric	Sherd Count	Comments
Context [520] – 15th/16th century?		
Ceramic		
LMW	2	Jugs. Ext. green glaze; int. brown glaze
Total	**2**	
Context [523] – 17th century or later		
Ceramic		
LMW	I	Jug. Int. green glaze
LMW	2	HW. Int. brown glaze. Ext. sooting
Clay pipe	(I)	
Misc. red tile/brick	(2)	Handmade bricks. Post-medieval
Total	**3**	
Context [527] – Post-medieval		
Ceramic		
Misc. red tile/brick	(2)	Handmade bricks. Post-medieval
Total	**0**	
Context [528] – 18th century or later		
Ceramic		
B/S slipped	I	Press-moulded dish. Ext. unglazed
Misc. red tile/brick	(3)	Handmade bricks. Post-medieval
Total	**I**	
Context [530] – Medieval/?post-medieval		
Ceramic		
LRT	(I)	Low cut crests
Total	**0**	

The castle west ditch excavation, 2003 (by Paul Courtney)

A total of 1,331 sherds of pottery was recovered from the excavation in the west ditch, outside the gatehouse, in 2003 (Figure 157; Table 7). Of this total, 342 sherds were medieval (25.7%), and of these 312 were 'local' (91.2%, i.e. 23.5% of the total sherd count from the castle), eleven sherds were English imports (3.2%, i.e. 0.9% of total) and nineteen sherds were continental imports (5.6%, i.e. 1.3% of total). The 470 Transitional sherds (late fifteenth/early sixteenth century) accounted for 35.3% of the total, and of these, 312 were English (66.4%, i.e. 23.5% of total) and 158 were continental imports (33.6%, i.e. 11.8% of total). There were also 137 sherds of early post-medieval pottery, from the late sixteenth/seventeenth centuries, constituting 10.3% of the total.

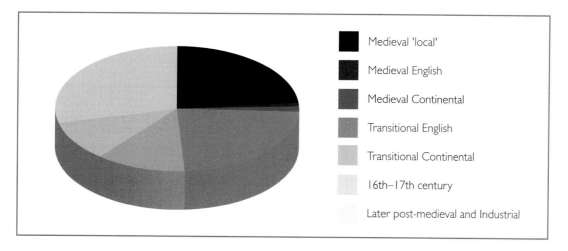

Medieval 'local'

Medieval English

Medieval Continental

Transitional English

Transitional Continental

16th–17th century

Later post-medieval and Industrial

Figure 157 Pottery fabric types from excavations in the west ditch, 2003

All the Transitional English imports that could be positively identified came from the west ditch excavation, as did the vast majority of continental imports and all the late sixteenth- and seventeenth-century wares (Table 1). In contrast, it produced the smallest percentage of late post-medieval wares, the majority coming from the fills of the South-west Tower and Square Tower cellar.

The lowest deposits were dominated by ceramics dating from the fifteenth and sixteenth centuries. These mainly comprised local wares (LMW) similar to Newport kiln products which may be fifteenth century (255 sherds), in which squat jugs and internally glazed vessels predominated. Specific recognisable forms include fish dishes, a skillet (context 065), storage vessels with applied thumbed collars to the neck (041 and 080), a bowl with applied prunts or rosettes on the rim, possibly copying northern vessels (044) and a chafing dish (048), the latter a variant in a fine reduced fabric but with the classic pitted glaze. Also numerous were late fifteenth–sixteenth-century Cistercian wares (216 sherds); late sixteenth–early seventeenth-century Somerset wares (130 sherds); fifteenth-/sixteenth-century Malvernian ware (91 sherds) and Merida ware (79 sherds). Two Tudor Green sherds possibly come from a cup and jug. There was also a scattering of continental imports of the first half of the sixteenth century, a not uncommon feature in urban and high-status assemblages from southern Wales in this period. Some of these could also come from privateering rather than trade. A small amount of residual medieval ceramics (Local, Ham Green, Bristol Redcliffe, Saintonge and northern French) was also recovered. The northern French wares (MWW) included a bowl fragment from context (047) with a bright green interior and external glaze, of medieval–sixteenth-century date. Two sherds of MWW (contexts 018 and 065) come from a polychrome jug of an identical type to a more complete example found at Langstone Court, Monmouthshire, and probably dating to the sixteenth century.[19] A green-glazed MWW applied prunt (026) parallels that on a fifteenth-/sixteenth-century French drinking vessel from Haverfordwest Priory, and is also present on Beauvais cups from the fourteenth century.[20]

Table 7 *West ditch ceramics and glass: catalogue by context*

Fabric	Sherd Count	Weight	Comments
Below wall [031] – 19th century or later			
Ceramic			
LMW	2	10 g.	Int. glaze
Cistercian	1	4 g.	Cup
Malvernian	1	24 g.	Jug
Saint. Green	1	1 g.	Jug
Somerset	3	12 g.	Inc. slipped DV
NDGT	7	177 g.	Jars/bowls
NDGF	4	34 g.	HW/FW
ND Sgraf	1	11 g.	HW
ND Slip	1	26 g.	Dish
LRE	2	7 g.	HW. Black glaze
DWW	3	5 g.	
Clay pipe	(2)		
LRT	(1)	39 g.	
Misc. red tile/brick	(1)		
Total	**26**		
Context [007] – Mid-17th century or later			
Ceramic			
ND Sgraf	1	9 g.	Dish
Total	**1**		
Fill of [134] – 19th century or later			
Ceramic			
DWW	7	25 g.	Transfer wares
Total	**7**		
U/S fill of Cellar 1 – 19th century or later			
Ceramic			
NDGT	1	3 g.	FW
IBW	1	15 g.	HW base
SGSW	2	8 g.	Bowl?
Pearlware	1	7 g.	Bowl; painted
DWW	1	3 g.	FW. Transfer
Clay pipe	(9)		
Clay marble	(1)		

Fabric	Sherd Count	Weight	Comments
Bead	(1)		Imitation pearl
Total	**6**		
Glass			
Bottle	1		Green
Total	**1**		

Context [001] – 17th century or later

Ceramic

Clay pipe	(2)		
Total	**0**		

Context [002] – 19th century or later

Ceramic

NDGT	2	27 g.	FW
NDGF	2	19 g.	Jug?
ND Slip	2	18 g.	Jugs
B/S mottled	1	1 g.	Tankard
LRE	1		FW. Unsourced. Int. and ext. slip-trail dec.
Creamware	3	2 g.	Inc. handle
Eng. Porcelain	2	2 g.	
SGSW	1	1 g.	DV?
DWW	1	1 g.	
Clay pipe	(2)		
Misc. Red tile/brick	(1)		Mod. Reconstituted rock/mock marble
Total	**15**		

Glass

Bottle	1		Green
Total	**1**		

Context [003] – 19th century or later

Ceramic

NDGT	2	50 g.	
NDGF	1	4 g.	
B/S mottled	1	2 g.	Tankard
Pearlware	15	106 g.	Dish
DWW	1	9 g.	Dish
Clay pipe	(2)		
Total	**20**		

Table 7 (continued)

Fabric	Sherd Count	Weight	Comments
Context [008] – 19th century or later			
Ceramic			
NDGT	2	48 g.	Jar, FW
ESW	1	5 g.	Jar. Trace of brown wash
DWW	1	12 g.	Teapot lid. Brown glaze
Clay pipe	(1)		
Total	**4**		
Context [009] – 19th century or later			
Ceramic			
NDGT	7	98 g.	FW
DWW	1	4 g.	Bowl? Mocha dec.
Mic. red tile/brick	(1)	13 g.	
Total	**8**		
Context [012] – 19th century or later			
Ceramic			
Pearlware	4	4 g.	FW and HW. Banded; transfer
DWW	3	7 g.	HW
Total	7		
Glass			
Bottle	1		Green
Total	**1**		
Context [016] – Late 17th century or later			
Ceramic			
Cistercian	1	1 g.	Cup
NDGT	2	16 g.	FW
ND Sgraf	1	5 g.	Dish
B/S slipped	1	10 g.	Moulded dish
Total	**5**		
Context [018] – 19th century or later			
Ceramic			
LMW	23	842 g.	Fish dishes. Int. glaze
Cistercian	5	11 g.	Cups
Malvernian	9	177 g.	Bowls, jugs, mug
Bristol Redcliffe	1	26 g.	Jug
Merida	5	58 g.	Jars

Fabric	Sherd Count	Weight	Comments
Saint. Poly	1	2 g.	Jug
MWW	3	16 g.	Jugs. 1 polychrome, Cu green/yellow
Martincamp I	2	6 g.	Flask
Italo-Neths. flower vase	1	2 g.	Flower-vase. Blue dec.
Somerset	2	8 g.	HW base
NDGF	1	18 g.	Small jar
SGSW	1	26 g.	Plate
Pearlware	5	13 g.	Plate, bowl, jug?
ESW	6	48 g.	Transfer. 19th century
DWW	7	24 g.	
LRT	(13)	437 g.	
Clay pipe	(3)	38 g.	
Total	**72**		

Glass

Bottle	2		Green
Total	**2**		

Context [019] – 17th century or later

Ceramic

Cistercian	1	11 g.	Cup. Stamped design on white pad
NDGT	1	48 g.	Bowl? Sooted
Saint. post-med.	1	9 g.	Base of lobed cup, worn
Beauvais Green	1	1 g.	Jug?
Somerset	1	4 g.	Beaker-like rim. Slipped
Clay pipe	(4)		
Clay marble	(1)		
Total	**5**		

Context [020] – 19th century or later

Ceramic

French redware?	1	88 g.	Hooked rim
ND Slip	2	35 g.	Dishes
Creamware	2	8 g.	Bowls, banded decoration.
Pearlware	3	6 g.	HW plain
DWW	12	27 g.	Transfer. 19th century
Clay pipe	(6)		
Total	**19**		

Table 7 *(continued)*

Fabric	Sherd Count	Weight	Comments
Glass			
Bottle; cylindrical	1		Green. Late 18th/early 19th century
Total	**1**		

Context [025] – Late 18th century or later

Fabric	Sherd Count	Weight	Comments
Ceramic			
LGW	3	25 g.	Jugs, Int. glaze
LMW	10	65 g.	Jugs, Int. glaze
Cistercian	2	8 g.	Cups
Malvernian	2	24 g.	Jugs
Misc. B	1	5 g.	Jar. Date and provenance uncertain
Merida	1	3 g.	HW
Beauvais Green	1	8 g.	HW
Somerset	3	16 g.	HW. Ext. white slip; unglazed?
NDGT	37	847 g.	Assorted
NDGF	7	108 g.	Jars
ND Sgraf	1	128 g.	Dish
ND Slip	5	19 g.	Dishes
B/S YW	1	2 g.	Mug?
B/S mottled	2	62 g.	Mug
LRE	2	11 g.	Slip-trail. Glamorgan? 17th/19th century
Pearlware	2	1 g.	FW. Green-edged. Late 18th century +
Eng. Porcelain	1	1 g.	Cup?
Clay pipe	(2)		
Normandy FT	(1)	110 g.	
Misc. red tile/brick	(1)		
Total	**81**		
Glass			
Bottle; cylindrical	3		Green. Late 18th/early 19th century
Total	**3**		

Context [026] – 1740s or later

Fabric	Sherd Count	Weight	Comments
Ceramic			
LGW	5	28 g.	
LMW	17	242 g.	Pancheon/bowl. Int. glaze
Cistercian	12	150 g.	DV? 2 ridged/carinated; 1 with appl. pad
Malvernian	3	24 g.	Jug. Applied band

Fabric	Sherd Count	Weight	Comments
Merida	1	6 g.	Jar
Saint. Green	1	3 g.	Jug
Raeren	1	6 g.	Mug. Cylindrical neck
Frechen SW	1	8 g.	Mug
Cologne-type SW	2	35 g	Jug neck
Beauvais Green	1	4 g.	Mug
MWW	2	10 g.	Prunt DV/Jug. Appl. roulette. 16th century?
Seville Maiolica	1	2 g.	Bowl. Ext. green glaze
N. Italian Marbled	1	11 g.	Dish
Saint. post-med.	1	14 g.	Polychrome bowl. Ext. knife trimming
Somerset	4	33 g. +	Jars
NDGT	33	1020 g.	Jugs, bowls, jars
NDGF	31	732 g.	Jars, bowls
ND Sgraf.	6	163 g.	Dishes
ND Slip	2	64 g.	Dishes
B/S slipped	1	3 g.	DV
LRE	2	45 g.	Bowl, small hand
Creamware	8	150 g.	Dish
Clay pipe	(3)		
LRT	(1)	105 g.	
Malvernian RT	(3)	71 g.	
NDGT RT	(1)	48 g.	
Micaceous medieval tile	(1)	30 g.	Applied glazed pyramid
Normandy FT	(2)	310 g.	
Total	**136**		
Glass			
Beaker	1		Green
Total	**1**		

Context [034] – 16th century or later

Ceramic

Fabric	Sherd Count	Weight	Comments
LMW	1	10 g.	Int. and ext. glaze
Cistercian	3	3 g.	Cups
Malvernian	1		Cup?
Martincamp I	1	15 g.	Flask
Somerset	1		HW. Glazed

Table 7 (continued)

Fabric	Sherd Count	Weight	Comments
Malvernian RT	(1)	54 g.	
Total	**7**		

Context [039] – Late 16th century or later

Ceramic

Fabric	Sherd Count	Weight	Comments
LGW	6	46 g.	Jugs. Int. glaze
LMW	9	224 g.	Jugs. Int. glaze
LMW	2	1328 g.	Fish dishes. Rims, 1 with handle
Cistercian	11	80 g.	Cups
Malvernian	5	137 g.	Jars? 1 with thumbed neck ring
Misc. A	1	49 g.	Jug. Pale fabric
Merida	3	22 g.	HW. 1 with handle
Martincamp 1	1	2 g.	Flask
Raeren	1	3 g.	Mug
Seville Maiolica	1	12 g.	Bowl
MWW	1	13 g.	Cup handle?
Somerset	7	98 g.	HW/FW. Slip and glaze. 1 pierced ?handle
LRT	(3)	325 g.	
Total	**48**		

Context [040] – 18th century or later

Ceramic

Fabric	Sherd Count	Weight	Comments
LGW	12	143 g.	Jugs
Bristol Redcliffe	1	2 g.	Jug
Saint. Green	5	19 g.	Jugs. 3 with vert. appl. strips
Saint. Unglazed?	3	12 g.	Jugs; unglazed?
Saint. Poly	1	5 g.	Jug
Frechen SW	1	4 g.	Mug
ESW	1	3 g.	HW. 18th century or later
LRT	(11)	521 g.	Inc. 1 crest
Total	**24**		

Glass

Fabric	Sherd Count	Weight	Comments
Lead glass	1		Green
Total	**1**		

Context [041] – 17th century or later

Ceramic

Fabric	Sherd Count	Weight	Comments
LCP	1	10 g.	
LGW	3	28 g.	Jugs. Int. glaze

Fabric	Sherd Count	Weight	Comments
LMW	16	592 g.	Jugs. Int. glaze
LMW	4	715 g.	Fish dishes
LMW	1	200 g.	Storage vessel. Coarse fabric
Cistercian	16	122 g.	Cups
Malvernian	9	337 g.	Bowls/Jugs
Merida	7	319 g.	Jars/Lid
Saint. Green	1	1 g.	Jug
Martincamp I	1	75 g.	Flask
Somerset	2	44 g.	
NDGT	1	35 g.	FW. Int. glaze
LRT	(9)	530 g.	
LFT	(1)	209 g.	No glaze survives. Appl. band
Clay pipe	(1)		17th century or later
Misc. red tile/brick	(2)		
Total	62		

Context [043] – 16th century or later

Ceramic			
LCP	1	10 g.	Cup
LGW	4	13 g.	Jugs
LMW	18	362 g.	Jugs. Int, glaze
Cistercian	45	234 g.	Glob. cups. 1 with white appl. pad
Malvernian	3	249 g.	Jugs
Misc A	1	24 g.	Foot of tripod pitcher
Merida	3	31 g.	Flask; HW
LRT	(1)	106 g.	
Misc. red tile/brick	(8)	75 g.	
Total	75		

Context [044] – Late 16th century or later

Ceramic			
Llansteffan	1	6 g.	Jug. Reduced
LMW	21	677 g.	Jugs/bowl. Rosette dec. Fig. 158
LMW	5	430 g.	Fish dishes
Cistercian	22	230 g.	Glob. Cups. 3 with appl. white spots
Malvernian	6	125 g.	Jugs/bowl/cup
Misc B	1	10 g.	Jar. Pink fabric

Table 7 (continued)

Fabric	Sherd Count	Weight	Comments
Merida	2	11 g.	Jar/HW
Martincamp I	4	25 g.	Flask
Somerset	17	339 g.	HW. Slipped
Misc red tile/brick	(5)	121 g.	
Total	**79**		

Context [045] – 16th century or later

Ceramic

Fabric	Sherd Count	Weight	Comments
LCP	2	33 g.	I sooted
LGW	I	6 g.	Jug. Combed dec. and ?ext. slip
Ham Green	I	8 g.	Jug
Bristol Redcliffe	I	5 g.	Jug
Malvernian	2	39 g.	Int. glaze
Saint. Green	I	3 g.	Jug
Saint. Poly	I	I g.	Jug?
NDGT	I	14 g.	FW
Total	**10**		

Context [046] – 17th century or later

Ceramic

Fabric	Sherd Count	Weight	Comments
LMW	9	122 g.	Int. glaze. I from chafing dish?
Cistercian	10	54 g.	Cups
Malvernian	2	30 g.	Jugs
Merida	6	136 g.	Flask, costrel
Saint. Green	I		Jug
Frechen SW	3	62 g.	Jugs. 17th century or later
Beauvais Green	2	8 g.	Mug handle
Beauvais Yellow	2	4 g.	Mug
Seville Maiolica	I	8 g.	Bowl/dish. Int. pink glaze and ext. green glaze
Somerset	19	330 g.	Pancheon; jars; small handle
NDGT	2	11 g.	Int. glaze
LRT	(8)	419 g.	
Malvernian RT	(4)	155 g.	
Normandy FT	(1)	279 g.	
Total	**41**		

Fabric	Sherd Count	Weight	Comments
Context [047] – Late 16th century or later			
Ceramic			
LCP	3	16 g.	
LGW	8	28 g.	Jugs. Int. glaze
LMW	52	1066 g.	Jugs; chafing dish(es). Int. glaze
Cistercian	35	148 g.	Glob cups
Malvernian	25	457 g.	Jugs; Costrel. Int. glaze
Bristol Redcliffe	1	10 g.	Jug
North Devon med?	1		Rim
Misc. A	2	27 g.	Jugs. Pale fabric
Tudor Green	1	4 g.	Cup?
Merida	35	275 g.	Flasks and bowls
Saint. Green	1	3 g.	Jug
Raeren	5	91 g.	Mugs
Beauvais SW	3	16 g.	Mugs
Beauvais Double Slip	1	3 g.	FW
MWW	7	26 g.	Jugs/DV
MWW?	1	14 g.	Bowl
Isabella Polychrome	8	41 g.	Jar?
Somerset	39	404 g.	HW
NDGT	2	104 g.	Dish. Int. glaze
Clay pipe	(1)		
LRT	(31)	1368 g.	Inc. 'disc'
Malvernian.RT	(1)	39 g.	
NDGT RT	(3)	380 g.	
Normandy FT	(1)	204 g.	
Misc. red tile/brick	(1)	15 g.	
Total	**230**		

Fabric	Sherd Count	Weight	Comments
Context [048] – 18th century or later			
Ceramic			
LGW	1	19 g.	Int. glaze
LMW	13	294 g.	Jugs: chafing dish. Int. glaze. Fig. 158
Cistercian	9	61 g.	Cups
Malvernian	4	69 g.	Inc. jar
Merida	4	103 g.	Lid; bowl; HW

Table 7 (continued)

Fabric	Sherd Count	Weight	Comments
Seville Maiolica	1	6 g.	Bowl?
MWW	2	6 g.	Jugs
Creamware	1	9 g.	Rim – jug? 18th century or later
LRT	(1)	28 g.	
Total	**35**		

Context [062] – 16th century or later

Ceramic

LCP	1	13 g.	Rim
LMW	2	7 g.	Inc. small handle. Int. glaze
Cistercian	1	1 g.	Cup
Malvernian	2	25 g.	Jug?; FW
LRT	(3)	30 g.	Crest
Malvernian RT	(1)	46 g.	
Total	**6**		

Context [064] – 16th century or later

Ceramic

LMW	4	168 g.	Jug. Int. glaze
Cistercian	5	25 g.	Cups
Malvernian	2	67 g.	Jugs
Bristol Redcliffe	2	5 g.	Jugs
Merida	1	21 g.	Jar base?
Raeren	1	11 g.	Mug handle
Total	**15**		

Context [065] – Late 16th cenury or later

Ceramic

LMW	11	335 g.	Jugs; skillet handle. Int. glaze. Fig. 158
LMW	1	203 g.	Fish dish
Cistercian	5	38 g.	Cup/costrel?
Tudor Green	1	6 g.	DV rim
Merida	3	5 g.	HW
MWW	3	51 g.	Jugs. 1 polychrome
Somerset	7	30 g.	HW; cup; jars?
LRT	(13)	375 g.	Crest
Total	**31**		

Fabric	Sherd Count	Weight	Comments
Context [066] – 20th century			
Ceramic			
NDGT	1	4 g.	
Somerset	1	4 g.	DV. Slipped
LRE	3	33 g.	Jar/bowl
ESW	2	67 g.	Jars
Eng. Porcelain	1		Gilt dec.
DWW	9	206 g.	Red and blue transfer; banded
Misc. red tile/brick	(1)		20th century
Total	**17**		
Glass			
	-		19th/20th century
Total	**-**		
Context [067] – 17th century or later			
Ceramic			
LGW	1	9 g.	HW, with strap-handle. Newport-type
LMW	12	174 g.	Int. glaze
Cistercian	9	42 g.	Cups
Malvernian	1	8 g.	Int. glaze
Merida	1	5 g.	HW
Saint. Green	4	63 g.	Jugs. Poor glazes. Late med.
MWW	1	6 g.	DV
Somerset	1	12 g.	Jug/jar
LRT	(2)	68 g.	
Clay pipe	(1)		17th century or later
Total	**30**		
Context [075] – Mid-18th century or later			
Ceramic			
Cistercian	2	45 g.	Cup, flared; inc. handle
Malvernian	1	17 g.	Jug base?
Minety	1	23 g.	Tripod pitcher? Combed dec.
Creamware	1	1 g.	HW. Mid-18th century or later
Total	**5**		

Table 7 *(continued)*

Fabric	Sherd Count	Weight	Comments
Context [076] – Mid-17th century or later			
Ceramic			
Cistercian	1	1 g.	Cup
Malvernian	3	66 g.	Jugs
Somerset	1	27 g.	Jar or jug. Slipped
ND Sgraf	1	1 g.	Dish
Total	**6**		
Context [077] – Late 16th century or later			
Ceramic			
Cistercian	2	45 g.	Cups. 1 copy of Raeren
Saint. Green	1	11 g.	Jug, part of 'parrot' rim. Mottled glaze
Somerset	6	154 g.	Jugs? Slip; int. glaze
Total	**9**		
Context [079] – Late medieval or later			
Ceramic			
LMW	1	320 g.	Jug, squat, with rod handle. Fig. 158
Total	**1**		
Context [080] – Late medieval or later			
Ceramic			
LMW	2	142 g.	Jar. Int. glaze. Thumbed band. Fig. 158
Malvernian	1	11 g.	
Total	**3**		
Context [084] – Late medieval or later			
Ceramic			
LMW	4	239 g.	Int. glaze
Total	**4**		
Context [085] – 16th century or later			
Ceramic			
LGW	3	79 g.	Jugs
Cistercian	1	6 g.	Cup handle
Merida	1	5 g.	
MWW	1	6 g.	Handle, small
Misc. red brick/tile	(1)	51 g.	16th century or later
Total	**6**		

Fabric	Sherd Count	Weight	Comments
Context [088] – 16th century or later			
Ceramic			
Misc. red brick/tile	(3)	296 g.	
Total	**0**		
Context [092] – Mid-17th century or later			
Ceramic			
Somerset	2	32 g.	Jar? Applied
NDGT	3	11 g.	FW
NDGF	1	19 g.	Jar?
ND Sgraf	1	9 g.	Dish
Clay pipe	(4)		
Total	**7**		
Context [094] – 19th century or later			
Ceramic			
Somerset	1	3 g.	Jar. Slip decorated. Applied white spot on ext.
NDGT	11	623 g.	Inc. fish dish and handle. Int. glaze
NDGF	8	180 g.	Jars
Blackware	1	3 g.	Tankard
DWW	1	12 g.	Jug? Transfer print
Total	**22**		
Context [095] – 19th century or later			
Ceramic			
Creamware	1	5 g.	Handle
DWW	1	5 g.	Blue-edged plate
Clay pipe	(35)		Some glazed
Total	**2**		
Context [096] – 18th century or later			
Ceramic			
Creamware	7	31 g.	Jug
Clay pipe	(9)		
Total	**7**		

Table 7 (continued)

Fabric	Sherd Count	Weight	Comments
Context [099] – Late 18th century or later			
Ceramic			
LMW	2	70 g.	Int. glaze
Cistercian	3	28 g.	Cups
Beauvais Green	1		Mug?
MWW	3		Moulded dec.
Somerset	3	29 g.	HW/FW
NDGT	2	47 g.	Bowl/dish?; handle
B/S slipped	1	6 g.	Moulded dish
LRE	2	6 g.	FW. Slip dec.
SGSW	3	3 g.	Tankard/plate
ESW	2	1 g.	DV
Creamware	2	3 g.	Plates
Pearlware	1	1 g.	Small handle
Clay pipe	(3)		
Misc. red brick/tile	(1)	56 g.	
Total	**25**		
Glass			
Bottle	1		White. Appliqué; green glaze. 16th century?
Bottle	2		Green? Moulded; green glaze. French. 19th century?
Bottle	33		
Total	**36**		
Context [100] – 19th century or later			
Ceramic			
Creamware	2	2 g.	
Pearlware	2	14 g.	Blue-edged plate
IYW	1	9 g.	Teapot lid; encrusted surface
DWW	1	1 g.	
Clay pipe	(5)		
Total	**6**		
Context [105] – Late 17th century or later			
Ceramic			
LMW	1	13 g.	Jug
Cistercian	3	13 g.	Cups
Malvernian	4	43 g.	Jugs

Fabric	Sherd Count	Weight	Comments
Merida	1	9 g.	Jar/flask
Somerset	4	115 g.	Jug(s);?skillet handle, twisted, unglazed
NDGT	4	112 g.	Bowls or jars
NDGF	4	374 g.	Jars
ND Sgraf.	3	110 g.	Dishes
ND Slip	2	8 g.	Dishes
B/S Mottled	3	6 g.	Tankard
Clay pipe	(5)		
Total	**27**		

Context [106] – 18th century or later

Ceramic

LMW	2	16 g.	Jug
Cistercian	1	1 g.	Cup
Malvernian	2	53 g.	Jugs
Merida	1	5 g.	
Raeren	1	22 g.	Mug
Somerset	3	60 g.	Jug/jars
NDGT	4	66 g.	Bowls?
ND Slip	1	3 g.	Small jar
B/S YW	2	5 g.	Cup/mug
TGE	1	4 g.	Drug jar? Blue dec.
Creamware	1	65 g	Oval dish
ESW	1	5 g.	Base of ?mug
LRT	(1)	84 g.	
Total	**21**		

Context [107] – 16th century or later

Ceramic

LMW	1	7 g.	Int. glaze
Cistercian	5	60 g.	Cups
Malvernian	2	74 g.	Jugs
Merida	3	15 g.	Jars
Beauvais Sgraf	1	5 g.	Bowl rim
Beauvais Yellow	1	2 g.	Mug
Montelupo	1	5 g.	Bowl
Somerset	2	9 g.	HW, jars?
Total	**16**		

Table 7 (continued)

Fabric	Sherd Count	Weight	Comments
Context [113] – 16th century or later			
Ceramic			
LGW	1	1 g.	Jug? Int. glaze?
LMW	1	252 g.	Fish dish
Cistercian	1	2 g.	Cup
Merida	1	1 g.	
LRT	(2)	14 g.	
Malvernian RT	(1)	16 g.	
Total	**4**		

Fabric	Sherd Count	Weight	Comments
Context [114] – 17th century or later			
Ceramic			
LMW	3	43 g.	Jugs
Cistercian	3	2 g.	Cups
Blackware	2	21 g.	DV. Slip dec.
Clay pipe	(1)		
Total	**8**		

Fabric	Sherd Count	Weight	Comments
Context [115] – 16th century or later			
Ceramic			
LMW	5	239 g.	Int. glaze
Cistercian	1	4 g.	Cup? Reduced
Malvernian	3	13 g.	FW/HW
Raeren	1	6 g.	Mug
Beauvais SW	2	51 g.	Mug inc. handle; jug?
Martincamp I	1	3 g.	Flask
Somerset	3	19 g.	HW, inc. white-slipped jar/jug rim
Total	**16**		

Fabric	Sherd Count	Weight	Comments
Context [116] – Mid-17th century or later			
Ceramic			
NDGF	2	22 g.	Int. glaze
ND Sgraf	1	24 g.	Dish
LRT	(1)	63 g.	Applied crest, stabbed
Total	**3**		

Also recovered were 101 sherds of locally made ridge-tiles of probable medieval date. A small number of Malvernian and North Devon ridge-tiles were also recovered. A single sherd, which might be a medieval tile crest, was in a micaceous fabric typical of Herefordshire or Monmouthshire.

Likely late fifteenth-/early sixteenth-century imports included Raeren and Cologne-type mugs, the latter represented by two sherds from context (026), from a single mug neck with characteristic neck cordon. They also included Spanish maiolica from Seville (an Isabella Polychrome jug from context 046), and both plain white, and white-and-green, dishes or bowls including four sherds of Seville maiolica ware from contexts (026), (039), (046), (048), those from 026 and 046 with partial green glaze on exterior. An Italo-Dutch maiolica flower vase (one sherd from context 018), and a sherd of Italo-Dutch Montelupo ware from context (107) were of similar date, as were several Martincamp I flasks, Beauvais stoneware (probably at least two mugs and a jug), Beauvais single slip (one sherd) and double slip sgraffito (one sherd), Beauvais green-and-yellow-glazed earthenware mugs, and post-medieval Saintonge, notably a lobed cup and polychrome bowl. Later imports included Frechen stoneware, a redware bowl identified as either Normandy earthenware or under-fired stoneware, and a sherd from a north Italian (Pisan) marbled bowl. Five fragments of early sixteenth-century Normandy-type green- or yellow-glazed tiles were also recovered.

Nevertheless, only four sherds of the pre-nineteenth-century pottery from the west ditch excavations came from deposits that could be securely identified as *in situ*, represented by the three large sherds of LMW (Figure 158) and one Malvernian ware sherd, from contexts 079 and 080. They were large, forming part of the deposit that contained the leather shoes and bowls and which was probably derived from a domestic property occupying the ditch (see below). The rest of the deposits appear to be secondary, and were probably derived from a rubbish dump during the late seventeenth–late eighteenth century (see Chapter 3). However, the assemblage as a whole is of interest in its own right. It adds to the material from Carmarthen's Franciscan friary to provide one of the largest groups of post-medieval pottery in south Wales, but also highlights the need for more groups of more or less contemporary ceramics in order that the changing patterns of supply and usage from the fifteenth century to the early seventeenth century can be more accurately determined.

ORGANICS AND METALWORK FROM MEDIEVAL DEPOSITS
(MARK REDKNAP)

Organics and metalwork from stratified deposits that can be dated to the medieval period are confined to the west ditch, where they occurred in four contexts – 078, 079, 080/086 and 081 – alongside late medieval pottery, described above. The last was the fill of a probable post-medieval wall-construction trench, cut through the other four deposits (see Chapter 3).

The leather includes offcuts as well as used shoe parts, indicating a cobbler's dump as one possible component. The wooden bowls are well preserved, and again point to a single primary dump. In character, the assemblages are reminiscent of the larger deposits from

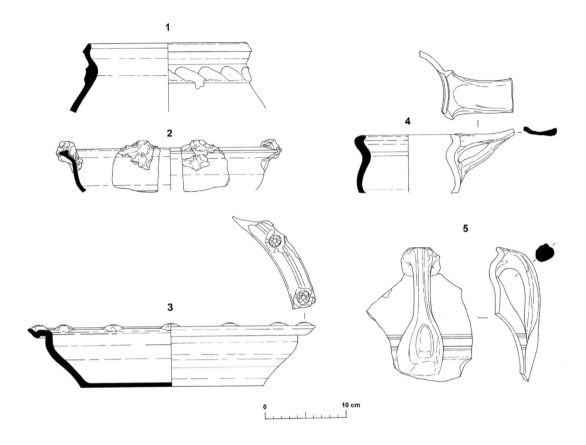

Figure 158 Some of the late medieval ware (LMW) from the west ditch:

1.   Storage vessel with thumbed applied shoulder piece, internally glazed with thin bright green splashed glaze, orange-red fabric with buff surfaces. Rim diameter 24 cm. Late medieval. Context 080 (primary deposit, c.1500)

2.   Chafing dish, glossy olive-green glaze with brown pitting over reduced dark grey fabric. Rim diameter 27 cm. Late medieval. Context 048 (secondary deposit); probable sherds from same vessel from secondary deposits 046 and 047

3.   Bowl with rosettes on rim. Olive-green glaze with brown flecks on interior, fabric oxidised but reduced on interior with small splashes of glaze on external dark buff surfaces. Rim diameter 36 cm. Late medieval. Context 044 (secondary deposit)

4.   Skillet handle, thin and pitted, splashed light green glaze on interior, fabric mostly oxidised orange with dark buff surfaces. Late medieval. Context 065 (secondary deposit)

5.   Jug, rod handle with single lower thumb mark, mostly oxidised dark orange fabric with pale- to dark-buff surfaces. Splashed and pitted light green to brown glaze with a few splashes on exterior. Late medieval. Context 079 (primary deposit, c.1500)

Coventry town wall ditch, interpreted as slipped dump bank deposits of *c*.1450–1534, containing leather shoes, straps and wooden bowl fragments.[21] The date range for 079 and 080, based on leather and aiglets, is 1480–1550, supported by the pottery. Context 078, based on the wooden bowl, may be late fifteenth century. On balance, a broad date of *c*.1500 is suggested for the dumping event.

Leather objects (Figs. 159-60; Table 8)

All the leather was examined following freeze-drying by Cardiff University. Species identification by grain pattern was undertaken by Mark Lewis, who writes: 'All the surviving grain patterns indicate bovine origin for the leather reported here. The coarse fibre bundles and patterns present in the shoe soles also indicate cattle skin. Many of the shoe upper fragments have grain patterns with an overall appearance and follicle spacing consistent with calfskin rather than skins of mature cattle.'

Shoe sizes were calculated using modern shoe-size scales, with a 5 per cent allowance for shrinkage. Leather finds were treated using a 20 per cent glycerol pre-treatment followed by freeze-drying. Measurements have found that this typically results in shrinkages of 0–3.5 per cent from wet leather.[22] However, it should be borne in mind that the wet leather is swollen with water and actual original size of the leather is likely to lie between these two values.[23]

Context 079

1. Near-complete slip-on left turnshoe in three-piece construction; pointed toe, wide joint, narrow waist and small seat; vamp with butt seams on the vamp wings, and no indication of fastening. The quarters are in two pieces, one longer piece running along the inside and around the complete heel, and a short section infilling on the remaining outside. One section of the outside quarter is missing. The plain-cut top edge of the upper reached just below the ankle. The turnshoe construction is equivalent to York Type 2,[24] with rand inserted between sole and upper to produce a stronger, more waterproof join. Soles of this type from York (York type e3) have been dated from the early thirteenth century onwards, especially the fourteenth and fifteenth centuries.[25] The shoe type is equivalent to Coventry Type 3.[26] Max. sole length 240 mm (+5 per cent = 252 mm), modern English size 6.5–7.5, continental size 38–39.5; widest part of forepart 75.5 mm; narrow waist width 27.9 mm; edge/flesh seam holes 4 mm apart; grain/flesh seam holes 4 mm apart. Slight wear at toe. Late fifteenth century, post-1450 (Figures 159 and 160).

2. Near-complete upper/vamp with slashed opening centre front; and rand fragment from a left turnshoe; rounded toe; fastening is a narrow leather tie (width 5 mm) passed though two holes either side of the central slash. Length about 220–30 mm (+5 per cent = 221–41 mm), modern English size 5½–6½, continental size 36.5–38; grain/flesh seam holes 3-4 mm apart. Equivalent to Coventry Type 4.[27] Late fifteenth century (Figure 159).

3.   Near-complete upper/vamp from a two-piece turnshoe cut high at throat with a slashed opening centre front, fastened across the instep by a narrow leather strap passing through small slits (those on the right slit for buckle pin); the straps are tab-ended to prevent them being pulled through. The buckle strap is threaded through two small slits in the outside vamp wing. Rounded toe. Surviving length 262 mm (slightly flattened); edge/flesh seam holes for missing quarters 2 mm apart; grain/flesh seam holes for sole 5 mm apart. Late fifteenth century. A similar lace-and-buckle arrangement occurs on a shoe stratigraphically attributed to the last quarter of the fifteenth century, from Finsbury Circus, London[28] (Figures 159 and 160).

4.   Near-complete sole from a left turnshoe; oval toe; narrow waist, small heel. Max. length 255 mm (+5 per cent = 268 mm), modern English size 8–9½, continental size 39.5–41; edge/flesh seam holes 5 mm apart. This sole pattern with rounded toe continues into the sixteenth century, being found, for example, on the *Mary Rose* (lost 1545).[29] This suggests a date *c.*1500 for the Carmarthen example (Figure 159).

5.   Near-complete sole from a left turnshoe; rounded toe; narrow waist, small heel. Length 218 mm (+5 per cent = 228.9 mm), modern English size 5–6½, continental size 36–37.5; narrow waist width 30 mm; edge/flesh seam holes 4 mm apart. Also five rand fragments (lengths 95, 113, 90, 80, 37 mm), grain/flesh holes 4 mm apart. Late fifteenth or early sixteenth century (Figure 159).

6.   Near-complete sole from a small child's right turnshoe (toe end missing); narrow waist, small heel (damaged). Max. length now 178 mm (originally about 210 mm; +5 per cent = 220.5 mm). It is not possible to calculate shoe size accurately, but it may have been in the order of modern English size 1½–3, continental size 34–6. Narrow waist width 18 mm; edge/flesh seam holes 3 mm apart; four fragments of rand (lengths 19.2, 47, 26, 25 mm); also ten fragments of upper (insufficient to identify form; some with bind stitching at 2 mm spacing), and one fragment of wood. The general sole form is paralleled by one from Gun and Shot Wharf, London, dated by associated ceramics to *c.*1480–1550[30] (Figure 159).

7.   Complete sole from a small child's left turnshoe; rounded toe; narrow waist, small heel. Max. length 127 mm (+5 per cent = 133.35 mm), modern English size 4½–6½, continental size 21–2; narrow waist width 23 mm; edge/flesh seam holes 5.5–6 mm apart (Figure 159).

8.   Mid-section of a sole from right turnshoe; pointed toe missing, wide joint, narrow waist, heel/seat missing. Surviving sole length 152 mm; widest part of forepart 88 mm; narrow waist width 35 mm; grain/flesh seam holes 3 mm apart (Figure 159).

9.   Offcut from the upper from pointed turnshoe, with three secondary cuts (max. length 80 x 76 mm; grain/flesh holes 2–3 mm apart).

10.   Near-complete upper from a slip-on turnshoe (not slashed). Rounded toe. Edge/flesh seam holes (for quarters) 2.5 mm apart; flesh/grain holes for sole 4 mm apart.

11.   Near-complete upper from a two- or three-piece slip-on turnshoe with pointed toe. Approximate dimensions 75 x max. width 150 mm in semi-flattened state. Edge/flesh seam holes for quarters 2 mm apart; flesh/grain sole holes at 4 mm spacing (Figure 160).

12.   Front part of what looks like a single-piece right sole (to narrow waist only) with a long pointed toe. However, while there are grain/flesh stitches 4–5 mm apart along the left side, there is diagonal bind stitching along the curved right edge (at 3 mm spacing), suggesting that this may not be a sole (or if it is, it may be reused). Length 215 mm. Max. width at ball 72 mm. The pointed toe form resembles those on pattens from London dated by association with ceramics to c.1480–1550.[31]

13.   Five fragments of leather, including two 'buttons', one with nine small stitch-holes (31 x 29 mm), the other with six small stitch-holes (29 x 29 mm). Some may be waste from leather-working. The buttons are similar to one found in the pocket of a leather jerkin from the *Mary Rose* which had been covered in silk[32] (Figures 159 and 160).

14.   Four small fragments of shoe leather (40 x 25 mm; 12 x 9 mm; 8 x 8 mm; 17 x 12 mm); one possible rand, 77 x max. 13 mm, grain/flesh holes 4 mm apart; one probable sole fragment 46 x 22 mm, grain/flesh holes 3 mm apart.

> Turnshoe offcut (77 x max. 18 mm); rand fragment (flesh/grain stitches 2 mm apart); triangular fragment of upper (70 x 77 x 110 mm along edges).
>
> Triangular off-cut, reuse probably from a shoe sole. Max. L 96 x 3 mm.
>
> Small fragments of shoe leather (mostly upper). Largest fragment 80 x 78 mm.
>
> Six small strap-like fragments of leather (widths 5–10 mm), and two edges of upper (grain/flesh stitching at 3–4 mm spacing).
>
> Six very small fragments of leather.
>
> Six fragments of upper.
>
> One large fragment of incomplete upper (length 163 mm); twelve smaller fragments of upper; one offcut; moss stuffing with rounded edge (from shoe lining?). Three different mixed woodland mosses have been reported used as stuffing for medieval shoes from London, while those from Gloucester have used riverine mosses[33] (Figure 160).

Small rectangular repair patch (47 x 20 mm). Small grain/flesh stitches at 2 mm spacing; four small offcuts; fragment of upper from a round-toed shoe (surviving length 173 mm); seven smaller fragments of upper.

Seven fragments of leather, including one rand and two upper fragments. Waste from leather working.

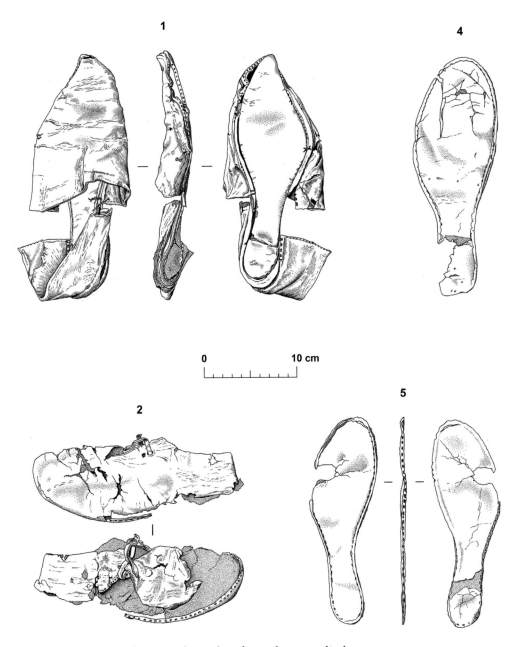

Figure 159 *(above and opposite) Leather from the west ditch*

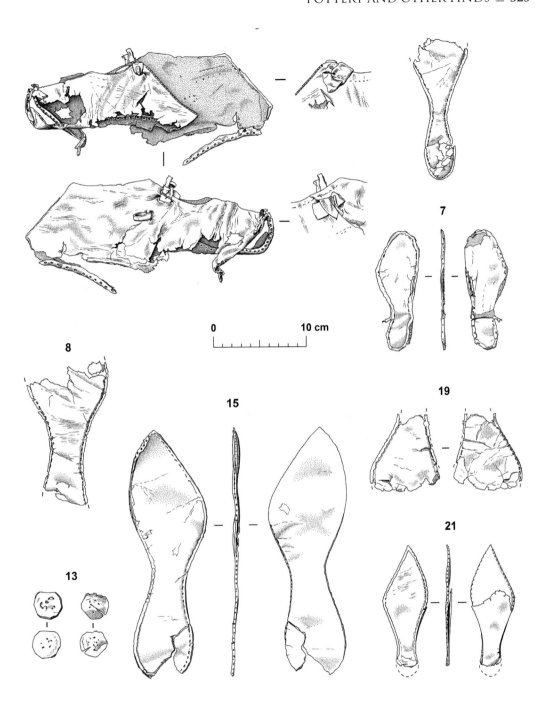

0   10 cm

Context 080

15. Near-complete sole from right turnshoe, and small fragment of vamp; pointed toe, wide joint, narrow waist and small seat. One small section of heel missing. Soles of this type from York (type e3) have been dated from early thirteenth century onwards, especially the fourteenth and fifteenth centuries.[34] Max. sole length 257 mm

(originally 258/9 mm), modern English size 8½, continental size 40–1, widest part of forepart 82 mm; narrow waist width 37 mm; heel width 63 mm; edge/flesh seam holes 4 mm apart. Post-1450.

16.   Twenty-two fragments of leather, including three small upper fragments and three rand fragments. Waste from leather-working (six strips of various shapes, one triangular cut, one 'tear-drop' offcut).

17.   Fourteen fragments of leather, including one fragment of upper (flesh/grain holes 4 mm apart). Waste from leather-working (including one strip 11 x 6 mm, and one triangular offcut 50 x 71mm).

18.   Two very small fragments of leather.

Context 081 (construction trench, probably post-medieval)

19.   Front part of the sole from a right turnshoe, with pointed toe and wide joint (surviving length 86 mm; width 75 mm). Narrow waist and heel missing.

20.   Three offcuts of leather (one 110 x 23mm; another 76 x 13mm; another max. length 120 x width 21 mm). Four small upper fragments, and eleven smaller fragments of shoe leather (not offcuts).

Context 086 (possibly same as 080)

21.   Near-complete sole from a small child's left turnshoe; pointed toe; narrow waist, half of heel missing. Max. length now 127 mm (originally about 140 mm; +5 per cent = 147 mm), about modern English size 6–7, continental size 23–4; narrow waist width 21 mm; edge/flesh seam holes 3 mm apart.

Comments

The assemblage comprises turnshoes, with single soles, made inside out. It includes seven complete/near-complete soles and fragmentary remains of two, along with fragments of uppers. Some are randed, with a wide rand incorporated in the sole seam between the upper and sole. At least six are from left shoes and four are from right shoes. Some leather had been cut up for secondary use or repair work, e.g. context 079, No. 4, but no repairs were visible though some shoes show signs of wear. The calfskin/cattle-hide uppers are difficult to reconstruct, but are characterized by butted edge/flesh seams.

Pointed or 'piked' shoes became popular again in the 1460s, though an English sumptuary law of 1463–4 against 'pike or poulaine' limited lengths to 2 inches.[35] Some of the shoes from Carmarthen have short pointed toes, 'petal-shaped treads' and relatively narrow waists, a style popular from the 1460s and 1470s. The method of shoe

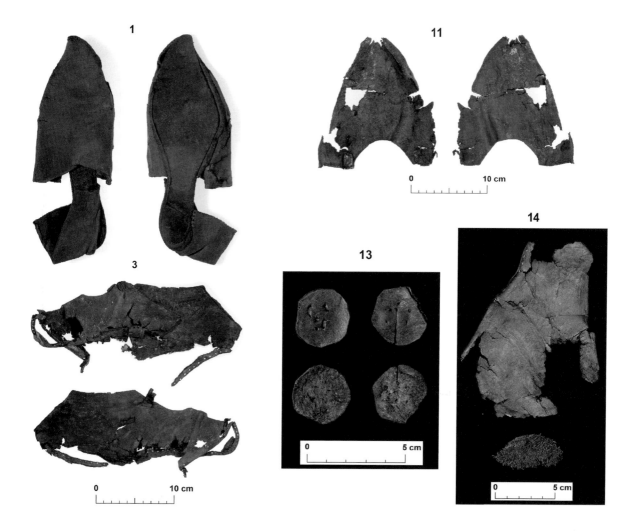

Figure 160 Leather from the west ditch (photographed by NMW)

construction, sole shapes and upper styles suggests a mid- to late fifteenth-century date for some of the assemblage. Some uppers have slashed throats, eg. context 079, No. 2, and would have been fastened with small buckles, possibly of iron or lead-tin alloy. By the 1490s pointed toes were no longer fashionable, and welted construction was over-taking turnshoe. Rounded-toe shoes dominate the Carmarthen assemblage, but they are narrow (almost oval) rather than broad. The absence of Tudor broad and rounded, square or eared toe styles, popular *c*.1500–50, may be significant. It seems unlikely that there was a significant time-lapse in new styles reaching Carmarthen, with its regular links with Bristol and London society (particularly around the castle), though time-lapses for iso-lated rural communities may have been longer. Similar shoes have been published from Wainfleet St Mary, Lincolnshire.[36]

Table 8 Leather: guide to shoe sizes represented

Context and item no.	Length mm (length corrected)	Approximate UK shoe size	Approximate Continental shoe size	Chart group used
079 1	240 (252)	6½–7½	38–39.5	Adult chart (M)
079 2	220–230 (221–241)	5½–6½	36.5–38	Adult (FM)
079 4	255 (268)	8–9½	39.5–41	Adult (M)
079 5	218 (229)	5–6½	36–37.5	Adult
079 6	210 (221)	1½–3	34–36	Youth
079 7	127 (133)	4½–6½	21–22	Child
080 1	257 (259)	8½	40–41	Adult
086	140 (147)	6–7	23–24	Child

Wooden objects (Figures 161–2)

The wood was pre-treated with a two stage PEG 400/PEG 4000 process and then freeze-dried by Cardiff University.[37] Species identification by grain pattern was undertaken by Paul Atkin and Robin Wood, but identifications are provisional, as end grains were not clear.

Context 078

1. Mid-section of lathe-turned bowl. Diameter 200 mm+ (rim missing). Surface blackened inside and out; unidentified, possibly ash or alder. One narrow incised line midway up the external wall surface, and similar deeper-turned groove at the junction of wall and base. Otherwise, only concentric grooves on the interior marking circumference of the flat base (Figures 161 and 162).

2. Wood waste (two pieces, one a chip of oak with sapwood).

Contexts 079 and 080

3. Lathe-turned bowl or deep platter in five fragments (ash). Everted rim (flattened tip); concentric grooves on the interior marking circumference of the flat base. Diameter 220–30 mm. Height about 60 mm (now distorted) (Figures 161 and 162).

Context 079

4. Small lathe-turned drinking cup or ladle bowl with a rounded profile and plain rim. Diameter about 120 mm (slightly distorted rim). Close-grained wood with a blackened surface on interior and partly on the exterior (unidentified). Thick wall (max. 11.5 mm). The diameter is closer to the frequency of the group from York defined as 'cups' rather than bowls[38] (Figures 161 and 162).

Context 080

5.   Wood waste (five offcuts with axe marks). One triangular worked piece, possibly a wooden lug from a small bucket stave, with traces of a cross-cut perforation. 43 x 62 mm x thickness 10 mm.

6.   Five wood fragments (small, probably a small twig).

Context 081

7.   Wood waste (nine pieces split along rays); oak.

Comments

The Carmarthen group of lathe-turned vessels provides a rare glimpse of the late medieval table in south-west Wales, a period in which it is thought that wooden vessels often occupied a position as important as pottery, particularly for drinking. The vessel from context 079 is either a simple palm cup, or the bowl from a large wooden ladle. Until the early sixteenth century, earthenware cups were rare, wooden vessels being more usual.[39] 'Ashen cups' are often mentioned in orders, for example when they were replaced by pottery cups at the London Inns of Court during the reign of Henry VIII.[40]

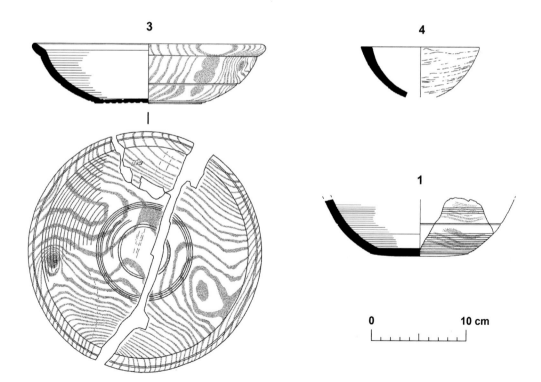

Figure 161 Wooden vessels from the west ditch

Figure 162 Wooden vessels from the west ditch (photographed by NMW)

Though unusual for Wales, the Carmarthen group is comparatively small – groups of between eight and eighteen vessels have been recovered from three excavations in London and Leicester.[41] Other assemblages have been recovered from urban excavations including Waterford,[42] Exeter[43] and Winchester.[44] Flat rims occur in the Waterford assemblage,[45] but are not common. One of the best-known Welsh items is a fifteenth-century burr-maple mazer, with engraved silver gilt rim-binding, which may have once belonged to the collegiate foundation at Clynnog Fawr (Caernarfonshire). The Newport Ship, thought to have been dismantled in the 1460s, yielded a small lathe-turned wooden bowl with an everted flat rim.[46]

The Carmarthen bowls are of a simple design with plain rims, and none have markings on them. Such bowls however continued to be used into the 1540s, for instance on the *Mary Rose* where their durability was an advantage. There they were made from elm, beech, alder, birch, and had carinated rim edges. The nineteen examples with measurable diameters ranged from 110 to 465 mm, and of these seven belonged to the 230–40 mm range.[47] Fifty-two bowls with diameters of less than 260 mm were also recovered; of these twenty five were beech, four birch, eighteen alder and the remainder unidentified.[48] A close parallel to the Carmarthen bowls is from medieval Coventry and has similar grooves midway up the body and at the base angle;[49] it was attributed to the early/mid-fifteenth century. Flat-topped everted rims occur on two medieval bowls from Exeter, both with blackened surfaces. One was of elm and associated with pottery dated *c*.1300, the other being of lime.[50]

Lead objects
Context 080
Folded mass of lead, possibly destined for recycling. The visible areas of tracery and triangular cross sections suggest a crumpled ventilator lattice or similar, cast in a simple open mould, rather than casting sprues or window cames. There appears to be a maker's mark or similar at one edge of the grille, in the form of a quartered heraldic shield within a single border (possibly crowned). 82 x 34.5 mm (Figure 163).

Cast openwork lead window ventilators, with characteristic triangular or diamond-shaped cross-sections, have been found in Wales at monastic sites such as Carmarthen Friary,[51] Haverfordwest Priory[52] and Llanthony Priory, Monmouthshire (from a fifteenth-century building context),[53] while a stone mould for a small square ventilator is known from Neath Abbey.[54] Lead ventilators are also known from the abbeys at Rievaulx, Roche and Byland (all Yorkshire).[55] Heraldic stamps on lead include those on an ingot from Criccieth Castle (Caernarfonshire).[56] The west ditch item's openwork tracery shares elements with the Llanthony Priory grille, and they may be of similar date. Whether it is associated with work at the castle is however uncertain.

Copper alloy objects
Context 079
1. Brass pin with wound wire head. Length 37 mm; head diameter 1.8 mm. Similar pins were recovered from pre-Dissolution deposits at Carmarthen Friary[57] (Figure 163).

Context 080
Lead ventilator

Context 079
Copper alloy aiglet

0   2 cm

Context 079
Brass pin

0   3 cm

0   5 cm

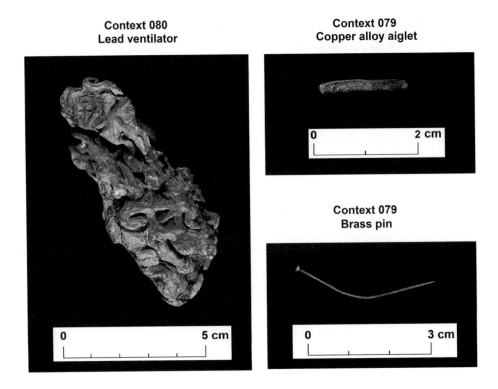

Figure 163 Metal objects from medieval contexts in the west ditch (photographed by NMW)

2. Sheet copper-alloy seam-butted aiglet or lace chape, with two opposed indents at one end, the other end partially closed. Length 18.3 mm; diameter 2.1 mm. Medieval or sixteenth century. The *Mary Rose* yielded 165 aiglets, varying in length from 16 to 28 mm.[58] Examples were also excavated at Coventry Whitefriars[59] (Figure 163).

SMALL FINDS FROM POST-MEDIEVAL DEPOSITS
(MARK REDKNAP, DEE WILLIAMS AND EDWARD BESLY)

Few other artefacts were recovered from the structured investigations, and were confined to post-medieval deposits (Table 9). Those from the west ditch include some interesting items, of medieval/early post-medieval date, but all from the secondary deposits described above, which were derived from an unknown source.[60]

Finds from the west ditch
   Context 039 (post-medieval Phase 2): thimble in sheet copper alloy with a basal band of stamped stylized flowers alternating with diamond punch marks with central pellets, between single-row 'roulette-pattern' borders. Height 23.2 mm; max. diam. 18.5 mm. Probably sixteenth/seventeenth century (Figure 164).

Table 9 *Finds from post-medieval contexts: catalogue by area*

Area	Context no. and date	Material	Qty.	Type	Date of object
Shell-keep	003 (C19+)	Copper alloy	1	Strip	?
Trenches B and C	008 (C20)	Iron	1	Nail	?
	012 (C16+)	Lead	1	Strip	Medieval?
		Iron	3	Nail	?
	014 (?)	Iron	1	Nail	?
	017 (?)	Iron	5	Nails	?
	018 (C18+)	Iron	22	?	?
		Iron	2	Slag	?
	035 (C20)	Iron	2	?	?
		Bone	1	Handle	C19?
		Rubber	1	Cap	C20
South-west Tower	007 (C19+)	Leather	1	Strap	Post-medieval?
	008 (C19+)	Iron	1	Nail	?
		Iron	1	Buckle	Post-medieval
	010 (C16+)	Slate	1	Roofing	?
Square Tower cellar	006 (C20)	Lead	1	Waste	C19/20
		Lead	1	Bar	C19/20
		Iron	1	Nail	C19/20
		Marble	1	Tile	C19/20
	007 (C20)	Leather	7	Boots	C20
		Plastic	1	Comb	C20
	008 (C20)	Iron	1	Buckle	C19/20
		Bone	1	Tab	C19/20
Gate passage	510 (C16+)	Iron	5	Nails	Post-medieval
West ditch	018 (C18+)	Lead	1	Disc	C16–C18?
	019 (C19+)	Copper alloy	1	Coin	C19
	023 (C19+)	Copper alloy	1	Button	C19
	026 (C18+)	Copper alloy	1	Aiglet	C15/16
		Copper alloy	1	Wire	Post-medieval
	039 (C16+)	Copper alloy	1	Strip	C16?
	041 (C17+)	Copper alloy	1	Pin	Post-medieval
	044 (C16+)	Copper alloy	1	Thimble	C16/17
		Copper alloy	1	Buckle	C16?
		Bone	1	Awl	Medieval?
	045 (C16+)	Bone	1	Tuning-peg	Medieval
	046 (C17+)	Copper alloy	1	Aiglet	C16/17
		Copper alloy	3	Pins	Post-medieval

Table 9 *(continued)*

Area	Context no. and date	Material	Quantity	Type	Date of object
West ditch *(cont.)*	064 (C16+)	Copper alloy	1	Buckle	C16+
	065 (C16+)	Slate	1	Disc	?
	066 (C20)	Plastic	3	Various	C20
	067 (C17+)	Copper alloy	1	Coin	Medieval
		Leather	1	Strip	?
	099 (C18+)	Copper alloy	3	Rods	Post-medieval
	U/S	Copper alloy	1	Key	C19
		Copper alloy	1	Spigot	C19

Context 044 (post-medieval Phase 2): bone awl with a roughly worked head, tapering to a sharp, smooth point, possibly for leather working. Polished towards the point. Length 111.6 mm; max width at head 9.7 mm. Possibly late medieval?

S-shaped copper-alloy binding strip with sharp, asymmetrical U-shaped cross-section, in two fragments: one well preserved with two holes for small nails or tacks at either end; the other heavily corroded, sides pinched together at one end. Dimensions: length: 116 mm, max. depth 10 mm; length 51.8 mm, depth 6.2 mm. Probably from a leather-covered wooden object. The curvature corresponds to the binding on the front arch or cantle of a saddle frame. Sixteenth century? (Figure 164).

Context 045 (post-medieval Phase 2): medieval bone tuning-peg from a stringed instrument. It was tapered, square in cross-section at key end, and circular in cross-section along the shaft. It had a transverse rectangular slot (instead of a drilled hole) at the end, through which the string passed. Probably fifteenth century. Other Welsh examples are known from Carmarthen Friary,[61] Usk and Monmouth, while there are a number of English and Irish examples of fourteenth-/fifteenth-century date (Figure 164).

Context 064 (post-medieval Phase 1): broken, U-shaped copper-alloy arm from a locking buckle, with a brambled head terminal; shaft of flattened oval cross-section. Such a buckle may have been used to suspend a purse: 39.2 x 23 mm. The form of the terminals suggests an early sixteenth-century date, though they can be later (Figure 164).

Context 067 (post-medieval Phase 2) – Edward III (1327-77), penny, Durham mint; Post-Treaty Coinage, 1369–77. *Obv.* + [EDWARDVS] REX ANGLIE. *Rev.* CIVI – TAS – DVN – OLM. Worn and clipped; 0.61 g. From its condition, it had seen considerable circulation and its loss is likely to be fifteenth-century (Figure 164).

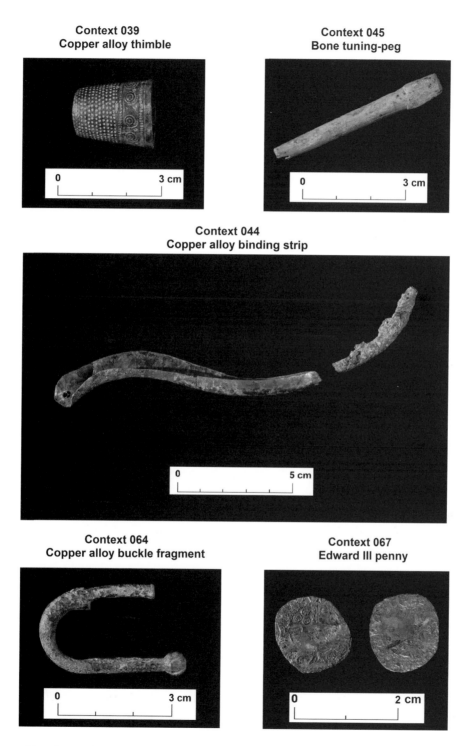

Figure 164 *Objects from post-medieval contexts in the west ditch (photographed by NMW)*

NOTES

1   D. Austin (ed.), 'The Carew Castle archaeological project: 1993 season interim report' (unpublished report, University of Wales Lampeter, 1995), 16–18; P. Webster, 'Pottery', in C. Caple, *Excavations at Dryslwyn Castle 1980–95*, SMA Monograph 26 (London, 2007), pp. 236–45; K. Murphy, 'The Castle and Borough of Wiston, Pembrokeshire', *Archaeologia Cambrensis*, 144 (1995), 88–91.

2   D. Schlee, 'Carmarthen Castle: excavations outside the gatehouse, June–August 2003' (unpublished DAT report, 2004), Appendix 3, 99–108.

3   C. O'Mahoney, 'Excavation at Carmarthen Greyfriars 1983–1990, Topic Report 2: pottery, ridge tile and ceramic water pipe' (unpublished DAT report, 1995).

4   See C. Papazian and E. Campbell, 'Medieval Pottery and Roof Tiles in Wales AD 1100–1600', *Medieval and Later Pottery in Wales,* 13 (1992), 56–9.

5   V. Early and D. Morgan, 'A Medieval Pottery Kiln Site at Newcastle Emlyn', *Archaeology in Wales,* 44 (2004), 97–100.

6   G. L. Good and V. E. J. Russett, 'Common Types of Earthenware Found in the Bristol Area', *Bristol and Avon Archaeology,* 6 (1987), 37–8.

7   P. Courtney, *Medieval and Later Usk: Report on the Excavations at Usk 1965–1976* (Cardiff: UWP, 1994), p. 57.

8   J. G. Hurst, D. S. Neal and H. J. E. van Beuningen, *Pottery Produced and Traded in North-West Europe, 1350–1650*, Rotterdam Papers 6 (Rotterdam, 1986).

9   O'Mahoney, 'Excavation at Carmarthen Greyfriars', 34.

10   Frechen is a German town to which Cologne potters migrated in *c*.1550.

11   A. Gutiérez, *Mediterranean Pottery in Wessex Households (13th–17th Centuries)*, *BAR* British Series, 306 (Oxford: British Archaeological Reports, 2000), p. 47.

12   Ibid., pp. 46–8 'Seville blue and purple'.

13   P. Icowicz, 'Martincamp Ware: A Problem of Attribution', *Medieval Ceramics,* 17 (1993), 51–60.

14   Good and Russett, 'Common Types of Earthenware', 39–40; G. L. Good, 'The Excavation of Two Docks at Narrow Quay, Bristol, 1978–9', *Post-Medieval Archaeology,* 21 (1987), 25–126.

15   B. Straube, Jamestown, VA, pers. comm.

16   J. M. Lewis, *The Medieval Tiles of Wales* (Cardiff: NMW, 1999), pp. 10, 73–4 (Group 31).

17   T. James and D. Brennan, 'Excavation at Carmarthen Greyfriars 1983–1990, Topic Report 1: 13th–16th century earthenware and oolitic limestone floor tiles' (unpublished DAT report, 1991), 28: Type 8.

18   D. Brennan, G. Evans, H. James and E. Dale-Jones, 'Excavations in Carmarthen, Dyfed, 1976–1990: finds from the seventeenth to the nineteenth centuries: pottery, glass, clay pipes and bone', *Medieval and Later Pottery in Wales,* 14 (1996), 15–108.

19   P. Courtney, 'The pottery' in K. Blockley. 'Langstone Castle Motte: Excavations by L. Alcock in 1964', *Archaeology in Wales,* 34 (1994), 21–2 (Figure 3, No. 8).

20   J. Cartier, *Céramiques de l'Oise* (Paris: Somogy, 2001), Nos. 77 and 79.

21   J. Bateman and M. Redknap, *Coventry: Excavations on the Town Wall 1976–78,* Coventry Museums Monograph Series, 2 (Coventry, 1986), p. 57.

22   H. Ganiaris, S. Keene and K. Starly, 'A Comparison for Some Treatments for Excavated Leather', *The Conservator,* 6 (1982), 12-23.

23   Phil Parkes (University of Wales), pers. comm.

24   Q. Mould, I. Carlisle and E. Cameron, *Leather and Leatherworking in Anglo-Scandinavian and Medieval York*, York Archaeological Trust/CBA: The Archaeology of York 17/16 (York, 2003), Figure 3269.

25 Ibid., Figure 1594. For an example on an early fifteenth-century side-laced boot, from London, see F. Grew and M. de Neergaard, *Shoes and Pattens, Medieval Finds from Excavations in London,* 2 (Museum of London, 1988), p. 74.

26 S. Thomas, *Medieval Footwear from Coventry: A Catalogue of the Collection of Coventry Museum* (Coventry: Herbert Art Gallery and Museum, 1980), Figure 1.

27 Ibid., Figure 15.

28 F. Lambert, 'Some Recent Excavations in London', *Archaeologia,* 71 (1921), 102 and Figure 24.

29 N. Evans and Q. Mould, 'Footwear', in G. Egan (ed.), *Material Culture in London in an Age of Transition: Tudor and Stuart Period Finds c.1450–c.1700 from Excavations at Riverside Sites in Southwark,* MoLAS Monograph 19 (London, 2005), Figure 2.66.

30 Nailer, A., 'Items of dress', in Egan, *Material Culture,* p. 25, No. 9.

31 Ibid., p. 29, No. 50 and Figure 13.

32 M. Richards, 'Aiglets, twisted wire loops, buttons, clasps and laces', in J. Gardiner (ed.), *Before the Mast. Life and Death aboard the Mary Rose* (Oxford: Mary Rose Trust, 2005), Figure 2.75, No. 81A4731.

33 Grew and de Neergaard, *Shoes and Pattens,* pp. 88–9.

34 Mould *et al., Leather and Leatherworking,* Figure 1594.

35 Grew and de Neergaard, *Shoes and Pattens,* p. 117.

36 Q. Mould, 'The leather', in F. McAvoy, 'Marine salt extraction: the excavation of Salterns at Wainfleet St Mary, Lincolnshire', *Medieval Archaeology,* 38 (1994), 152–8.

37 Phil Parkes, pers. comm.

38 C. A. Morris, *Wood and Woodworking in Anglo-Scandinavian and Medieval York,* York Archaeological Trust/CBA: The Archaeology of York 17/13 (York, 2000), No. 2179, Figure 1001.

39 P. C. D. Brears, *The English Country Pottery: Its History and Techniques* (Newton Abbot: David and Charles, 1971), p. 13.

40 L. G. Matthews and H. J. M. Green, 'Post-medieval Pottery of the Inns of Court', *Post-Medieval Archaeology,* 3 (1970), 1.

41 See e.g. C. Thomas, B. Sloane and C. Phillpotts, *Excavations at the Priory and Hospital of St Mary Spital, London,* MoLAS Monograph 1 (London, 1997), p. 204, Table 48; P. Clay, 'The small finds – non-structural', in J. Mellor and T. Pearce (eds), *The Austin Friars, Leicester,* CBA Research Report 35 (London, 1981), pp. 139–42.

42 M. F. Hurley, O. M. B. Scully and S. W. J. McCutcheon, *Late Viking Age and Medieval Waterford. Excavations 1986-1992* (Waterford: Institute of Public Administration, 1997), pp. 560–4.

43 J. P. Allan and C. Morris, '1. Wooden objects', in J. P. Allan (ed.), *Medieval and Post-medieval Finds from Exeter 1971–1980,* Exeter Archaeological Reports 3 (Exeter, 1984), pp. 305–6.

44 D. Keene, 'Wooden vessels', in M. Biddle (ed.), *Object and Economy in Medieval Winchester: Artefacts from Medieval Winchester,* Winchester Studies 7/2 (Oxford, 1990), Nos. 959–65.

45 Hurley *et al., Medieval Waterford,* Figures 16:2, 16:4.

46 Redknap, M. (in prep.), 'The wooden objects', in the Newport Medieval Ship Project Report.

47 R. Weinstein, 'Messing items', in Gardiner, *Before the Mast,* p. 446.

48 Ibid., p. 448.

49 Bateman and Redknap, *Coventry,* p. 155, No. 1.

50 Allan and Morris, 'Wooden objects', Figure 173, Nos. 1 and 8.

51 T. James (ed.), 'Excavations at Carmarthen Greyfriars 1983–1990, Topic Report No. 4: the small finds and other artefacts' (unpublished DAT report, 2001), 38, Nos. 79–83.

52   A. W. Clapham, 'Haverfordwest Priory. Report on the Excavations of June, 1922', *Archaeologia Cambrensis*, 77 (1922), 334; NMW Acc. No. 23.111.

53   D. H. Evans, 'Excavations at Llanthony Priory, Gwent, 1978', *The Monmouthshire Antiquary*, 4 (1980), 5–34, Figure 27.

54   S. E. Rigold, 'A Mould for Lead Ventilators from Neath Abbey, South Wales', *Antiquaries Journal,* 57 (1977), 334–6; NMW Acc. No. 77.38H.

55   Evans, *Llanthony Priory*, 29.

56   B. H. St J. O'Neil, 'Criccieth Castle, Caernarvonshire', *Archaeologia Cambrensis*, 98 (1945), 42, Figure 5; NMW Acc. No. 38.835/2.

57   James, 'Carmarthen Greyfriars', 31, No. 74a ('Type A').

58   Richards, 'Aiglets, twisted wire loops', 94–9.

59   C. Woodfield, 'Finds from the Free Grammar School at the Whitefriars, Coventry, *c*.1545–*c*.1557/8', *Post-Medieval Archaeology*, 15 (1981), 91–3 and 98–9.

60   The reader is referred to the full archive report (M. Redknap, 'Finds from Carmarthen Castle 2003' (unpublished DAT report, 2012).

61   James, 'Carmarthen Greyfriars', 47–8.

CHAPTER SEVEN

EPILOGUE:
THE CASTLE REDISCOVERED

FOR OVER 300 years, the remains of Carmarthen Castle were largely hidden from view. Beginning in the early 1970s, they have been re-exposed and once more dominate the town and surrounding country. The castle's striking visual presence can again be appreciated, particularly from the main, southern approaches, and is complemented by County Hall – itself symbolic of the castle's endurance as a seat of local government.[1]

Much has been discovered during the recent work, chiefly from study of the castle's standing remains and the source material relating to its development. And the limited below-ground archaeological interventions yielded a high return of information relative to comparatively minor disturbance. A number of key research issues, identified at the outset of the project, can now be clarified.

We have, so far, looked at Carmarthen Castle in the past. This chapter offers some reflections on the castle's continuing role in the present, and the future.

THE CASTLE IN THE PRESENT

The subject of neither poetry, song nor fiction – perhaps surprisingly, given the town's Arthurian associations[2] – and not a particular favourite among artists, Carmarthen Castle's cultural impact has largely been local. The various functions that it fulfilled over the centuries have nevertheless been crucial in defining the identity of the town and region, and its inhabitants. Their sense of history and place, their government and, formerly, their punishment, have been dictated from this site. Now made safe, and with improved access, the castle can fulfil a further role as cultural amenity and visitor attraction. On-site interpretation includes panels, booklets and leaflets, and displays in the Old Police Station (Castle House) which, in 2011, became the Tourist Information Centre for the town.

We have seen that the castle was intrinsic to the 'landscape of consciousness', as a visible symbol of Anglo-Norman, royal authority. The gaol was similarly symbolic – *mae*

Dai wedi myn'd i'r castell ('Dai has gone to the castle') was a saying commonly heard in the region during the nineteenth century[3] – while there is evidence that its very visibility was exploited in the name of deterrence. It follows that the castle is also the main vantage point for views over the surrounding region, and the historic town. The latter can be particularly appreciated from the motte, where the informal nature of the development of medieval burgage plots has resulted in a roofscape of great complexity and interest. It is here, as well, that the radial system of boundaries can best be seen, allowing the historic centrality of the castle to be appreciated.

A castle in Wales

What has emerged, in summary, from the work? And where does Carmarthen Castle stand in British, and specifically Welsh, castle studies? Its layout, and its development relative to its various functions – military, administrative and residential – has been reconstructed, and compared with that of other similar sites. Is it representative of British – and Crown – castles? To what extent did it follow developmental trends? Is there anything particularly unique about its design and development? Is it noticeably 'Welsh'?

I suggest that the castle was founded soon after the abandonment of the nearby baronial castle at 'Rhydygors' in 1106. This earlier castle may have stood to the west of the River Tywi, rather than its more widely accepted location on the east bank. It was held, in 1102–5, by a Welsh chieftain in what is, to my knowledge, the earliest recorded Welsh occupation of a castle.

We can now be a little more certain of the form that Carmarthen Castle took during its early, timber-built years. A motte, with two baileys separated by a deep cross-ditch, appears to have been present from the first. The motte is characteristic of Carmarthenshire, where the rectangular inner ward also has parallels, which may suggest planning and supervision at a regional rather than central level. The inner ward appears to have been defended by substantial earthen banks, on which the curtain walls were later built, but they were probably rather unstable – banks and curtains have both largely gone. The outer ward may have begun as a hornwork, protecting the rear of the castle, but the possibility exists that it contained the main entrance, and that the castle was 'turned around' to face the town when refortified in stone. The castle's infrastructure during the twelfth century, like the composition of its household, remain uncertain. We also know very little about its internal arrangements. And while we may be a little closer to understanding the nature of the twelfth-/early thirteenth-century episodes of Welsh occupation, their influence on the castle's development has yet to be established.

Comparisons with contemporary work in Wales and the Marches, especially by the Crown and its major tenants, can now be advanced. The possible half-timbered round tower on the motte was an unexpected discovery. Although it cannot be dated, it appears to be earlier than the shell-keep and is therefore probably twelfth century – and if a tower, it is a very early example of the circular form. It may plausibly have been of Welsh construction, although no similar structures have yet been firmly attributed to the Princes of Deheubarth.

The shell-keep partly revets the motte and features three lobes or turrets, unusual attributes that are most closely paralleled at Berkeley, in Gloucestershire – a county to which Carmarthen was closely tied. The Berkeley keep was built on the orders of Henry II in 1153–6, while the Carmarthen keep was probably a product of documented Crown expenditure in the early 1180s. Although it may instead belong to the 1220–1230s, the construction of entirely new shell-keeps was, by this time, on the wane.

Comparison with other sites has also influenced the dating of other surviving castle structures, offering new suggestions for its builders. By the mid-thirteenth century, architectural trends in British castles were being increasingly set by the works of the Crown,[4] but during the early part of the century at least, baronial castles could remain a source of influence. This is nowhere more apparent than in the building works of the Marshal earls and Hubert de Burgh,[5] who held Carmarthen Castle as Marcher lords and were responsible for its reconstruction in stone. The inner ward comprised five round towers, comparable with similar work by both the Marshals and de Burgh. The South-west Tower however has spur-buttresses of a type almost endemic to south Wales, but normally of late thirteenth-century date. Other detail, internal arrangements and the surviving source material nevertheless suggest that the tower may have been built in the 1230s, and it may have influenced the design of the very similar north tower at Cardigan Castle, built in the 1240s–1260s when both castles were under Crown control. Nevertheless, the sheer scale and height of the spur-buttresses mean that doubts must remain. A second tower, the 'King's Tower', was apparently completed by Henry III and may have been larger than the rest; it probably contained private chambers. The sources suggest that it lay towards the south-east corner of the inner ward – possibly flanking the bailey like the large D-shaped towers at Montgomery and Helmsley, of similar date – where it would have dominated the view when approached from the Welsh-held territories. Two of the other three towers may have been represented by a twin-towered gatehouse, while the fifth tower is probably the one shown by Speed at the north-east apex of the inner ward. These masonry defences, with their advanced design, were substantially complete before Carmarthen was recovered by the Crown in 1241.

Building continued under the Crown but was more limited, concentrating on domestic accommodation. Henry III added a great hall, which may have been primarily ceremonial and administrative, and an adjoining chamber, both built as a unit with the King's Tower. Edward I appears to have added the chamber for 'knights and esquires', which probably lay against the south wall of the inner ward, and the 'Queen's Chamber', which may be the long building, against the north-east side of the bailey, suggested by eighteenth-century maps. The gatehouse appears to have been extended into the bailey, with a corner stair-turret(s). In addition, the sources suggest that the outer ward was walled in stone during the 1280–1290s; two of its D-shaped towers are shown by the Buck Brothers. It may have housed the 'large stable' which appears to have been contemporary, and it was entered from Spilman Street to the north; a gate-tower had been added by the 1320s, which may have been protected by a barbican.

As a result of the recent work we can speak with more confidence about the castle's political development. It is clear that, for the Crown, it was primarily a buffer to the Welsh princes, and Marcher lords, during the twelfth and early thirteenth centuries. It was held as a manorial lordship, under a custodian who held the courts at the castle and saw to its defence. The lordship was not fiscally autonomous, being attached to the exchequer at Gloucester. We have seen, moreover, that it was intermittently granted to royal favourites as an independent Marcher lordship. After 1241, it was held as a feudal county, but remained under the control of a single officer, the custodian, although a separate constable was appointed in 1277. However, no sheriffs were appointed until the Edwardian conquest, when, with the addition of further territory, the county was reorganised as a royal domain, Carmarthenshire. Castle and shire were, along with all Crown territories in south Wales, controlled by the justiciar of south Wales and became fiscally independent, with an exchequer and chamberlain. The castle did not, then, properly emerge as a centre of regional government until the 1280s, and particularly after 1301 when the administrative machinery in the Principality was overhauled by Prince Edward. As a royal castle, and centre of Crown administration, it fulfilled a range of functions that were rather different from the Marcher castles, and which in Wales were only really paralleled at Caernarfon.

In addition, the domestic and administrative infrastructure of later medieval Carmarthen Castle – its households, courts, staff and lodgings – has been clarified. The custodian's was the sole resident household until the late thirteenth century, when the figure rose to three. In addition, as many as six separate courts existed at the castle during the early fourteenth century. This period accordingly saw a massive expansion of its residential and clerical accommodation. The constable and his household occupied the customary first-floor chamber in the gatehouse. However, the new apartments built for the households of the other Crown officials, the justiciar and chamberlain, appear to have been ranges of buildings in the late medieval 'courtyard-house' tradition. Documentary and physical evidence suggest that the chamberlain's lodging, or 'mansion', occupied the south-west quarter of the inner ward, together with the new exchequer. The Justiciar's Mansion meanwhile appears to have stood north of the gatehouse, where a building, fossilised in the west curtain, may represent his courthouse. Nothing really comparable to these official complexes is known at any other British castle, while, in general, architectural patronage by royal servants diminished appreciably during the political instability of Edward II's reign.[6] They may be contrasted with Caernarfon, where officials occupied the spacious towers and had begun, moreover, to move out into the town by the fifteenth century – unlike at Carmarthen, where the persistence of a large resident population is suggested in the sources.

The remodelling of the motte – which, though a massive undertaking, goes unremarked in published studies – appears to have accompanied this development. The Justiciar's Mansion overlies the motte ditch, which was infilled with material derived from cutting back the entire south-east quadrant of the motte, flush with the shell-keep which was then extended down to bailey level; the surviving 'forebuilding' may be contemporary. Such treatment is, as far as I know, unique. The suggested motte tower appears to have survived until this period, when it was replaced by a range of lightly constructed buildings. Around the same time, a second chapel was built for the king's private use – probably in the south-east corner of the inner ward – and the gateway between the baileys was given a tower. The fourteenth century was also a time of considerable repair work, but expenditure was sporadic. Much of the medieval walling appears to have been built directly upon the substrate, without footings, but this is far from unusual in a local context (cf., for example, Nevern Castle). Nevertheless, it was evidently prone to collapse, particularly the southern curtain walls which were built on the unstable gravel terrace.

Carmarthen Castle, like other castles of similar function, acquired a number of distinct, but overlapping identities. It was a symbol of authority and prestige, a military base, a centre of government, a manorial centre, a lordly residence(s) and, in its most public identity, a judicial centre. There is also some evidence that it became zoned according to these identities. The southern half of the inner ward was primarily reserved for the king, and was separated from the northern half by a cross-wall, shown in eighteenth-century maps and prints. The northern half contained the justiciar's lodgings and courthouse, while the buildings on the motte were perhaps of relatively low status.

Evidence for damage during the Glyndŵr revolt (1403–6) was observed in the surviving stretch of west curtain, which was apparently truncated at the same time as the documented destruction of the gatehouse. Both were rebuilt in the early fifteenth century. The gatehouse is remarkably grand for a royal castle of the period and is among the last of its kind, (cf. the contemporary gatehouses at Kidwelly and Lancaster also built for Henry IV). It represents a considerable investment and more than a passing Crown interest in its west Wales dominions. It may be the 'Skidmore's Tower' of the sources, taking its name from an early fifteenth-century constable. Later medieval work was otherwise more or less confined to rebuilding and repairs. The courthouse was rebuilt as the 'Justiciar's Hall'. The surviving Square Tower on the inner ward south wall is stylistically late medieval, and a similar tower is shown by Speed between the gatehouse and South-west Tower where both bank and curtain wall have unfortunately been truncated. Both probably reflect the fifteenth-century fashion for square towers. Excavation suggests that the gatehouse was approached via a timber bridge supported by two masonry piers. Speed shows a twin-towered barbican in front of the bridge, which may have replaced an earlier barbican enclosure. A remarkable assemblage of leather and wooden artefacts was retrieved from a late medieval midden deposit beneath the bridge.

Finds and documentary evidence have been brought together to clarify the castle's position in the regional economy, and in the wider world of trade and supply. Basic provisioning was local, from the lordship, while much of the building stone and domestic ceramics were locally sourced. However, provisions and building supplies were also obtained by sea, primarily from the West Country, with Bristol the main *entrepôt*. Similarly the influence of the castle on the landscape has been assessed. The introduction of Anglo-Norman agricultural practices had a profound effect on the hinterland, as did the late thirteenth-century creation of a royal forest in north Carmarthenshire, administered by – and for the use of – the castle officials. Moreover the Anglo-Norman borough of Carmarthen originated from the castle, which exerted a powerful influence on its layout and development. On a fundamental level, the castle was built to be seen – its natural visibility was enhanced by the motte and, it seems, the King's Tower, and by the documented whitewashing of its walls.

The survival of an institution

A significant result of the recent research has been the presentation, for the first time, of a full narrative for the castle's post-medieval decline, disuse and disposal. Although a momentous time of transition for British castles, it has been neglected in the past[7] and is an important avenue for future research in castle studies. Carmarthen's administrative functions diminished under the Acts of Union of the 1530–1540s, and by the late sixteenth century it appears both to have lost its courts, which moved to the Borough Guildhall, and its resident household. The site was demised by the Crown in the early seventeenth century, and was granted, in 1634, to Sir Henry Browne and John Cliffe, who were busily acquiring a lot of former Crown land. The lease passed to local landowners, the Vaughans of Golden Grove, in 1639. Only two buildings may by this time have been habitable, and Carmarthen Castle henceforth existed solely as a prison, administered by the county authorities. The castle changed hands three times during the Civil War, when the town was fortified and the castle was possibly strengthened; the gate-towers have been infilled with masonry, and a secondary defensive bank may exist along the southern flank. We now know that the castle was garrisoned into the 1650s under the Parliamentary governor Rowland Dawkins – a figure largely absent from published histories of the town – and a document from 1652 describes it as still 'defensible and strong'. Although the event is unrecorded, it is clear that the castle was subsequently slighted, possibly after the Restoration in early 1660; it had been 'quite demolished' by the end of the year. The field evidence suggests that slighting targeted the curtain walls, which appear largely to have occupied unstable banks and were easily brought down, rather than the towers, whose damage may have been incidental. Domestic development in the west ditch appears to have been cleared prior to slighting.

The developmental sequence of the post-slighting gaol has also been clarified. Antique maps and prints show that it was confined to the northern half of the inner ward, of which the north curtain, cross-wall, the northern half of the west curtain, and a wall to the east – possibly from the Queen's Chamber – survived. The gatehouse had been retained and now housed the prisoners. By the early eighteenth century, the site had been divided into three parcels: the gaol, a garden south of the cross-wall – both of which were held by the county – and the outer ward, which was held by the Vaughans. Some new building was recorded in the 1770s, when the evidence suggests that the present shell-wall was also built. The outer ward, as 'Castle Green', was developed with housing alongside a thoroughfare within the medieval cross-ditch, which led onto Bridge Street through a former postern in the outer curtain. Bridge Street similarly saw domestic development, which encroached into the bodies of both the South-west Tower and Square Tower. John Nash's late eighteenth-century gaol was slightly larger than its predecessor, and the medieval east wall was demolished, followed by the rear half of the gatehouse, while the South-west Tower was altered. The last traces of the castle's internal divisions were lost in 1868–72, when the new gaol was built over its entire site. A number of detailed plans of both gaols have herein been brought together and show the layout of the gaol buildings; one of Nash's cell blocks was also revealed through excavation. Nash's frontage, facing Spilman Street, was retained for the new gaol but was lost when it was demolished to make way for County Hall. The old County Police Station, built next to the gaol in the 1880s, however, survived.

In its continuing history as a prison and centre of government, Carmarthen stands apart from the majority of Welsh castles. It is not unique in Britain – the sites of the castles at Chester, Oxford, Winchester and York are well known as administrative, judicial and penal centres. Monmouth Castle retained it assizes until 1939, while Haverfordwest Castle was used as a gaol until 1878. Nevertheless neither is still the centre of local government, and Carmarthen is the only Welsh castle that now houses the headquarters of the county authorities. While this continuity of use means that the castle has survived as an institution, it has inevitably been destructive to the earlier remains, in contrast to those castles which were allowed to become ruins.

The recent work was not without its surprises. Removal of the fill in the South-west Tower, for instance, revealed more fabric than it was ever hoped could survive, as well as the post-medieval reuse which threatened its very stability. The survival of bridge piers in front of the Great Gatehouse, only inches below a busy thoroughfare, was equally un-expected. Some of these discoveries make an important contribution to castle studies, and are of national importance, including the bridge, the probable early date of the spurred South-west Tower, the late medieval remodelling of the motte, its possible round tower and the affinities of the shell-keep, the evidence – physical and documentary – for the extensive development of governmental buildings during the fourteenth century and the medieval leather and wooden artefacts from the castle ditch which are among the best national assemblages of this material. Part of the surviving gaol perimeter wall, more-over, has been demonstrated to belong to the only surviving gaol building by John Nash, while the Old Police Station is the only county police station and lock-up that still exists in Wales.

THE CASTLE IN THE FUTURE

The full archaeological potential of the site has yet to be fully evaluated, having been sampled only in a few small areas, mainly on the periphery of the castle. The interior, which is now mainly a level tarmac area occupied by County Hall and its car park, has been subject to very little investigation, and there has been none within the outer ward area. However, the archaeological interventions, though limited, allow a general assessment of the extent of damage to the physical resource, and suggest areas where buried archaeology still survives.

Slighting was comprehensive, and subsequent losses of *standing* fabric to gaol development appear to have been confined to the gatehouse rear section, most of the inner ward east wall and its cross-wall. The loss of between twelve and twenty metres from the eastern flank of the outer ward through road widening (Figure 165; see Chapter 5) will have removed some internal deposits and, it seems, any evidence for the outer curtain. Further losses followed in the mid-1960s, when Coracle Way was constructed. Approximately 5 per cent of internal deposits were lost from the south-east corner of the inner ward, along with its south-east and east walls, which may have retained medieval fabric. The southern flank of the outer ward and any surviving evidence for its postern were also swept away; some evidence may however survive beneath the sloping revetment that was built around the southern side of the site. No formal record was made during any of these works. A small landslip, during the later twentieth century, meant the loss of some internal deposits between the South-west Tower and Square Tower (see Chapter 3). An unknown percentage of the castle interior was also lost to, or disturbed by, the late nineteenth-century gaol, and perhaps more was destroyed when County Hall was built; deposits may have been entirely removed beneath its footprint, which occupies over a third of the interior. A number of service trenches exist – in the car park, in the yard east of the gatehouse, and in the bridge area – and there will undoubtedly be many others. In addition there are the losses to recent archaeological investigation.

We saw in Chapter 3 that the natural profile slopes gently downhill across the castle site, from north-west to south-east, with a fall in medieval horizons of at least a metre (see Figures 12b and 12e). This means that at least some deposits north-west of County Hall will have been truncated when the car park was laid out (see Figure 165). However, it also means that medieval contexts survive at the south-west corner of the inner ward, where they also slope downhill to the east to lie 2 m above car park level next to the South-west Tower, but 1.5 m beneath this level next to the Square Tower (Figure 165). They appear to have suffered some truncation, but lower horizons may be relatively undisturbed beneath the southern two-thirds of the car park. Deposits also survive in the north–south strip between the west curtain and the gaol wall, 0.5 m beneath the surface, but they lie nearly 1 m above car park level, so some truncation may have taken place east of the gaol wall; preservation is clearly best in the peripheral areas between the gaol wall and the former curtains. However, archaeology also survives in a 5 m-wide strip along the foot of the north curtain, just beneath the present surface (Figures 12–14). Medieval deposits survive within the shell-keep, 1.5 m beneath modern ground level, although earlier post-medieval horizons have been truncated; the body of the motte outside the shell-keep appears also to be undamaged (see Figures 12, 14 and 21). The possible presence of human burials on the motte (and elsewhere in the castle?) of course represents a constraint, as well as an opportunity.

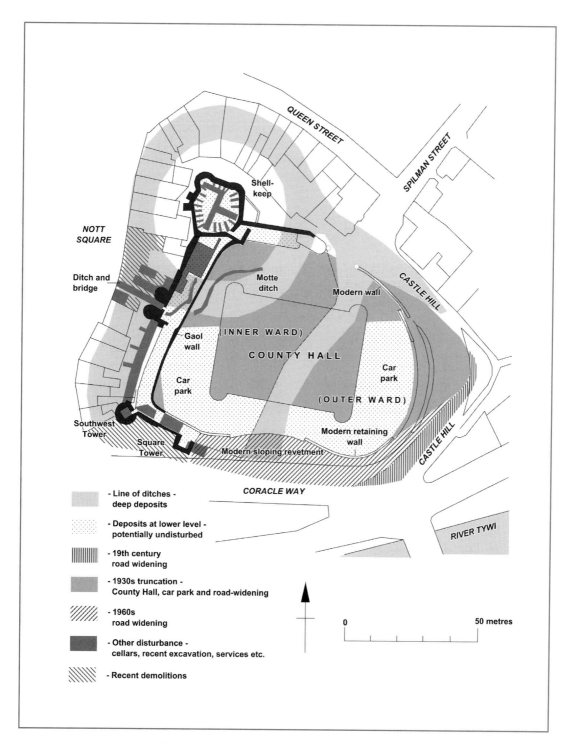

Figure 165 *Plan of the entire castle site showing archaeological potential, and losses to development*

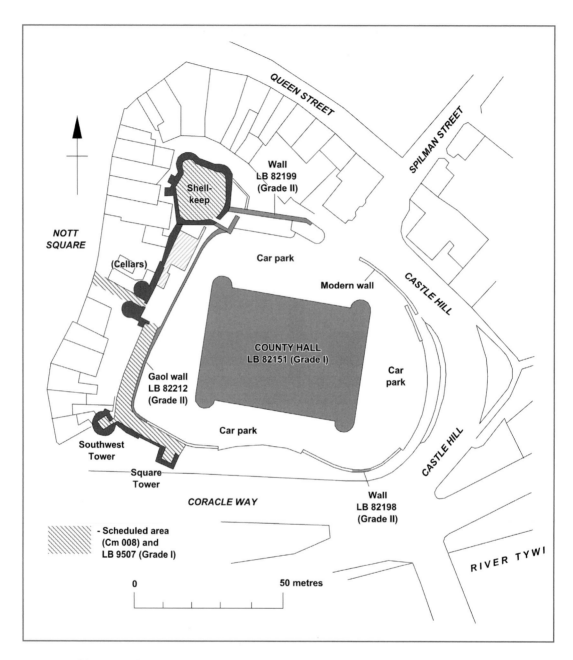

Figure 166 Plan of the castle site showing the scheduled area and listed buildings

Survival will presumably be better in the castle ditches (Figure 165). The motte ditch, where it underlies the car park, was probably at least 5 m deep, and its lower horizons, at least, may lie beneath County Hall foundation level (Figure 12b). The cross-ditch between the inner and outer wards, where waterlogged deposits appear to have survived the construction of the late nineteenth-century gaol, may be similarly preserved. We have seen

Table 10 *Summary of known buried archaeological deposits in the castle*

Location	Depth	Nature and quality	Underlying/sealed by
Shell-keep interior	1.5m	Walls and deposits. Very good	Garden soil; debris
Shell-keep exterior/motte summit	0.1m	Deposits and structures. Very good	Turf
Strip at foot of internal face of north curtain	0.1m – ?0.5m	Walls (post-medieval). Very good.	Modern surfacing
Strip between former west curtain and gaol wall	0.5m	Walls and deposits. Good – some damage	Modern surfacing and make-up
Strip between southern retaining wall and gaol wall	0.2m – 1.7m	Walls and deposits. Good – truncated?	Modern surfacing and dumping
Castle interior – northwest quarter	0.2m	Uncharacterised. Truncated	Modern tarmac surface
West ditch (gatehouse area)	0.2m	Mainly deposits; causeway walls. Good	Modern surfacing

that there is excellent survival in the west ditch, despite post-medieval development, and presumably these deposits will continue around the motte exterior. The northern periphery of the site – including any northern ditch – may also be relatively undisturbed. See Figure 12 for suggested levels of archaeological horizons.

So the overall potential for the survival of below-ground archaeological deposits may yet be reasonably good. The standing medieval remains have been subject to much post-medieval alteration – the shell-wall was practically rebuilt, the north curtain may only be partly medieval, while the South-west Tower and Square Tower have been truncated and altered. Nevertheless a good percentage of the west curtain may be medieval, and as the west wall of the Old Police Station is free-standing, its internal face may be unaltered (Figure 151). Meanwhile the gatehouse – or at least its outer half – is substantially intact.

The medieval remains are a Scheduled Ancient Monument and a Grade I listed building (SAM No. Cm 008; LB No. 9507: see Fig. 166). The scheduled area takes in the bridge piers outside the Great Gatehouse and areas of known buried archaeology. The north 'curtain' wall, however, is not scheduled, and is only Grade II listed (LB No. 82199; DAT PRN 61706). The remains of the post-medieval gaol perimeter wall are similarly Grade II listed (LB No. 82212; DAT PRN 61717), as is County Hall (LB No. 82151). A further, small section of perimeter walling at the south-eastern corner of County Hall car park is also Grade II listed (LB No. 82198; DAT PRN 61705), but contrary to the suggestion in the Cadw LB database,[8] it is early nineteenth century and not medieval (see Chapters 3 and 5). Scheduling ensures that the future management of the site and its status will be subject to regular review. The story of the castle's development may be far from over, and further opportunities for investigation may yet arise.[9]

NOTES

1 County Hall has become almost iconic and is the image most used to illustrate Carmarthen, and Carmarthenshire, in the press and on TV.

2 In Geoffrey of Monmouth's *History of the Kings of Britain*, Merlin is born in Carmarthen to a princess and an incubus.

3 F. Green, 'Carmarthen Castle. A Collection of Historical Documents relating to Carmarthen Castle from the Earliest Times to the Close of the Reign of Henry VIII', *WWHR*, 3 (1913), 6.

4 J. Goodall, *The English Castle 1066–1650* (Newhaven and London: Yale University Press, 2011), p. 198 and passim.

5 See, for example, R. Avent, 'William Marshal's castle at Chepstow and its place in military architecture', in R. Turner and A. Johnson (eds), *Chepstow Castle: Its History and Buildings* (Almeley: Logaston, 2006), pp. 81–90.

6 Goodall, *English Castle*, p. 233.

7 See J. R. Kenyon, review of *The Decline of the Castle* by M. W. Thompson, *Medieval Archaeology*, 33 (1989), pp. 262–4.

8 Cadw, LB No. 82198 (retaining wall), Cadw LB database accessed via END, July 2006.

9 For example, structural engineering works may become necessary on the northern periphery of the site, and the northern ditch, so there may be further opportunities for archaeological investigation in this area.

APPENDIX

DOCUMENTED DEVELOPMENT

The surviving building accounts are summarised below, along with other documentary sources from the medieval period that relate to work at the castle. An overview of these sources is given in the introduction to Chapter 4.

THE TWELFTH CENTURY

1106/9
Carmarthen Castle was first established; it was possibly complete by 1109: see Chapter 2 (Jones, 1971, p. 109).

1116
Castle attacked. A contemporary account gives some clues as to the nature of the castle, as the *rhag-gastell* – meaning the outworks or bailey – were burnt, but the attackers failed to capture the *tŵr*, or the motte and keep: *gwedy llosgi y raccastell heb uynet y mywn y'r tŵr*, or 'after burning the outer castle without entering the keep' (Jones 1955, 88–9).

1137
Carmarthen Castle 'burnt' and taken in Welsh attack. It was possibly left vacant, or at least not rebuilt (Jones 1952, 52; Jones 1971, 147).

1145
Carmarthen Castle was 'built', presumably meaning 'rebuilt', suggesting that it had been left in decay after 1137 (Jones 1952, 54).

1150
Carmarthen Castle was repaired by Cadell ap Gruffudd 'for the strength and splendour of his kingdom' (Jones 1952, 57).

1158–76

Castle chapel first specifically mentioned – 'Grant and confirmation by Henry II . . . to [Carmarthen Priory] . . . of the church of St Peter . . . with the chapel of my castle of Carmarthen, and all other chapels to the same church belonging' (Daniel-Tyssen 1878, 4–6, from *Charter Roll* 31 Hen. III; Davies 1946, 283).

The priory had been granted to Battle Abbey in 1120–5, along with St Peter's Church and its other appurtenances (Davies 1946, 245–6) which may be assumed, by this time, to have included the castle chapel. Henry II's charter, inspected and confirmed by Henry III, is dated by Davies to 1154–76. However, the castle probably remained in Welsh hands until 1158 (see Chapter 2).

1181–3

Henry II spends £160 on 'our castle of Carmarthen'. No details given (*Pipe Roll* 27 Hen. II, 5, 15; *Pipe Roll* 28 Hen. II., 108; *Pipe Roll* 29 Hen. II., 27, 141).

The *History of the King's Works* gives a total of £170 (Colvin 1963, 600). However, the Pipe Rolls differentiate between payments to keepers for custody of the castle (*pro custodia*), which total £40, and for building work (*ad operationem*), which total £160, with a grand total of £200 – which is incidentally the figure assigned to building work by Armitage (1908), 15.

THE EARLY THIRTEENTH CENTURY

1223

William Marshal II 'repaired' Carmarthen Castle (Jones 1952, 100; Jones 1955, 225).

1224–6

Custody of Carmarthen and Cardigan Castles appears to have cost William Marshal II 300 marks (£198) yearly between 1224 and 1226 (Green 1913, 10, from *Close Roll* 10 Hen. III), which was spent on their fabric. The king made this figure up to £800 (King 1988a, 54 n.14).

1226

Carmarthen and Cardigan Castles relinquished to the Crown. Repairs were undertaken by the king's carpenters: 50 marks (£33) were spent on 'works' at the castles, and 45s. paid to two carpenters for sixty days' work (Colvin 1963, 600; Green 1913, 32, from *Close Roll* 10 Hen. III).

1227

Another 50 marks (£33) were spent on the repair of the 'bridges' at Carmarthen and Cardigan Castles (*CLR* 1226–40, 17). Further 'divers payments' were made for the keeping and 'repair' of Carmarthen Castle, while two carpenters undertook 'certain works' at Carmarthen and Cardigan castles (Green 1913, 10, 32, from *Close Roll* 11 Hen. III).

1228-32
Carmarthen held by Hubert de Burgh (*CChR* 1 1226–1257, 100).

1241
The Crown recovers Carmarthen and Cardigan (Green 1913, 12, from *Pat. Roll* 26 Hen. III).

1247
38 marks (£25 2s.) spent on repairing the 'King's tower' at Carmarthen. A further 20 marks (£13 6s.) spent on the 'king's works in the castle' (*CLR* 1245–1251, 134–5).

1250
40 marks (£26 8s.) spent on building the 'hall for the King' at Carmarthen (*CLR* 1245–1251, 303–4).

*c.*1250
Two smiths, nine quarrymen and twenty-four masons sent to Carmarthen from Bristol, for five days, along with 1,000 nails 'called spikings', 4,000 floor-nails and 2,000 wall-nails (TNA: PRO SC 1/11/118, Indenture, *c.*1250).

1251-2
Four 'fothers' of lead for roofing the 'King's Tower' – £6 7s. 6d (*CLR* 1251–1260, 43).

1252
Order to spend 200 marks (£132 8s.) on 'making a hall and chamber for the King's use at Carmarthen' (TNA: PRO E 372/96, Pipe Roll 36 Hen. III).

1248-54
Expenditure on 'new building the King's Hall and Chamber at Carmarthen' had included £140 8s. 3d, and £41 15s. had been spent fitting the 'tower of Carmarthen' with joists, roofing it with lead and whitewashing it (*CLR* 1260–1267, 40; also see TNA: PRO E 372/104, Pipe Roll 44 Hen. III).

THE LATE THIRTEENTH CENTURY

*c.*1257-9
The burgesses of Carmarthen petitioned King Henry III that the castle was 'weakened and collapsing in several places, and is in great peril' (TNA: PRO SC 1/3/1, Letter to Henry III, n.d. *c.*1257–9).

1265-79

'Eight hundredweight of iron, six seams of lead (each seam of four cartloads)' and 3,000 nails sent from Bristol to Carmarthen Castle, 'by order of the Lord Edmund'. Six smiths hired for eight days, twenty-four workmen for five days, and three smiths. Sum: £25 14s. 11d (TNA: PRO C 47/10/43/14, Indenture, *c*.1265–79).

1275

'Extent of the manors of Carmarthen and Cardigan:
'There is [at Carmarthen] a certain castle in which is a certain good dungeon constructed from five small towers (*in quo est quedam bona Dungeo, ex quinque parvis turribus constructa*), which is in want of repair as well as keeping up.
'A certain great tower is there (*Est ibi quedam magna turris*), which is much in want of reparation; one convenient hall with a chamber (*una aula competens cum camera*) also require repairing as the above.
'The chapel, stable and kitchen are decayed, and the gate of the castle (*Capella, Stabulum et Coquina debiles, et porta Castri*), so as to be of no value.
'The castle wall towards the water for the length of 8 perches and the wall from the castle gate unto the western corner (*et murus a porta Castri usque ad angulum occidentalem*), for the length of 10 perches appear in a ruinous state and have partly fallen down.
'All the defects as well of the towers and walls, can be amended and newly repaired for 100 marks' (£66 13s. 4d) (Daniel-Tyssen 1878, 45, from Inquisitions, Edward I, June 1275, 84).
This Inquisition had previously been seen by local historian Alcwyn Evans, who had made notes from it prior to addressing the Carmarthenshire Antiquarian Society in 1875. Where Daniel-Tyssen gives both the Latin and English as 'western corner' (i.e. '*angulum occidentalem*'), Evans had noted it as 'western *tower*' (Holmes 1908, 21). I have not seen the original manuscript.

1275

It was estimated that 'the buildings of [Carmarthen and Cardigan castles] can be put in repair for 100 marks; neither castle can be maintained in time of peace for less than 40 marks' (*Cal. Inq. Misc.* 1219–1307, 305).

1277

Mandate the Constable and Mayor of Bristol to send to Carmarthen and Cardigan 'two good smiths and four other smiths, together with 40 *summae* of iron and four *magnae carratae* of lead' (Edwards 1935, 158).

1279+

Order for '3 smiths, 9 stone cutters, 24 workmen for 5 days, 1,000 nails called "spikings"', 4,000 floor-nails and 2,000 wall-nails. The nails to be put on a ship at Bristol, and taken to Carmarthen (Edwards 1935, 114; n.d., after 1279. NB: this is more-or-less identical with TNA: PRO SC 1/11/118 above, dated *c*.1250).

1280

'Extent of Carmarthen:

'A certain castle is there in which a certain good (dungeon) is constructed out of five small towers' (Daniel-Tyssen 1878, 51–4, from Exchequer Records, Bag 1 Wallia, No. 14).

1287–8

Fourteen carats of lead sent from Bristol Castle to Carmarthen Castle for roofing the houses of the castle – £31 7s. 8d (TNA: PRO E 159/61, Memoranda Roll 16 Edw. I, 1287–8; also see Fryde 1974, 4).

1288–9

Expenditure includes:

Quarrying and carrying stone, lime and roofing slates – £46 13s. 6d

'Making a new wall below the castle towards the Bridge of Towey [Tywi], on both sides of the postern' – 115s

Work on the new stable, including masonry walls, 'doors, mangers, and other necessaries', '5,000 laths' and carpentry – £10 5s. 5d

Repairing and 'whitening' the walls of 'the entire castle' – 40s.

Wages for work on the leadwork on the 'five towers' – 40s.

Wages for work on the freestone of two windows in the hall – 20s.

Wages for work on the freestone of two windows in the 'tower above the gate' – 20s.

Sum – £169 15s. 3d (Green 1913, 46–8, from *Pipe Roll* 17 Edw. I).

1289

Mandate to spend up to £30 on the 'thatched (*foragio coopertas*) houses' in Carmarthen Castle, in repairing them and reroofing them 'with stone' (*CCcR* 1277–1326, 321; also see Daniel-Tyssen 1878, 57).

THE EARLY FOURTEENTH CENTURY

1300

Order to repair 'the houses of the King's castles in West Wales', including Carmarthen (Green 1913, 49, from *Close Roll* 28 Edw. I).

1300–1

£1 12s. 0½d spent on works at the castle. No particulars (Green 1914, 65).

1303-4

The 'land and castles' of Carmarthen were 'surveyed and ordered' (*Cal. Inq. Misc.* 1307–1349, 19). £8 14s. 1d spent on works (Green 1914, 65).

1304-5

£1 0s. 1d spent on works at castle (Green 1914, 65).

1306

Works include:
'Repairing the Queen's Chamber' – 19s.
And a 'certain porch of the Large Hall' – 9s.
And 'the Exchequer' – 3s.
And 'the 5 towers, the Justiciar's Kitchen, the ceiling of the chamber over the Pantry'.
Carpenter's wages for 'making a certain *fumerell*' (narrow chimney) . . . and locks for the gate of the five towers [i.e. the Great Gatehouse]' (Green 1913, 49–50, from Exchequer K. R. Account, 486/19).

1307-8

£4 11s. 4d spent on works (Green 1914, 65).

1308

The king's castles in north, west and south Wales were ordered to be 'surveyed and fortified' (*CFR* 1307–1319, 13).

1309-10

Works include:
A 'house newly built in [Carmarthen] castle next to the great gate . . . by order of Roger de Mortimer justiciar of Wales' – 75s. 8½d
A 'certain house newly built and ordained for the kitchen of the Chamberlain' – 47s. 2d
And 'another house newly built in the said castle by order of the Justiciar, the first part being a dresser, the second part a kitchen, the third part a larder and the fourth part a bakehouse and brewhouse with a kiln' – £21 12s.
A 'house newly put up . . . between the King's chamber and the Knights' chamber, which house was ordained for the chapel'
Sum – £27 14s. 10½d (TNA: PRO E 372/159, Enrolled Account, 1309–10).

1310-11

£1628 19s. 10½d spent on the five royal castles of south-west Wales (Fryde 1974, 33, from TNA: PRO E 368/82/261).

1314-15

£7 8s. 2d spent on 'timber, stone, lime, lead, divers ironwork, boards, wages of masons, carpenters, smiths and other labourers' on the repair of lodgings at Carmarthen Castle (retrospective) (TNA: PRO E 159/92, Memoranda Roll 12 Edw. II, 1318–19).

1315

Order for 'the houses, walls, towers, and other buildings . . . to be repaired' (Green 1913, 51, from *Close Roll* 9 Edw. II).

1315-16

Works include 'the repair of the lodgings and other things' – £4 19s. 7½d. For 18½ft of lead for the works – 42s. 10d (TNA: PRO SC 6/1219/1, Chamberlain's Account, 1315–16).

1317

£15 0s. 2½d spent on the repair of 'the lodgings, walls and the New Bridge' (TNA: PRO E 159/92).

1317-18

Account for expenses on various lead works – £44 5s. 2½d (TNA: PRO SC 6/1219/8, Chamberlain's Account, 1317–18).

1318

Order to spend £100 in repairing the castle, as 'repairs are much needed' (Green 1913, 16, from *Close Roll* 12 Edw. II).

1318-19

Account of the 'repair of the lodgings' of Carmarthen Castle – £54 4s. 8d, i.e. half of the £100 ordered to be spent (TNA: PRO SC 6/1219/9, Chamberlain's Account, 1318–19).

1319-20

Account of 'divers expenses . . . on the works at Carmarthen Castle' – £27 17s. 11d. Two tilers, for the 'repair of the roofing of the old houses' – 16s. (TNA: PRO SC 6/1219/10, Chamberlain's Account, 1319–20).

1320-1

Allowance to the prior of Carmarthen for money spent repairing Carmarthen Castle (Fryde 1974, 50, from PRO E 368/91/414).

1321

Condition survey:
The 'King's hall . . . ought to be repaired partly with new timber. And the gutters . . . repaired with lead'.

The 'chamberlain's hall and kitchen ought to be repaired with timber at the top, and the gutters towards the sea . . . repaired with lead'.

Of 'the 5 towers, the floors . . . [of the] . . . tower there (where prisoners should be kept) ought to be repaired with new joists, and the other floors ought to be repaired with new lead'.

The 'four high towers with the watch-tower (*garit*) ought to be repaired with new joists and lead'.

The hall 'where the great lords (*grauntz seigneurs*) usually stay [the Knights' Chamber?] . . . ought to be repaired a little'.

Also 'all the stairs and passages of the said towers ought to be repaired, together with foundation of an enclosure opposite the gate of the said towers [i.e. a barbican?]'.

(This account, BL Harl. Roll 7198, was transcribed and published by Francis Green who dated it to 1340 (1913, 61). Stephen Priestley however dates it to 1321.)

1326-7

Expenses on works at the castle – £4 0s. 10d. Tiler appointed 'for the repair of the reroofing of the stone houses in the castle', taking '16s. for his annual fee' (TNA: PRO SC 6/1220/3, Chamberlain's Account, 1326–7). The account for 1327–8 is identical (TNA: PRO SC 6/1220/5, Chamberlain's Account, 1327–8).

1331

Order to the chamberlain to 'supervise the king's works' commenced in the castles of Carmarthen and Dinefwr 'and cause them to be completed' (Green 1913, 17, 53, from *Close Roll* 5 Edw. III).

1335

Expenses on works – £5 7s. 3d. Tiler's annual fee – 16s. (TNA: PRO SC 6/1220/8, Chamberlain's Account, 1335).

1335-6

£2 2s. 1d spent on works at the castle. No particulars. Tiler's annual fee – 16s. (Green 1914, 66 and n. 2).

1336

Order to the chamberlain to spend 'up to £40 in repairing the defects' in Carmarthen Castle (Green 1913, 54, from *Close Roll* 10 Edw. III).

1336-7

For 'various expenses' on the 'necessary works' – £ 3 14s 10½d.

For 'divers expenses incurred on the repair and mending of the Castle . . . towards the river Tewy [Tywi] ruined and collapsed during this present year' – no further sum given (TNA: PRO SC 6/1220/10, Chamberlain's Account, 1336; Green 1914, 66).

1338
Order to repair the castle for £20, in response to French threats and storm damage (Green 1913, 17, 54, from *Close Roll* 12 Edw. III). Carried out in 1338–9, after admonishment from the king – see the following.

1338-9
'Lime bought for the mason-work upon . . . the ruined walls, towers, and houses, unroofed and destroyed by wind and storm . . . to wit, the King's hall and chamber, the knights' and esquires' chamber, and the chapel there'.

Also for nine boatloads of stone 'towards the defects of a certain outer wall of the said castle between the town and the castle aforesaid, destroyed on account of its age'.

To two masons, for a week and a day, for 'making anew a wall 26ft long and 8ft high for one pinion [gable?] between the kitchen and the bakehouse . . . the greater part of the said bakehouse, decayed through age and a bad foundation, had fallen beyond the castle wall towards the River Towey' – 4s. 6d.

And to three carpenters for 'boarding anew the floors of the said kitchen and bakehouse, and a pinion of the said kitchen, and for refitting the King's large stable . . . and making and mending divers doors and windows in the chambers of the King, Queen, Knights, and Esquires, and of the granary, pantry and buttery, for 9 weeks' – 48s.

Also to four quarriers 'in the quarry, digging and cutting . . . slates for covering the roofs of the aforesaid bakehouse and kitchen, and for mending and repairing all the defects of all houses in the said castle, for 30 working days' – 25s.

And for three tilers working on the same roofs – 60s.

To the mason for 'making a wall on both sides of the entrance of the King's Hall there, and making and mending the wall of the King's chapel', for four working days – 12d.

To two freemasons, for 'repairing, and mending defects of the wall in the Chamberlain's enclosure there, and of the five towers, and making anew . . . a certain portion of the outer wall between the castle and the town, near the outer gate', for eleven weeks – 66s. 8d.

Sum – £19 15s. 1½d.

Sum of the works at Carmarthen – £58 6s. 7d (Green 1913, 17, 55–60, from Exchequer K. R. Account, 487/9, 3).

1339-40
'Works of the castle of Carmarthen and of the County Hall there. Paid for the repair of the castle for one year, 48s. 11½d'.

'Paid for the works and repair of the King's County Hall of Carmarthen for holding the pleas of the English and Welsh Counties and the Justiciar's Sessions there, 66s. 7d'. Sum – £5 5s. 6½d (Green 1913, 60, from Min. Acc. 1221/3).

1340

Order to 'expend up to £40 in repairing that part of the wall of [Carmarthen] Castle which is now destroyed' (Green 1913, 18, 61–2, from *Close Roll* 14 Edw. III).

THE MID-FOURTEENTH CENTURY

1343

Survey of Carmarthen Castle on behalf of the Black Prince:
'Concerning the defects . . . the Chamberlain's House . . . and a certain tower next to the said house which greatly need repair cannot be repaired for less than £30.'
'Also that the stable, kitchen, bakehouse and brewhouse in the same castle fallen to the ground cannot be repaired unless built anew'. Estimated cost £40.
'And that the King's and Queen's chambers and the garderobe of the Queen's Chamber with a garret adjoining the said chamber and five turrets of the great tower (*quinque turrel in magna turr'*) that are decayed . . . cannot be repaired . . . for less than £6'.
'And that a certain chapel and a certain old stable with the bridge of the great gate (*ponte magne porte*) which is very decayed and ruined for lack of repair cannot be repaired for less than £6'.
'Also that 6 rods in length and 7ft in width of walling between the Postern tower and the great hall which has been begun and not finished can be completed at a cost of 100 marks'.
'Also that the defects of the masonry in walls, steps, corbels and other things . . . can be repaired . . . for 100 marks'.
Total estimate – £215 6s. 8d (TNA: PRO E 163/4/42, Survey of Carmarthen Castle, 1343).

1348-9

'Repairs of the houses of Carmarthen Castle':
The 'large hall'
The 'large chamber there'
The 'house above the Exchequer'
The 'Chamberlain's hall and kitchen'
The 'armourer's chamber'
Two slaters, for 43 days, 21s. 6d
The 'repair of the house above the well, to wit, in roofing it round' – 3s. 4d
Repair 'of a portion of the castle wall at the head of the Chamberlain's kitchen' – 3s. 7½d

'The hire of 1 carpenter for . . . repairing the houses (dorm.) of the Large gate' – 5s.
Sum – £2 2s. 1½d (Green 1913, 62, from Min. Acc. 1221/8).

1352–3

£2 3s. 7½d spent on works (Green 1914, 66, from Min. Acc. 1158/3).
Canvas was bought for the windows of the 'County Hall' in the castle (Griffiths 1972, 22;
Rees 1941, 267).

1354–5

Repairing 'the Constable's chamber above the gate, and the pentice of the said chamber,
together with the repair of the large wall of the castle towards the east and other divers
necessaries, 22s. 3d.'
Paid to 'divers masons making divers repairs there, 9s. 7d'.
Paid to 'divers tilers tiling the pentice near the chamber above the outer gate, and other
houses in the castle, 35s. 6d'.
Sum – £22 3s. 9½d (Green 1913, 63, from Min. Acc. 1221/9).
Additional costs for two plumbers working 'on the castle, the Hall of the Chamberlain
facing the town and the chamber over the outer gate' (TNA: PRO SC 6/1221/9, Chamberlain's Account, 1354–5).

1355–6

Paid 'to divers masons for making a certain wine cellar under the Chamberlain's chamber
and repairing other necessaries, together with the stone-flooring of the Constable's chamber over the Large Gate . . . 17s. 9d'.
'Making a certain pentice of the Chamberlain's chamber'.
And making 'the windows of the hall of the inner bailey (*aule interioris ballivae*) . . . and
palice [fence?] made opposite the Chamberlain's hall' – 17s. 4½d.
Sum – £2 4s. 5½d (Green 1913, 63–4, from Min. Acc. 1221/10).

1356–60

During this four-year period, £158 10s. 0d was spent on works at the castle, mainly on
wages of carpenters, masons, tilers and others, and for nails, boards, laths and hooks. No
particulars (Green 1914, 66).

1360–1

Making 'a new kitchen for the constable . . . with one chamber in the said kitchen, and a
prison below the said kitchen, and divers other repairs necessary'.
Sum – £36 7s. 10d.
'100 marks to be expended yearly upon the repair of all the [royal] castles in South
Wales' except Haverfordwest, Aberystwyth and Dinefwr (Green 1913, 64, from Min. Acc.
1221/13).

THE LATE FOURTEENTH CENTURY

1377-85

During this eight-year period, only £50 3s. 9¼d was spent on works at the castle (Green 1914, 67), including 'money paid to . . . carpenters, masons, tilers and others . . . repairing many defects' (TNA: PRO SC 6/1221/14, Chamberlain's Account, 1379–80).

1385-6

'Repair of the New Wall [*sic*] of the Castle of Carmarthen' – Sum £45 5s. 9½d.
'Ordinary repairs' to Carmarthen and Dinefwr Castles – Sum £11 2s. 2d (Green 1913, 67, from Min. Acc. 1221/1).

1387-8

For 'plastering the broken wall of the castle, 2 men for 8 days'.
Expenses on the chapel, 'cords for the big bell', and 'repairing the window'.
Locks for the 'Justiciar and Chamberlain's stable'.
Materials, and non-specific minor repairs, comprising 'laths' and 'nails', mending timber-work and tile roofs.
Sum – £ 4 3s. 6d (Green 1913, 67–8, from Min. Acc. 1222/3).

1389-90

Minor repairs including work on the 'Exchequer House' and 'Chamberlain's chamber', and the 'Reception Hall (*hospitium*) of the Chamberlain and Justiciar'. Sum –
£4 9s. 0d. The carpenter/tiler was retained for twenty-one weeks (Green 1913, 69–70, from Min. Acc. 1306/5).

1390-1

Non-itemised repairs – 'divers masons, carpenters, and divers other workers repairing, amending and cleaning divers towers, houses, walls and well'. The 'Chamberlain's hostel' (*hospitium*) is singled out. Sum – £21 14s. 10d.
The 'costs of the prison of the castle' include 'locks and keys for divers doors of the 5 towers, and for gyves' etc., 8s. 2d. And iron 'for making fetters' etc., £1 19s. 1½d. Chapel expenses – 6s. 1d (Green 1913, 70, from Min. Acc. 1222/5).

1394-5

Payment to 'divers masons, carpenters, tilers, quarrymen' etc. making a 'certain gate with a crenellated chamber made anew upon it between the inner ward and the outer ward' – £6 4s. 1d. There are no particulars for an additional expenditure of £8 19s. 8½d (Green 1913, 70–1, from Min. Acc. 1222/6; Green 1914, 68).

1395-6

£5 3s. 7d spent on works at the castle (Green 1914, 68). No particulars.

1396-7

The 'building of a certain part of the wall of the castle, 145ft long . . . which part was in entire decay before it was amended'. Paid to John Hirde of Pembroke, mason – £20. Materials – £23 7s. 1½d. There are no particulars for an additional expenditure of £5 6s. 0d (Green 1913, 72, from Min. Acc. 1222/8; Green 1914, 68).

1397-8

£8 7s. 11d spent on works at the castle (Green 1914, 68). No particulars.

THE EARLY FIFTEENTH CENTURY

1400-1

Payment to 'divers quarrymen . . . masons, carpenters, slaters, smiths' and other workers, 'on the new Exchequer building and the Chamberlain's mansion'. Sum – £28 6s. 6½d. 'The ordinary repairs of the castle of Carmarthen – divers masons, carpenters . . . and other labourers repairing and mending of defects there'. Sum – £2 14s. 6½d (Green 1914, 1–2, from Min. Acc. 1222/9).

1409-10

Paid for 'the first building and repair of the castle' – £90 9s. 10½d.
Also 'for the repair of five towers, houses and other divers necessaries' – £191 10s. 3d.
'Costs of the Prince's castle of Carmarthen and of his boat there' – £5 6s. 2d.
A plumber was engaged for one month, making gutters for 'John Skidmore's Tower', and the 'armourer's tower [both in the Great Gatehouse?]', and 'fixing the same' (Green 1914, 16–17, from Min. Acc. 1222/10; also see Colvin 1963, 601).

1410-11

For the 'repair of the New Gate [the Great Gatehouse] . . . and of the tower above le postern, and other necessaries' – £98 14s. 2d (Green 1914, 17, from Min. Acc. 1222/12; also see Colvin 1963, 601).

1413-14

'Building and repairing the new house over the prison near the gate of the castle' – £28 0s. 0¾d.
Paid to 'the King's plumber, for working in the castle . . . for 194 days' – £4 17s.
A large coffer for keeping the 'Record Rolls' in 'the King's Treasury within Carmarthen Castle' was purchased (Green 1914, 18, from Min. Acc. 1222/13).

1414-15

Paid to 'the King's plumber, working in the castles of Carmarthen and Aberystwyth for 365 days' – £9 2s. 6d.

'Costs of the castle of Carmarthen. Paid for covering the tower of the gate . . . with boards under lead', and making one new gable for the 'new chambers above the prison', and other necessaries – £11 11s. 7½d (Green 1914, 18–19, from Min. Acc. 1222/14).

1416-17

£5 6s. 8d spent on works at the castle, limited to the chapel (Green 1914, 69).

1418-19

'For making the Chamberlain's stable anew, repairing the Auditor's Hall and other necessaries' – £27 13s. 1½d (Green 1914, 69 n. 2).

1420-1

'Paid for making and erecting one pentice of the Chamberlain's hall' and the 'repair of several defects' – £4 3s. 8d (Green 1914, 19, from Min. Acc. 1223/3).

1421

Boards, lime, hinges etc. 'used upon the doors and windows of the Chamberlain's mansion' and 'the carriage of one large stone from the priory . . . and laid in the Chamberlain's Hall for placing a fireplace thereon', and other sundries – 39s. 4d (Green 1914, 19–20, from Min. Acc. 1223/4).

1422

John Matthew, chaplain, granted a chantry within Carmarthen Castle chapel (Green 1914, 20, from *Pat. Roll* I Hen. VI).

1424

Minor repairs, but a number of buildings are mentioned for the first time.

Repairs include the louvre of the Chamberlain's Hall (i.e. for an open hearth), the chamber below the Chamberlain's Hall (the 'wine cellar' of 1355–6?), the chamberlain's kitchen and stable, the large stable, the 'new stable', the chambers above and below the exchequer, the latter with two windows, the 'new' Justiciar's Hall, the 'new cellar at the end of the Justiciar's hall', the Auditor's Chamber, the 'chamber of the King's armoury' or 'armoury chamber' (the 'armourer's tower' of 1409–10?), and 'Greyndour's Tower'. New stairs were made from the Chamberlain's Chamber to the chamber beneath the exchequer, 'and a trap-door there'.

A number of chimneys were repaired, including one in the Chamberlain's Kitchen, one each in the Justiciar's Chamber and Chamberlain's Chamber, another 'near' the exchequer, and two in the Armoury Chamber.

Also repaired were 'the 'bridge of the . . . castle, one fireplace of the kitchen there, and of 2 other fireplaces of the armoury chamber' and 'one other fireplace in the chief chamber of the Justice'.
Sum – £8 14s. 5½d (Green 1914, 21–7, from Exchequer Q. R. Account, 487/17 and Min. Acc. 1223/5).

1424-5

Materials and wages of carpenters, masons, tilers and other labourers 'for making' the new Justiciar's Hall, and the 'repair of the said hall' during 1421–4 – £34 4s. 1½d.
Goods 'for making one small stable'.
Repairing 'divers defects in the King's Chapel'.
Other expenses were incurred in the pantry, the Armoury Chamber, the chambers above and below the exchequer, the chamber below the Chamberlain's Hall, the Auditor's Chamber, the Justiciar's Chamber and the Chamberlain's Stable.
Sum – £37 7s. 2½d (Green 1914, 28–32, from Min. Acc. 1223/6).

1428-9

Works include 'making the louver [sic] of the Constable's hall', repairing 'the large lock of the Chamberlain's gate [i.e. of the mansion enclosure]', and various roof repairs. Sum – 42s. 6d (Green 1914, 32–4, from Exchequer K. R. Account, 487/18).

1430-2

Carpenter and plumber engaged in the repair of 'Greyndory's Tower'.
Lime-pointing in the large stable, the hall, the exchequer and 'the two towers above the "dayree" [sic] and above "the middle gate" of the castle'.
'5,000 stones, called slate-stones', for the 'thatching . . . of the aforesaid houses'.
Other materials and carriage.
Sum – £6 3s. 6d.
The 'Costs of the Castle Chapel' include:
A 'small cord for ringing the chapel bell'
'Working at a wall on the north side of the chapel, and one step at the entrance of the chamber of the castle chapel'
'pointing and roofing the chapel'.
Sum – 33s. 3½d (Green 1914, 34–40, from BL Add. MS, Ch. Roll 26, 596).

1432-3

Minor works include repairing the stairs in the Justiciar's Hall, purchase of a lock for 'the chamber of Jenkin Maredudd' and boards for 'the cellar over [sic] the Janitor's House', 'making a cellar there within the Chamberlain's mansion' and 'the repair of rackes in the stables, both of the Justiciar and the Chamberlain'. Sum – £1 19s. 1½d (Green 1914, 40–1, from Min. Acc. 1223/8).

1433-5

Minor works include making a porch for the chapel and reroofing the 'large gate [Great Gatehouse]' in lead. Materials etc. Sum – £6 3s. 10½d.

'Repairs of the Prison and of the chamber above the said prison' included 'making a fireplace in the chamber above the prison near the large gate . . . and strengthening the walls on the west side there', also 'making . . . one window there, as well as the roof of the said chamber'.

Materials etc. Sum – £10 1s. 3½d

'Repairs of divers houses within the Chamberlain and Justice's mansions' included pointing the Justiciar's Hall and 'making and mending divers louvers and other defects in the halls, kitchens, and stables of the Justice and Chamberlain'. The postern 'towards the bridge of Carmarthen' is mentioned. Sum – 30s. 5d.

Total sum – £17 15s. 7d.

The 'Dead Store' included '1 spruce coffer . . . for keeping the records, minister's accounts' etc. (Green 1914, 41–6, from Min. Acc. 1223/9).

THE MID-FIFTEENTH CENTURY

1435-6

Repairing 'the stairs leading to the Constable's hall, one lavatory in the constable's chamber, and making the ends of one pinion [gable?] in the new chamber there'.

Covering 'the Constable's Hall with stone tiles'.

Repairing 'the Chamberlain's Exchequer hall and kitchen'.

Repairing 'the Justiciar's hall and the great chamber there, and the draught-chamber [i.e. a smoke-bay for an open hearth?], together with the roof of the lavatory there, and the stable at the end of the large hall'.

Repairing 'the cellar above [sic] the prison house'.

And '6,000 tile-stones for covering the chamber above the prison'.

Other sundries.

Sum – £4 17s. 6d (Green 1914, 48–50, from Exchequer Q. R. Account, 487/21).

1435-7

To the 'repair of the Chapel House' for the chaplain:

'the making a certain ceiling below the chamber and the cellar where the chaplain in the King's chapel dwells', wages for two carpenters, and for boards, planks and nails, and for two 'stained cloths' for the altar.

Sum – 18s. 2½d.

The same document refers to the hall, chamber, exchequer and kitchen within the 'mansion of the constable', but it is clear from its content that the Chamberlain's Mansion is meant. Its repairs, along with those to the 'hall, chambers, stables and other necessaries within the Justiciar's Mansions [*sic*]', and to the 'houses and chambers over the king's prison' totalled £4 17s. 6d (Green 1914, 46–8, from Min. Acc. 1223/9).

1447-8

Minor works, including the construction of a 'new parlour (*parclose*) in the Exchequer [i.e. a screened-off area]' for housing the account rolls and other 'King's records'.
Sum – £20 5s. 9d (Green 1914, 50–1, from Min. Acc. 1306/7).

1448-9

Paid for '10 tons of stones called 'freestones' bought at Bristol . . . for the execution of work on two chambers and one stable at the north end of the Justice's chamber, for the said Justice and other of the King's officers there, and for other divers repairs', and wages.
Sum – £9 0s. 7d (Green 1914, 51–2, from Min. Acc. 1224/4).

1452-3

Costs for the 'stonework of one tower in the castle . . . over the gate there called the Postern'.
Making 'anew of two large gates for the entrance of the ward of the Justiciar and the King's auditors there [i.e. the justiciar's enclosure?]'.
Repair of 'two stables in the castle . . . for the King's Officers [i.e. the Chamberlain's and Justiciar's stables?]'.
Making 'anew divers iron-fittings of several windows of the Exchequer . . . for the safe custody of the King's evidences and records'.
Materials and wages.
Sum – £63 5s. 11d (Green 1914, 52, from Min. Acc. 1224/1).

1461-2

'Cost of repairs of the castle of Carmarthen and the Shire Hall there':
The 'repair and mending of divers houses, chambers, and stables in the castle and Exchequer of Carmarthen, and also in the King's Shire Hall'.
And 'the glass of two large windows in the Exchequer'.
And for wages, 'tiles . . . shingles . . . and other materials'.
Sum – £36 8s. 7d.
The 'Round Tower' in the castle is mentioned (Green 1914, 53–4, from Min. Acc. 1224/6).

1462-3

£18 15s. 1½d spent on minor works at the castle. No detailed particulars (Green 1914, 55, from Min. Acc. 1224/7).

1464-5

£17 13s. 4d paid to 'stonecutters to make and fortify the [castle] walls . . . between the chapel and the gate there called the Postern'. Also to other minor repairs, materials and wages. Sum – £34 17s. 10½d (Green 1914, 55–6, from Min. Acc. 1224/8).

THE LATE FIFTEENTH CENTURY

1465-81

£73 14s. 4d spent on works. No particulars. Individual sums average £6, but £31 7s. 0½d spent in 1466–7 (Green 1914, 70–1).

c.1488-9

The 'making anew of a house in the castle'. Sum – £194 15s. 10d.
'Sir Rice [Rhys] ap Thomas, has of late repaired the newe place within oure castell of Kermerdyn [Carmarthen] in the Southside' (Green 1914, 57–8, from Min. Acc. Hen. VII, 1613).

1490

£5 12s. 0d spent on works at the castle. No particulars (Green 1914, 71).

1490-1

Minor repairs, mainly for roofing including 30,000 tiles and 1,300 shingles, but including 'glass for the window(s) of the Exchequer'. Sum – £6 7s. 10d (Green 1914, 58, from Min. Acc. Hen. VII, 1615).

1491-2

Costs of £4 4s. include 9,000 tiles and 1,000 shingles (Green 1914, 58, from Min. Acc. Hen. VII, 1616).

THE SIXTEENTH CENTURY

1520-1

For the 'repair of the King's gaol in the castle, the chapel, and the King's Chamberlain's chamber there, and the chamber in the said gaol called "le maynipryce [mainprize]" chamber, and of another chamber called Hopkin ap Rhys's Chamber' – 21,500 tiles, 48 ridge-tiles, lime, sand, timber and nails etc. Sum – £20 17s. 2½d (Green 1914, 59, from Min. Acc. 12–13 Hen. VIII).

1534

John Leland, writing in the 1530s described the castle as very fair and double-walled (i.e. two baileys), implying that it was still occupied and in use (Smith 1906, 59).

1542–6

£25 3s. spent on works. No particulars (Green 1914, 71).

1578

Condition survey and estimate, mainly concerning roofing materials with the general comment that the existing slates were too thin to 'endure the force of the wind', and that their use in 'times past hath . . . brought the present ruin'.

'The kitchen' – 16,000 *Laughdony* slates, 36 ridge-tiles, materials and labour. Estimate – £13 18s. 8d.

'There is a pynnyon [gable?] to be made up betwixt the hall and the kitchen, the lack whereof hath caused the hall roof to remove a foot from the other end.'

'The Hall' – 20,000 slates 'as above', etc. Estimate – £22 4s. 8d

'The chamber next the hall for the covering like the kitchen'. Estimate – £13 13s. 8d.

'The Auditor's Chamber' – 'there must be a new frame for the roof'. Old slates to be reused. Materials etc. Estimate – £7 5s. 4d.

The 'long Roofe': the 'frame for the most part must be new'. New slates, which will cost as much as the kitchen, hall and chamber together. 'The wall on the west side to be made new'. Estimate – £88 8s. 8d.

'The stable': slate from 'old store'. A 'new pynnyon at one end'. Materials etc. Estimate – £12 2s.

'The Gatehouse and Exchequer and other Rooms': slate from 'old store'. 'There is a great piece of a wall fallen, the charge of setting up a slender wall in place of it.' Materials etc. Estimate – £23 6s. 8d

'A void room having walls but not covered. The timber . . . taken from the long house [the 'long Roofe'?] will serve, and there will be slate enough.' Materials etc. Estimate – £5 4s. 4d.

Sum of all repairs – £233 6s. 8d (Green 1914, 60–4, from Exchequer K. R. Account, 489/20).

BIBLIOGRAPHY

MAP SOURCES

Ordnance Survey 1" Old Series, Sheet 41, 1831 (revised 1865).
Ordnance Survey 1:500, Carmarthenshire Sheet XXIX.7.6, 1895.
Ordnance Survey 1:2500, First Edition, Carmarthenshire Sheet XXIX.7, 1886.
Ordnance Survey 1:2500, Second Edition, Carmarthenshire Sheet XXIX.7, 1906.
Ordnance Survey 1:2500, plans SN4019 and SN4119, 1969.

Carmarthenshire Archive Service (Carmarthen Record Office; GB0211)
CRO, Acc. 7812, Block plan of gaol, 1898.
CRO, Cawdor maps –
    38. 'Plan of the Castle Green in Carmarthen, 20 August 1845'.
    39. 'Plan of Carmarthen showing County Gaol (Castle Green)', 1846.
    40. 'Plan of part of Carmarthen (Bridge Street – Gaol), 5 April 1858'.
    41. 'Plan of part of Carmarthen showing County Gaol and premises', n.d., *c.*1857.
    42. 'Plan of part of Carmarthen showing property belonging to the Earl of Cawdor', *c.*1867.
    43. 'Plan of County Gaol and premises', 1818.
    219. Map of Vaughan etc. property in Carmarthen, by Thomas Lewis, 1786.
CRO, Cawdor 2/112, 'Plan of the County Gaol etc.', 24 August 1819.
CRO2 (M) 5, Map of Morgan properties in Carmarthen, by Thomas Lewis, 1786.
CRO2 (M) 21, Plan of Carmarthen by John Speed, *c.*1610.
CRO (M) 459a, Map of Morgan properties in Carmarthen, by Thomas Lewis, 1786.
CRO (M) 786, Map of Carmarthen by John Wood, 1834.
CRO, Misc. Maps 1, Plans, elevations, agreement etc. for building a new chapel in the gaol, 1859.

CRO, MS 19:

> 'Plan showing boundary of Carmarthen Gaol and land belonging to the County' (n.d.,1858–66).
>
> Plans and elevation of new police station at Carmarthen, n.d.
>
> 'Plan showing proposed alteration at Carmarthen County Gaol, 30 June 1866'.
>
> Plan of proposed alterations to frontage of Carmarthen Gaol, n.d.
>
> Plan of proposed new lock-up at Carmarthen, 27 April 1880.

PICTORIAL SOURCES

Carmarthenshire Museums Service

CAASG 1975/0037, original drawing for the south-east view of Carmarthen, by S. and N. Buck, 1748.

CAASG 1976/1695, 'The south-east view of Carmarthen', by S. and N. Buck, 1748.

CAASG 1976/1864, Carmarthen Castle and bridge from south-east, by Hugh Hughes, *c.*1850.

CAASG 1976/1964, 'South view of Carmarthen Castle', by S. and N. Buck, 1740.

CAASG 1976/2394, Gaol Governor's House (n.d.).

CAASG 1987/0074, aerial photograph of the gaol, *c.*1935.

CAASG 2003/0069, view looking east through the gatehouse passage, *c.*1920.

CAASG 2005/0817/2, Carmarthen Gaol frontage, 1922.

CAASG 2006/0332, 'Carmarthen Quay and Castle', by Alfred Keene, 1840s.

Carmarthenshire Archive Service

CRO, CAC/PL/11, Section drawings of Carmarthen Gaol, 1937.

CRO Mus. vol. 36, 'CAS Scrapbook', 124, Gaol from south-east, 1931.

National Library of Wales (NLW)

NLW, Drawing vol. 64, 9a, 'Carmarthen Castle (rear view of tower)', 1857.

NLW, Drawing vol. 404 p. 21, PG 321, 'Carmarthen Castle' by Rev. E. Edwards, 1829.

NLW, Carm. Top. A5, A007, 'Carmarthen by Henri Gastineau', 1830.

NLW, Carm. Top. A5, A009, 'Carmarthen Castle, South Wales', 1792.

NLW, Carm. Top. A5, A011, 'Carmarthen Castle, Metcalf sculpt.', *c.*1785.

NLW, Carm. Top. A5, A013, 'South view of Carmarthen Castle and Town', *c.*1820.

National Monuments Record (NMR)

NMR, B42/1502, Gaol debtor's block from south-east, n.d., 1930s.

Private collections
Carmarthen Castle gatehouse from the west, by Mary Ellen Bagnall Oakley, *c.*1860
  (Mrs Suzanne Hayes).

PRIMARY SOURCES, UNPUBLISHED

Carmarthenshire Archive Service
CRO, CAC/CL/32, File relating to the completion and opening of County Hall.
CRO, Carmarthen Borough 331, Acc. 5570, Lime Grove Chapel 1938.
CRO, Cawdor 2/71, Rental of Vaughan properties, 1819.
CRO, Cawdor 2/54, Writ to the keeper of the gaol, 1669.
CRO, Cawdor 21/613, Inspeximus of deeds, 1639.
CRO, Cawdor 22/659, 'Specification of the manors and lordships of the late Lady Anne
  Vaughan', 1753.
CRO, Cawdor 63/6602, Letter dated 26 January 1761.
CRO, Cawdor 103/8056, Schedule of leases in Co. Borough of Carmarthen, *c.*1750.
CRO, Cawdor 112/8400, Rental of Vaughan properties in the Borough of Carmarthen etc.,
  1669.
CRO, Cawdor 125/8647, Notebook including transcription of presentments of Grand Jury
  of Carmarthen *re* boundaries of the liberties of Carmarthen Castle, 1753.
CRO, Cawdor Papers, vol. IV, Manorial Records, 1275–1814.
CRO (M) 49, Presentment on properties within Carmarthen, 1657.
CRO (M) 155, 156 and 156a, Corporation Order Books ('Books of Ordinances').
CRO (M) 420, Deeds and documents relating to properties in Carmarthen, 1647–1835.
CRO (M) 693, Vote in House of Commons *re* building of Carmarthen Gaol, 1783.
CRO, Mus. vol. A4, 'Carmarthen: book of the bridge'.
CRO, William Morris Papers, 27/9.

Early English Books Online, Thomason Tracts
Thomason 669, f.10, Lists of Parliamentary victories by Joseph Ricraft, 1646.
Thomason E46.8, *The Parliament Scout*, by John Dillingham, 1643–5.
Thomason E84.34, Declaration by Parliament concerning Lincolnshire, 9 January 1643.
Thomason E307.15, Letter from Maj.-Gen. Laugharne to the House of Commons,
  28 October 1645.
Thomason E307.25, Journal of Matthew Walbancke, 1644–6.
Thomason E435.9, Declaration of Col. Poyer, 10 April 1648.
Thomason E441.6, 'The particular relation of another great fight in south Wales', by
  Thomas Hill, Cornet, 3 May 1648.
Thomason E442.11, Declaration of Maj.-Gen. Laugharne and Col. Rice Powell, 15 May
  1648.

Thomason E993.33, *The Weekly Post*, by D. Border, 1659–60.

Thomason E1075.13, 'An act for the speedy disbanding of the army and garrisons of this kingdome', 15 September 1660.

Thomason E1432.2, Account of a journey through Wales in 1652, by John Taylor, 1653.

National Library of Wales (NLW)

NLW, Records of the Great Sessions ('Gaol Files').

NLW, Handlist of MSS at NLW, 8 (MSS acquired 1981–91).

NLW, Llangunnor parish tithe schedule, 1841.

NLW, MS 2258C, 'A journal of a tour in Wales', by Sir Christopher Sykes, Bart., 1796 (typescript copy).

NLW, MS 12358D, Records of the Corporate Borough of Carmarthen, 1590–1764 (transcribed by Alcwyn Evans, 1851–3).

NLW, MSS 12364D and 12365D, 'Collectanea concerning Caermarthen', 1 and 2, transcribed by Alcwyn Evans.

NLW, MS 12367D, 'Carmarthen borough records, charters etc. 1581–1610, 1738–1835', transcribed by Alcwyn Evans.

The National Archives, Public Record Office

TNA: PRO C 47/10/43/14, Indenture, n.d. (*c.*1265–79).

TNA: PRO E 101/683/54, Letter of Adam Scot, tiler (1336).

TNA: PRO E 159/61, Memoranda Roll 16 Edw. I (1287–8).

TNA: PRO E 159/92, Memoranda Roll 12 Edw. II (1318–19).

TNA: PRO E 163/4/42, Survey of Carmarthen Castle (1343).

TNA: PRO E 372/96, Pipe Roll 36 Hen. III (1251–2).

TNA: PRO E 372/104, Pipe Roll 44 Hen. III (1259–60).

TNA: PRO E 372/159, Enrolled Account (1309–10).

TNA: PRO SC 1/3/1, Letter to Henry III (n.d., *c.*1257–9).

TNA: PRO SC 1/11/118, Indenture (*c.*1250).

TNA: PRO SC 6/1219/1, Chamberlain's Account (1315–16).

TNA: PRO SC 6/1219/8, Chamberlain's Account (1317–18).

TNA: PRO SC 6/1219/9, Chamberlain's Account (1318–19).

TNA: PRO SC 6/1219/10, Chamberlain's Account (1319–20).

TNA: PRO SC 6/1220/3, Chamberlain's Account (1326–7).

TNA: PRO SC 6/1220/5, Chamberlain's Account (1327–8).

TNA: PRO SC 6/1220/8, Chamberlain's Account (1335).

TNA: PRO SC 6/1220/10, Chamberlain's Account (1336).

TNA: PRO SC 6/1221/9, Chamberlain's Account (1354–5).

TNA: PRO SC 6/1221/14, Chamberlain's Account (1379–80).

PRIMARY SOURCES, PUBLISHED

Anon. (ed.), 'A Carmarthenshire Diary, AD 1829, 1830', *Trans. Carms. Antiq. Soc. and Field Club*, 9 (1914), 16–18.

Blome, R., *Britannia or, a Geographical Description of the Kingdoms of England, Scotland and Ireland, with the Isles and Territories thereto Belonging* (London: Thomas Roycroft for Richard Blome, 1673).

Calendar of Chancery Rolls (Supplementary Close Rolls, Welsh Rolls, Scutage Rolls), 1277–1326 (London: HMSO, 1912).

Calendars of Charter Rolls (London: HMSO):
    1, Hen. III, 1226–1257 (1903).
    2, Hen. III–Edw. I, 1257–1300 (1906).
    3, Edw. I, Edw. II, 1300–1326 (1908).
    4, 1–14 Edw. III, 1327–1341 (1912).
    5, 15 Edw. III–5 Hen. V, 1341–1417 (1916).
    6, 5 Hen. VI–8 Hen. VIII, 1427–1516 (1927).

Calendars of Close Rolls (London: HMSO):
    Hen. III 2, 1231–1234 (1908).
    Hen. III 4, 1237–1242 (1911).
    Hen. III 6, 1247–1251 (1922).
    Edw. II 1, 1307–1313 (1892).
    Edw. III 8, 1369–1374 (1910).
    Rich. II 2, 1381–1385 (1920).
    Rich. II 4, 1389–1392 (1922).
    Rich. II 6, 1396–1399 (1927).

Calendars of Fine Rolls (London: HMSO):
    1, Edw. I, 1272–1307 (1911).
    3, Edw. II, 1319–1327 (1912).
    5, Edw. III, 1337–1347 (1915).

Calendar of Inquisitions Miscellaneous (Chancery), 2, 1307–1349 (London: HMSO, 1916).

Calendars of Liberate Rolls (London: HMSO):
    Hen. III, 1, 1226–1240 (1916).
    Hen. III, 3, 1245–1251 (1937).
    Hen. III, 4, 1251–1260 (1959).
    Hen. III, 5, 1260–1267 (1961).
    Hen. III, 6, 1267–1272 (1964).

Calendars of Patent Rolls (London: HMSO):
    Hen. III, 1216–1225 (1901).
    Hen. III, 1225–1232 (1903).
    Hen. III, 1258–1266 (1910).
    Hen. III, 1266–1272 (1913).

Edw. I, 1301–1307 (1898).

Edw. III 16, 1374–1377 (1916).

Rich. II 3, 1385–1389 (1900).

Hen. V 1, 1413–1416 (1910).

Hen. VI 2, 1429–1436 (1907).

Hen. VI 3, 1436–1441 (1907).

Hen. VI 5, 1446–1452 (1909).

Hen. VI 6, 1452–1461 (1910).

Hen. VII 1, 1485–1494 (1914).

Hen. VII 2, 1494–1509 (1916).

Philip and Mary 1, 1553–1554 (1937).

Elizabeth I 2, 1560–1563 (1948).

Elizabeth I 3, 1563–1566 (1960).

Calendar of State Papers (Domestic), James I, 1603–1610 (London: HMSO, 1857).

Carlisle, N., *A Topographical Dictionary of the Dominion of Wales* (London: Nicholas Carlisle, 1811).

The Carmarthen Journal, passim.

The Daily Express, 30 May 1931.

Daniel-Tyssen, J. R. (ed.), *Royal Charters and Historic Documents relating to the Town and County of Carmarthen* (Carmarthen: William Spurrell, 1878).

Davies, J. (ed.), *The Carmarthen Book of Ordinances 1569–1606* (Llandybïe: Carmarthenshire Antiquarian Society, 1996).

Davies, J. C. (ed.), *Episcopal Acts relating to the Welsh Dioceses 1066–1272*, 1 (Cardiff: Historical Society of the Church in Wales, 1946).

Dawes, M. C. B. (ed.), *Registers of Edward the Black Prince*, 1: *1346–1348* (London: HMSO, 1930).

Dawes, M. C. B. (ed.), *Registers of Edward the Black Prince*, 3: *1351–1365* (London: HMSO, 1932).

Defoe, D., *A Tour through the Whole Island of Great Britain* (London: Longman, 1962 edn).

Dineley, T., *The Account of the Official Progress of His Grace Henry the First Duke of Beaufort through Wales in 1684* (London: Blades and Blades, 1888 facsimile edn).

Dodridge, J., *An Historical Account of the Ancient and Modern State of the Principality of Wales, Duchy of Cornwall and Earldom of Chester* (London: J. Roberts, 1630, second print 1714).

Donovan, E., *Descriptive Excursions through South Wales and Monmouthshire in the Year 1804, and the Four Preceding Summers*, 2 (London: Edward Donovan, 1805).

Edwards, J. G. (ed.), *Calendar of Ancient Correspondence relating to Wales* (Cardiff: University of Wales Press, 1935).

Evans, G. E. (ed.), 'Caermarthen, 1764–1797', *Trans. Carms. Antiq. Soc. and Field Club*, 1 (1906), 101–2.

Evans, G. E. (ed.), 'Carmarthen Local Events AD 1547–1836', *Yr Encilion*, 1/1 (1912), 8–29

Evans, G. E. (ed.), 'The Cwmgwili Manuscripts', *Trans. Carms. Antiq. Soc. and Field Club*, 23 (1932), 90–3.

Evans, G. E. (ed.), 'The Cwmgwili Manuscripts', *Trans. Carms. Antiq. Soc. and Field Club*, 26 (1936), 26–31.

Evans, G. E. (ed.), 'Carmarthen. Documents relating to the Town from the Earliest Times to the Close of the Reign of Henry VIII', *Trans. Carms. Antiq. Soc. and Field Club*, 17 (1924), 61–72.

Evans, G. E. (ed.), 'Carmarthen. Documents relating to the Town from the Earliest Times to the Close of the Reign of Henry VIII', *Trans. Carms. Antiq. Soc. and Field Club*, 18 (1925), 1–8, 18–22.

Firth, C. H., and Rait, R. S. (eds), *Acts and Ordinances of the Interregnum, 1642–1660* (London: History of Parliament Trust, 1911).

Fisher, J. (ed.), *Tours in Wales (1804–1813) by Richard Fenton* (London; Bedford Press, 1917).

Fryde, N. (ed.), *List of Welsh Entries in the Memoranda Rolls, 1282–1343* (Cardiff: University of Wales Press, 1974).

The Gentleman's Magazine, 24 November 1755.

Green, F. (ed.), 'Carmarthen Castle: A Collection of Historical Documents relating to Carmarthen Castle from the Earliest Times to the Close of the Reign of Henry VIII', *West Wales Historical Records*, 3 (1913), 1–72.

Green, F. (ed.), 'Carmarthen Castle: A Collection of Historical Documents relating to Carmarthen Castle from the Earliest Times to the Close of the Reign of Henry VIII', *West Wales Historical Records*, 4 (1914), 1–71.

Howard, J., *The State of the Prisons in England and Wales, with Preliminary Observations, and an Account of some Foreign Prisons* (Warrington: William Eyres, 1777).

Hunter, J. (ed.), *The Pipe Roll of 31 Henry I* (London: Record Commission, 1929 edn).

Jones, E. D. (ed.), 'Survey of South Wales Chantries, 1546', *Archaeoogia Cambrensis*, 89 (1934), 135–55.

Jones, E. G. (ed.), *Exchequer Proceedings (Equity) concerning Wales, Henry VIII–Elizabeth* (Cardiff: University of Wales Press, 1939).

Jones, T. (ed.), *Brut y Tywysogyon: Peniarth MS. 20 Version* (Cardiff: University of Wales Press, 1952).

Jones, T. (ed.), *Brut y Tywysogyon: Red Book of Hergest Version* (Cardiff: University of Wales Press, 1955).

Jones, T. (ed.), *Brenhinedd y Saesson, or The Kings of the Saxons* (Cardiff: University of Wales Press, 1971).

Journal of the House of Commons (London: History of Parliament Trust):
    5, 1646–1648 (1802).
    7, 1651–1660 (1802).
    8, 1660–1667 (1802).

Kirby, J. L. (ed.), *Calendar of Signet Letters of Henry IV and Henry V, 1399–1422* (London: HMSO, 1978).

Lewis, S., *A Topographical Dictionary of Wales*, 1 and 2 (London: S. Lewis and Co., 1849).

Malkin, B. H, *The Scenery, Antiquities and Biography of South Wales*, 2 (London: Longman and Rees, 1807).

Neild, J., *An Account of the Rise, Progress and Present State, of the Society for the Discharge and Relief of Persons Imprisoned for Small Debts throughout England and Wales* (London: John Nichols and Son, 1808).

Nicolas, H. (ed.), *Proceedings and Ordinances of the Privy Council of England, 1, 1386–1410* (London: Record Commission/Eyre and Spottiswoode, 1834).

Owen, H. (ed.), *A Calendar of the Public Records Relating to Pembrokeshire*, 2 (London: Honourable Society of Cymmrodorion, 1914).

Owen, H. (ed.), *The Description of Pembrokeshire by George Owen of Henllys*, 4, Cymmrodorion Record Series 1 (London, 1936).

Phillipps, T. (ed.), *Cartularium St Johannis Baptistae de Caermarthen* (Cheltenham: John Lowe, 1865).

Pipe Rolls (London: Pipe Roll Society):
24 Hen. II, 1177–1178 (1906).
27 Hen. II, 1180–1181 (1909).
28 Hen. II, 1181–1182 (1910).
29 Hen. II, 1182–1183 (1911).
1 John, 1199 (1933).
2 John, 1200 (1934).

Pryce, H. (ed.), *The Acts of Welsh Rulers 1120–1283* (Cardiff: University of Wales Press, 2005).

Rees, W. (ed.), 'Ministers' Accounts of West Wales, 1352–3', *Bulletin of the Board of Celtic Studies,* 10 (1941), 60–82, 139–55, 256–70.

Rees, W. (ed.), *A Survey of the Duchy of Lancaster Lordships in Wales 1609–1613* (Cardiff: University of Wales Press, 1953).

Rees, W. (ed.), *Calendar of Ancient Petitions relating to Wales* (Cardiff: University of Wales Press, 1975)

Shaw, W. A. (ed.), *Calendar of Treasury Books, 1, 1660–1667* (London: Institute of Historical Research, 1904)

Smith, L. T. (ed.), *The Itinerary in Wales of John Leland in or about the Years 1536–1539* (London: George Bell and Sons, 1906).

Thompson, M. W. (ed.), *The Journeys of Sir Richard Colt Hoare through Wales and England, 1793–1810* (Gloucester: Sutton Publishing Ltd, 1983).

Thorpe, L. (ed.), *Gerald of Wales: The Journey through Wales/The Description of Wales* (Harmondsworth: Penguin, 1978).

Vicars, J., *God in the Mount or, England's Parliamentary Chronicle 1 and 2* (London: J. Rothwell and T. Underhill, 1644).

Vicars, J., *God's Arke overtopping the World's Waves or, the Third Part of the Parliamentary Chronicle* (London: J. Rothwell and T. Underhill, 1646).

Vicars, J., *The Burning-bush not Consumed or, the Fourth and Last Part of the Parliamentarie-Chronicle* (London: J. Rothwell and T. Underhill, 1646).

Williams ab Ithel, J. (ed.), *Annales Cambriae*, Rolls Series (London: Longman, Green, Longman and Roberts, 1860).

SECONDARY SOURCES, UNPUBLISHED

Austin, D. (ed.), 'The Carew Castle archaeological project: 1993 season interim report' (University of Wales, Lampeter, 1995).

Cadw Listed Buildings database, accessed via Extended National Database.

King, D. J. C., 'Carmarthen Castle' (unpublished field notebooks held in the Society of Antiquaries of London Library, Burlington House, 1949, 19–20, and 1950, 53).

Opus International Consultants UK Ltd, 'Carmarthen Castle phase 4: ground investigation report for base of shell keep walls' (2007; ref. CS7058-01-GIR-1.0).

Parry, G. 'A guide to the records of the Great Sessions in Wales' (Aberystwyth: National Library of Wales, 1995).

Rae, E., 'Archaeological investigations at the former Cattle Market, Carmarthen, Carmarthenshire, October 2007–May 2008' (unpublished report by Northamptonshire Archaeology, 2009; copy held in DAT HER).

Spurgeon, C. J., 'Llandovery Castle' (NMR record file (NPRN 92751), RCAHMW Aberystwyth, 1980).

Unpublished Dyfed Archaeological Trust reports; copies held in DAT HER

Austin, L., Hill, C., James, H., James, T. and Poucher, P., 'Carmarthen historic town survey: understanding and protecting the archaeology of Wales' oldest town' (2005).

Crane, P., 'Carmarthen Castle Square Tower: evaluation and watching brief, 1993' (1994).

Crane, P., 'Carmarthen Castle, phase 3 interim report, October 2001' (2001).

James, H., 'Carmarthen Castle excavations, Sept.–Oct. 1980: interim excavation report' (typescript, 1980; Detailed Record File PRN 57).

James, T. (ed.), 'Excavations at Carmarthen Greyfriars 1983–1990, Topic Report No. 4: the small finds and other artefacts' (2001).

James, T. and Brennan, D., 'Excavation at Carmarthen Greyfriars 1983–1990, Topic Report No. 1: 13th–16th century earthenware and oolitic limestone floor tiles' (1991).

Ludlow, N. D., 'Carmarthen Castle Southwest Tower: recording and watching brief, 1994' (1994).

Ludlow, N. D., 'Carmarthen Castle: archaeological recording and watching brief 1995–6' (1996).

Ludlow, N. D., 'Carmarthen Castle: phase 3 archaeological work, 2001–2003' (2004).

Ludlow, N. D. and Allen, B., 'Carmarthen Castle: archaeological evaluation within the shell-keep, 1997' (1997).

Murphy, K. and Ludlow, N., 'Carmarthenshire historic landscape characterisation: Black Mountain and Mynydd Myddfai/Tywi Valley/Dolaucothi/Taf and Tywi Estuary', vol. 1 (2000).

Murphy, K. and Sambrook, P., 'South-east Dyfed minerals: a survey of the archaeological resource threatened by mineral extraction' (1994).

O'Mahoney, C., 'Excavation at Carmarthen Greyfriars 1983–1990, Topic Report No. 2: pottery, ridge tile and ceramic water pipe' (1995).

Page, N., 'Carmarthen Castle shell-keep, archaeological evaluation, 1998' (1998).

Redknap, M., 'Finds from Carmarthen Castle 2003' (2012).

Sambrook, P., 'Mineral extraction at Pedair Heol, Kidwelly and Llandyfan, Llandybie' (1995).

Schlee, D., 'Carmarthen Castle: excavations outside the gatehouse, June–August 2003' (2004).

SECONDARY SOURCES, PUBLISHED

Allan, J. P. and Morris, C., '1. Wooden objects', in J. P. Allan (ed.), *Medieval and Post-medieval Finds from Exeter 1971–1980*, Exeter Archaeological Reports, 3 (1984), pp. 305–15.

Anon., 'Carmarthen Meeting', *Archaeologia Cambrensis*, 6 (1875), 403–30.

Anon., 'Long Loans', *Trans. Carms. Antiq. Soc. and Field Club*, 11 (1917), 82.

Anon., 'County Council Action', *Trans. Carms. Antiq. Soc. and Field Club*, 18 (1925), 47.

Armitage, E., 'Carmarthen Castle', *Trans. Carms. Antiq. Soc. and Field Club*, 2 (1907), 196–7.

Armitage, E., 'Carmarthen Castle', *Trans. Carms. Antiq. Soc. and Field Club*, 3 (1908), 14–15.

Ashbee, J., *Conwy Castle and Town Walls* (Cardiff: Cadw, 2007).

Ashbee, J., *Goodrich Castle* (London: English Heritage, 2009).

Austin, D., *Acts of Perception: A Study of Barnard Castle in Teesdale*, 1, English Heritage/ Architectural and Archaeological Society of Durham and Northumberland Research Report 6 (London, 2007).

Avent, R., 'The early development of three coastal castles', in H. James (1991), pp. 167–88.

Avent, R., *Laugharne Castle* (Cardiff: Cadw, 1995).

Avent, R., 'William Marshal's castle at Chepstow and its place in military architecture', in Turner and Johnson (2006), pp. 81–90.

Baddeley, W. St C., 'Berkeley Castle', *Trans. Bristol and Gloucs. Archaeol. Soc.*, 48 (1926), 133–79.

Baker-Jones, D. L., 'John Nash, Architect and Builder', *Carmarthenshire Antiquary*, 3 (1961), 157–60.

Barker, P. A. and Higham, R., *Hen Domen, Montgomery: A Timber Castle on the English–Welsh Border. Excavations 1960–1988: A Summary Report* (London: Royal Archaeological Institute, 1988).

Barnett, C., 'Carmarthen Castle: The Chamberlain's Hall', *Trans. Carms. Antiq. Soc. And Field Club*, 26 (1936), 18.

Bateman, J. and Redknap, M., *Coventry: Excavations on the Town Wall 1976–78*, Coventry Museums Monograph Series, 2 (1986).

Brears, P. C. D., *The English Country Pottery: Its History and Techniques* (Newton Abbot: David and Charles, 1971).

Brennan, D., Evans, G., James, H. and Dale-Jones, E., 'Excavations in Carmarthen, Dyfed, 1976–1990. Finds from the Seventeenth to the Nineteenth Centuries: Pottery, Glass, Clay Pipes and Bone', *Medieval and Later Pottery in Wales*, 14 (1996), 15–108.

Brown, R. A., *English Castles* (London: Batsford, 1976 edn).

Browne, A. L., 'George Phetiplace, Justice of South Wales, 1574–1577', *Trans. Carms. Antiq. Soc. and Field Club*, 24 (1933), 38–42.

Butler, L., *Pickering Castle* (London: English Heritage, 1993).

Butler, L., 'The castles of the princes of Gwynedd', in Williams and Kenyon (2010), pp. 27–36.

Butler, L. and Knight, J. K., *Dolforwyn Castle/Montgomery Castle* (Cardiff: Cadw, 2004).

Bythell, D. and Leyland, M., *Durham Castle: University College, Durham* (Norwich: University College, Durham and Jarrold, 1992).

Caple, C., *Excavations at Dryslwyn Castle 1980–95*, Soc. Med. Archaeol. Monograph 26 (London, 2007).

Caple, C., 'Nevern Castle: Searching for the First Masonry Castle in Wales', *Medieval Archaeology*, 55 (2011), 326–34.

Capp, B. S., *The World of John Taylor the Water Poet, 1578–1653* (Oxford University Press, 1994).

Cartier, J., *Céramiques de l'Oise* (Paris: Somogy, 2001).

Champness, J., *Lancaster Castle: A Brief History* (Preston: Lancashire County Books, 1993).

Clapham, A. W., 'Haverfordwest Priory: Report on the Excavations of June, 1922', *Archaeologia Cambrensis*, 77 (1922), 327–34.

Clark, J., *Helmsley Castle* (London: English Heritage, 2004).

Clark, J., *Clifford's Tower and the Castle of York* (London: English Heritage, 2010).

Clay, P., 'The small finds – non-structural', in J. Mellor and T. Pearce (eds), *The Austin Friars, Leicester*, CBA Research Report 35 (London, 1981), pp. 130–45.

Coad, J., *Dover Castle* (London: English Heritage, 2007).

Colvin, H. M. (ed.), *A History of the King's Works*, 1 and 2: *The Middle Ages* (London: HMSO, 1963).

Coplestone-Crow, B., 'Ystlwyf/Oysterlow: Welsh Commote and Norman Lordship', *Carms. Antiq.*, 46 (2010), 5–11.

Coulson, C., *Castles in Medieval Society: Fortresses in England, France and Ireland in the Central Middle Ages* (Oxford University Press, 2003).

Courtney, P. *Medieval and Later Usk: Report on the Excavations at Usk 1965–1976* (Cardiff: University of Wales Press, 1994).

Courtney, P. 'The pottery', in K. Blockley. 'Langstone Castle Motte: Excavations by L. Alcock in 1964', *Archaeology in Wales*, 34 (1994), 21–2.

Craster, O. E., 'Skenfrith Castle: When Was it Built?', *Archaeologia Cambrensis*, 116 (1967), 133–58.

Creighton, O. and Higham R., *Medieval Town Walls: An Archaeology and Social History of Urban Defence* (Stroud: Tempus, 2002).

Crossley, A. and Elrington, C. R. (eds), *A History of the County of Oxford*, 12 (Oxford University Press, 1990).

Darwen, M., *Lincoln Castle* (Lincoln: Lincs. County Council, n.d.).

Davies, R. R., *The Revolt of Owain Glyn Dŵr* (Oxford University Press, 1995).

Dorsett, A., 'Artist's depictions of Carmarthen quay', in H. James and P. Moore (eds), *Carmarthenshire and Beyond: Studies in History and Archaeology in Memory of Terry James* (Carmarthen: Carms. Antiq. Soc., 2009), pp. 61–6.

Drage, C., 'Urban castles', in J. Schofield and R. Leach (eds), *Urban Archaeology in Britain*, CBA Research Report 61 (1987), pp. 117–32.

Early, V. and Morgan, D., 'A Medieval Pottery Kiln Site at Newcastle Emlyn', *Archaeology in Wales*, 44 (2004), 97–100.

Egan, G. (ed.), *Material Culture in London in an Age of Transition: Tudor and Stuart Period Finds c.1450–c.1700 from Excavations at Riverside Sites in Southwark*, MoLAS Monograph 19 (London, 2005).

English Heritage, *Restormel Castle* (London: English Heritage, 1996).

Evans, D. H., 'Excavations at Llanthony Priory, Gwent, 1978', *The Monmouthshire Antiquary*, 4 (1980), 5–34.

Evans, G. E., 'Carmarthen Castle', *Trans. Carms. Antiq. Soc. and Field Club*, 1 (1906), 27.

Evans, G. E., 'Llanllwch: AD 1404–1462', *Trans. Carms. Antiq. Soc. and Field Club*, 5 (1910), 64.

Evans, G. E., 'Carmarthen: Castle Green', *Trans. Carms. Antiq. Soc. and Field Club*, 24 (1933), 9.

Evans, G. E., 'Castle Hill and Carmarthen Bridge Works', *Trans. Carms. Antiq. Soc. and Field Club*, 27 (1937), 43.

Evans, J. W., 'Aspects of the early church in Carmarthenshire', in H. James (1991), pp. 239–54.

Evans, N. and Mould, Q., 'Footwear', in Egan (2005), pp. 59–94.

Ganiaris, H., Keene S. and Starly, K., 'A Comparison for some Treatments for Excavated Leather', *The Conservator*, 6 (1982), 12-23.

Gardiner, J. (ed.), *Before the Mast: Life and Death aboard the Mary Rose* (Oxford: Mary Rose Trust, 2005).

Geear, G., Priestley, S. and Turner, R., 'After the Restoration', in Turner and Johnson (2006), pp. 229–42.

Giggins, B. L., 'Northampton's Forgotten Castle', *Castle Studies Group Bulletin*, 18 (2005), 185–7.

Good, G. L., 'The Excavation of Two Docks at Narrow Quay, Bristol, 1978–9', *Post-Medieval Archaeology*, 21 (1987), 25–126.

Good, G. L. and Russett, V. E. J, 'Common Types of Earthenware Found in the Bristol Area', *Bristol and Avon Archaeology*, 6 (1987), 35–43.

Goodall, J., *Pevensey Castle* (London: English Heritage, 1999).

Goodall, J., *Richmond Castle/Easby Abbey* (London: English Heritage, 2001).

Goodall, J., *The English Castle 1066–1650* (Newhaven and London: Yale University Press, 2011).

Goodall, P. J. R., *The Black Flag over Carmarthen: Over Three Centuries of Barbarism, Crime, Murder, Punishment and Executions* (Llanrwst: Gwasg Carreg Gwalch, 2005).

Grew, F. and de Neergaard, M., *Shoes and Pattens: Medieval Finds from Excavations in London*, 2 (Museum of London, 1988).

Griffiths, R. A., *The Principality of Wales in the Later Middle Ages: The Structure and Personnel of Government*, 1, *South Wales 1277–1536* (Cardiff: University of Wales Press, 1972).

Griffiths, R. A., 'The Making of Medieval Carmarthen', *Carmarthenshire Antiquary*, 9 (1973), 83–101.

Griffiths, R. A., 'Carmarthen', in R. A. Griffiths (ed.), *Boroughs of Mediaeval Wales* (Cardiff: University of Wales Press, 1978), pp. 130–63.

Griffiths, R. A., 'The Making of Medieval Cardigan', *Ceredigion*, 11/2 (1990), 97–133.

Griffiths, R. A. and Thomas, R. S., *The Making of the Tudor Dynasty* (Stroud: Alan Sutton Publishing, 2005).

Gutiérez, A., *Mediterranean Pottery in Wessex Households, 13th–17th Centuries*, British Archaeology Reports, British Series, 306 (Oxford, 2000).

Guy, N. (ed.), 'News: Northampton Castle', *Castle Studies Group Bulletin*, 18 (2005), 99.

Harraden, R. B., *History of the University of Cambridge* (Cambridge: Harraden and Son, 1814).

Higham, R. and Barker, P., *Timber Castles* (London: Batsford, 1992).

Hilling, J. B., *The Historic Architecture of Wales* (Cardiff: University of Wales Press, 1976).

Hilling, J. B., *Cilgerran Castle/St Dogmaels Abbey* (Cardiff: Cadw, 1992).

Holmes, H. S., 'Carmarthen Castle', *Trans. Carms. Antiq. Soc. and Field Club*, 3 (1908), 21–2.

Howe, J. A., *The Geology of Building Stones* (London: Edward Arnold. 1910).

Hurley, M. F., Scully, O. M. B. and McCutcheon, S. W. J., *Late Viking Age and Medieval Waterford. Excavations 1986-1992* (Waterford: Institute of Public Administration, 1997).

Hurst, J. G., Neal, D. S. and van Beuningen, H. J. E., *Pottery Produced and Traded in North-west Europe, 1350–1650*, Rotterdam Papers, 6 (Rotterdam: 1986).

Icowicz, P., 'Martincamp Ware: A Problem of Attribution', *Medieval Ceramics,* 17 (1993), 51–60.

Impey, E. and Parnell, G., *The Tower of London: The Official Illustrated History* (London and New York: Merrell, 2011).

Ireland, R. W., *'A Want of Order and Good Discipline': Rules, Discretion and the Victorian Prison* (Cardiff: University of Wales Press, 2007).

James, H. (ed.), *Sir Gâr: Studies in Carmarthenshire History* (Carmarthen: Carms. Antiq. Soc., 1991).

James, H., 'Carmarthen', in E. P. Dennison (ed.), *Conservation and Change in Historic Towns*, CBA Research Report 122 (1999), pp. 158–68.

James, H., *Roman Carmarthen: Excavations 1978–1993*, Britannia Monograph Series, 20 (London: 2003).

James, T., 'Excavations at the Augustinian Priory of St John and St Teulyddog, Carmarthen, 1979', *Archaeologia Cambrensis*, 134 (1985), 120–61.

James, T., 'Medieval Carmarthen and its Burgesses: A Study of Town Growth and Burgess Families in the Later Thirteenth Century', *Carmarthenshire Antiq.*, 25 (1989), 9–26.

James, T., 'Carmarthen's Civil War Defences', *Carmarthenshire Antiq.*, 27 (1991), 21–30.

James, T., 'Where sea meets land: the changing Carmarthenshire coastline', in H. James (1991), pp. 143–66.

James, T., 'Excavations at Carmarthen Greyfriars, 1983–1990', *Medieval Archaeology*, 41 (1997), 100–94.

James, T. A., *Carmarthen: An Archaeological and Topographical Survey*, Carms. Antiq. Soc. Monograph 2 (Carmarthen, 1980).

Jones, J. F., 'Common Law Records: Carmarthenshire', *Trans. Carms. Antiq. Soc. and Field Club*, 24 (1933), 36–8.

Jones, J. F., 'Carmarthen Stylus', *Carmarthenshire Antiq.*, 2 (1957), 46–7.

Jones, J. F., 'Carmarthen Gaol, 1808', *Carmarthenshire Antiq.*, 4 (1962), 87–8.

Jones, J. F., 'Carmarthen "Mount"', *Carmarthenshire Antiq.*, 5 (1963), 188.

Jones, M. H., 'Report of the First Field Day', *Trans. Carms. Antiq. Soc. and Field Club*, 2 (1907), 149.

Keene, D., 'Wooden vessels', in M. Biddle (ed.), *Object and Economy in Medieval Winchester: Artefacts from Medieval Winchester*, Winchester Studies, 7/2 (Oxford, 1990), pp. 461–3.

Kenyon, J. R., review of *The Decline of the Castle* by M. W. Thompson, *Medieval Archaeology*, 33 (1989), 262–4.

Kenyon, J. R., *Medieval Fortifications* (Leicester University Press, 1990).

Kenyon, J. R., *Kidwelly Castle* (Cardiff: Cadw, 2007).

Kenyon, J. R., and Avent, R. (eds), *Castles in Wales and the Marches: Essays in Honour of D. J. Cathcart King* (Cardiff: University of Wales Press, 1987).

Kenyon, J. R. and Spurgeon, C. J., *Coity Castle/Ogmore Castle/Newcastle* (Cardiff: Cadw, 2001).

King, D. J. C., 'Pembroke Castle', *Archaeologia Cambrensis*, 127 (1978), 75–121.

King, D. J. C., *Castellarium Anglicanum* (New York: Kraus International, 1983).

King, D. J. C., *The Castle in England and Wales* (London: Croom Helm, 1988).

King, D. J. C. and Perks, J. C., 'Manorbier Castle, Pembrokeshire', *Archaeologia Cambrensis*, 119 (1970), 83–118.

Knight, J. K., 'The road to Harlech: aspects of some early thirteenth-century Welsh castles', in Kenyon and Avent (1987), pp. 75–88.

Knight, J. K., 'Excavations at Montgomery Castle, part I', *Archaeologia Cambrensis*, 142 (1992), 97–180.

Knight, J., 'Civil War and Commonwealth', in Turner and Johnson (2006), pp. 221–8.

Knight, J. K., *The Three Castles: Grosmont Castle/Skenfrith Castle/White Castle* (Cardiff: Cadw, 2009).

Knight, J. K. and Johnson, A. (eds), *Usk Castle, Priory and Town* (Almeley: Logaston, 2008).

Lambert, F., 'Some Recent Excavations in London', *Archaeologia*, 71 (1921), 55–112.

Leach, A. L., *The History of the Civil War (1642–1649) in Pembrokeshire and on its Borders* (London: H. F. and G. Witherby, 1937).

Lewis, A. H. T., 'The Early Effects of Carmarthenshire's Turnpike Trusts', *Carmarthenshire Historian*, 4 (1967), 41–54.

Lewis, J. M., *The Medieval Tiles of Wales* (Cardiff: National Museum of Wales, 1999).

Liddiard, R. and McGuicken, R., *Beeston Castle* (London: English Heritage, 2007).

Lloyd, J. D. K. and Knight, J. K., *Montgomery Castle* (Cardiff: HMSO, 1981).

Lloyd, J. E. (ed.), *A History of Carmarthenshire*, 1 (London: London Carmarthenshire Society, 1935).

Lloyd, J. E. (ed.), *A History of Carmarthenshire*, 2 (London: London Carmarthenshire Society, 1939).

Lloyd, T., Orbach, J. and Scourfield, R., *The Buildings of Wales: Carmarthenshire and Ceredigion* (London: Yale University Press, 2006).

Lodwick, J., and Lodwick, V., *The Story of Carmarthen* (Carmarthen: V. G. Lodwick and Sons Ltd, 1972).

Lord, P., 'Artisan Painters in Carmarthen', *Carms. Antiq.*, 27 (1991), 47–60.

Ludlow, N. D., 'Pembroke Castle and Town Walls', *Fortress*, 8 (1991), 25–30.

Mahany, C., *Stamford Castle and Town*, South Lincolnshire Archaeology, 2 (Stamford, 1978).

Malden, H. E (ed.), *A History of the County of Surrey*, 3 (London: Constable, 1911).

Mathias, R., 'The Second Civil War and Interregnum', in B. Howells (ed.), *Pembrokeshire County History, 3: Early Modern Pembrokeshire 1536–1815* (Haverfordwest: Pembrokeshire Historical Society, 1987), pp. 197–224.

Matthews, L. G. and Green, H. J. M., 'Post-medieval Pottery of the Inns of Court', *Post-Medieval Archaeology*, 3 (1970), 1–17.

Morgan, W. L. and Spurrell, W., 'Carmarthen Castle Mount', *Trans. Carms. Antiq. Soc. and Field Club*, 10 (1915), 61–2.

Morris, C. A., *Wood and Woodworking in Anglo-Scandinavian and Medieval York*, The Archaeology of York, 17/13 (York Archaeological Trust/CBA, 2000).

Morris, J. E., *The Welsh Wars of Edward I* (Oxford: Clarendon Press, 1901).

Mould, Q., 'The Leather', in F. McAvoy, 'Marine Salt Extraction: The Excavation of Salterns at Wainfleet St Mary, Lincolnshire', *Medieval Archaeology*, 38 (1994), 152–8.

Mould, Q., Carlisle, I. and Cameron, E., *Leather and Leatherworking in Anglo-Scandinavian and Medieval York*, The Archaeology of York, 17/16 (York Archaeological Trust/ CBA: 2003).

Murphy, K., 'The Castle and Borough of Wiston, Pembrokeshire', *Archaeologia Cambrensis*, 144 (1995), 71–102.

Murphy, K. and O'Mahoney, C., 'Excavation and Survey at Cardigan Castle', *Ceredigion*, 10/2 (1985), 190–218.

Nailer, A., 'Items of dress', in Egan (2005), pp. 17–32.

O'Neil, B. H. St J., 'The Bulwarks, Carmarthen', *Archaeologia Cambrensis,* 93 (1938), 126–30.

O'Neil, B. H. St J., 'Criccieth Castle, Caernarvonshire', *Archaeologia Cambrensis*, 98 (1945), 1–51.

Oxley, J. (ed.), *Excavations at Southampton Castle* (Stroud: Alan Sutton/Southampton City Museums, 1986).

Page, W., *A History of the County of Middlesex*, 2 (London: Constable, 1911).

Papazian, C. and Campbell, E., 'Medieval Pottery and Roof Tiles in Wales AD 1100–1600', *Medieval and Later Pottery in Wales,* 13 (1992), 1–107.

Parry, C., 'Survey and Excavation at Newcastle Emlyn Castle', *Carmarthenshire Antiq.*, 23 (1987), 11–28.

Phillips, J. R., *Memoirs of the Civil War in Wales and the Marches 1642–1649*, 1 and 2 (London: Longmans, Green and Co., 1874).

Pounds, N. J. G., *The Medieval Castle in England and Wales: A Social and Political History* (Cambridge University Press, 1990).

Prestwich, M., 'Edward I and Wales', in Williams and Kenyon (2010), pp. 1–8.

Radford, C. A. R., *White Castle* (London: HMSO, 1962).

Rees, D., 'The Forest of Glyncothi', *Carmarthenshire Antiq.*, 31 (1995), 45–55.

Rees, S. E. and Caple, C., *Dinefwr Castle/Dryswlyn Castle* (Cardiff: Cadw, 2007).

Rees, W., *Industry before the Industrial Revolution*, 1 (Cardiff: University of Wales Press, 1968).

Renn, D. F., 'Mottes: A Classification', *Antiquity*, 33 (1959), 106–12.

Renn, D. F., *Clifford's Tower and the Castles of York* (London: HMSO, 1971).

Renn, D. F., *Norman Castles in Britain* (London: John Baker, 1973 edn).

Renn, D. F., 'An Angevin Gatehouse at Skipton Castle', *Château Gaillard*, 7 (1975), 173–82.

Renn, D. F., *Caerphilly Castle* (Cardiff: Cadw, 1997).

Richards, A. J., *A Gazetteer of the Welsh Slate Industry* (Llanrwst: Gwasg Carreg Gwalch, 1991).

Richards, M., 'Aiglets, twisted wire loops, buttons, clasps and laces', in Gardiner (2005), pp. 94–9.

Rickard, J., *The Castle Community: The Personnel of English and Welsh Castles, 1272–1422* (Woodbridge: Boydell Press, 2002).

Rigold, S. E., *Totnes Castle* (London: HMSO, 1975).

Rigold, S. E., 'A Mould for Lead Ventilators from Neath Abbey, South Wales', *Antiquaries Journal,* 57 (1977), 334–6.

Roberts, S. K., 'Dawkins, Rowland (1618–1691)', *Oxford Dictionary of National Biography* (OUP, 2004; online edn, 2008).

Robinson, D. M., *Tretower Court and Castle* (Cardiff: Cadw, 2010).

Royal Commission on the Ancient and Historical Monuments of Wales, *Inventory of Ancient Monuments*, V: *County of Carmarthen* (London: HMSO, 1917).

Saul, N., *Richard II* (New Haven and London: Yale University Press, 1997)

Saunders, A., *Excavations at Launceston Castle, Cornwall*, Soc. Med. Archaeol. Monograph 24 (London, 2006).

Spurrell, W., *Carmarthen and its Neighbourhood* (Carmarthen: Spurrell and Co., 1879).

Strahan, A., Cantrill, T. C., Dixon, E. and Thomas, H. H., *The Geology of the South Wales Coalfield*, Part X: *The Country around Carmarthen* (London: Memoirs of the Geological Survey, 1909).

Suggett, R., *John Nash, Architect in Wales* (Aberystwyth: RCAHMW/NLW, 1995).

Sussex Archaeological Society, 'Lewes Castle and Brack Mount', *Castle Studies Group Bulletin,* 18 (2005), 160–5.

Taylor, A. J., *Monmouth Castle and Great Castle House* (London: HMSO, 1951).

Taylor, A. J., *Caernarvon Castle and Town Walls* (London: HMSO, 1953).

Taylor, A. J., *Caernarfon Castle and Town Walls* (Cardiff: Cadw, 2008).

Thomas, C., Sloane, B. and Phillpotts, C., *Excavations at the Priory and Hospital of St Mary Spital, London*, MoLAS Monograph 1 (London:, 1997).

Thomas, G. J., 'Carmarthen Gaols, 1774, 1788', *Trans. Carms. Antiq. Soc. and Field Club*, 29 (1939), 104–5.

Thomas, S., *Medieval Footwear from Coventry: A Catalogue of the Collection of Coventry Museum* (Coventry: Herbert Art Gallery and Museum, 1980).

Thompson, M. W., *Farnham Castle Keep* (London: HMSO, 1961).

Thompson, M. W., *The Decline of the Castle* (Cambridge University Press, 1987).

Turner, R., *Wiston Castle* (Cardiff: Cadw, 1996).

Turner, R., *Lamphey Bishop's Palace/Llawhaden Castle* (Cardiff: Cadw, 2000).

Turner, R., 'The Upper Bailey', in Turner and Johnson (2006), pp. 71–80.

Turner, R., 'The Upper Barbican', in Turner and Johnson (2006), pp. 113–18.

Turner, R. and Johnson, A. (eds), *Chepstow Castle: its History and Buildings* (Almeley: Logaston, 2006).

Turvey, R., 'The Defences of Twelfth-century Deheubarth and the Castle Strategy of the Lord Rhys', *Archaeologia Cambrensis*, 144 (1997), 103–32.

Turvey, R., 'Twelve Days that Shook South-west Wales: The Royal Letters, Owain Glyndŵr and the Campaign of July 1403', *Carmarthenshire Antiq.*, 37 (2001), 5–20.

Webster, P., 'Pottery', in Caple (2007), pp. 236–45.

Weinstein, R., 'Messing items', in Gardiner (2005), pp. 440–8.

Williams, D. M. and Kenyon, J. R. (eds), *The Impact of the Edwardian Castles in Wales* (Oxford: Oxbow, 2010).

Williams, M. I., 'Carmarthenshire's Maritime Trade in the 16th and 17th Centuries', *Carmarthenshire Antiq.*, 14 (1978), 61–70.

Woodfield, C., 'Finds from the Free Grammar School at the Whitefriars, Coventry, *c*.1545–*c*.1557/8', *Post-Medieval Archaeology*, 15 (1981), 81–160.

Woolgar, C. M., *The Great Household in Late Medieval England* (New Haven and London: Yale University Press, 1999).

Young, C., *Carisbrooke Castle* (London: English Heritage, 2003).

Conjectural reconstruction of Carmarthen Castle, from the south-west, as it may have appeared in c.1500. ©Neil Ludlow, 2012.

INDEX